ETHNICITY IN COLLEGE

ETHNICITY IN COLLEGE

Advancing Theory and Improving
Diversity Practices on Campus

Anna M. Ortiz and Silvia J. Santos

STERLING, VIRGINIA

Sty/us

COPYRIGHT © 2009 BY STYLUS PUBLISHING, LLC.

Published by Stylus Publishing, LLC
22883 Quicksilver Drive
Sterling, Virginia 20166-2102

Cover photo by Victoria Sanchez, California State University, Long Beach

Library of Congress Cataloging-in-Publication Data
Ortiz, Anna Marie, 1963-
   Ethnicity in college : advancing theory and improving diversity practices on campus / Anna M. Ortiz and Silvia J. Santos.—1st ed.
      p.   cm.
   Includes bibliographical references and index.
   ISBN 978-1-57922-051-8 (hardcover : alk. paper)—
ISBN 978-1-57922-332-8 (pbk. : alk. paper)   1. Minorities—Education (Higher)—United States.   2. Minority college students—United States.   3. Ethnicity—United States.
I. Santos, Silvia J., 1963–   II. Title.
LC3731.O78   2009
378.1′982—dc22   2008054640

13-digit ISBN: 978-1-57922-051-8 (cloth)
13-digit ISBN: 978-1-57922-322-8 (paper)

Printed in the United States of America

All first editions printed on acid free paper that meets the American National Standards Institute Z39-48 Standard.

Bulk Purchases

Quantity discounts are available for use in workshops and for staff development.
Call 1-800-232-0223

First Edition, 2009

10   9   8   7   6   5   4   3   2   1

To my parents, John and Barbara Ortiz, and siblings John, Elizabeth, and Michael for their support and encouragement in all that I do.

—Anna M. Ortiz

To my husband, Lewis, and children, Gabriela and Armando, who patiently endured my many absences as I labored over the ideas and findings presented in this book; their belief in me and the importance of what I was doing meant the world to me. To my parents and other family members, I am also grateful for their unwavering support in my life.

—Silvia J. Santos

CONTENTS

W hat led us to address ethnic identity development in diverse contexts and compelled us ultimately to write a book on this topic?
We found that the research and theoretical models at the time
of the study were limited in their multicultural perspective of ethnic identity
development in young adulthood and college students in general. Such theoretical models as presented by Cross (1971), Helms and Cook (1999), and
Phinney (1990) all assumed that people of color, primarily African Americans, grow and develop in predominantly White contexts. When Asian
Americans and Latinos/as were studied, this same narrow view of ethnic evolution persisted. While the field of psychology and the study of racial and
ethnic identity benefited greatly from these early perspectives, we found that
these traditions did not help to predict or explain the experiences of students
with whom we interacted daily.

Accordingly, we also acknowledge that our own experiences and evolution of ethnicity has not only been in reference to mainstream White culture.
We have been influenced by our ethnic-other family and friends in ways that
are just as meaningful as those offered by our participation in mainstream or
predominantly White culture. At the same time, because we live in environments that allow regular contact with our cultural group and its institutions,
we are frequently reminded how ethnicity shapes our self-concept, world-
view(s), behaviors, and values. This amalgamation of formative ethnic experiences is made possible because we live in a multicultural context that results
in unique realities that differ from those presented in the ethnic identity literature, especially earlier empirical works.

We bring to the study our higher education experiences as teachers and
administrators and our differing disciplinary traditions of social psychology
and student affairs in higher education. These allowed us to offer a multidis-
ciplinary perspective to the research question of how students develop ethnic
identities in multicultural contexts. This question necessitated a grounding
in the theoretical traditions of psychology, where theories of ethnic identity
have evolved and which has been the primary location of empirical study.

However, using higher education perspectives on student developmental and environmental forces helped to contextualize the study and enabled us to make meaning of the influence of the social and academic environment where students live and learn.

Previous research on racial and ethnic identity has often used college students as research participants, through the ubiquitous extra credit for undergraduate courses, but few have considered the college context as a vehicle for ethnic identity development and change. The limit of survey research using psychometric inventories or scales results in an examination of the individual with findings that may or may not be interpreted within the college setting. Thus, our goal was to produce a study that used both the standards of the research tradition (survey research) and the opportunities qualitative research offers. Studies relying on surveys or psychometric inventories view the college influence and the dynamic and fluid nature of ethnic identity narrowly. Through qualitative inquiry we were able to capture the many ways in which being in college affects students, where students could describe a wide spectrum of experiences, how those experiences influenced them as changing and evolving ethnic persons, and how they as ethnic persons affected others in the college community.

In embarking on the study, it was important to capture both the college context and the individual experiences students had with their ethnicity. This resulted in descriptions of the four major "umbrella" groups often studied in both higher education and psychological research. Through data analyses, we create descriptions of how African Americans, Asian Americans, Latinos/as, and White students come to develop meaningful ethnic self-concepts and experience their ethnicity in college and in the racially and ethnically diverse environment of Southern California. In Southern California, as in other large urban areas in the United States, ethnic and racial groups have created ways to maintain their cultures through ethnic enclaves and ethnic-specific institutions such as churches, clubs, and culture-based schools, thus making this book very place-bound, that is, more relevant in its application to urban settings and universities.

The combination of the college environment, different ethnic participants, and a culturally and racially diverse societal context enabled us to see unique patterns in the ways students experienced and developed their ethnic identities. We observed how the ethnic composition of the neighborhoods in which students grew up and the high schools they attended enabled them to have ethnic identity. However, when in contact with ethnic–others, many experienced a loss of ethnicity and eventually reclaimed their ethnic identity while in college—thus highlighting the critical role peers played in the ethnic identity process. We also saw that students were negotiating their ethnic identity within the process of becoming an adult, thus noting the intersection of two strong developmental processes. For Asian Americans and Latino/a students this was emphasized by the strength of the family as a supporter of ethnic identity and how, by gaining independence and a more individualized self-concept, students feared a loss of ethnic identity. For African Americans the familial influence was more likely to include how, through strengthening their ethnic identity and pride in being African American, they were preparing for future generations. Meanwhile, for White students the task was to understand the role of their upbringing juxtaposed with their role as ethnic players in a diverse society where ethnicity clearly mattered and could not be ignored. Not surprising, another major influence on students' ethnic identities was the sociohistorical forces that surrounded their educational experience. These underscore the importance of looking at ethnic identity in a contemporary time frame, in a specific region or community and political climate. While this study took place in the late 1990s, many of the issues of the day—affirmative action, immigration rights, bilingual education, and ethnic politics on campus—are very much alive today and at the forefront of the national agenda. Finally, the data directed us to contemplate the very real differences between terms and concepts so readily interchanged in the sociological and psychological literature—race, culture, and ethnicity.

We must acknowledge that we are both Latinas and have considered the role our own ethnic identity had on the analysis of the data and development of this book. It is important to note that a multiethnic team of researchers was involved in the origins of the study, which included developing the interview protocol and other instruments, the initial coding scheme for data analysis, conducting interviews, and training other members of the interview team. Likewise, the many graduate and undergraduate students who participated in different phases of the data analysis came from diverse ethnic backgrounds. Additionally, professional colleagues from each of the four ethnic groups acted as peer debriefers at different points in the writing process. While all of these measures helped to buffer the influence of our common ethnic identity, we recognize that what is presented in this book cannot be completely devoid of bias. As is the case with qualitative research, the credibility and generalizability of the research is ultimately a judgment of the reader.

This book is to be used not only as a volume on cultural diversity for upper-division or graduate courses on pluralism, but also as a resource for researchers and practitioners in psychology and higher education. Student affairs and higher education administrators and leaders will also be urged to consider the ways in which their campus policies and practices can positively influence development of more supportive campus climates that draw on the strengths of each ethnic group to create an overarching pluralistic culture. The book presents not only new research findings on the four major ethnic groups—African Americans, Asian Americans, Latinos/as, and Whites, but also a new model of thinking about ethnic identity that pushes theoretical development in a more holistic way rather than isolating it as one of the many social identities students construct during early adulthood. Embracing a multimethod approach and studying multiple groups at the same time allowed us to discover similarities and differences in more meaningful ways.

Many individuals in the more than 10 years since the project's inception have contributed to the end product presented here. Jeanette Diaz-Veizades, Ericka Yamasaki, and Stacy Sinclair were all a part of the original research team that conceptualized the project and executed the data collection phase. We are indebted to the many undergraduate and graduate students who served on the interview team, allowing us to match ethnicity and, thereby, giving us the insider perspective we so valued. In this effort, we recognize in particular Robert Dutile and Astrid Reina, who served as head research assistants for the California State University Dominguez Hills interview team. Our data analysis team, Alex Morales, Monica Rosales, Judd Hark, Pamela Eddy, and Diane Johnson, worked tirelessly to analyze data from more than 120 hours of interviews and surveys. Their work was instrumental to completion of this book. We also acknowledge other students who have contributed to conference presentations, such as Aisha Patten, Diana Dowds, Jennifer Doucett, Noemi Lirios, Saddiyah Abdul, Sonia Garcia, and Victor Rico. Johanna Masse and Susana Marin, graduate research assistants, were invaluable in the final stages of the writing. We also acknowledge the insight of our professional colleagues who read drafts of chapters and discussed issues with which we grappled, permitting us to see and interpret our findings better.

We also thank our institutions that provided financial support for the project, namely California State Dominguez Hills, Michigan State University, and California State University, Long Beach. Finally, we are deeply indebted to the 120 students who participated in the qualitative interviews. Their willingness to share their stories and experiences in deeply candid ways made it possible for us to peer into the lives of students in ways we are not typically privileged to see. This has permitted all who have been a part of the study and all who read this book insight that only "in group" members typically have access to.

We would also like to thank our families and friends for their support throughout this process. Their willingness to help us in practical and emotional ways made the work possible. Silvia's family hosted several research "retreats," allowing us concentrated time to work on the book. Our sisters and Silvia's mother actually contributed to the research process by assisting us in the development of our thinking about the findings through conversations about students' commentaries and in transcribing interviews. Finally, we are especially grateful to our partners and to our parents for their support and belief in our abilities.

INTRODUCTION
TO THE STUDY

On paper, I'd probably put myself as White, 'cuz when they give you the options . . . they don't have an option for Armenian, so I just answer White. But if someone were to ask me, I'd say I'm Armenian. . . . Race isn't a very important thing, but I'm proud to be what I am. I try to make more of an effort to seem like I know more about my own race, when I'm around Armenians. I'm afraid of being looked down upon, 'cuz I use to know how to read and write Armenian. I can only speak it now . . . I don't know as much as I should about my own culture . . . some people get on me for that. I get on myself for that. I kind of feel embarrassed.

I wouldn't listen to Mexican music. I would try not to talk Spanish. For example, on a holiday, I wouldn't even mention it or anything because of the fact that my friends wouldn't be familiar with it. But now, here, it's like my friends celebrate it, my friends listen to that music and they speak Spanish. So I guess that I've changed a lot . . . I became more familiar with my identity. I was taking Chicano Studies courses and the Mexican American experience. I became more in tune with like my identity. And I feel that now, it means a lot to me . . . I think that now [my identity] is starting to be significant in my life. And I want to pass it on to my kids.

I didn't have a lot of close friends who were Black, and so I didn't have a very strong ethnic identity at all. I don't think I had any ethnic identity at that time. It wasn't until I got into situations as a young adult entering college when I realized, for a lot of non-Black people, the bottom line was that I would always be Black regardless of "You're my best friend" or "You're my girlfriend." When it comes right down to it, I always felt like it was going to be Black and White issues that are divided. I think when I became older, because of these experiences when I was younger, I began to seek out my cultural identity. [I felt that to] really know, I should get information to try and make myself positive about who I was. [Reading books] helped me better understand my identity, and I have fully embraced all of the positive things and reevaluated who I am on my own terms and not attempt to define myself by the terms that the mainstream society puts out. [Now I feel] stronger and I feel beautiful for the first time, inside and out . . . nothing will stop me from achieving my goals.

My culture has made me the person I am, because it taught me how to respect my parents. It taught me how to appreciate what they're doing to get me here. My dad's still in Vietnam, he'd be retired a long time ago, but he's still working to support me. It taught me to have greater respect for the elderly and for my parents, and basically gave me lot of inner drive. 'Cause I'm in a different country, I have to make it here or else I'll be just a nobody. So it gives me a lot of push. My culture gives me a lot of confidence, so I know that I can make it, as long as I know who I am and I keep what I believe in and not forget that I am Vietnamese. Some people, they come and they try to forget that they're Vietnamese, they forget the language or they try to forget their culture. Then twenty years down the line, they really want to learn about it, it's too late. So I want to keep it now, and then, then years later, I won't start flipping through the books trying to find out who I am 'cause I already know. And so it helps me to be a stronger person inside and outside. Once I'm strong, I can succeed and I can do anything.

These students are all expressing different conceptions of their own ethnic identity and how it has an impact on how they see themselves and the world around them. In these quotations students show how they attempt to maintain their culture despite pressure to acculturate to a more generic American identity. We also see how college is an opportunity for students to revisit and develop their ethnic identity more fully after turning away from it in high school. In the first student, there appears to be a tension to deny the importance of race in society, yet the need to embrace ethnicity[1] as an important aspect of the self. These students struggle with race and ethnicity regardless of background and experiences

---

1. Definitions of race and ethnicity are presented in Chapter 2.

because, as colleges and universities continue to become racial places, even the seemingly benign American identity is challenged. However, these students also demonstrate how closely connected a strong sense of ethnic identity is to their confidence as college students and to their becoming successful adults.

In this book we explore the importance and construction of ethnic identity to these and other college students. We also explore how ethnicity interfaces with students' interactions on campus and the communities in which they live. We develop a dynamic portrayal of how ethnicity affects students' identity and their experiences in college. The experiences shared in this volume represent the change that has already taken place on many of our campuses and previews the transformation that awaits all colleges and universities. The lessons we can learn from these students are infinite, but they strongly indicate that multicultural learning environments have the potential to increase significantly a broad range of traditional and nontraditional student learning outcomes. Although much research has begun to document the positive outcomes associated with diverse learning environments (as outlined in Hurtado et al., 1999; Hurtado, 2007), this study emphasizes and more closely delineates just how these outcomes come to be. In addition, the study reveals how the freedom to express and develop ethnic identity, which multicultural environments ideally support, promotes student confidence and achievement in ways students themselves can articulate.

This chapter includes an introduction to the relevance of ethnicity in higher education and the importance that identity development processes play in the development of college students and their experiences in higher education institutions. The study presented in this volume is introduced here in terms of sample characteristics, site descriptions to contextualize the findings of the study, and an overview of study methods. We conclude with an overview of subsequent chapters in the book.

Ethnicity in Contemporary Higher Education

Since the dawn of the civil rights era, ethnicity and race in higher education have assumed a central position in political, intellectual, and social debates about the purposes and intents of higher education itself. "Balkanization," "separatism," and "turf wars" describe the early discourse on entities such as ethnic studies, ethnic student organizations, and culturally focused residence halls. Early resistance to multiculturalism called for a focus on our similarities rather than on our differences. But the continuing transformation of the nation would not sustain this line of reasoning as ethnic groups grew, attained visibility, and established communities with social and economic systems that maintained the distinctions of ethnic groups rather than their assimilation. The strength of ethnic enclaves and their substantial role in our urban centers is well documented in the work of Alejandro Portes and his associates (Portes & Bach, 1985; Portes & Rumbaut, 1996; Portes & Stepick, 1993). In the Los Angeles area, where the study presented here was conducted, residential segregation of ethnic groups also sustains distinct ethnic group communities. In the communities with the largest proportions of Latinos/as, less than 10% of the households are White. This proportion is even smaller (4%) for the areas with the largest concentrations of African Americans. Meanwhile, there are distinct communities with Asian American populations that reach almost 45% (Charles, 2000). The millennial census demonstrates the increasing presence of ethnic groups in the United States, especially in California, where Whites are now only 59.5% of the population and Latinos/as are nearly a third of the state population. There are 3 times the proportion of Asian Americans in California (10.9%) as there are in the U.S. population (3.6%). However, African Americans, who account for 12.1% of the total U.S. population, comprise only 6.7% of Californians (U.S. Census Bureau, 2000). California's demographic characteristics make it different from most states in the union, but similar trends can be seen in New York, Florida, Texas, Arizona, Illinois, New Mexico, and Arizona.

In higher education the growth of ethnic groups in the national student population created opportunities and tensions that mirrored events in society. Because many of our communities remain essentially segregated, higher education has seen the ethnic mix in ways that other societal institutions have yet to experience fully. The increasing number of non-White students in higher education was accompanied by increasing criticism of affirmative action that arose out of the 1979 *Regents of the University of California v. Bakke* Supreme Court decision, which ended the use of quotas in college and university admissions. Spurred by this victory, critics of multiculturalism and ethnic studies campaigned to prevent the establishment of ethnic studies programs and to end student support services targeted to non-White students. These controversies brought a spotlight to ethnicity and race on campus that was new for many institutions and, for some, reminiscent of the ethnic studies movement of the late 1960s. These two streams, criticism of multiculturalism and the growth of ethnic groups on campus, created fertile ground for ethnic identity as a political identity rather than one more closely associated with family, culture, and traditions.

Conservative criticism often targeted the student support programs and services that served as gathering places for the emerging importance of ethnicity and race in students' everyday lives. Organizations such as the campus Black Student Association, Movimiento Estudiantil Chicano de Axtlán (MEChA), and Native and Asian American student associations became places where students gathered, some would argue, for shelter from hostile campus climates, but also for friendship, affiliation, and activism. Ethnic studies programs also served as locations for students to reclaim their group's histories and catalyze individuals to strengthen the importance of ethnic background to their public and private selves.

Ethnic students became active in their campus environments by demanding the hiring of diverse faculty and staff, establishment and growth in ethnic studies programs, diversification of curricula, equal funding for student organizations, equal access to top campus offices for ethnic student group leaders, and challenging racist behavior on campus. Many of the struggles became well known in higher education and in the local media. The students at Rutgers "sat in" during a National Collegiate Athletic Association (NCAA) basketball game because their president made public remarks asserting that racial differences in standardized test scores reflected genetic differences (Rhoads, 1998). Chicano students at the University of California, Los Angeles (UCLA) created a tent city and went on a hunger strike to protest the denial of department status to the Chicano Studies Program (Rhoads, 1998). More recently, Chicano students at Michigan State University checked out thousands of history books from the library in a single day to demonstrate what it is like to go to an institution where you feel your history is denied. The continuing protests of students and faculty at the University of Illinois over the use of a Native American mascot gives evidence to the persistence of ethnic politics on America's college campuses.

Programs to support ethnic students also supported continued exploration of ethnic identity for new cohorts of students entering higher education. Diversification of the curriculum, as well as the push for categorization and the need or pressure to belong—two long-held characteristics of adolescence—have made nearly every college student consider his or her ethnicity in some way. Ethnic student organizations prompted some White students to consider establishing their own groups. Ethnic studies requirements or broadening of general education curricula has introduced diverse literature, history, and social justice topics to many college students. Although data show that only 16.7% of faculty have diversified their courses by including writings on racial or ethnic issues (Sax, Astin, Korn, & Gilmartin, 1999), a much higher proportion of students reported having taken ethnic studies courses or participated in discussions on race and ethnicity (Chang, 2001; Hurtado, 2007). It is rare that students progress through the college without considering what ethnicity means from an academic and personal perspective.

Identity and College Students

It is logical that students would gravitate toward the notion of ethnicity in developing their identity, not only because of the past several decades' focus on race and ethnicity, but also because establishing one's identity has long been established as a task of the college years. Although Erik Erikson (1968) conceived of his Identity vs. Role Confusion stage as confined primarily to the traditional adolescent teenage years, elongation of adolescence by the pursuit of an undergraduate degree has extended the length of time college students spend in the Identity v. Role Confusion stage. Chickering in 1969, and, later, with Reisser in 1993, has studied this stage in particular with application to the college years. Marcia's (1980) ego identity statuses also have direct application to ethnic identity (indeed, they have been the theoretical foundation of many of the ethnic identity theories) and support the presence of identity development as a task of the college years.

Erikson's (1968) work gives theoretical strength to the presence of ethnic identity as a growing concern of college students. An intense focus on how one is defined in relationship to others at a time when social, family, and societal roles are shifting at a rapid pace characterizes adolescence in the United States. Also distinctive is the tendency for youth to turn away from family and parents as sources of affirmation of behavior and educational or occupational choices. Increasingly, peers become the referent for the emerging adult identity: "[adolescents] are sometimes morbidly, often curiously, preoccupied with what they appear to be to the eyes of others as compared with what they feel they are" (p. 128). This constant comparison between self and peers gives students the opportunity to define identity by "projecting one's diffused self-image on another and by seeing it thus reflected and gradually clarified" (p. 132). When exposed to peers who are ethnically different from themselves or to peer groups where there are significant numbers of coethnics, students make ethnicity a part of their self-image that is reflected and clarified. Thus, the result, whether it be a strengthening of ethnicity or denial of it, is dependent on the available peer group.

The tension between the influence of peers and that of family has implications for the development of ethnicity as an integral component of identity. When pressure from the peer group is contradictory to the ethnic tradition of the home, there is the risk that students will turn away from ethnicity to be accepted by their peers. Erikson suggests that the adolescent "would rather act shamelessly in the eyes of his elders, out of free choice, than be forced into activities which would be shameful in his own eyes or in those of his peers" (1968, p. 129). However, students who connect with coethnic peer groups often find that ethnicity is strengthened and sustained, in many ways providing a defense structure that provides support in time of attack and sustains loyalties when values are in conflict (Erikson, 1968).

Chickering and Reisser's "7 Vectors of Student Development" isolates and expands on Erikson's theory, specifically addressing his developmental stages of Identity vs. Role Confusion and Intimacy vs. Isolation. The vectors encompass developmental tasks necessary for successful identity development and for students to benefit optimally from college experiences. Chickering and Reisser (1993) describe this trajectory as:

> The primary element is that a solid sense of self, that inner feeling of mastery and ownership that takes shape as the developmental tasks for competence, emotions, autonomy and relationships are undertaken with some success, and that, as it becomes firmer provides a framework for purpose and integrity, as well as for more progress along the other vectors. (p. 181)

Each vector encompasses more specific tasks that, once accomplished, give rise to a sense of having achieved the vector. Early vectors, which are commonly achieved in concert with one another, include development of intellectual, interpersonal, physical, and manual competence; management of positive and negative emotions; and becoming autonomous enough to live as an adult, yet realizing that adult life requires interdependent relationships.

The central vectors focus more on development of a unique identity with acknowledgment and support of mature interpersonal relationships. This unique identity allows for the appreciation of the diversity of others and the realization of the impact of culture on the self. In addition, the identity constructed through achieving all of these vectors promotes the development necessary in the final two: developing purpose and developing integrity.

There are several instances in this theory of college student development that lend credence to the claim that ethnic identity development is also a task of the college years. Chickering and Reisser (1993) operationalize the vector of Establishing Identity by identifying seven attributes that are characteristic of a solid sense of self:

1. Comfort with body and appearance
2. Comfort with gender and sexual orientation
3. Sense of self in a social, historical, and cultural context
4. Clarification of self-concept through roles and lifestyles
5. Sense of self in response to feedback from valued others
6. Self-acceptance and self-esteem
7. Personal stability and integration

As will be evident throughout the chapters of this book, where students express their own concerns and experiences around their ethnic identity, all of these attributes play a role in an evolving sense of self. For a person in environments where ethnicity plays a role in the social system, ethnicity becomes a part of the internal and external dynamics of identity development.

Ethnic identity development can be illustrated in each of the attributes listed above. Phenotype plays a role in identity development if students grasp an ethnicity that does not match their outer appearance. Not only does phenotype (light versus dark skin, for instance) play a role in the level of comfort students have in themselves, but phenotype also may affect how peers respond to students who embrace an ethnicity that is in conflict with their phenotypes. Many women in the study noted how gender role expectations, dictated by their ethnic group traditions, challenged their concept of themselves as independent, capable women.

For students who had experienced few repercussions from their ethnic heritage, balkanization, discrimination, and racism experienced in college challenged them to integrate their sense of self with the social context. Students who were introduced to the history or literature of diverse groups in college also encountered the historical context that has helped to shape their current realities. Roles and lifestyles are affected by ethnicity when students immerse themselves in peer groups defined by ethnic heritage or if they make commitments to careers that assist their ethnic group. Peers play a significant role all along the way: they "permit" access to ethnic student organizations, they see through false or temporary displays of identity, and they reject (or embrace) friends whose affiliation groups change dramatically. As students learn ways to express ethnic identity in college, the reactions they encounter affect their self-esteem and self-concept in significant ways. Indeed, foundational to theories of ethnic identity development is the idea that self-loathing and rejection of the ethnic self are consequences of overidentification with the majority group (Whites). These theories are also consistent with Chickering and Reisser's (1993) last attribute, personal stability and integration, as they delineate the process by which students integrate ethnicity into their other social identities and roles and develop a self that is stable enough to withstand challenge and criticism. Chapter 2 explores these connections in greater depth.

James Marcia's (1980) model of ego identity development encompasses the notion of crisis present in Erikson's theory, and the notion of task, in that commitments about identity must be made. The process of the theory is one where the crisis precipitates movement toward an end point of identity achievement or diffusion. He posits that at any point, an individual is in one of four statuses that describe the current style of coping with the identity development process. Like Erikson's (1968) and Chickering and Reisser's (1993), Marcia's theory also embraces the dynamic interplay among the individual, the social environment, and the influence of significant others. Students who are *identity diffused* have not made commitments about their identity and may not have encountered a crisis of identity. To these students, any way of being, any belief system, and any career choice is just as valid as another. They are unable to make these decisions because their sense of self is ill-defined. Students who are *foreclosed* have not had an identity crisis and, as a result, conform to their parents' values and expectations without examination. The focus here is on the lack of exploration of identity issues rather than on the inability to make choices, decisions, or commitments congruent with identity. The *moratorium* status reflects the active exploration that follows the crisis. Decisions have yet to be made, but the exploration is appropriate and active. The final status, *identity-achieved*, reflects the student's ability to endure an identity crisis and make commitments independently consistent with the renewed identity.

Marcia's model of identity development is foundational to the epigenesis of most ethnic identity theories, thus making the direct application of ethnicity to identity development readily evident. Typically, identity diffusion characterizes a student who is undecided about the personal meaning of ethnicity and may find him- or herself unable to embrace fully membership in the appropriate ethnic group or in the dominant group. This may be more characteristic of students of color, but White students may also feel this way about their own ethnicity. Students who have a foreclosed identity have taken, unexamined, the ethnic identity of those important to them (a referent). This could be either parents or the dominant societal group, but the distinction is the unexplored acceptance of the ethnic identity. Students in moratorium are at the threshold of making commitments about the place of ethnicity in their lives, but they are still actively exploring the manifestations. Students who have achieved identity, like the final phase of the other theories, have integrated their ethnicity into their broader sense of self. Therefore, the work of these three theories (Erikson, Marcia, and Chickering and Reisser) highlights that elements of the self, societal, and family roles find resolution in their relationship to one another in achieved, adult identities. The extended latency period that college offers enables exploration of these in ways that may be truncated for those with more immediate adult responsibilities such as parenting and employment.

Overview of the Study

The study highlighted in this book was conducted in Southern California over a 3-year period in the late 1990s. Our goal was to discover how college students made meaning of their ethnicity in a multicultural world. We were interested in how living in an environment where there were critical masses of many ethnic groups and less of a White majority group dominance affected the development of ethnicity and how that ethnicity interfaces with the college experience. The students who participated in the study attended one of two public universities in Southern California. These campuses are characterized by their diversity and the fact that Whites on those campuses, at the time of the study, comprised less than 50% of the student population. At one campus, 31% of the students were African American, making it the largest ethnic group at that school. Whites comprised 30% of the student population, and Latinos/as made up 24% of the student population. Only 9% of students were Asian Americans, and many of those were Pacific Islanders or Southeast Asian, not of Chinese or Japanese origin. At the second campus, Whites (37%) and Asian Americans (35%) were the clear majority. In contrast, Latinos/as and African Americans accounted for a much smaller proportion of the student population (16% and 6%, respectively). Ethnicity is an issue on these campuses, one of which had 162 student organizations affiliated with particular ethnic or racial groups, including many representing specific European ethnicities and 75 different Asian American student organizations.

Students typically grew up in communities with significant numbers of people from their own ethnic group and perhaps only one or two other ethnic groups. For Latinos/as and African Americans, the data revealed that they continue to live in relatively segregated areas. The mean composition of the neighborhood for African Americans was predominantly African American—81.33%. Not one student lived in a predominantly White neighborhood, and only one lived in a neighborhood that was not majority African American. Latinos/as also lived in predominantly Latino/a neighborhoods, with the neighborhood composition being 56.45% Latino/a. Latinos/as also responded that about 25.1% of their neighborhoods were majority African American. Both Latinos/as and African Americans reported low proportions of Asian Americans in their neighborhoods. Asian Americans and Whites lived in predominantly White areas. Not surprising, the group with the highest proportion of Asian Americans in their neighborhoods was Asian Americans. The high school ethnic composition resembled that of the neighborhood. However, the high schools were not as heavily segregated as the neighborhoods of Latinos/as and African Americans. One probable reason is that in Los Angeles, students can be bused to schools outside their neighborhoods. Although students were not asked directly about having been bused, a cursory look at the differences between the composition of the neighborhood and that of the high school revealed that as many as a quarter of the Latino/a students and one-third of the African American students may have been bused during high school. Table 1.1 provides a more in-depth analysis of the ethnic composition of the neighborhoods and high schools in which student participants lived and were educated. The table is structured to provide a sense of representational proportion of ethnic groups in comparison to the students' own group. Therefore, the first section of figures reflects the percentage of specific ethnic group members who grew up in neighborhoods or attended high schools where there was no one like them in the environment. The second section of figures reflects the percentage of student participants who lived and attended schools in environments where they were members of minority groups. The third section of figures represents the proportion of students from neighborhoods and high schools where their ethnic group was at parity with their proportion in the U.S. population. Finally, the fourth section tells us what percentage of students were from neighborhoods and high schools where their own group were in the clear majority.

One hundred twenty students participated in the study. Of them, 24 were African American (20%); 26, Asian American (22%); 34, Latino/a (28%); and 36, Caucasian or White (30%). Although only 1 student identified as mixed race, 6 students indicated, by identifying the ethnic background of their parents, that they were biracial. Within the four broad ethnic categories used in this book, students indicated a number of ethnic backgrounds that were more descriptive. The Asian American category was composed of students who identified as Korean, Vietnamese, Chinese, Cambodian, Japanese, Taiwanese, Filipino, and Indian. Latino/a students identified as Mexican American, Puerto Rican, Dominican, and Ecuadorian. White students identified their ethnic heritage as coming from a wide range of European countries, such as Italy, Germany, France, England, Scotland, Ireland, Sweden, Poland, Spain, Czech Republic, and Hungary. African Americans identified as Black, Ethiopian, or African American. Ethnic labels are discussed in greater detail in later chapters.

The sample spanned a wide age range, 18–35, though the average age of the sample was 21.3 years. Most students were in either their junior or senior year of college. More women than men participated in the study (64%). Three-quarters of the students indicated their socioeconomic status as working class, lower middle class, or middle class. Forty-one percent of students said they worked full time, 36% worked part time, and 24% were not employed. Approximately half of the students (42%) lived with family, while

TABLE 1.1
Ethnic Composition of Neighborhoods and High Schools

	No Representation of Ethnic Group in Neighborhood				Ethnic Group Is in the Minority in Neighborhood				Ethnic Group Approximates Parity in Neighborhood				Ethnic Group Is in the Majority in Neighborhood			
	AfAm	AsAm	Lat	Whit	AfAm	AsAm	Lat	Whit	AfAm	AsAm	Lat	Whit	AfAm	AsAm	Lat	Whit
African Americans	0	54.5	36.1	13.6	13.5	45.3	54.3	40.8	13.6	0	22.7	9	72.5	0	9	13.2
Asian Americans	40	9.1	13	22.7	36.3	45.5	49.9	22.7	22.7	31.1	22.6	13.5	0	13.6	4.5	49.7
Latinos/as	26	41.2	26	5.9	38.1	44	11.7	38.3	20.6	8.8	29.4	14.6	17.6	5.8	32.8	20.6
Whites	35	35	0	50	50	37.4	32.3	8.7	11.7	20.6	8.7	14.6	2.9	5.8	5.9	76.3
Total Sample	**26**	**35.5**	**17**	**23.9**	**36.3**	**42.6**	**19.6**	**23.9**	**16.9**	**15.9**	**20.4**	**13.4**	**20.5**	**6.3**	**20.5**	**42.7**

	No Representation of Ethnic Group in High School				Ethnic Group Is in the Minority in High School				Ethnic Group Approximates Parity in High School				Ethnic Group Is in the Majority in High School			
	AfAm	AsAm	Lat	Wht	AfAm	AsAm	Lat	Wht	AfAm	AsAm	Lat	Wht	AfAm	AsAm	Lat	Wht
African Americans	0	36.4	0	13.6	18.1	54.5	54.5	36.4	40.7	9	26.7	27.1	40.7	0	18	22.6
Asian Americans	4.5	0	4.5	4.5	54.5	40.8	49.9	18.1	40.9	45.3	35.8	40.9	0	13.5	9	36.1
Latinos/as	8.8	17.6	2.9	11.8	47	80.5	4.7	44	38.1	8.7	23.4	26.3	5.9	2.9	38	17.6
Whites	8.8	11.8	17.6	0	67.6	46.9	64.6	8.8	20.9	35.2	16.7	26.4	2.9	5.8	0	67.4
Total Sample	**6.2**	**15.9**	**7.1**	**7.1**	**49.5**	**54.2**	**44.3**	**25.6**	**33.7**	**24.9**	**31.9**	**28.7**	**10.7**	**5.4**	**17**	**38.4**

Note: No representation = 0% group; minority = 1%–19% group representation; approximating parity = 20–49% group representation; majority = 50+% group representation.

39% lived in an apartment, and 24% lived in campus residence halls. One-third of the sample spoke a language other than English, with 67% of the participants reporting they were native English speakers. Almost half of the students were either first- (born in another country) or second-generation (born in the United States of parents born in another country) citizens. Almost 44% of students in the sample were the first in their families to attend college.

We used a multimethod approach to address the varied influences of ethnically diverse university communities on students' personal and ethnic identity development and adaptation to the university culture. The center-piece of the study was the qualitative interview in which each student participated. Of the 120 participants, we analyzed 102 interviews, which included 30 Whites (29%), 26 Latinos/as (25%), 23 African Americans (23%), and 23 Asians (23%). These interviews asked students to talk about their ethnic background; how they participated in the activities and traditions of that background; and how that background has affected their personalities, values, and aspirations. In addition, many questions focused on student experiences with their peers from other ethnic groups on campus and in their home communities. Students were also asked about how politics, social or historical movements, and issues associated with ethnicity had an effect on their lives as students and citizens. A number of survey instruments were administered to gather additional information about students' degree of ethnic identity, self-esteem, college experiences, and general demographic characteristics. A full account of the methods used in the study are outlined in the appendix.

The survey data ($N = 120$) allowed us to examine the extent to which participants constructed their ethnic identity with respect to established overarching components of ethnicity and how these components are related to students' personal self-esteem and adjustment to college. More specifically, we used a multidimensional measure of ethnic identity (Luhtanen & Crocker, 1992) to tap into students' (1) private acceptance of ethnicity, (2) perceived public acceptance of their ethnic group, (3) membership group esteem, and (4) integration of ethnicity into the self-concept. Furthermore, a college self-efficacy questionnaire (Solberg, O'Brien, Kennel, & Davis, 1993) was used to measure students' level of confidence in handling the demands of college life in terms of (a) meeting academic requirements, (b) interacting with faculty and peers, and (c) living with roommates. Finally, we used a self-esteem scale (Rosenberg, 1979) as a global measure of one's personal self-worth. (Refer to the appendix for a more detailed description of the survey instruments and their psychometric properties.) Including these measures enhanced our confidence in the triangulation of the qualitative data and the validity of the reported research findings, especially when interpreting the interview data of students who may have been at different levels of development concerning their ethnic identity.

Consequences of Ethnic Identity Development

Much of the psychological research literature on ethnic identity development focuses on the relationships between positive or negative ethnic identity and a host of psychological and academic outcomes. The underlying assumption of these studies is that individuals with positive, well-developed ethnic identities are likely to achieve vital, healthy personalities. Self-esteem is the most studied correlate of a positive ethnic identity. When students have pride in their ethnicity, feel a sense of belonging to members of their ethnic group, and participate in behaviors associated with their ethnicity, they have higher self-esteem than do students who experience a disconnect with their ethnicity (Phelps, Taylor, & Gerard, 2001; Phinney & Chavira, 1992; Robinson, 2000). This finding holds across ethnic groups, as the positive association between ethnic identity and self-esteem has been found to be true for Latinos/as, African Americans, and Whites (Phinney, Cantu, & Kurtz, 1997). Coping ability, mastery, and optimism have also been shown to have positive associations with ethnic identity (Roberts, Phinney, & Masse, 1999). Even healthy behaviors, such as less substance abuse, better nutrition, and more exercise are associated with positive ethnic identity (Walsh & McGrath, 2000). Conversely, negative or undeveloped ethnic identities are assumed to be symptomatic of dysfunctional personalities and problematic behavior.

Ethnic identity is also associated with an increased awareness of the role of race and ethnicity in American society. For instance, heightened ethnic consciousness is negatively correlated with conservative values (Brown & Johnson, 1999), and increases in ethnicity exploration resulted in the perception of more discrimination and negative attitudes toward members of ethnic groups. A positive sense of belonging to one's ethnic group led to positive attitudes toward members of other ethnic groups as well (Romero & Roberts, 1998). In addition, ethnic diversity in out-of-school settings led to more out-group interaction in school, which then led to an increase in positive attitudes toward members of other ethnic groups (Phinney, Ferguson, & Tate, 1997).

In the study presented in this book, correlational analyses were also used to examine the multidimensional aspects of ethnic identity with other variables (see Table 1.2). Different dimensions of ethnic identity emerged as important correlates of college self-efficacy. Membership identity (i.e., a sense of worth that stems from one's ability to contribute positively to the ethnic group) was significantly associated with overall college self-efficacy, academic self-efficacy, and social self-efficacy in university students. Hence, those students who felt worthy of contributing to their ethnic group also benefited from having greater confidence in their ability to integrate socially into campus life and handle demanding academic requirements, which were associated with a positive sense of college self-efficacy. Second, the results showed a significant correspondence between public acceptance identity (i.e., social judgments of one's ethnic group) and academic self-efficacy. This suggests that students were not immune to public judgments of their ethnic group, and those who perceived a high level of public acceptance were also more likely to have greater confidence in their ability to handle academic requirements. This finding mirrors the research on campus climate and stereotype threat, which indicates that a "hostile" or "friendly" campus climate can predict either academic success or failure in students (Hurtado, Milem, Clayton-Pedersen, & Allen, 1999; Reid & Radhakrishnan, 2003). Therefore,

TABLE 1.2
Correlation Matrix of Variables for Total Sample

	College Efficacy	Social Efficacy	Academic Efficacy	Self-Esteem
Ethnic Identity	.127*	.131*	.107	.380**
Private Acceptance	.015	.060	.060	.365**
Public Acceptance	.106	.050	.114*	.110
Personal Identity	.001	.131*	.107	.286**
Membership Identity	.200**	.229**	.220**	.468**

*$p < .10$
** $p < .05$

it is within the context of a "friendly" campus climate (high perceived ethnic acceptance) that students may be less inclined to question their ability to succeed academically and experience low academic self-efficacy. Third, the correlational analysis also revealed a relationship between personal ethnic identity (i.e., the importance of ethnic identity to one's self-definition) and social self-efficacy in college. This result implies that, when ethnicity is well integrated into the self-concept, it relates positively to how well students perceive themselves as being capable of adapting to the campus culture. It appears that knowing who they were in ethnic terms gave students the added self-confidence to negotiate various social circles on campus effectively, from interacting with peers to interacting with professors.

In reference to self-esteem, private-, personal-, and membership-ethnic identity were positively linked to a strong sense of personal self-worth in students. The fact that public acceptance was not a significant correlate of self-esteem in students is consistent with earlier research (Crocker & Major, 1989), suggesting that individuals distance themselves personally from negative societal images of their group. This is a protective mechanism against potential threats to one's personal self-esteem that stem from social devaluation of one's ethnic group.

Overall, the findings of the correlational analyses highlight the multidimensional facet of ethnic identity and how its components may relate differently to various aspects of psychological functioning.

In this study we also conducted a series of group comparison analyses on the ethnic identity measures, college self-efficacy measures, and self-esteem by ethnic background of students. These analyses identified significant ethnic group differences on four of the ethnic identity measures: overall ethnic identity, private acceptance ethnic identity, personal ethnic identity, and membership identity. The results of the comparison of mean tests (see Table 1.3) conducted on the ethnic identity measures revealed that White students scored significantly lower than did African American, Asian, and Latino/a students on overall ethnic identity. White participants also had significantly lower scores on private acceptance and personal ethnic identity compared to their African American, Asian, and Latino/a peers. Likewise, White students reported lower membership ethnic identity scores relative to Latinos/as. These findings are in line with earlier research indicating that White students consistently score lower on global ethnic identity measures than do ethnic minority students (Alba, 1990; Phinney & Alipuria, 1990;

TABLE 1.3

Analysis of Variance and Duncan's Post-Hoc Test of Group Mean on Ethnic Identity Measures, Self-Esteem, and College Self-Efficacy Measure

	African American	Asian American	Latino/a American	White American
Ethnic Identity	91.90_b	87.83_b	91.03_b	79.59_a
$F(3,105) = 6.73, p < .0001$				
Private Acceptance	26.55_b	24.64_{ab}	25.68_b	22.78_a
$F(3,113) = 6.23, p < .001$				
Public Acceptance	18.61_a	21.48_a	20.97_a	20.54_a
n.s. *				
Personal Identity	21.88_b	19.67_b	20.82_b	14.68_a
$F(3,113) = 14.41, p < .0001$				
Self-Esteem	63.39_b	58.28_a	63.15_b	59.56_{ab}
$F(3,113) = 3.32, p < .05$				
College Self- Efficacy	$*94.93_a$	89.39_a	101.43_a	97.45_a
n.s.				
Academic	40.83_a	36.44_a	40.28_a	41.03_a
n.s.				
Social	38.20_a	32.21_a	38.09_a	35.41_a
n.s.				
Roommate	19.53_a	20.00_a	20.35_a	21.45_a
n.s.				

$*n.s.$ = analyses of variance not significant, or $p > .05$.
Note: All Duncan post-hoc test are significant at $p < .05$; same subscript = no significant difference; different subscript = significant difference.

Wright & Littleford, 2002). In the case of White students, ethnicity was not as crucial to their definition of self-concept (i.e., personal identity) as was the case for ethnic minority students. Similarly, ethnicity did not appear to give White students a strong basis for self-worth and pride (i.e., private acceptance). It has been argued that this "lack of awareness on the part of White students may make it difficult for them to understand the attitudes and behaviors of ethnic minority students and may hamper their efforts to interact with ethnic students on a more intimate basis" (Mack et al., 1997, p. 259). Finally, African American students had significantly higher membership identity scores than did White, Asian, and Latino/a students. Membership identity speaks directly to one's self-worth in terms of ability to contribute positively to one's ethnic group. "For many minority students, and often most saliently for African Americans, the historical reality of oppression and their own current experiences of racism and discrimination" is a truism with which they must learn to cope (Wright & Littleford, 2002, p. 4). African American students' higher scores on membership identity tell of the proactive manner in which these individuals choose to achieve ethnic dignity and a secure ethnic identity (Wright & Littleford, 2002).

In regard to self-esteem (see Table 1.3), the analysis revealed that Asian American students scored lower on self-esteem than did African American and Latino/a students. This finding is consistent with the work conducted by Yeh and Huang (1996), which points to lower personal self-esteem among Asian students, where a "collective" self-esteem is culturally more germane for this population. White students' self-esteem scores were between those for African American and Latino/a students on the one hand, and Asian students on the other, hence they did not differ statistically from other groups. Therefore, the findings suggest that comparable levels of positive self-worth were revealed across all groups studied. Finally, as demonstrated in Table 1.3, there were no ethnic group differences for college self-efficacy. These findings highlight ethnic group differences in ethnic identity development for the groups of students in the study, largely confirm findings in the research, and point to the mediating effects of a positive ethnic identity for important outcomes such as self-esteem and college self-efficacy.

Overview of the Book

The book is structured in 3 parts. Chapter 2 provides a comprehensive review of the theoretical and research literature related to general ethnic and racial identity development, and for specific ethnic groups, thus establishing the psychological foundations of ethnic identity. Chapters 3–6, which describe the ethnic identity of Asian Americans, African Americans, Latinos/as, and Whites, provide an overview of each ethnic group, the distinctiveness of each, and each one's major cultural influences on students. In these chapters, we use unique themes for each of the groups to present the qualitative findings. Chapter 7 explores more deeply the college experience, specifically illustrating the positive and negative facets associated with diverse learning communities for students' ethnic identity development and interethnic relations. The final chapter synthesizes the study's major findings and their implications for theory and offers practical implications for university personnel and faculty.

2

ETHNIC IDENTITY'S
THEORETICAL AND
RESEARCH TRADITIONS

E thnic identity is perhaps best conceptualized as an enduring and fundamental aspect of the self-concept that derives from a sense of membership in an ethnic group, along with the "value and emotional significance attached to that group membership" (Tajfel, 1981, p. 225). Included in the meaning of ethnic identity are the attitudes, beliefs, values, behavioral norms, and expectations that members of a specific group share and that form the basis for differentiating and setting groups apart in society (Keefe, 1992; Phinney, 1990; Uba, 1994). This definition of ethnic identity clearly points to a complex and multidimensional construct comprising various internal (feelings and thoughts) and external (behaviors) elements (Phinney, 1996; Sodowsky, Kwan, & Pannu, 1995). Also captured in the literature is the view of ethnic identity as a dynamic and unfolding process that changes over time and context as a person examines and explores the meaning of his or her ethnic and/or racial group membership (Helms & Cook, 1999; Lee & Zane, 1998; Phinney, 1996; Ponterotto, Casas, Suzuki, & Alexander, 1995). Although the *content* of ethnic identity and the process of ethnic identity *formation* are interrelated, for the stake of clarity we address them separately. Furthermore, this chapter attempts to distinguish between ethnic and racial identity development.

Ethnic Identity—A Focus on Content and Context

Much attention has been given to examining the content of ethnic identity among American ethnic minority groups.[1] When addressing the content of ethnic identity and its relevant components, the focus has been on the state of an individual's identification at a given time. The most pertinent components of ethnic identity include (1) self-identification as a group member; (2) personal attitudes and feelings of oneself as an ethnic group member; (3) the scope and breadth of ethnic knowledge, and (4) the scope and breath of ethnic behaviors and practices (Phinney, 1990, 1995, 1996). These components reflect the universal aspects of ethnic identity found across groups (Phinney, 1990). In addition, ethnic identity has contextual aspects, such as a group's status, power, and salience; public attitudes toward the group by the larger society; and level of social acceptance (Phinney, 2000b; Sodowsky et al., 1995; Sue, Mak, & Sue, 1998). In this section we consider the content of ethnic identity, keeping in mind the contextual dimensions that shape its meaning.

In discussing the components of ethnic identity, self-identification refers to the ethnic label individuals use to identify themselves as an ethnic group member. For instance, a European American college student may refer to herself as White, and an African American student may choose to call herself Black. However, in the case of the African American student who is a member of a racially and culturally distinct group (i.e., group salience) from White Americans, self-identification is externally imposed to some extent (Phinney, 1990). Phinney states "that calling oneself Black or Asian American is less a self-categorization than recognition of imposed distinctions, and the issue is less whether to use an ethnic label than which ethnic label to adopt" (Phinney, 1990, p. 504). Persons of Mexican descent, for example, may choose the ethnic labels of Mexicano, Mexican American, Chicano/a, Indio/a, Hispanic, or Latino/a, each label connoting a somewhat different national, binational, political, or cultural ethnic identity orientation and a unique personal meaning (Buriel, 1987; Buriel & De Ment, 1997; Comas-Diaz, 2001; Hurtado, Gurin, & Peng, 1994). A student in the study illustrated this point well.

---

1. The term "ethnic minority groups" refers to non-European groups in American society, such as African, Asian, and Native Americans; Pacific Islanders; and Latinos/as, and is used to distinguish such people (who in many areas are no longer the numerical minority) from the dominant White majority (Phinney, 1996).

There's a big issue about are you Chicana, Chicano, Latino, Mexican American, or what? And I think that I identify more with Mexican American. I don't know, I guess that because I have been told that since I was young, but I see myself more as a Mexican American, and that is my heritage. To be Chicana, I think is more political. I think that it is a political term. I know about different issues that they do advocate, but I don't participate, so I don't feel comfortable calling myself Chicana. But there have been times that I have said that I am something else, because of the environment, you know, the moment I'm in. I was at a conference and I was helping, you know working with them, and everybody else called themselves Chicano and so I did. But I have to say that I can't identify myself as one.

Another factor influencing ethnic identity for visibly distinct groups is that self-identification may differ from the identity the larger society imposes. To illustrate, a Puerto Rican student who identifies as such may be labeled Black by others based on his or her phenotypic characteristics. Hence, self-identification can be a complex interaction of an individual's physical appearance, personal choice, the specific social context, and the available ethnic labels (Padilla, 2006; Phinney, 2000a, 2000b).

Researchers have also observed that the selection or choice of ethnic labels can change, depending on the social context and the existing ethnopolitical conditions (Comas-Diaz, 2001; Phinney, 1996; Phinney, 2000a; Tafoya, 2004/2005; Yip, 2005). To illustrate, a politically active Latina student may identify herself as Chicana within the confines of the university walls, but adopt the label of Mexican American when interacting with family members. Because of the unique meaning associated with the ethnic labels Chicano/a and Mexican American, the student in the earlier quote was able to convey a particular sense of her ethnicity (a political versus cultural orientation) in different situations by using different labels (Water, 1990). Therefore, an important factor in self-designation of ethnic labels is "gaining a voice and power to name one's identity and define one's reality" within a given social context (Comas-Diaz, 2001, p. 116). Rumbaut's (1995) research with adolescents attending inner-city, "minority" high schools in San Diego further exemplifies this dynamic. A pan-ethnic identification, that is, Asian or Hispanic, was found to be the ethnic label of choice among these adolescents. The shift in identification from smaller affiliations (Vietnamese or Mexican) to larger ones (pan-ethnic identity) can be seen as an attempt by these youths to protect and promote the collective interest of their group (Buriel & De Ment, 1997). Hence, contextual factors (social, political, and economic constraints) and subjective influences come to bear in important ways on the social identities and ethnic labels of individuals (Pizarro & Vera, 2001).

In addition to self-identification, personal attitudes and feelings about one's group are viewed as central aspects of ethnic identity. Positive personal attitudes of oneself as a group member are related to feelings of acceptance, pride, satisfaction, attachment, sense of belonging, and a general preference for and commitment to one's ethnic group (Yip & Fuligni, 2002). Conversely, the presence of negative attitudes is associated with feelings of displeasure, shame, or denial of one's ethnicity and a sense of ethnic inferiority (Phinney, 1990, 1995). Unfortunately, negative stereotypes and biased portrayals of ethnic minorities are prevalent in American society, and they affect the attitudes minorities have about themselves and other groups have toward them (Cohen & Garcia, 2005; Mobasher, 2006; Sinclair, Hardin, & Lowery, 2006; Sue et al., 1998). Public attitudes and social evaluations of one's group by the larger society are believed to influence the affective dimension of ethnic identity (Phinney, 1995; Tajfel & Turner, 1986). To illustrate, a Korean American university student who experiences repeated ethnic discrimination and social criticism by peers or a faculty professor may have difficulty feeling positive about his group membership in this context. Although there is much variability across individuals in the extent to which discrimination is perceived (Phinney, Madden, & Santos, 1996; Uba, 1994), a proactive approach to dealing with such issues (self-affirmation and discussions and efforts to disprove stereotypes) has been found to predict a secure ethnic identity and positive self-esteem in ethnic minority adolescents (Phinney & Chavira, 1995). Hence, ethnic identity is adversely affected by negative public attitudes to the extent that individuals internalize negative group messages as opposed to personally distancing themselves from such information and embracing positive group characteristics that engender ethnic esteem (Cohen & Garcia, 2005; Crocker, Luhtanen, Blain, & Broadnax, 1994; Crocker & Major, 1989).

The third component—ethnic knowledge—has been identified as an important cognitive aspect of ethnic identity. It reflects a person's level of "cultural awareness" or "ethnic consciousness" regarding his or her group's characteristics, that is, knowledge of ethnic history, cultural norms, values, traditions, mores, and behavioral expectations (Sue et al., 1998; Uba, 1994). According to researchers, ethnic knowledge provides the foundation for the construction of "ethnic schemas" (Sue et al., 1998; Uba, 1994)—cognitive structures that influence the manner in which individuals register, filter, and process "information, events and situations within their own group, other cultural groups and the dominant society" (Sue et al., 1998, p. 293). Factors known to invoke ethnic schemas include personal salience of ethnic identity for the individual, group salience within a specific social context, and social discrimination (Sue et al., 1998; Uba, 1994; Yip, 2005). For instance, a Latino student attending a predominantly White university (high group salience) may only feel comfortable expressing his ethnic identity under very specific situations—when interacting with coethnic peers—due to fear of social criticism, while another student in the same situation, but who has little invested in his ethnic identity (low personal salience), may regard his ethnicity as irrelevant in this context—his student identity predominates. Still, another Latino student who is highly committed to his ethnic group will invoke that identity across a broad range of situations (Uba, 1994). "Thus, to varying degrees, individuals' psychological reality is shaped by their knowledge . . . of their ethnic identity" (Sue et al., 1998, p. 293).

Last, ethnic behaviors and practices reflect the cultural aspects of ethnic identity and refer specifically to the level of "involvement in the social life and cultural practices of one's ethnic group" (Phinney, 1990, p. 505). For many Latinos/as and Asian Americans, this includes language (Sue et al., 1998; Yip, 2005). Researchers view language proficiency and use as being an important dimension of ethnic identity for many cultural groups and one that is closely tied to their sense of self as a group member (Giles, Bourhis, & Taylor, 1977; Phinney, 2000b). The inability to speak one's native language can be a source of much embarrassment for many individuals, engendering a sense of ethnic loss (Padilla, 2006). This is cogently illustrated by comments made by a student in our study.

> College group meetings are run in Korean, so I get the gist of it, but I really don't understand the specifics, so I am always whispering to someone to get a translation. So language is probably the key thing that makes me feel like I'm not as Korean as I should be.

Researchers have found that language use is not only a positive predictor of group pride among college students but is also related to choice of ethnic social affiliations (i.e., preferred friends) (Ontai-Grzebik & Raffaelli, 2004; Tsai, Ying, & Lee, 2001).

Other commonly studied indicators of ethnic involvement have included composition of social networks; religious affiliations and practices; and various cultural activities such as ethnic music, dance, literature, or foods and participation in ethnic celebrations (e.g., *Cinco de Mayo*). The literature has also examined the level of adherence to traditional gender roles and ethnic value orientations such as individualism, collectivism, and familialism (Halgunseth, Ispa, & Rudy, 2006; Inman, 2006; Phinney, 1990, 1996, 2000b; Yeh, Carter, & Pieterse, 2004). Once again, contextual aspects of the situation play an important role in maintaining ethnic culture, with residence in an ethnic community (ethnic enclave or barrio) being known to strengthen cultural awareness and involvement in ethnic practices (Juang, Nguyen, & Yunghui, 2006; Padilla, 2006; Ramirez & Castaneda, 1974; Uba, 1994). For instance, residence in a vital ethnic community was associated with greater observance of a Mexican Catholic ideology (as opposed to American Catholicism) and a strong familial and community orientation (collectivism) in Mexican Americans residing in Southern California (Ramirez & Castaneda, 1974). Likewise, frequent contact with other Mexican people was linked to having a Spanish-speaking identity and a strong family identity among Mexican Americans (Gurin, Hurtado, & Peng, 1994).

In examining the state of ethnic identity, it is assumed that in the strength of individuals' ethnic identification will differ. Ethnic identity varies along a continuum of high to low, with individuals falling somewhere between these two poles on relevant components (Phinney, 1995). This model of ethnic identity strength proposes that a high or strong ethnic identity is exemplified by someone who self-identifies as a group member (e.g., "I am Filipino"), evaluates the group positively, shows a preference for the group and is happy with his or her membership in the group, is knowledgeable about the group, and is involved in ethnic practices. On the other hand, a low or weak ethnic identity typifies a person who is unclear about his or her ethnic identity, who finds it problematic, or for whom ethnicity is of little importance. Such individuals may find it difficult to self-identify as ethnic group members (e.g., "I am a human being"), exhibit little ethnic knowledge or involvement in cultural practices, and/or have negative evaluations of the group and their membership in the group. Several questionnaires have been devised to assess the strength and structure of ethnic identity by examining its various components; most notable is the work conducted by Phinney and her colleagues (e.g., for Latinos/as, Garcia [1982] and Felix-Ortiz [1994]; for Asians, Suinn, Ahuna, & Hknoo [1992] and Tsai et al. [2001]; and for use with any group, Phinney [1992]).

Relationship Among Ethnic Identity Components

A major concern of researchers has been to identify the interrelationship among the various ethnic components, that is, to understand the relationship between "what people say they are (ethnic self-identification) and what they actually do (ethnic involvement) or how they feel (ethnic pride)" (Phinney, 1990, p. 506). The picture that emerges from the literature is that the various components of ethnic identity can operate independently of each other or interact to influence the strength and form that ethnic identity takes within a given context (Sue et al., 1998). For instance, just because an African American individual is quite knowledgeable about an ethnic-specific custom, such as the Kwanzaa celebration,[2] it does not mean that person will actually practice that tradition or derive group pride from this knowledge. Conversely, an African American person who actively participates in this yearly celebration is likely to be knowledgeable about this ethnic custom, engendering in that person a sense of ethnic pride (positive group attitude and feelings). Hence, there is great variability within groups in terms of how "individuals select and integrate certain cultural patterns and beliefs into their repertoire and invoke these ethnic schemata as found to be appropriate in specific social situations" (Sue et al., 1998, p. 294). Contextual factors (e.g., social acceptance or discrimination), along with individual differences in ethnic identity development, are believed to account for the variability observed across individuals in manifest ethnic identity (Phinney, 1995; Uba, 1994).

Despite individual variability in ethnicity identity, researchers have noted changes in the meaning or structure of ethnic identity as a function of generational status in contemporary American ethnic minority groups (Cardona, Busby, & Wampler, 2004). Work conducted with Chinese American adolescents revealed that ethnic knowledge and behaviors decrease between the first and second generation, but positive evaluations of the group and

---

2. Kwanzaa is a 7-day cultural festival that focuses on the principles of unity, self-determination, responsibility, economics, purpose, creativity, and faith.

group identification remains relatively constant (Rosenthal & Feldman, 1990). Similarly, research conducted with Latino/a samples also shows that awareness of Mexican culture diminishes with each successive generation; yet, loyalty to one's group (i.e., positive ethnic attitudes and feelings and ethnic preference) remains high (Keefe, 1992; Keefe & Padilla, 1987; Padilla, 2006). This phenomenon of strong ethnic identification despite low cultural awareness and involvement has been termed *ethnic loyalty* (Padilla, 2006). An accorded minority status[3] is believed to be a major force contributing to maintaining symbolic ethnicity and ethnic loyalty across generations in present-day ethnic minority groups. *Symbolic ethnicity* refers to claiming pride in ethnicity without the associated cultural knowledge and/or engagement in long-standing ethnic or cultural practices (Keefe & Padilla, 1987; Padilla, 2006; Phinney, 1996).

Finally, researchers have also observed that aspects of ethnic identity vary independently of each other and impinge differently on psychological outcomes. In general, a sense of belonging and preference for one's group, positive evaluations of one's ethnic group (group pride), and commitment to one's ethnic group contribute positively to self-esteem, while other aspects of ethnic identity, notably self-identification or ethnic labeling, ethnic knowledge, and ethnic practices, have shown an inconsistent association or no relation to self-esteem (Phinney, 1995; Phinney, Cantu, & Kurtz, 1997; Roberts, Phinney, & Masse, 1999; Tsai et al., 2001; Yip, 2005). It is not group membership per se (i.e., being Black, Latino/a, Asian, or White) but a person's personal identification (attitudes and feelings) with his or her ethnic group that is most important in understanding the psychological role that ethnicity plays in people's lives.

Psychological Salience of Ethnic Identity

The salience[4] or psychological centrality of ethnic identity varies across American ethnic groups. Research studies have consistently shown that ethnic identity is a more central and important component of the self-concept among ethnic minority groups than it is among White Americans (Alba,

---

3. The term "minority status" is usually linked to people of color and "carries with it the connotation of unequal relationships among groups within society, in which some groups are subjected to greater prejudice and discrimination" (Phinney, 1996, p. 923).

4. Ethnic identity salience refers to "the importance of ethnic identity within a conglomeration of identities" (Uba, 1994, p. 103).

1990; Crocker et al., 1994; Ellis, 2004; Kim-Ju & Liem, 2003; Negy, Shreve, Jensen, & Uddin; 2003; Phinney & Alipuria, 1990). The greater centrality of ethnic identity for ethnic groups of color is attributed to the visible and obvious characteristics (skin color and phenotypic differences) associated with their group membership and the stigma of having minority status. Because of their accorded dominant status, most White Americans tend not to think of themselves in ethnic terms and experience greater flexibility in choosing "what role, if any, it will have for them" (Phinney, 1996, p. 922). In fact, Perry (2001) notes that construction of "cultureless" identities among White Americans can be seen, even if unintentionally, as a means of acknowledging the superiority of their group status in the United States. To be cultureless or non-ethnic "implies that one is either the norm (the standard by which others are judged)" (p. 57) or a rational perspective where to be cultureless is considered a preferred status. Notwithstanding, changes in the ethnic diversification of university campuses across the country make it more probable that ethnicity will become a more salient and defining aspect of White students' identity. Phinney and colleagues (Phinney, Cantu, & Kurtz, 1997) support this notion by finding that, in the case of White students attending a predominantly ethnic minority high school, having a strong American identity correlated highly with ethnic identity and self-esteem. This highlights the unique meaning ethnic identity has for this group of White adolescents. An American identity may have engendered a sense of ethnic pride that stemmed from being associated with and belonging to the "dominant" group in society.

The Interplay Between Race and Ethnicity

Both ethnic and racial identity are seen as components of the larger social identity, with *racial identity* specifically referring to "the process by which individuals define themselves with regard to racial classification in their social contexts" (Pizarro & Vera, 2001, p. 94). Differentiating racial from ethnic identity has been the topic of much recent debate in the literature. Complicating this discussion is that the constructs of race, culture, and ethnicity are frequently used interchangeably and/or are confounded in identity research (Helms & Cook, 1999; Phinney, 1996). Many have noted that race is socially constructed, meaning that there is no factual basis or biological distinction between groups of people. They claim that race has been socially constructed due to exclusionary practices, stereotypes or mythology about groups of people, and the subsequent development of racism as an ideology. Although we do not advocate abolishing race through its deconstruction, we do want to acknowledge that racial categories are not distinct and are largely defined by individuals in particular contexts. Therefore, there is great variation within ethnic or racial categories and even greater variability when considering the interchange of the multiple social identities an individual may have, including multiple racial or ethnic identities due to mixed racial heritage (Miville, Constantine, Baysden, & So-Lloyd, 2005; Padilla, 2006; Renn, 2004; Suyemoto, 2004).

Because of ongoing disagreements among social scientists regarding the meaning and use of race, Phinney (1996), in her conceptual discussion of ethnicity, proposed that race and racial identity be encompassed within the construct of ethnicity. Although Phinney's work addresses aspects of identity formation that are specifically the result of racial influences, that is, a minority status (Pizarro & Vera, 2001), she argues that racial and ethnic identity development can be conceptualized as one process (Phinney & Kohatsu, 1997). Phinney's three-stage model of ethnic identity development is presented later in this chapter.

Notwithstanding that racial issues are likely to be intertwined with ethnic identity, it would seem advantageous to define race operationally as a psychological construct distinguishable from ethnicity (Helms & Talleyrand, 1997). Accordingly, Helms and Talleyrand (1997) proposed that "if ethnicity (and derivatives thereof) is intended to refer to dimensions of cultural socialization (i.e., socioculture and expression) and expressions (i.e., psychoculture) then freeing the term from the race-related baggage (e.g., 'minority status') that now obscures the meaning of ethnicity" would be valuable to researchers (p. 1247). The authors buttress their argument by explaining that individuals experience distinct forms of racial and ethnic socialization, with each type of socialization having different implications for individual and group behavior.

Furthermore, the authors note that the role race plays in American society is salient for visibly distinct groups, whereas ethnicity (i.e., socioculture) is less visible. Race is constantly used as means of categorizing individuals into distinct social groups. "People are treated as though they belong to a biologically defined racial group" on the basis of characteristics that society deems to be racial (i.e., skin color, hair texture, body size, and facial features), and regardless of one's cultural socialization, disadvantageous treatment most often occurs on the basis of phenotypic characteristics (Helms & Talleyrand, 1997, p. 1247). Supporting this view is research linking phenotypic differences within ethnic minority groups to experiences with discrimination and economic opportunities in this country. For instance, studies of African Americans and Latinos/as in the United States show that participants with lighter skin and more distinctly European features (i.e., thin lips, aquiline nose, light eyes, and straighter hair) experience higher income and educational levels and less discrimination than do their darker-skinned counterparts (Arce, Murguia, & Frisbie, 1987; Gomez, 2001; Hall, 1994; Russell, Wilson, & Hall, 1992). Similarly, researchers have also shown a link between skin color and mental health in Latino/a samples, with darker-skinned participants (i.e., those with a more indigenous phenotype) experiencing higher rates of depression regardless of proficiency in Spanish or English (Araujo & Borrell, 2006; Codina & Montalvo, 1994). Asians and Latinos/as have been portrayed to seem "less American" than African and White Americans (Cheryan & Monin, 2005). Hence, race, not ethnicity, is more likely to influence the quality of life and psychological well-being of individuals who are visibly distinct from White Americans (Pizarro & Vera, 2001).

Based on the above discussion, it is not surprising that many scholars view racial identity to be a central aspect of the social identity among people of color. The literature has proposed several models of racial identity development (Atkinson, Morten, & Sue, 1993; Helms, 1995; Helms & Cook, 1999), which are covered in some detail later in this chapter. In their conceptual analysis of ethnic identity, Sodowsky and colleagues (1995) were the first to outline explicitly the primary differences between models of racial and ethnic identity. They note that:

> *racial identity* is (a) based on a sociopolitical model of oppression, (b) based on a socially constructed definition of race, and (c) concerned with how individuals abandon the effects of disenfranchisement and develop respectful attitudes towards their racial group. On the other hand, *ethnic identity* (a) concerns one's attachment to, sense of belonging to, and identification with one ethnic group (e.g., Japanese, Vietnamese, Indian) and with one's ethnic culture; (b) does not have a theoretical emphasis on oppression/racism, but (c) may include the prejudices and cultural pressures that ethnic individuals experience when their ways of life come into conflict with those of the White dominant group. (p. 133)

To illustrate, an Asian or Latino/a student may experience social criticism from his or her peers because the student speaks with an accent, a prejudice that is more likely to have a negative impact on the student's sense of cultural identity. This student may attempt to minimize his or her accent by speaking English only, which may result in language loss, or the student may become very reluctant to speak English in this context for fear of being humiliated (e.g., publicly corrected as if he or she were a child).

To conclude, future studies that better delineate the dual influences of racial and ethnic identity will increase our understanding of how these two processes are interrelated and come to bear on identity formation. As noted by Pizarro and Vera (2001), many of the psychological concerns that ethnic minority groups in this country face are linked to experiences of discrimination and oppression; therefore, "understanding ethnic identity necessarily involves a clarification of what role race plays in the daily lives" of such individuals (p. 94).

Factors That Influence the Formation of Ethnic Identity

Ethnic identity is a fluid and dynamic experience that changes over time and across contexts. To understand the development of ethnic identity formation, it is important to consider first the role enculturation and acculturation play in this process.

Enculturation or ethnic socialization "is the process through which individuals learn that they have specific ethnic role behaviors (e.g., rituals, celebrations of holidays) that are based on unique ethnic knowledge and lead to ethnic preferences (e.g., for music, food, friends) and feelings" (Pizarro & Vera, 2001, p. 92). In essence, ethnic identity develops through enculturation—a process in which familial and nonfamilial influences (peers, teachers, community, the media, and larger institutions) play a significant role (Berry, 1990, 1993; Knight, Bernal, Cota, Garza, & Ocampo, 1993). More specifically, the social ecology of the family (socioeconomic status and generation in the United States, cultural knowledge, and family structure) is believed to interact with ethnopolitical conditions of the family's home community (minority-majority relations and public views of the group) to influence the content of ethnic socialization. Family members tend to focus more on teaching ethnic content (e.g., cultural values, gender roles, and behavioral expectations), while nonfamilial agents emphasize communicating social views about ethnicity and group membership (e.g., minority/majority status and group stereotypes) (Bernal & Martinelli, 1993; Knight et al., 1993; Padilla, 2006). This interplay between familial and nonfamilial socializing agents is believed to influence various aspects of ethnic identity formation directly. Finally, differences in parental ethnic socialization have been observed. Specifically, African American parents are more apt to discuss prejudice with their children than are Asian and Mexican American parents (Cross & Fhagen-Smith, 2001; Phinney & Chavira, 1995). Furthermore, African and Asian American parents are also more likely than are Mexican American parents to stress the importance of adapting to the dominant society.

In addition to enculturation, acculturation processes are believed to play an important role in ethnic identity development. Acculturation refers to how ethnic minority or immigrant groups adapt and relate to the dominant or host society. Specifically, *acculturation* concerns the changes in cultural attitudes, values, and behaviors that result when two distinct groups are in contact over time, a phenomenon characteristic of racially and ethnically heterogeneous pluralistic societies (Berry, 1993).

Two distinct models have primarily guided acculturation research when examining cultural change in American ethnic groups: a linear, bipolar model and a two-dimensional model of acculturation. The linear model of acculturation conceptualizes cultural change along a continuum of strong ethnic ties at one extreme to strong mainstream ties at the other (Buriel & De Ment, 1997; Phinney, 1990; Stonequist, 1937). The assumption underlying this model is that, as individuals strengthen their ties to and identification with the mainstream culture, acculturation inevitably involves a weakening of ethnic identity. The result of complete acculturation is *assimilation*, whereby individuals lose all trace of their ancestral identity and become indistinguishable members of the dominant society by assuming a new (superior) cultural identity. Although the ethnic culture continues to coexist with the dominant culture, the person is no longer a part of that cultural world, nor does he or she find it of value (Phinney & Devich-Navarro, 1997).

Given that America is a race- and color-conscious society, assimilation is not really a viable option for individuals of non-European extraction who are visibly distinct from White Americans (Buriel & De Ment, 1997). This is certainly the case for most present-day ethnic minority individuals. Regardless of how much assimilation takes place at a personal level, it does not mean that the larger society will view such individuals (e.g., indigenous-looking Latinos/as) as indistinguishable from the White majority (Cheryan & Monin, 2005; Pizarro & Vera, 2001). Hence, attempts to assimilate can come at a great psychological cost to the individual, that is, such individuals potentially face rejection not only by the dominant group but the ethnic in-group, whose members may view their actions as disloyal and having "sold out" to Whites (LaFrambroise, Coleman, & Gerton, 1995; Padilla, 2006).

It is clear that the linear or bipolar model of culture change is overly simplistic and fails to capture adequately the acculturative experience of contemporary ethnic minority groups. Several bidirectional models of acculturation that emerged in response to this problem have gained much wider acceptance in the literature (Berry, 1990; Buriel & De Ment, 1997). Most notable is Berry's (1990) model, which conceptualizes acculturation as a two-dimensional process in which an individual's relationship to the ethnic culture and to the dominant or majority culture are considered simultaneously. According to this perspective, individuals may have a strong or weak identification with either the mainstream culture or the ethnic culture, or they may exhibit strong or weak identification to both the mainstream culture and ethnic culture (Phinney, 1990). Hence, Berry's model proposes four possible ways that minority individuals can attempt to cope with membership in a diverse society.

Figure 2.1 illustrates the four different acculturative strategies. An exclusive identification with the dominant culture reflects *assimilation* (high mainstream identification, low cultural retention), while an exclusive identification to the traditional culture indicates separation (high cultural retention, low mainstream orientation). *Separation* implies that the individual is solely embedded in the ethnic culture and completely dissociates from mainstream culture, for example, he or she chooses to live in an ethnic enclave or barrio. Low identification with both the ethnic culture and the majority culture suggests marginality (low cultural retention, low mainstream orientation), a phenomenon descriptive of Ogbu's "caste-like" minority when referring to American youth gangs (1987b). *Marginality*[5] is the result of

---

5. Deculturation is "defined as a loss of one's ancestral identity coupled with a sense of alienation from the larger society" (Buriel & De Ment, 1997, p. 176). Research by Buriel and colleagues suggests that individuals with weak ties to their ancestral or immigrant culture are at greater risk of experiencing deculturation, which can lead to a marginalized state. They argue that, although marginalized individuals may continue to have a sense of identification with their ethnic group, they are more prone to adopt a

FIGURE 2.1
Illustration of a Bidirectional Model of Acculturation*

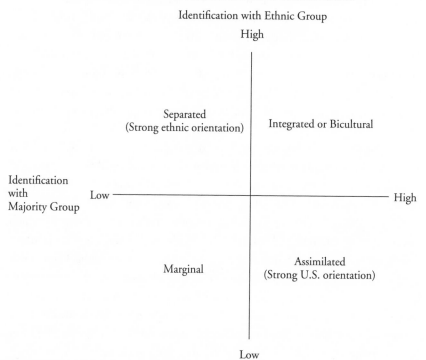

Identification with Ethnic Group
High

Separated
(Strong ethnic orientation)   Integrated or Bicultural

Identification
with   Low ————————————————————— High
Majority Group

Marginal   Assimilated
(Strong U.S. orientation)

Low

*Adapted from Berry, 1990; Buriel & De Ment, 1997.

deculturation and implies that an individual is in between two cultures and belongs to neither one, a state believed to engender great psychological distress in individuals, that is, identity confusion, ambiguity, and normlessness (Berry, 1990; LaFrambroise et al., 1995; Stonequist, 1937). Finally, a strong identification with and participation in both the ethnic and majority culture indicates *integration* or *biculturalism*. Integrated or bicultural individuals are those who retain their cultural identity while at the same time adopting cultural characteristics of mainstream culture, thereby effectively negotiating both worlds (Berry, 1990; LaFrambroise et al., 1995; Phinney & Devich-Navarro, 1997). Hence, establishing and maintaining positive relationships

---

distorted view of the group and internalize negative societal depictions and stereotypes of the group (e.g., Latinos are violent, illiterate, and deviant).

with the majority group does not necessitate a loss of ethnic identity. Biculturalism "permits individuals to meet the dual cultural expectations that characterize the lives of ethnic minorities as they move in and out of minority and majority cultural environments" (Buriel & De Ment, 1997, p. 174). There is evidence that an integrated or bicultural option is the most desirable for minority individuals, and a marginal orientation is the least favorable (Buriel & De Ment, 1997; Haritatos & Benet-Martinez, 2002; LaFrambroise et al., 1995; Lieber, Chin, Nihira, & Mink, 2001; Padilla, 2006; Phinney, 1990).

Sodowsky and colleagues (1995) modified Berry's bidirectional model of acculturation to explain ethnic identity processes among Asian Americans. Operating from the assumption that ethnic identity follows a bidirectional process, they proposed four ethnic identity orientations based on the degree to which "Whiteness" is adopted and sought and/or the degree to which "Asianness" is retained and valued. This model allows for a nonlinear trend over time and across situations so that "individuals can move back and forth among the four acculturation orientations (i.e., assimilation, integration, biculturalism, and marginalization), depending on the context" (p. 143). To illustrate, a first-generation female Japanese college student may express a *bicultural orientation* in her interpersonal interactions with White peers but have a *strong ethnic identity* orientation regarding such matters as marriage (is comfortable with the notion of an arranged marriage) and religion (she chooses to observe Buddhism in spite of being exposed to Christianity). Yet, in another context the student may feel *culturally marginalized* with regard to her views on gender, that is, she does not endorse a subservient female role, but neither does she agree with the agenda of White feminists (Sodowsky et al., 1995). Finally, this student may reflect a strong *U.S. White identity* orientation regarding views on democracy and governance. This model is important because it highlights the selective nature of acculturation across ethnicity's various internal (values, beliefs) and external (behavioral practices) aspects.

In conclusion, addressed in the enculturation and acculturation research are two important dimensions of ethnic identity formation: (1) a person's attitudes and feelings of belonging to the group, which are largely determined by enculturation or ethnic socialization, and (2) a person's attitudes and feelings of belonging to the larger society (other group attitudes), which are shaped primarily through acculturation experiences. It is this interplay between enculturative and acculturative processes that is believed to influence ethnic identity development so heavily, a dynamic that is played out most prominently during adolescence and early adulthood (Pizarro & Vera, 2001).

Models of Ethnic and Racial Identity Development

The literature has proposed a number of stage models of ethnic and racial identity in an effort to delineate more clearly the process of ethnic identity formation. In general, these models acknowledge the struggles and conflicts that ethnic individuals go through as they negotiate their own cultural orientation, influences of the dominant culture, and experiences with prejudice and discrimination (Sue et al., 1998). Table 2.1 illustrates the relationship between the different identity models and the terminology used for each model. Although these models focus on somewhat different issues and/or groups, they share structural similarities and parallels that are based on ego identity development theory. In this section we describe in detail only those models of ethnic and racial identity development that have been applied to high school and college-age students and touch briefly on new perspectives of racial identity that have emerged in the literature.

A Three-Stage Model of Ethnic Identity Development

Phinney's (1993) three-stage model of ethnic identity is grounded in Erikson's (1968) writings on ego identity formation and Marcia's (1980) work on ego identity statuses. Operating from the premise that identity formation is a central task of the adolescent years, Phinney "views ethnic and/or racial identity as an extension of ego identity" that should "run parallel to other components of ego identity development" (Cross & Fhagen-Smith, 2001, p. 247). Phinney's work is significant in that she was the first to examine ethnic and/or racial identity development during the adolescent and early adulthood years and to apply this perspective successfully across various ethnic groups. Although Phinney's model is applicable to Whites, she focuses primarily on the identity formation of ethnic minority groups (Phinney, 1995).

According to Phinney, the first stage of ethnic identity development—*Unexamined Ethnic Identity*—is characterized by a lack of exploration of one's ethnicity. At this point, the person has not yet examined or evaluated the meaning or implications of his or her ethnic group membership. Hence,

TABLE 2.1
Comparison of Ego Identity Theory With Models of Ethnic and Racial Identity Development*

Model	Initial Phase	Transition	Intermediate Phase	Final Phase
Ego Identity (Marcia, 1980)	Diffusion/Foreclosed	Identity Crisis	Moratorium	Identity Achievement
Ethnic Identity (Phinney, 1993)	Unexamined	Exposure/Experience	Exploration	Achievement
Black/People of Color Racial Identity (Helms, 1990, 1995)	Preencounter/ Conformity	Encounter/Dissonance	Resistance-Emersion	Internalized Commitment
White Racial Identity (Helms, 1995)	Contact	Disintegration & Reintegration	Pseudoindependent & Immersion-Emersion	Autonomy
Minority Identity Model (Atkinson, Morten, & Sue, 1993)	Conformity	Dissonance	Resistance & Emersion	Introspection & Integrative Awareness
Lifespan Model of Black Identity Development (Cross & Fhagen-Smith, 2001)	Infancy & Childhood Pre-Adolescence	Adolescence–Early Adulthood	Adult Nigrescence	Nigrescence Recycling
Asian American Identity Development Model (Kim, 2001)	Ethnic Awareness Childhood	White Identification	Awakening to Social-Political Consciousness	Redirection to an Asian American Consciousness

*Adapted from Phinney & Kohatsu, 1997.

the person has a poorly developed or weak identity (diffused status), marked by a lack of concern about or interest in his or her ethnicity (low personal salience), or has adopted a view (positive or negative) of ethnicity from his or her parents and other primary socializing agents (foreclosed status). A positive foreclosed ethnic identity is possible for persons embedded in a vital and cohesive ethnic community. However, in line with Erikson's (1968) notion of ego formation, an unexamined ethnic identity (a foreclosed or diffused status) reflects immaturity in the person's ego development.

The initial phase of ethnic identity development continues until the person experiences a "crisis" or encounters a situation that triggers the next stage, *Ethnic Identity Search* or *Moratorium*, in which the challenges and conflicts surrounding one's minority or ethnic status are examined and scrutinized. Individuals in the second stage are involved in a quest for knowledge; they become the ultimate explorers as they strive to understand the meaning of their ethnicity, which necessarily involves questioning previously held cultural perspectives and worldviews. This is exemplified by high school and college students who take ethnic courses and join politically oriented organizations (i.e., *Movimiento Estudiantil Chicano de Aztlán* [MEChA] or Asian American Club) to enhance their cultural awareness and political consciousness. According to Phinney (1993), the exploratory phase need not involve a pivotal event in the person's life or be marked by emotional turbulence, but a period of examination and reflection is essential for reaching an achieved identity.

The final stage, *Ethnic Identity Achieved*, is characterized by a sense of clarity and confidence regarding one's ethnicity that is associated with positive feelings about oneself as an ethnic group member. Specifically, an achieved ethnic identity is defined as a "secure commitment to one's group based on knowledge and understanding obtained through an active exploration of one's cultural background" (Phinney & Chavira, 1992, p. 272). This final stage involves a resolution of previous conflicts regarding retention of one's cultural heritage, the relationship of oneself to the dominant society, and the development of adaptive strategies for handling racism and discrimination (Phinney & Kohatsu, 1997). An achieved ethnic identity status is believed to be the most adaptive and desirable status for healthy development.

Early research by Phinney and her colleagues provided strong support for the validity of her three-stage model of ethnic identity development. In her seminal work with adolescents from Asian (Chinese, Filipino, Japanese, Korean, and Vietnamese), Mexican, and African American backgrounds, Phinney (1989) addressed the degree to which these minority youth had examined and resolved ethnic identity issues and the relationship of these processes to psychological adjustment. She found that those students who had an achieved ethnic identity status reported higher scores in self-evaluations, sense of mastery, social and peer interactions, and family relations than those who did not. Furthermore, ethnic identity statuses were related to ego identity development, with adolescents with an unexamined ethnic identity reporting the lowest ego identity scores and those with an achieved identity having the highest scores. This suggests that students who had the "clearest sense of themselves in terms of personal identity were also the most secure about their ethnicity and its meaning in their lives" (Phinney, 1993, p. 73). Furthermore, in a three-year longitudinal study of adolescents from three ethnic groups (Asian, Mexican, and African American students), Phinney and colleagues were able to demonstrate the progression of ethnic identity over time, "from an unexamined or diffuse stage to an achieved ethnic identity" (Phinney & Chavira, 1992, p. 271). Although they found that the majority of participants moved toward higher stages of ethnic identity development from ages 16 to 19, stability, progression, and regression in identity stages were also evident, pointing to individual differences in ethnic identity development. Even though more recent research seems to favor this linear movement in ethnic identity development, Phinney notes that ethnic identity formation need not evolve in a sequential and linear direction, but should be viewed in terms of dimensions along which individuals differ rather than in terms of categories in which to classify individuals and samples (Phinney, 1996).

In another study, Phinney and Alipuria (1990) examined ethnic identity search and commitment in college students from four ethnic groups—Asian, Mexican, African and White Americans—to determine the importance of ethnicity as a social identity compared to other identity domains (i.e., gender, occupational, political, and religious identities). Although gender and occupational identities were the most important identities for all groups, ethnic identity was the next highest for ethnic minorities. Only in the case of White students was ethnicity rated the least important. They also found that the quest for ethnic identity search was higher among ethnic minority groups, and that commitment to one's ethnicity was significantly and positively related to self-esteem in all four groups.

Phinney's early work led to the development of the Multigroup Ethnic Identity Measure (MEIM) (1992). The dimensions in the MEIM include self-identification or ethnic labels, ethnic behaviors and practices, affirmation and belonging (i.e., attitudes toward the group and sense of attachment and pride), and the statuses of ethnic identity achievement (i.e., exploration and resolution of ethnic identity issues). The MEIM has been shown to be a reliable and valid measure of ethnic identity that can be used with diverse ethnic groups (Phinney, 1992). The measure shows evidence of the developmental progression of ethnic identity, with college students scoring higher on the ethnic identity achievement factor of MEIM (the process and resolution of ethnic identity issues) than do high school students. In fact, the reliability of the measure was higher with college students, supporting the notion that ethnic identity becomes more consolidated with age. Furthermore, and adding support to the MEIM's validity, high ethnicity scores on this measure have been found to predict self-esteem in adolescent (Phinney, 1992; Phinney, Cantu & Kurtz, 1997; Roberts et al., 1999) and college-age samples (Phinney, 1992) from various ethnic groups (i.e., Asian, Latino/a, Black, and White students). In a study with Latino/a, African, and White American adolescent students, high ethnic identity scores on the MEIM (high group commitment and positive in-group attitudes) correlated positively with indicators of psychological well-being (i.e., coping skills, sense of mastery, and optimism) and correlated negatively with depression and loneliness (Roberts et al., 1999). Similarly, a study of Asian and multiethnic students found that high MEIM scores were related to advanced ego identity scores, particularly self-esteem (Yuh, 2005).

Helms's Theory of Racial Identity Development

Helms's (Helms, 1990, 1995; Helms & Cook, 1999) theory of racial identity development is considered to be one of the most influential models in the literature (Pizarro & Vera, 2001). His model includes three conceptualizations: the Black Racial Identity Theory, the People of Color Racial Identity Theory, and the White Racial Identity Theory. These three theories explain the transformative process that Whites, Blacks, and other people of color (i.e., Asian Americans and Pacific Islanders, Native Americans, and Latinos/as) go through to attain racial and ethnic self-actualization (Thompson &

Carter, 1997). The process of development is expressed through racial identity ego statuses that range from the most simplistic to the most complex in terms of how individuals manage racial stimuli. Helms (1995) writes:

> the general developmental issue for Whites is the abandonment of entitlement whereas . . . for people of color it is surmounting internalized racism. In both circumstances development occurs by way of an evolution or differentiation of successive racial identity statuses, where statuses are defined as the dynamic cognitive, emotional, and behavioral processes that govern a person's interpretation of racial information in his or her interpersonal environments. Statuses give rise to schemata which are the behavioral manifestations of the underlying status. It is schemata rather than the statuses per se that paper-and-pencil identity attitude scales presumably measure. (p. 184)

Helms (1995) notes that, although statuses are presumed to mature and evolve sequentially, they are expressed according to their level of dominance within the person's ego structure. In all three theories,

> achieving access to schemata and information-processing strategies of the final statuses means an increased likelihood of perceiving the realities of racism and other oppressive forces and, therefore, having the ability to cope with these realities using complex and higher level information processing strategies; a freeing from individual acts of racist behavior (for Whites) or from the attitudes and behaviors that reflect internalized racism (for People of Color); and a commitment toward the erosion of institutionalized and cultural racism, as well as other forms of oppression. (Thompson & Carter, 1997, p. 17)

People of Color Identity Development Theory

In her conceptualization of racial identity development in People of Color, Helms (1995) expanded her Theory of Black Racial Identity to encompass all racially marginalized groups. The People of Color Identity Theory reflects an integration of Cross's seminal work on the psychology of Nigrescence and Atkinson's Minority Identity Development Model. The differences between the Black and People of Color theories are minimal; that is, statuses are labeled differently, with the ego expressions and information-processing strategies remaining the same (Thompson & Carter, 1997). For the sake of clarity, the status labels used in the Black racial identity theory are presented in parenthesis.

Helms posits that all people of color move through five ego statuses. The first status, *Conformity* (*Preencounter* for Black people), is the least sophisticated schema and is characterized by an internalization of negative stereotypes of one's ethnic/racial group and a commitment to White standards, which is often accompanied by a devaluing of one's people and culture. Adaptation in this status is associated with attempts to assimilate and be accepted into White culture and the tendency to idealize all things White. "When the person is using the conformity schema or information processing strategy, he or she is oblivious to the racial dynamics in her or his environment, and if they are forced into the person's awareness, he or she may respond with selective perception in which information is nonconsciously distorted and minimized to favor the White group" (Helms & Cook, 1999, p. 86). For example, a Latino collage student operating within this status may blame his ethnic culture for Latinos/as' educational underachievement (e.g., Latino parents discourage their children from pursuing a college education).

The second ego status, *Dissonance* (*Encounter*), is marked by much confusion, ambivalence, and anxiety in response to an event, or series of events, that shatters a person's frame of reference and forces the person to question his or her place in a White world. The event(s) can be an uplifting experience (e.g., the Latino student discussed above takes a Chicano Studies course, which contradicts elements of his formal education and accepted notions of race-based social stratification) or a negative personal or social encounter (e.g., being discriminated against or witnessing racial discrimination against one's ethnic group). Persons in this stage begin to realize that no matter what they do, most Whites will always perceive them as persons of color. The primary information-processing strategy used to manage dissonant emotions is to repress anxiety-provoking racial messages (Helms, 1990). These dissonant emotions, however, are important because they plant the seed for transitioning into the next ego status, which involves examining one's ethnic/racial identity. In the final phase of the dissonance status, the person experiences a sense of euphoria that derives from the decision to explore his or her ethnic identity and to seek a "Black or Asian or Hispanic" identity (Thompson & Carter, 1997, p. 21).

The *Immersion/Emersion* (same label used for Black people) status encompasses two phases. In the immersion phase, minority individuals immerse themselves in their cultural group in an effort to reconstruct a new definition of what it means to be Black or Asian or Latino/a (Thompson & Carter, 1997). Characteristic of the immersion phase is a blind idealization of one's group and a denigration and rejection of White culture and White people. This phase can be highly reactive and marked by much guilt, anger, and hostility. Guilt arises out of self-blame for being ignorant of the social implications of one's race and for perpetuating attitudes, stereotypes, and values that degrade and devalue one's ethnicity and racial group. Anger and hostility may follow as the individual becomes increasingly more aware of the oppressive and exploitive nature of White-dominant society. Hence, in the immersion status, individuals struggle "through an interplay of comedy (by trying out a new identity in a superficial and often stereotypic manner); tragedy (by lashing out angrily against others, White, Black, or Asian); and romance (by "idealizing one's culture and ethnic group") (Thompson and Carter, 1997, p. 22). At this stage, persons' racial identities are still elusive and not well integrated into the larger ego identity structure. College students who align themselves to militant and reactive subgroups within various campus ethnic organizations may be operating in this status. The primary information-processing strategies persons in this status use include being hyper-vigilant toward racial information (race and racism are central themes) and simplistic thinking (e.g., one's group members are always right) as well as dichotomous thinking (e.g., viewing all people, ideas, scholarship, and organizations as being either pro-White or antiminority).

In the emersion phase, individuals become educated about their culture, which leads to a true understanding of its strengths and weaknesses, thereby affording these individuals a realistic worldview of the culture and the sociopolitical implications of being a person of color (Thompson & Carter, 1997). This is a cathartic experience, allowing the individual to become less reactive and angry and begin the transition to the next status (Thompson & Carter, 1997).

Achievement of the final *Internalization* (same label used for Black people) status occurs when the person of color "is able to merge the fully evolved [ethnic] identity into his or her repertoire of being" (Thompson & Carter, 1997, p. 22). Therefore, an internalized ethnic identity solidifies the total identity by balancing and synthesizing ethnicity with sexual, gender, occupational, religious, and other social identities. Internalization of a positive racial identity is marked by resolution of conflicts of earlier statuses and a reconstitution of a complex personality that reflects inner security, greater objectivity and receptivity, and less defensiveness. The person rejects all prejudices (even those directed at Whites) and is able to analyze the White culture objectively for its strengths and weaknesses and establish relationships with White persons who are nonracist. The internalized identity serves three primary functions: (1) to defend and protect the person from psychological distress related to racism; (2) to provide a sense of belonging and social grounding; and (3) to provide a personal reference from which to base cognitions and interactions beyond contexts explicitly derived from one's ethnicity and/or race (Cross, 1971).

The second phase of this status, *Internalization-Commitment phase* (*Internalized Awareness* for Black people), is marked by the capacity to embrace one's collective identities (e.g., racial, gender, sexual, and religious identities) and to collaborate with other People of Color to eliminate all forms of racism, discrimination, and oppression. Hence, an integrated awareness status reflects cognitive, behavioral, and emotional processes that are motivated by more globally humanistic and activist self-expressions. This is found in individuals who embrace a pluralistic reference group orientation and choose an ascribed pan-ethnic identity (Helms, 1990). For instance, instead of aligning themselves to the Latino/a, Asian, or Black Caucus, the students now see themselves as part of the rainbow coalition. Because this phase is not entirely differentiated from an internalization status, it is usually omitted from research studies (Thompson & Carter, 1997). Individuals with internalized statuses use flexible and complex information-processing strategies (analytical reasoning and intellectualization) to manage racial information.

Researchers have paid much attention to examining the relationship between racial identity development and psychological functioning in college students. Most of this research employs Helms's (1990, 1995) theory and its corresponding instruments (Black Racial Identity Attitude Scale [B-RIAS]; The People of Color Racial Identity Attitude Scale [PRIAS]) to tap into the five identity schemas discussed. This research has focused almost exclusively on African American students, and only very recently has Helms's theory been applied to other students of color, that is, Asian Americans (Alvarez & Helms, 2001; Chen, LePhuoc, Guzmán, Rude, & Dodd, 2006;

Kohatsu, 1992; Yeh, 1997) and Native Americans (Bryant & Baker, 2003). In general, these studies show that preencounter and immersion/emersion attitudes are associated with greater psychological distress in African American students (see, e.g., Mahalik, Pierre, & Wan, 2006). Specifically, "denial of the social importance of one's Blackness (preencounter attitudes)" and the immature "idealization of one's racial heritage (immersion/emersion attitudes)" has been linked to lower levels of self-esteem (Parham & Helms, 1985a) and self-actualization (Parham & Helms, 1985b); higher levels of anxiety, and hypersensitivity; and a sense of personal inadequacy (Parham & Helms, 1985b) in college students (Neville, Heppner, & Wang, 1997, p. 304).

Immersion/emersion attitudes (pro-Black/anti-White attitudes) have also been associated with greater perceived stress in students and the use of less effective problem-solving strategies (lack of confidence, avoiding problems, and suppressive coping styles). Similar findings were observed with Asian American college students in regard to collective self-esteem, with conformity attitudes (pro-White/anti-Asian) predicting a negative collective self-esteem or sense of "Asianness" in this group (Alvarez & Helms, 2001). On the other hand, internalization of a positive racial identity has been linked to better psychological adjustment in African American students (i.e., higher levels of ego development [Miville, Koonce, Darlington, & Whitlock, 2000], self-esteem [Lemon & Waehler, 1996], locus of control [Martin & Hall, 1992], general well-being [Wilson & Constantine, 1999], and goal-directed behavior [Jackson & Neville, 1998]) as well as to a positive collective self-esteem in Asian American students (Alvarez & Helms, 2001).

To conclude, Nghe and Mahalik's (2001) study examining the link between racial identity statuses and psychological defense mechanisms further validated Helms's theory. They found that African American students with lower racial identity statuses resorted to more immature defense mechanisms when coping with racial stimuli. To illustrate, college students who have preencounter attitudes (anti-Black/pro-White) were more likely to use principalization[6]

> to reinterpret the personal significance of perceived threats as a more abstract issue (e.g., "He was just raised that way"), reversal through unduly positive behavioral responses to frustrating or threatening events (e.g.,

---

6. A defense mechanism for coping with conflict "by splitting off affect from content and by then repressing the former" (Nghe & Mahalik, 2001, p. 14).

"Blacks don't experience racism in America since Colin Powell made it"), and less likely to use turning against objects through expression of direct or indirect aggression (e.g., not challenging racism). (Nghe & Mahalik, 2001, p. 15)

Furthermore, an immersion ego status was linked to immature psychological defenses (e.g., turning against others and projection through blaming others), while an emersion ego status was related to more mature psychological defenses. These findings are important because they support Helms's (1995) premise that racial identity statuses predict how persons manage painful affect.

White Racial Identity Development Theory

Helms's (1990, 1995) model of White racial identity rests on the premise that belonging to the White socioracial group contributes to a false sense of racial superiority and privilege (Helms & Cook, 1999). Her model describes the development of a healthy White racial identity in terms of progressing through six ego identity statuses, which culminate in the formation of a non-racist, White identity.

The first status, *Contact,* is characterized by White persons' denial of the benefits associated with their privileged position and a superficial acknowledgment of their membership in the White racial group. They generally accept the status quo where Whites tend to be oblivious to racism and how they may contribute inadvertently to or benefit from it. "The main theme of this status is that the White person does not simply acknowledge that differences exist between himself/herself and the Black person, rather, the Person of Color is seen as 'different' and is treated with trepidation, wonderment, or fear" (Thompson & Carter, 1997, p. 23). Hence, obliviousness is the primary information strategy contact status individuals use, in that anxiety-provoking information is avoided, especially if such information implies something derogatory or disparaging about Whites. For instance, students operating in this status may naively deny the existence of oppressive societal restrictions targeted against certain groups in this country, namely People of Color.

Disintegration evolves as a response to racial situations or incidents that force White individuals to acknowledge racial inequalities and their group's privileged status. For many White students, taking an Ethnic Studies course in college may generate a great deal of discomfort. Awareness of racial and ethnic inequalities presents them with the moral dilemma of choosing between humanism (justice, fairness, and equality) and loyalty to one's group. Unresolved racial moral dilemmas can provoke much anxiety and dissonance. Hence, persons operating in this status tend to suppress racial knowledge and show ambivalence when managing racial information.

Reintegration status evolves in response to the negative feelings of the previous status. The person "avoids personal anxiety by adopting the version of racism that exists in her or his socialization environments, which then relieves him or her of the responsibility for doing anything about it" (Helms & Cook, 1999, p. 92). Common themes of this status include a conscious identification with being White, viewing White people as superior to other racial groups (White people have earned their privilege status), and a general intolerance and devaluing of People of Color. Reintegration status is expressed in passive or active forms. *Passive* reintegration reflects persons who believe that racial stereotypes are essentially true, so they avoid contact with People of Color by deliberately removing themselves from situations where such encounters may occur; for example, a White student operating in this status may steer clear from campus dialogues on cultural diversity. It is interesting that such individuals may rationalize that they are not racist because of their associations and friendships with ethnic minority peers who share similar pro-White and antiminority perspectives, thereby validating their worldviews on race (Thompson & Carter, 1997). The notion that societal and institutional racism continue to hinder minority progress is dismissed with the belief that people essentially get what they deserve. *Active* reintegration describes persons who engage in acts of violence against people of color and/or who support societal restrictions against minorities that protect the White privilege system. Increases in the incidence of hate crimes on university campuses (Chan & Wang, 1991; Walker, 2001), as well as outlawing affirmative action policies within the state of California, may arguably illustrate the actions of persons operating within an active reintegration status (e.g., Weis, Proweller, & Centrie, 1997). Also recent anti-immigrant actions taken by the vigilante group, called the "Minute Men," along the U.S.-Mexican border, exemplify individuals at this stage of racial identity. The main information-processing strategies Whites in this status use are "selective perception and distortion of information in an own-group enhancing and out-group debasing manner" (Helms & Cook, 1999, p. 92).

A crisis (an identity-shattering experience or series of experiences) is needed to propel the person into *Pseudo-Independent status*, which marks the initial step toward constructing a positive, nonracist, White identity. In this status the person begins to abandon the belief in White superiority and adopts an intellectualized stance regarding racial issues. For example, students operating within this status are capable of acknowledging past and present racial wrongdoings by attributing these actions to some subgroups of Whites but not to themselves (i.e., they personally are not racist). Such persons may attempt to resolve the "race problem" by helping ethnic minorities to become more like Whites (Helms & Cook, 1999). For instance, by advocating the assimilation of ethnic minorities, these persons may argue against bilingual education (it interferes with educational achievement of minorities) and favor the English-only initiative. "Avoidance of negative information about oneself," selective perception of racial information, and a tendency to reshape reality to "fit one's liberal societal framework" are the main information-processing strategies used by persons in this status (p. 92).

Immersion/emersion status is marked by a search for or reeducation regarding what it means to be White and an examination of the "the personal meaning of racism and the way by which one benefits [from it]" (Helms, 1995, p. 185). Individuals in this status are no longer concerned with changing ethnic minorities but are now focused on encouraging other Whites to explore their racial identity and abandon their racist beliefs. Hyper-vigilance toward racial stimuli, engagement in political activism, and reshaping one's worldview (e.g., beginning to formulate a new internal definition of racial standards) are the information-processing strategies operating in this status.

Racial exploration transitions the person into the last status, *Autonomy*, which is marked by the person's sense of security and comfort with his or her Whiteness. Persons in this status have internalized a positive definition of Whiteness and are able to recognize actions within themselves and other Whites that perpetuate racism (Thompson & Carter, 1997). The autonomy-status person uses flexible and complex analytic information-processing strategies when responding to racial information. This person is no longer threatened by racial issues but seeks opportunities to eliminate all forms of oppression and to increase his or her cultural awareness. "Maintaining this identity is an ongoing process requiring continuous openness to learning about racial, cultural, social, and political issues as well as integrating proactive behaviors" (Richardson & Silvestri, 1999, p. 51).

The body of research examining the relationship of White racial identity to psychological functioning among college students is relatively scant. In general, the few studies conducted thus far using Helms's White Racial Identity Attitude Scale (W-RIAS) indicate that lower-level racial identity statuses are linked to poor adjustment. Specifically, self-esteem was found to be associated positively with pseudoindependence and autonomy statuses and negatively related to contact and disintegration (Lemon & Waehler, 1996). Furthermore, self-derogation was linked positively to disintegration attitudes and negatively to pseudoindependence. Likewise, more-developed racial identity statuses (e.g., autonomy) were related positively to self-actualization, while less-sophisticated identity statuses (e.g., contact and disintegration) were associated negatively with self-actualization (Tokar & Swanson, 1991). These findings point to the detrimental effect internalized racist attitudes and beliefs have on the psychological well-being of Whites.

Researchers have also examined the relationship between racism and racial identity development. This research shows that less-developed (or undifferentiated) racial identity statuses were predictive of racist attitudes among White students (Carter, 1990; Carter, Helms, & Juby, 2004; Pope-Davis & Ottavi, 1994; Silvestri & Richardson, 2001). Younger students have also been found to have higher levels of disintegration and reintegration attitudes than do older students, suggesting that racial awareness may be a function of age (Pope-Davis & Ottavi, 1994). Furthermore, one study reported that women were found to have higher pseudoindependence and autonomy scores than did men; conversely, men were found to have higher levels of disintegration and reintegration attitudes (Pope-Davis & Ottavi, 1994). This suggests that, perhaps, experiences with gender discrimination allow White women to understand the plight of ethnic minorities better. The observed relationship between racism and racial identity is important because it supports Helms's premise that as "Whites develop their racial identity, they begin to shed racist attitudes and form racist-free identities" (Silvestri & Richardson, 2001, p. 69).

Other Developmental Models of Racial and Ethnic Identity

Cross & Fhagen-Smith's (2001) and Kim's (2001) models of racial identity represent newer theoretical advances in the literature. Similar to the models discussed earlier, these theories address the developmental milestones that African Americans (Cross & Fhagen-Smith, 2001) and Asian Americans (Kim, 2001) undergo in the process of achieving a positive and healthy ethnic identity as racial minorities in the United States. They depart from earlier theoretical viewpoints in that they articulate a life span perspective of racial and ethnic identity development that begins in early childhood and continues through adolescence and into adulthood.

Cross and Fhagen-Smith's Life Span Model of Black Identity Development

Heavily influenced by the work of Erikson (1968), Cross and Fhagen-Smith's (1996, 2001) Life Span model describes three different Nigrescence outcomes that may occur over six sectors of an individual's life span. Nigresence refers to the process by which Black Americans achieve Black racial and ethnic identity (Cross & Fhagen-Smith, 2001). The Life Span model reflects a revision in Cross's original Nigresence Model of Adult Identity Conversion (1991), which took into account adult experiences only. The new model (Cross & Fhagen-Smith, 1996) describes three models of achieved Black identity: Nigresence Pattern A, in which formative childhood experiences influence the achievement of Blackness; Nigresence Pattern B, in which Blackness is an outcome of adult conversion experiences; and Nigresence Pattern C, in which ongoing identity modification, or Nigrescence Recycling (Parham, 1989), occurs.

Although not considered to be a strictly linear model, the Life Span model follows an individual's development through six sectors that reflect an age-wise progression. Sector One comprises infancy and childhood. In this sector, a combination of micro and macro influences shapes children's understanding of the world around them and their position in it. In this stage, according to Cross and Fhagen-Smith (2001), "Before racism can take its toll, the dreams and self-trajectories of Black children are likely to be as diverse, whimsical, fanciful and daring as those found among any group of American children" (p. 251). It is not until Sector Two: Preadolescence that children begin to manifest signs of an individual emergent identity.

Family dynamics play a key role in socializing preadolescents to the different ways Blackness can be lived in America. Children raised in households where Blackness is deemphasized may manifest what Cross and Fhagen-Smith (2001) call *Emergent Low Race Salience (LRS) Patterns*. On the other hand, more race-conscious parents may impart values of *Emergent High Race Salience (HRS) Patterns*, which can include features of Afrocentrism, biculturalism, or multiculturalism. Last in Sector Two, children can acquire feelings of *Internalized Racism (IR)* that can later develop into a damaged self-concept.

In Sector Three: Adolescence, each of the three patterns that emerge in Sector Two undergo further development. That is not to say that individuals follow a linear trajectory based on their preadolescent conditioning. Rather, during adolescence, Black youths' self-concept may undergo transformations, and identity patterns can shift. For example, children who have internalized many negative impressions of Black people could have positive experiences of Blackness in adolescence, thereby shifting their identity patterns from *Internalized Racism* to *High Race Salience*. Accordingly, individuals with emergent High Race Salience patterns in childhood may focus on other aspects of their identities in their adolescence and therefore demonstrate more *Low Race Salience Patterns*. Still others may maintain the same patterns of understanding they developed as children.

By the time individuals reach Early Adulthood (Sector Four), the race salience patterns that emerged at younger ages coalesce into more fundamental reference group orientations that undergird ongoing racial and ethnic identity development (Cross & Fhagen-Smith, 2001). Again, Black adults in this sector may demonstrate identities comprising *Low Race Salience, High Race Salience*, or *Internalized Racism*. Cross and Fhagen-Smith posit that individuals who enter Early Adulthood with *Low Race Salience* may experience the Nigresence Conversion Process in Sector Five: Adult Nigresence when they encounter experiences that cause them to question their beliefs about race and identity. Similarly, individuals with Internalized Racism may have a Nigresence conversion later in life. Young adults with *High Race Salience* may have experienced a Nigresence conversion earlier in their lives; thus, further Black identity development for them may occur in Sector Six: Nigresence Recycling. It is important to note that some Black people never experience a Nigresence Conversion, but remain unchanged in *Low Race Salience* or *Internalized Racism* identities.

The actual conversion process of Adult Nigresence—that is, Nigresence Pattern B—takes place in Sector Five. People with *Low Race Salience* or *Internalized Racism* identities remain in the *Preencounter* stage until an *Encounter* "that challenges the person to rethink his or her attitudes, feelings, and behavior concerning race and Black culture" (Cross & Fhagen-Smith, 2001, p. 262). Individuals will struggle to negotiate these new insights with their previously held beliefs during the *Immersion-Emersion* Stage. Successful integration of a more race-salient understanding of the self will result in *Internalization*. Finally, long-term commitment to an achieved Black identity results in *Internalization-Commitment*. Blacks who reach this stage in Sector Five demonstrate similar group orientations as do those who achieved Nigresence in childhood or adolescence (*Nigresence Pattern A*); that is, Afrocentrism, biculturalism, or multiculturalism.

Sector Six: Nigresence Recycling, based on the work of Parham (1989), describes additional explorations of Blackness that occur throughout the life span. Through identity recycling, individuals further enhance their Black identity as a result of what Cross and Fhagen-Smith (2001) call *Life Span Encounters*. These *Encounters* differ from *Encounters* in Sector Five in that they do not trigger a Nigresence conversion, but rather provide additional multidimensionality to one's understanding of his or her Black identity. Cross and Fhagen-Smith describe the ongoing process of identity development *Nigresence Pattern C*.

Empirical support for the Life Span Model of Black Identity has centered on the Adult Nigresence sector, where the RAIS Inventory has been used to evaluate stages or statuses of racial identity. These findings were reported earlier in this section; however, other developmental phases of this life span perspective of racial identity development have yet to be tested.

Asian American Identity Development

Kim's (2001) Asian American Identity Development (AAID) theory can be characterized as the process by which Asian Americans negotiate their identities within predominantly White society. The AAID model assumes that: (1) Asian American identity is intrinsically linked to the legacy of White racism in America; (2) the process of shedding internalized racism does not happen automatically; and (3) psychological well-being is achieved when Asian Americans transform their negative racial identities into positive identities (Kim, 2001). While Kim presents the model in five stages, individuals do not necessarily progress in a linear fashion through these stages to an achieved identity. Qualitative empirical support for the Asian American Model of Identity Development is based on Kim's (1981) doctoral dissertation thesis.

Stage One of the AAID model, Ethnic Awareness, generally lasts until children are ready to enter school. In this stage, children's primary reference group is their family. Individuals' identity ego statuses may vary to the degree that they are exposed to ethnic "others," but the families' ethnic identities remain the fundamental basis for ethnic awareness. Participation in a strong ethnic community is associated with a positive self-concept and a clear sense that one is a person of Asian heritage, while less participation in an ethnic community "is related to a neutral self concept and confused ego identity," where the child is unclear about the meaning of his or her Asian heritage (Kim 2001, p. 73).

Children typically enter Stage Two: White Identification when they attend school and begin to associate with larger numbers of White peers. Kim (2001) argues that Asian American children at this stage first encounter feelings of "difference" that contribute to a negative self-concept. This negative self-concept may manifest as either Active or Passive White Identification. Active White Identification is typical of people who minimize their Asianness and consider themselves to be similar to Whites. Passive White Identification is more typical of individuals who enter Stage Two with a stronger sense of Asian identity (i.e., they grew up in predominately Asian or mixed communities) than those with Active White Identification. Unlike the Active White Identified, they are also more likely to enter this stage later, while in junior high rather than elementary school, which most often characterizes the adaptation strategies of first-generation Asians who immigrated to the United States before their teen years. Children and youth with Passive White Identification accept Whiteness as the norm but do not completely abandon other Asians. Asian Americans in both types of White Identification attempt to "fit in" or "pass" as White. A collective group orientation and cultural values regarding public shame strongly influence Asians' desire to assimilate at all costs (Kim, 2001). "As long as Asian Americans believe they can be fully assimilated into White society, they will remain in this stage of White Identification" (Kim, 2001, p. 76). At this stage, Asian Americans are likely to deny racism or discrimination as societal and cultural restrictions that affect their racial group and/or themselves personally.

To move into Stage Three: Awakening to Social Political Consciousness, individuals must become aware of White racism to develop a positive Asian self-concept. This is most likely to occur during late adolescence and early adulthood during which environmental factors such as exposure to campus racial politics and sociopolitical issues propel the person into this stage. Kim (2001) describes this change in awareness as a paradigm shift from personalizing encounters with racism to contextualizing them within an oppressive society. She also argues that heightened political action, affinity with other oppressed minority groups, and reactions against White people are typical of this stage. By Stage Four: Redirection to an Asian American Consciousness, Asian Americans begin to immerse themselves in specific Asian American experiences and develop a sense of pride in their ethnic heritage. A key aspect of this stage is to "figure out what parts of themselves are Asian and what parts are American" and "acquiring pride and a positive self-concept as Americans with Asian heritage" (Kim, 2001, p. 79). In Stage Five of the AAID model, *Incorporation*, individuals have confidence in their Asian American identity as one important aspect of their overall social identities. They also no longer feel threatened by encounters with non-Asians out of fear losing one's Asian identity.

Critique of Ethnic/Racial Identity Models

The models of ethnic and racial identity development discussed here have had a major impact on the field of psychology and education and in the practice of multicultural training within the counseling arena, academia, and public organizations. Notwithstanding the positive contribution this work has made to our overall understanding of ethnic and racial issues, it is important to address some of the weaknesses we see inherent in these perspectives.

First, when considering the ethnic or racial identity development of groups of color, these models use an ethnic minority-dominant perspective where Whites are the primary reference group and the standard from which all ethnic and racial identity processes evolve. That is, conflicts and resolutions related to ethnic and/or racial identity for ethnic minority groups are primarily in reference to the dominant White group. These models center on the reactions of ethnic minorities to experiences of oppression and are criticized "for construing ethnic identity" primarily "as the consequence of this reaction" (Yi & Shorter-Gooden, 1999, p. 17).

Second, current identity models do not consider the influences that growing up in a multiethnic context may have on ethnic identity processes, nor do they address the issue that, within such contexts, Whites may not be the primary reference group for people of color. To illustrate, Latino/a students who grow up in a predominantly Black-Latino/a community, such as

Compton, California, are likely to use African Americans as their primary reference group. Likewise, when discussing ethnic or racial identity development in Whites, present identity models assume that these persons are primarily in contact with other Whites, but these models fail to address how ethnic identity development may differ for Whites raised in close proximity to Blacks, Latinos/as, or a mix of ethnicities. Given the changing face of our communities, schools, and universities, particularly in Southern California, this perspective is shortsighted. Future ethnic identity research must seriously consider the multiethnic and multicultural context in which present-day ethnic identity processes are evolving and the impact this is having on interethnic relations and the psychological adjustment of persons.

Third, specifically addressing Helms's theory of White racial identity development, this model has been faulted for applying an "oppression-adaptive" perspective of minority ethnic development to Whites, which may be inappropriate for understanding the experiences of a racially dominant group (Hardiman, 2001; Rowe, Behrens, & Leach, 1995). That is, a White person's sense of racial identity may develop along different pathways from that of ethnic minorities (Rowe et al., 1995). Furthermore, the focus of Helms's model is not on the formation of a White identity per se but on "how Whites develop different levels of sensitivity and appreciation of other racial/ ethnic groups," thereby providing "little insight into the attributes of a White identity" (Rowe et al., 1995, p. 224). As Hardiman (2001) notes, "a model of White identity should help us understand how Whites feel, think and reflect upon their Whiteness and their own racial group, as well as how they relate to other races" (p. 124).

Last, traditional stage models of ethnic and racial identity have been criticized for failing to consider how a person's ethnic identity is situated within multiple identities (e.g., gender, occupation, sexual orientation, socioeconomic status) and how these identities interact to influence the meaning and form of ethnic identity (Casas & Pytluk, 1995; Lee, 2006; Vera & De Los Santos, 2005; Yi & Shorter-Gooden, 1999). To illustrate, the sense of ethnic and gender identity in an Asian American female student raised in a traditional Chinese home is likely to be strongly interwoven, shaping the meaning of what it is for her to be a Chinese American woman. Furthermore, stage theories in general have received much criticism lately for their

(a) emphasis on linearity, which makes it difficult to account for the complexity of human development; (b) emphasis on invariant sequences of structural unfolding, which cannot easily account for important situational influences in the developmental process; and (c) emphasis on invariant sequences for "ideal" or "normal" development, leading to implicit pathologizing of diversity of developmental outcomes among individuals. (Yi & Shorter-Gooden, 1999, p. 18)

Therefore, instead of conceptualizing identity primarily as a linear, sequential unfolding, Yi and Shorter-Gooden (1999) propose that ethnic identity development be viewed as a fluid and dynamic process that is constructed in a relational (interpersonal) context and "shaped by contemporary and historical exchanges with one's family, friends, institutions, and the broader culture" (p. 16).

Other Perspectives on Racial Identity

The models discussed in this section are departures from developmental perspectives and assess people at particular points in time. We present them because we believe they highlight the interpersonal context of racial identity development and the variability observed within groups regarding this process.

Types of White Racial Consciousness

Rowe and colleagues (Rowe et al., 1995; Rowe, Bennett, & Atkinson, 1994) have proposed an alternate model of White racial identity to Helms's. They conceive of White racial consciousness "as the characteristic attitudes held by a person regarding the significance of being White, particularly in terms of what that implies in relation to those who do not share White group membership" (Rowe et al., 1995, p. 225). These authors propose seven types of White racial consciousness or attitude types, which are encompassed under two forms of identity statuses—achieved versus unachieved. Included within the achieved statuses are attitude types that necessitate an exploration and commitment on the part of the person to his or her ethnicity and to racial issues (i.e., the person has committed to some position on these matters), while unachieved statuses include attitude types that are common to persons who have not reflected or explored such issues (Rowe et al., 1995). The authors do not make any claims regarding the sequence of White racial consciousness development and address this issue solely in terms of achieved or unachieved attitude types. Specifically:

Achieved statuses are characterized by four relatively stable internalized attitude types. *Dominative* attitudes refer to strong ethnocentric perspectives that justify the oppression of minority groups. *Conflictive* attitudes reflect opposition to discriminatory practices and opposition to programs designed to reduce or eliminate such discriminatory practices (discrimination is a thing of the past). *Reactive* attitudes entail a recognition that White society wrongly benefits from and promotes discriminatory practices. *Integrative* attitudes refer to comfort with one's Whiteness and with minority groups. Within the unachieved status, the three attitude types share a noninternalized set of expressed racial attitudes. *Dependent* attitudes reflect the reliance on others to define one's own racial attitudes. *Avoidant* attitudes are characterized by a lack of interest in one's own White identity and a lack of concern for issues surrounding race. Last, *Dissonant* attitudes entail uncertainty about one's sense of racial consciousness and racial issues. Moreover, a person experiences dissonance between previously held beliefs and recent personal experiences. (Richardson & Silvestri, 1999, pp. 51–52)

Unlike Helms's theory of White racial identity, the model of White racial consciousness focuses primarily on Whites' attitudes toward their own group rather than just their attitudes toward other racial and ethnic groups (Rowe et al., 1995). In this sense, the model provides an important contribution to the study of "Whiteness," an area of research that only recently has begun to receive increased attention in the social sciences (Warren & Hytten, 2004).

Latino/a Model of Racial Identity Orientation

Ferdman and Gallegos (2001) have introduced a new paradigm of Latino/a identity and proposed a model that describes the "orientations" or responses that Latinos/as make in attempting to define themselves in the U.S. racial system. They argue that current identity models fail to capture the diversity of the Latino/a experience, an eclectic group that defies current social constructions of race and racial-categorization (e.g., Latino/a races range from White to Mestizo to Indian or Black). Ferdman and Gallegos's model describes six different Latino/a racial identity orientations; however, the authors make no claims regarding the sequence or progression of development across orientations.

Described first is the *Latino/a-Integrated* orientation, which characterizes those who have integrated their Latino/a identity with other social identities (gender, class, professional) and are able to consider the importance of their group membership without its becoming the most salient identity. Latino/a-integrated persons see themselves, as well as other Latinos/as, "as one of many groups coexisting in the multicultural fabric of the United States" (Ferdman & Gallegos, 2001, p. 51). Next are persons with a *Latino/a-identified orientation*, who tend to have a pan-ethnic and activist identification in which all Latino/a subgroups are viewed as constituting one distinct race (*La Raza*), which is regarded very positively. Whites are seen as a distinct racial category whose members may present barriers or be allies to their inclusion in the U.S. social order. Third are Latinos/as with a *Subgroup-identified* orientation, who define themselves primarily in terms of their national-origin subgroup (e.g., Mexican or Puerto Rican), which is viewed as distinct from Whites, but they do not identify with other Latino/a subgroups, which they may regard positively or negatively. Race is not a central organizational concept for *subgroup-identified* individuals, whereas culture and ethnicity are prominent to their Latino/a identity. Fourth are persons with an *Other* orientation, which is characteristic of Latinos/as who are unaware of their specific Latino/a background, but because of their phenotypic characteristics, see themselves as distinct from Whites. They do not necessarily adhere to Latino/a cultural norms and expectations, and their orientation is framed by external factors (i.e., public views of the group). Fifth is an *Undifferentiated* Latino/a orientation that characterizes persons who view themselves and other persons as just "people," and who do not associate with any particular Latino/a subgroup. They claim to be color-blind and are oblivious to racial differences. Sixth is a *White-identified* orientation. These Latinos/as "see themselves racially as White, and distinct from, and generally superior to, people of color" (p. 53); such persons adhere to a *mejorar La Raza*[7] perspective, thereby favoring marriage to Whites but not to darker groups. This orientation characterizes assimilated Latinos/as or those persons who identify with a specific subgroup (e.g., Cubans, Mexicans, or Puerto Ricans) but deny any connection to other Latino/a groups, which they may regard negatively.

Ferdman and Gallegos's (2001) descriptive model of racial identity is significant in that it is grounded in descriptive methodologies (survey and personal narratives) and represents an initial attempt by the authors to capture

---

7. A term that refers to seeing marriage to "Whites as a way of improving" the Latino race, while marriage to "Blacks or Browns diminishes the group" (Ferdman & Gallegos, 2001, p. 54).

the richness and diversity of the Latino/a experience in this country and their "orientation towards race and racial identity" (p. 55).

Summary and Conclusions

This chapter covers pertinent theoretical frameworks and empirical research relating to the ethnic identity development of ethnic groups in American society. We discussed ethnic identity as a multidimensional construct that encompasses a person's thoughts, feelings, and behaviors regarding his or her ethnic group membership (Phinney, 1990). Its meaning for individuals is largely shaped by contextual factors related to family (enculturation), community (ethnic density and cohesiveness), and the nature of minority-majority social relations in the larger society (i.e., group salience, power and status, and existing ethnopolitical and social conditions). Acculturative processes, that is, how a person adapts to the dominant society, were also noted as playing an influential role in determining the nature of ethnic identity for ethnic minorities. The social construction of race was distinguished from ethnic identity in that the latter is based primarily on a sociopolitical model of oppression in which ethnic minorities leave behind the negative effects of disenfranchisement and develop positive racial identities. We presented various models of ethnic and racial identity development, which provided valuable insight for understanding the identity development of different ethnic groups and pointed to the significance of ethnic identity in the psychological adjustment of persons. Nonetheless, we argued that these models are far too simplistic in their focus to capture the diversity of experiences that shape ethnic identity formation in contemporary American ethnic groups.

In conclusion, the body of literature examined in this chapter points to the complexity of understanding the meaning of ethnic identity and the need to contextualize its study further through qualitative analyses. As Sue and colleagues note (1998), researchers need to begin to look at ethnic identity "at multiple levels (personal, social, political, economic and cultural), in multiple areas (feelings, attitudes, values, knowledge, and practice), and in multiple settings (being alone, being with members of own ethnic group, other ethno-cultural groups, the dominant group, or a mix)" (p. 312). A greater reliance on descriptive techniques would allow researchers to better capture the multiplicity of ethnic identity-shaping experiences that affect the lives of ethnic groups in this country (Phinney, 2000b; Yi & Shorter-Gooden, 1999). The work conducted by Ferdman and Gallegos (2001) on Latino/a racial identity orientations is a step in that direction. Further, to study ethnic identity development in college students, we not only need to turn to the study of specific nationality-based ethnic subgroups, but we also must consider the dynamic environment that is present on nearly all college campuses, where opportunities for involvement in immersion experiences, intergroup interactions, current events, and structural characteristics of the campus must be examined to assess the impact of these factors on students' evolving ethnic identity (Santos, Ortiz, Morales, & Rosales, 2007).

3

ASIAN AMERICANS
Feet in Two Worlds, Making a Third

The term "Asian American" is typically used as a pan-ethnic descriptor of individuals who come from Asian and Pacific Rim countries. The students in this study are quite clear that they are both Asian Americans and, more specifically, individuals of specific ethnic backgrounds. Therefore, students were more likely to call themselves Japanese American or Filipino than they were to use the term Asian American. In fact, only one student, who was of Vietnamese background, identified as Asian. The only student in the study who identified as biracial was a White and Vietnamese American. Labels students chose to describe themselves are of consequence because they reflect evolving political attitudes and orientations and the impact of generational status. The importance of using specific ethnic labels was especially salient among Asian Americans. Assuming that any pan-ethnic group is monolithic often leads to relational difficulties with student groups and an inability to attend to specific needs and issues of the diverse ethnic groups that collectively comprise Asian Americans. Students in this study reflected both the diversity of the pan-ethnic Asian American group and the problematic nature of identifying the differences within the group. The only Indian American in the study describes the tension involved in ethnic labels:

> What really bothers me is when it comes to politically correct labeling. We're from Asia. India is in Asia, quite obviously in Asia. But Asian Americans and all my Oriental/Pacific Rim friends, or whatever you want to say, they're all, "You're Asian American?" Yeah, I am. India is very obviously in Asia, look at the map. But it's not when you say Pacific Rim. Or you could say Southeast Asian, but they think that's wrong, but we are

considered Southeast Asian. But they're like, "No, that's Thailand, Cambodia, and Laos." So they've come up with "subcontinental," which I think is most horrible. I'd say I'm Asian, but people are going to think Asian is what you look like. They're going to think automatically [that] an Asian person looks Japanese or Chinese, not look Indian. They think we're Middle Eastern. We're not Middle Eastern, we're Asian.

Other students reflected the contradictions this student experienced from her Asian American friends. A Filipino student stressed the diversity within that island nation and how islands are different from each other in language and culture. A second Filipino student also noted that she faced confusion from others who would look at her with puzzled faces when they heard her Spanish surname. Additionally, a Korean student stressed the religious differences within the group and how Korean communities often organize themselves around churches or temples that may be Christian, Catholic, or Buddhist.

Of the 23 Asian American students interviewed, 5 were Korean, 5 were Filipino, 4 were Japanese, 3 were Vietnamese (including one biracial student), 3 were Chinese, and there was 1 Cambodian American, 1 Taiwanese, and 1 Indian American. Fully half of these students were immigrants themselves, having come to the United States as young children. The other half were second generation and the first members of their family to have been born in this country. More than African Americans or Latinos/as, Asian American students were likely to have lived in predominantly White neighborhoods and have attended predominantly White high schools. However, in both of these locations, Asian Americans would be considered to represent, on average, a critical mass. The average neighborhood was composed of 22% Asian American families, and the average Asian American composition in high school was nearly 25%. Both of these are considerably higher than the 3.6% of Asian Americans in the U.S. population (U.S. Census Bureau, 2000).

The interview data for Asian American reflected three dominant themes, the most prevalent of which was the impact of the family system on ethnic identity and other important issues that college students experience. The second theme was the role of language and culture in ethnic identity and group pride. Within this theme the importance of language and maintenance of ethnicity is clear. Finally, the third theme was the transformation of the students' own cultures by becoming American. Most Asian American students could clearly articulate the ways in which they saw themselves becoming less Filipino, Korean, etc., and more like mainstream Americans, creating what many termed the best of both cultures.

The Family System and Its Impact on Ethnic Identity

Nearly every Asian American student in the study highlighted the importance of family. While most traditional-age college students still have strong connections to their families, these students articulated the connection between family (including extended families), the development of ethnic identity, the establishment of cultural values, and how these forces shaped their educational and career values. In addition, students shared what they believed to be cultural constructions of the family system they thought were unique to Asian American families, regardless of a student's specific ethnic background. Generally, students spoke of these as positive forces and attributes. However, some students noted that family dynamics and structure were not always positive qualities in light of traditional gender roles and the deference to parents and elders that was expected in the home. Thus, subthemes for this section of the chapter are close family ties, the presence of extended family structures, familial obligations, and familial complexities.

Close Family Ties

Close family ties (identified by 20 of 23 Asian American students) have been associated with high ethnic salience (Yip, 2005), as is ethnic pride, which is generally included in theories of ethnic identity and measures of the construct (Parham & Helms, 1985b; Luhtanen and Crocker, 1992; Phinney, 1992). For Asian American students, family was the place where pride was developed. One student said, "I'm proud of the culture that we have, like how we're so close to our family, we're like a unit. We have very close ties to parents; I'm proud of that." The connection of family to culture and pride in the ethnic group was a pervasive feeling among these students. Students even felt that other ethnic groups looked positively on their own group because of the strength of family: "Someone who is Filipino feels a bond with their family and that is positive. My Caucasian friends look on people of my own ethnic group positively because of that." Likewise, comparisons were made to the role of family in U.S. culture as students noted differences in expectations between their cultures and the host culture, as expressed by a Cambodian woman.

> Cambodian Americans don't like the children to separate. For example, if you're over eighteen, you're out in American culture. It's not like that in our culture. For example, my father would like me to stay close to him. Even now, when I'm in school, he wants me to just go to school and then come home and not go out. Especially because I'm a woman, he wants me to stay closer to home.

Students acknowledged that family was of the utmost importance and that the close nature of Asian families is a force they expected to have an impact on their lives beyond college. Two students contributed the following:

> Filipinos expect you to keep your kids at home and hold on to them as tight as possible and never let go. My dad wants to build a west or east wing where we will live forever. I feel like I'm more independent and that I should want to set out on my own for a while—if I can do it on my own. But my mom says, "When you get married, if I buy you a house, you'll stay with me, right?"

> I think it's in our culture (Vietnamese) to be close to the family. It's in our culture to not stray away from a family unit. It's always close; even when you're grown-up and married with your own life, you're always close. You don't see your family once in a year. You're always nearby, even when you move out. So, every weekend you will see them, most likely. . . . My friends still haven't moved out. In my boyfriend's family, his sisters are all grown-up and they're still living with their parents. His sisters that are married, they [are] still around the premises. They still live close to the parents' home.

For others close ties to the family were perceived to be a result of historical forces, where the presence of family helped individuals to endure adversity.

> Family is an important value. I guess it's very important to the culture. Because sometimes, like when during the World War when everyone was sent out to concentration camps, the only thing they had was their family. So I guess that's something very important.

For still others family was a basic cultural value that enabled family to endure through generations.

> In Chinese society the family is the unit of society. The family is the source of support, the family is always there for each other. That seems different from Western cultures. It's not necessarily the norm, but in Chinese families you have several generations living in the same household; you don't often see that in other families.

Despite coming from four different ethnic backgrounds, each of these students had strikingly similar perspectives on their families and the expectations about how they constructed their lives during and after college, even after achieving the markers of adulthood in U.S. culture. Another male student offered, "When you're married, even when you have to move away from the family, if you need help, you can call your family. They are right there to help you, and the whole family deals with the problem."

The notable importance of physical proximity and tight maintenance of the family unit is remarkably similar among these Asian American students regardless of ethnic background. Generational status probably contributes to this, with a stronger commitment to maintain close family ties the closer the family is to the time of immigration.

Extended Families

For over half of the Asian American students, the sense and structure of family included the extended family of grandparents, aunts, uncles, and cousins. In many cases students came from multigenerational households. These families not only served as sources of general support as indicated above, but they also sustained ethnic identity or acted as the source of ethnic identity.

> The community I grew up in was predominantly White. I did not have any other Filipino friends, much less Asian friends, so for me it was like my family was the only source of ethnicity that I have. I have not a huge, but an extended family, which lives within an hour of me. That's where I get all my ethnic background. All my friends were either White or maybe one or two other Asian friends, and they were not Filipino.

In this student's case, the family prevented a loss of ethnic identity that might have resulted from living in a predominantly White environment. In the protection of ethnicity it is important to combat the strong influence of assimilation that ethnic students in predominantly White neighborhoods and schools often experience. It has been theorized that a core process of Asian American identity development is initially identifying with, and then later resisting, White culture (Kim, 2001). The student above recognized how her strong family connection helped her resist what Kim calls "Active White Identification." Similarly this student considered close, extended families a characteristic of her ethnic group.

> Family is a positive aspect of being Chinese. In Chinese society the family is the unit of society. The family is the source of support; the family is always there for each other. That seems different from Western cultures. It's not necessarily the norm, but in Chinese families you have several generations living in the same household. You don't often see that in other families. That's an example of how we are supported or unified.

In addition to supporting ethnicity, extended family members shared parenting responsibility. This type of experience helped this student to develop a sense of being part of a larger system.

> I was talking to my friend, and he's Chinese and he's just like telling me, "Gosh, you know Filipinos, they always have their grandparents living with them." I never noticed that until I started seeing my friends and thinking, "Oh, that's true." Because my parents and my grandparents lived with me and I was raised by my grandparents and so I know, I can tell that it's not really just the immediate family that's important, but it's more.

These two students, one Chinese and the other Filipino, also reveal how Asian American students perceive the uniqueness of ethnic groups and the diversity within ethnic groups. The first student sees extended families as a characteristic of Chinese society and culture. However, in the second quote, the Filipino student reports that his Chinese friend does not perceive multigenerational households as a Chinese experience at all, but one that is more characteristic of Filipinos. These differences of perception can be attributed to a number of factors, such as immigration experiences (the first of an extended family to come to the United States) or generational status (later generations becoming more assimilated).

Respect for elders was another ethnic value and experience voiced by many students in the study. One Vietnamese student said, "We have more respect for our parents, for our elders, compared to how Americans are. They just yell at their parents. They're like, they put their old grandmother in the home." She went on to say that this respect continued throughout their lives, and that parents always have a say in how the children live their lives. Students were expected to show deference to older family members, as this student explains. Respect and deference were intimately part of the family dynamic, which maintained the power relations characteristic of hierarchical and collectivistic family units. This ensures a willingness among younger generations to be influenced by elders and key figures within the family.

> Anybody older than you, you have to treat them with respect, don't talk back to them. Even when you talk to a younger person who is older than you, you show them a certain amount of respect. You don't say, "Hey, you!" You call them by their name. My mom made sure, all throughout her life, that my brother, who is five years younger than me, called me "Sister Marie." In Vietnamese there's something called Chi-Marie, which means big sister Marie. She made him interpret it into English and call me that, for respect. Sometimes it's hard to show respect unless you verbally say it.

Although there are negative implications of absolute deference to elders, these students experienced respect for elders as a positive aspect of being a member of their specific Asian ethnic group. When one student, a Filipina, was asked how she practiced her ethnicity on daily basis, she said, "Helping the elders . . . showing respect, we always respect each other." Family values remained a central element of being Korean for the following student, despite the acquisition of Western values, such as independence.

> I have all the good things that you get from being a Korean, respecting the elders, putting the importance of family values first is very important and I feel very strongly about that. But at the same time I also have Western values. Again the independence and really being able to talk just as easy to a three-year-old as you could talk to an eighty-year-old.

There is the sense that the value of independence has permitted this student to communicate more easily with elders, which may have been contrary to the traditional relationships of elders in the family.

Other students also felt that respect and deference for family has affected additional values and traits that they have. A Japanese student felt that respect for parents and country resulted in the development of loyalty and honesty as shared values for Japanese. A Korean student felt that the value of parents and elders has led her to be "more conservative, more passive, more introverted, in order to be proper." However, she later noted that these characteristics are "more based on the beliefs they hold," than on those she has chosen personally. Her sentiment foreshadows what was also a common theme among students, the sense of critique that students hold about the family dynamics and the influence of family on their evolving sense of self that primarily arose out of a sense of obligation they felt to their families.

Familial Obligation

These closely connected families also came with responsibility and obligations. Almost a third of the students felt duty to the family was a cultural value that was distinct from mainstream American culture.

> I think the American culture stresses independence so much that, if you're independent you can't be with family, 'cause family ties you down. So that I think, because of that, you could get away from the chain that your parents have on you. So that it's less likely for American kids to live with their parents after they're eighteen or live with their elderly parents. They don't do this, 'cause they've learned to be self-sufficient at a young age. So when they're older, they don't have the closeness to their families like the Asian family would have. It's sort of like they would have the heart to let their parents into the rest home or let their elderly parents live by themselves, you know. I don't think Asian families can do that.

This student seems to be conflicted, almost critical of both "American" families and Asian families, implying that parents use "chains" to hold on to their children and that "American" families lack "heart." Students understood and embraced responsibilities, as they saw they were "paying back" for the benefits they gained from the family while growing up. While the student above expected to take care of his parents as they aged, other students felt their educational decisions, daily behavior, and more immediate career plans were heavily influenced by a sense of obligation to family. This Korean woman has had to interrupt her college education a number of times due to family obligations.

> My mother immigrated here, so it was a struggle for her. She is also an abused wife, so that was a big thing. She's tried to rebuild her life, she got

a business of her own because she was dependent on him. I also have a brother and a sister, and she depended on us for help and because that was our only source of income. My brother, who is the oldest, decided that he didn't want to do it anymore so stepped out of the picture. I guess you can say that I had to let my education go more and more. I became more involved with the family and more so, my mother became dependent on me in a lot ways. I guess you can say my sister and I pretty much operate the whole business knowing how dependent she is on us and relying on our help. It would be very hard to walk away from it, so the business has become our hope . . . Family is my biggest obligation. The situation within our family, where education had to be put aside for awhile due to the family, allowed education to get lost in the process. I lost focus, and after a while it was a struggle for me, and so now I just try to take advantage of everything I can as far as getting my education.

Responsibility and obligation to the family and parents as a cultural value was connected to important aspects of students' drive to achieve in college and in other aspects of life. The following quote outlines the connection among culture, responsibility, and motivation.

My culture has made me the person I am, because it taught me how to respect my parents. It taught me how to appreciate what they're doing to get me here. My dad's still in Vietnam. He'd be retired a long time ago and yet he's still working to support me. It taught me to have greater respect for the elderly and for my parents, and basically gave me a lot of inner drive.

This young woman's respect for her parents has translated to an obligation to do well and achieve, due to the sacrifices they made for her to live in the United States. The sense of overcoming adversity in this student's statement was also found in a Cambodian American whose family also stayed behind in order for her to have better opportunities: "[their sacrifices] made me strong and that's why I keep thinking to get more education and keep believing in myself." The strong messages students heard from their parents and other family members about educational expectations, desired occupations, and markers of success were intimately coupled with a sense of obligation to the family and to the effort the entire family system has made to ensure the prosperity of successive generations, which echoes similar findings from Kawaguchi's (2003) qualitative study of Asian Pacific American college students. As persons who benefited from the sacrifices made by family, students

were acutely aware that their successes and failures in education would ultimately bring pride or shame to their respective families. Even when all family
members were in the United States, the sacrifices of the immigrant experience served as motivators for students, as illustrated by this Korean student:

> They just expect, since they're immigrants from Korea, for me to go to
> school in America and to strive. Be the best at what I could do. They were
> always encouraging me and always telling me to study, and even for school
> activities and stuff, they're always encouraging me. They are very strong
> about education, being educated, and using your education in the future.
> My dad graduated from a really prestigious college in Korea, he has a
> chemical engineering degree, and he wasn't able to use that degree for his
> career here. They had to come here and start from scratch with nothing
> and start a business. But a lot of my close friends are Korean, and unless
> they're really quote-unquote Americanized, then they're basically in the
> same position as I am. Their parents always encourage education, and want
> them to study, and get a good job, and just live a happy and successful life.

This student went on to compare these experiences with her "American"
peers: "their parents encourage them to just, you know, do whatever you
want, your life is the way you create it, and they don't really have expectations as much as Koreans." A Filipina noted her parents' strict rules that
supported her education:

> [My parents] stressed education so much that when I was in high school,
> when most of the kids went to work, they wouldn't let me work. They
> think that it would detract from my studying time. They wouldn't let me
> have a boyfriend. You know you're young and you're impressionable and
> you get easily distracted. So you know you fall in puppy love and all that
> stuff. You don't concentrate in school.

Later in the interview, when she was asked to summarize the importance of
being Filipino in the development of her personality or identity, she said,
"the most important thing to me is education, and that has been stressed
upon me by my Filipino background."

Even when students felt support, rather than pressure to do well in
school, the underlying message is clear, as this student conveys:

> My parents are very supportive in the way that, whatever I do is good, as
> long as I try my best. It's okay if I fail; it's okay if I didn't get the straight

As, you know. They're still proud of what I accomplished. They don't put me down when I don't do well. You know, whatever I get, they always say, "At least you did your best, or at least you tried." I think a lot of Asian parents put a lot of stress, a lot of emphasis on how they have to be a doctor, they have to go to medical school. You know, that's the number one dream of Asian parents. I see a lot of my friends, they are so stressed. When they find themselves not making the grade, they're not getting what their parents want. I often see them break down, they aren't doing what their parents want them to do. [But mine] don't force me to do something that I don't want to do.

Although this student did not feel the pressure to succeed that he reports other Asians experience, the message about the general expectation of success in school was confirmed by another student who felt the expectation to do well in school was communicated through Asian communities: "Keeping their families together and getting an education is so highly valued and stressed in the Asian community. Because you see it and hear about it in Asian groups, you know what's expected of you." Culture, family, responsibility, and education were so enmeshed for students that, as one student said, "I think education is bonded to my molecules. I can't separate from it. It's a part of being Filipino." Some researchers suggest that this core value of educational achievement perpetuated within Asian families is at least partially responsible for the genesis of the Asian "model minority" myth (Kawaguchi, 2003).

Familial Complexities

About 40% of students reported that many of their families' high expectations for education, personal behavior, and maintaining traditional gender roles were indicative of being raised in strict households. Students experienced this as both a positive and negative aspect of being a member of their ethnic group. Some students appreciated the impact of strict parenting on their lives, and some even wanted to replicate it despite pressure to modernize. One Japanese American woman explained this dilemma:

My family is real father-dominated, so when I'm with my friends, my Caucasian friends, I'm really reserved when it comes to different things, just little things. And they are like, "Why don't you say something?" And I'm like, "Because I can't!" And they are like, "Why not?" And I'm like,

"'Cause my parents raised me not to say things like that." Little things like that always happen. Or we will be talking about what our husbands are going to be like. I'm like, "Yeah, I'll go and do this and that for them," and they are like, "No, Gina, you have to learn not be dominated by the man." And I'm like, "Well that's the way I want my husband to be." I want him to have more control, to be smarter than me. Because that is the way I see my dad and that is the way I want my husband to be. I don't care if I have to clean; that doesn't bother me. That is what I am supposed to do . . . if my husband is Japanese then he will know, they have been raised in the same way, their parents are strict.

The dominance of fathers in families was a persistent theme for women, regardless of their ethnic group membership. Women analyzed this from a variety of viewpoints—the dutiful daughter who meets parental expectations, a player in lifetime relationships with reciprocal obligations where they "pay back" parents for the sacrifices made for them, or by idealizing future marital relationships.

I think in the Korean culture it's very strong that the male is the dominant figure and the female is the subservient one. I see this with my parents, and this really upsets me. My dad will be downstairs watching TV and I'm upstairs doing something and he'll call me. And I come thinking it's important, and he'll be like, "Can you get me some water?" And I think, why do you do that? I can't personally say anything back to him, because that's just what I'm supposed to be doing as a daughter. If he says, "Do this," then I'm supposed to do it. So that's one thing that kind of upsets me. It burns me up, but if I show any sign of being pissed off, then he gets mad at me, like, "What's the big deal? I can't even ask you for a cup of water?" So you just deal with it.

Another woman hoped that in her own family she would reverse some of the practices she saw as being culturally related:

I have a difficult time communicating with my father . . . there is a tradition, carried on through thousands of years, and the elder, being older, has such a high consequence because of the hierarchical type of culture. A lot of times they use physical discipline, physical abuse, so those are negative parts of the culture. . . . I could try to bring about the best of two cultures rather than the worst of two cultures. I want to try to solve that [problem], in not only myself, but in people around me and hopefully my family as well.

A Vietnamese woman related a more resigned account of the gender roles in her house, but felt that the deference shown to the father was more a function of being Christian than of being Vietnamese. However, this Filipina and others like her felt that strict parenting helped to form solid values, which stood in stark contrast to their more American peers:

> As far as the family and how strict they may seem, I think in the long run that's just for your own good and stuff. And growing up I kind of learned that it led me the right way. Some of my friends growing up weren't given that treatment from their parents. I see the difference between them and me now and it's like I'm really glad my parents did that.

However, not all students experienced adherence to traditional gender roles and strict application of rules and expectations as ultimately positive. As is evident later in this chapter, moving away from strict households and structured gender roles is a part of how students experienced becoming more American. This student alludes to difficult family dynamics, a sentiment expressed by others in the study:

> I think the reason why Asians do so well in school is because that's their escape from their own home lives. I found that we all share the same or similar experiences of hurt in our home so that school was our way of escaping . . . [it was] our therapy session.

In fact, some students did disclose that there was physical punishment in the home and high expectations that children remain passive in parent-child relationships. For these students, becoming more American was how they saw themselves changing family dynamics for future generations.

The Role of Language and Culture in Personal and Group Pride

Students expressed an overwhelming sense of legacy based on culture and history that helped them to develop pride in their ethnic groups and gave them a connection to something beyond their own families and experiences in the United States. Students took a great deal of pride in the rich, cultural histories of their ethnic groups: histories filled with emperors of Japan, the mix of colonizers that gave rise to the Filipino culture, and the legacy of survival as a result of political struggles and war in Southeast Asian countries. Strong associations to home countries led to students' having a deep understanding of the importance and desirability of maintaining individual cultures. Students who felt they lacked knowledge or language had a sense of urgency about working to gain what was lost. Students maintained their individual cultures through learning the history of their ethnic group, visiting the country from which they or their parents came, and maintaining or renewing their language. All of these efforts to maintain culture were often supported by the presence of coethnic peers, who came to serve as places where language was practiced and cultural activities were cultivated.

Language

The use of their native, non-English languages was one of the key attributes that students used to measure the degree of their ethnic identity. In fact, almost two-thirds of students either were fluent in their ethnic language or knew enough of it to communicate with monolingual family members. One student said, "Speaking Chinese identifies your ethnic background, it tells you that you are Chinese." Another who listed activities he participated in that were Chinese said, "Most importantly, I speak the language and I have a lot of friends that I speak Chinese with." As he suggests, language may be perceived as a cultural signifier for high ethnic salience (Yip, 2005). Fourteen of the 23 Asian Americans in the study spoke their non-English language. Knowing and speaking the language of their family and ethnic group was a source of pride for those with language capacity and a source of shame for those who never knew the language or those who lost it over time.

Most students, like the Chinese man above, emphasized using their native language as a primary expression of their ethnic identity. A woman who was born in Korea said,

> I was born in Korea, but I did my growing up here. So it's kind of confusing [in terms] of what it means to be Korean. Basically, for me, I guess what it means to be Korean is just [that] the culture and definitely the language has a really strong thing to do with it. . . . They taught us how to speak Korean at home and how to write and read and all that stuff.

The high concentration of Asian Americans, especially at the research university, allowed students to maintain their language by taking academic courses, participating in ethnically based student organizations, or living with coethnics. A Vietnamese woman roomed with three other Vietnamese students. As a result,

> most of the time we speak to each other in Vietnamese. . . . They're more
> Americanized since they all came over when they were really, really young.
> . . . I came over here when I was eight so I know a lot more. I still keep a
> lot of it, so I think my vocabulary compared to them is a lot higher.

In college, she was able craft an almost exclusively Vietnamese experience—she and her roommates almost always ate Vietnamese food, went to Vietnamese nightclubs, watched Vietnamese movies, and listened to Vietnamese music.

In addition to the self-evaluation of ethnic identity as it related to using the native language, students felt that coethnics judged their level of ethnic identity by language as well. When a loss of language occurred, it was primarily due to entrance into the school system and an associated deemphasis of the language in the family.

> When I was small I used to speak Japanese really well, but then I guess
> when I entered school everybody spoke English and I had to go to an ESL
> (English as a second language) program. So, after that, I think I started to
> lose my Japanese. It started to become worse and worse, and my English
> became better. I even started speaking English to my parents little by little.

Other students had a similar experience:

> I learned my language when I was little, and then my parents just stopped
> teaching me. They didn't want my language to get mixed up with the
> English. But you don't know what the advantage of having that language
> is. Knowing the language, knowing your heritage, and being proud of
> where you came from.

These students demonstrated the common experience of many whose parents stopped using their native languages when their children entered the school system. In many instances, students reported that parents felt their inability to speak English well had interfered with their ability to do well in the United States and did not want their children to experience language-related barriers and associated discrimination. This, coupled with participation in English as a Second Language programs, produced an environment where the value of the native language was lost.

Later, when students entered college, the cost of the loss of language surfaced in a new way, demonstrated by this woman:

> We'd have these college group meetings and they're run in Korean. I get the gist of it, but I really don't understand the specifics, so I'm always whispering, trying to get a translation or whatever. And so language is probably the key thing that makes me feel like I'm not as Korean as I should be.

A common experience among the Asian American, Latino/a, and African American students in the study was a fear of not being "ethnic enough." For Asian Americans, as for the Latinos/as, language was a primary indicator used by coethnics to measure strength of ethnic identity. Peers often communicated that, without knowledge of the group's language, an individual did not pass the ethnic litmus test. This translated to a sense of shame for participants who had lost or had never known their language. For students who were fluent in their group's language, use and knowledge of the language was closely connected to a sense of culture and pride. And for those who were in the process of losing the language, the loss became significant.

> When I started elementary school, I was learning English, but my parents wanted me to keep my Japanese. So they sent me to Japanese school because they wanted me to pick it up someplace. I understand almost everything, but when I'm talking, I can just get by.

> I used to speak [my Filipino dialect] when I was younger. I picked it up in comic books. I used to keep the comic books, so I somehow learned to understand it. I also try to watch the Filipino news half-hour. They speak a different dialect, but I'm trying to understand it just the same.

Students were cognizant of the slow disintegration of language, and they were quick to link a loss of language to a loss of culture, as this Korean woman describes:

> When I was growing up, my nationality was reinforced by going to church and learning the Korean language and writing. But after a certain period

of time it sort of faded, and my ethnicity, not just my ethnicity, but my culture, well, it went out the back door.

Another student made regular visits to the Philippines with her family. In this setting, her inability to speak the local dialect caused a sense of uneasiness in her and her siblings.

> My mom and dad would always speak [the language], it was always a part of my life. I could understand what they were saying, but I cannot speak it. So I feel pretty weird when I go the Philippines because there is that barrier between me and the family. They all speak English, but I would rather speak the native dialect. I'm sorry we have to speak English.

Although there were many reasons for losing language, one Japanese American student put it simply when he said, "A lot of third or fourth generation don't speak the language fluently." For the ethnic groups whose immigration was long enough ago to have three or more generations in the states, the loss of language was common. Given the patterns of immigration in the United States, Japanese and Chinese were most likely to be fourth generation (or more), so they were more likely to have experienced the loss of language.

Cultural Attributes Contributing to Ethnicity

Almost three-quarters of students also felt that elements of their culture supported and provided an avenue for expression of their ethnic identity. Many of their cultural attributes can be considered to be fairly straightforward, such as food, holidays, or other traditions. Others spoke of attributes that represented interconnections they perceived among themselves, their home countries, and the history and people of these countries. Even an attribute such as the food students ate had cultural meaning to them, as demonstrated by this student: "We share something the same, like we love the same food. Food, sharing, eating are very important parts of the Filipino culture, and when we eat together it's like we're communing together." Holidays and traditions they celebrated also enabled them to join with families and other community members. Participation in cultural rituals has been linked to higher levels of ethnic salience, perhaps as a result of the reconnections with family, community, or both that holidays invite (Yip, 2005; Yip & Fuligni, 2002). Examples of these include the various New Year celebrations or the boys and girls day of Japanese culture. As mentioned earlier, coethnics helped to maintain these cultural attributes.

Religion as an Expression of Ethnicity

Religion was also an expression of ethnicity for two-thirds of the students (especially if the student maintained the religion of the home country). Buddhist or Hindu students had prayer rooms or small temples in their homes or were associated with local congregations. Due to the high concentration of coethnics in students' communities, students who were Christian also had the opportunity to attend religious services that were often composed of only their coethnics, for example, a Baptist church for Korean Americans. In these cases, Christian students associated religion with ethnicity, as noted by a Christian student, who said, "I see my religious values as being an extension of my ethnicity." A Korean woman who said, "Religion is really important to me," was asked by the interviewer if religion was related to her culture. She responded:

> Well, yes, I think so. My parents are both Christian, my dad's side of the family practices a lot. My grandfather always calls and tells me to go to church and stuff, so I think it's really important. They think of it as very important, too. Yeah, I would consider that a part of my culture too.

Students who practiced religions traditionally associated with their ethnic group described that practice as being a part of their ethnicity.

> I identify my religion a lot with my ethnicity. I am Catholic, and that is very big in the Philippines. My mom and dad belong to an um . . . a group for Filipinos. I go to sessions because it is a family thing and that's another aspect that I thought was really Filipino.

Another student said, "I'm Buddhist, I think that's part of being Japanese, to be Buddhist." One student who was Christian noted that learning more about Buddhism was one of the ways she was learning more about her Vietnamese culture, thus making religion a method of reconnecting or connecting with culture. Finally, one student even used religious affiliation to describe the types of Koreans who attended her university. She reported, "There are two groups of Koreans. There are the Catholic or Christian group—they are very devout, they go to church . . . and then there is the group that goes to the Korean Christian Student group or the Korean Christian Network and Korean bible study as much as possible. Then you have that other group like the Korean Student Association and they are just like clubs, drinking, parties, and smoking, you know?"

History, A Sense of Common Destiny

Perhaps the most interesting data that revealed the impact of culture and history on students was found in the more than 40% of students who were able to connect culture and history to their own identity, sense of legacy, and family heritage. Some students were just beginning this journey, as demonstrated by a Korean woman who is working to strengthen her ethnicity in college: "I volunteer to take Korean classes, I'm trying to get into more East Asian culture classes to find out more about history, and what not." She attributed this not so much to peer influence, but to an age-related change—something that has happened since getting older. Others took pride in the history of their people, an example of which a Vietnamese woman provided: "I like how we have had such a strong history for a thousand years. I'm proud of that, I'm proud of the culture we have." Another woman talked about a historical perspective that served to ground her in a bicultural place:

> I feel like I have two lives. You know what I mean? I feel like I have two pasts. Like I have the American past and the Japanese past. So I can . . . it's kind of sad because I could never really relate to just one. You know, I'm kind of like double-sided. So I am kind of caught in between two places. But I think it's just really, it makes me proud to know that I have a history and I have some ties that go back. Like when I went back to Japan, I felt like that. Like, wow people, you know, my past, I have these people in my blood. Yeah, you know, it feels good. And I know that like in America it seems like a lot of people don't know where they came from. Like because they are mixed, so many different ethnicities that they don't even know what they are. I feel like I have something to hold on to. I have a language and the cultural things that I can always hold on to.

Ethnicity acted as an anchor in this student's life. There is a sense that her ethnicity is the connection between her two pasts. Her Japanese past and the connection to others of Japanese descent give her a sense of pride and centeredness. The lack of conflict between these two pasts and the present they create demonstrates the negotiation many students experienced in becoming Asian American. History, legacy, and connection to others are also demonstrated by this student:

> I'm proud of the culture that we have, like how we're so close to our family, we're like a unit. We have very close ties to parents, and we have a strong history for a thousand years. I'm proud of that. I try to understand the holidays that we celebrate. My dad, he's starting to tell me about it now. A couple of years back, he tells me about it and I never really listen to him. It was a bore. Now, whenever he tells me, I love it when he starts talking about the myths we used to have. It's so interesting. I appreciate them a lot more than before. My culture gives me a lot of confidence, so I know that I can make it as, as long as I know who I am and I keep what I believe in and not forget that I am Vietnamese. Some people they come and they try to forget that they're Vietnamese, they forget the language, or they try to forget their culture. Then twenty years down the line, when they really want to learn about it, it's too late. So I want to keep it now and then, then years later I won't start flipping through the books trying to find out who I am 'cause I already know. And so it helps me to be a stronger person inside and outside. Once I'm strong, I can succeed, and I can do anything.

This student discloses how the role of culture and history has changed as he has grown older. He now realizes the critical role culture and ethnicity plays in his life. He can connect his relationship to his culture and the pride he has in being Vietnamese with specific outcomes such as confidence and a drive to succeed. The direct connection the student articulates also provides motivation to retain cultural knowledge. He alludes to other important outcomes, such as a closer relationship with his father and ethnicity. A Cambodian woman echoed this by saying, "[Being Cambodian] has made me stronger, I would fight for it. Whatever happened in the past when I was younger made me stronger; that's why I keep thinking to get more education and keep believing in myself."

Connection to coethnics, knowledge of cultural history, and home country visits all strengthen ethnicity for students and help to ground them. The student below is able to pinpoint the psychological and emotional assistance that being Japanese represents to her.

> I think being Japanese had a huge part in me developing psychologically, mentally, emotionally. A lot of the values that I hold now are a lot based

on my parents and like their background. Like with ethnic identity, I think that everyone should have some past. It's important, you know? You want to always feel connected to something, I think. For me, like going to Japan, is this huge thing because I felt that I belonged somewhere. Even though I probably could never live there, it felt like, "Wow! These are my people!" Even though they probably don't look like me, they still have my blood. You know what I mean? And I'm different than everyone else, because I have their blood. So you feel good because you are a part of something. I value the feeling.

The sense of connection and belonging—being part of something larger than herself—was critical to how this student felt about herself. It appears that her ethnic identity provides a solid foundation and a comforting home for her to return to when sustenance is needed.

Not only did students take pride in the histories of their countries of origin, but they also took pride in the fact that many of their families and coethnics were immigrants who have found success in the United States despite the many obstacles they encountered. One man reflected on the historical forces that have shaped the Japanese American experience:

Like when the Japanese got interned . . . that really made an impact when I read about that. And about the battalion totally made up of Japanese Americans. They became very distinguished during their service, and this made me feel real proud because it just shows that the Japanese could be just as good as any other race.

Another spoke more specifically of the immigrant experience and generalized that experience to all Asians.

My family and most of my friends—they were all immigrants. They came over and started with nothing. Everyone has these totally negative stereotypes like, "All you people are rich. All Indian people are rich. All Asian people are rich. All of you drive Mercedes." When my family and friends came here, they had nothing. Half of them didn't even speak English and they're doing incredibly well. Obviously it's because they worked totally hard. I'm like [Americans] have the raddest opportunities; they've lived here all of their lives. Their families came on the Mayflower. They should have more.

This student suggests that the emerging legacy and history of recently immigrated groups in assimilating into our society will be a story of overcoming the adversity of the immigrant experience. She contrasts her family's ability to achieve success so rapidly with the situation of "Americans," who have had generations to become successful in the United States.

Values Associated With Culture

There was also a persistent sense among most students that values were also a reflection of ethnicity and culture. As we described earlier, many students associated how they valued education with their cultures. In the interviews students were asked about values they held dear and then asked to reflect on whether those would be common to their ethnic group. One man confirmed:

> The beliefs my parents have affected how they raised me, so [the influence] is more indirectly Korean, it has a more indirect affect on my personality. I'm more conservative. I'm more passive. I'm more introverted, just to be proper. Those are more based on the beliefs they [my parents] hold.

Many in the study also mentioned an inclination toward conservative values and behavior.

> Besides speaking the language, eating Chinese food, listening to the music, having Chinese friends . . . I think what comes to my mind, the main difference [between me and my non-Chinese friends] is, I think Chinese are more conservative, more conservative in just like everything.

Similarly, when a student was asked where his values of loyalty and honesty came from, he said,

> I think my parents pretty much instilled this in me. They made me feel bad if I wasn't honest, or if I said something about a friend that would betray that friendship, then they would tell me about that—"You should be more loyal to that friend." It was really emphasized and I think I wanted to be, I really wanted to be more outspoken because I'm kind of a quiet person. It's really hard to, even in class, it's really hard to raise my hand . . . [I think the Japanese] share the value of loyalty and honesty, but I don't think they value being outspoken. I think the most quiet people in the world would be the Japanese.

When asked how he knew these values were shared, he said,

> I went to Japanese school and I had a lot of Japanese friends; their parents
> also seemed the same way. And again, it's just the history of Japan. They
> seem very loyal to the emperor and stuff and willing to sacrifice their life
> for the emperors.

He later said, "I just think that the identity with me being Japanese, my
parents really instilled in me a lot of traditional Japanese values and I think
that's what made me, what really shaped my personality."

This last student connected his values to the values of his Japanese culture and to the history of that country. He saw honesty, loyalty, and a quiet
reserve all as being a part of the Japanese experience, and this was buttressed
by what he learned in Japanese school and by the coethnic friends he met
there. Other students in the study shared the notion of coethnics supporting
ethnicity and culture.

Coethnics as Ethnicity Supporters

Almost half of the Asian American students interviewed found themselves in
friendship groups that were composed primarily of members of their own
ethnic groups. This finding is demonstrated in exemplars elsewhere in this
chapter and they are important reminders about the pervasiveness of these
themes. Coethnics served as places to practice language, they were preferred
roommates where ethnic food and pop culture were shared, and as individuals they served as a referent point as students contemplated the connection
among family structure, values, and ethnicity. Two students in the study
described their need for coethnic friendships in these ways.

> I don't usually hang around with people, but when I do it's mostly my
> own ethnic group . . . I'm basically a shy person, so it's really hard to find
> a person who can associate with me from another cultural group. Tradi-
> tionally, Chinese have been pretty shy, and I guess I fit into that category.
> So it's easier to have someone from your own cultural background to relate
> to you. That's why it's easier to have a friend who is a member of your
> own cultural background.

> The Vietnamese culture in me is still so strong that I need the other person
> to understand what I'm going through or what I'm feeling, because I don't

think that there's an American person who understands. Sometimes I think you need them to know what I feel, understand what I feel and I don't [think] that anybody besides Vietnamese would understand it. Sometimes I would want to speak Vietnamese to them, and I wouldn't be able to do that if they weren't Vietnamese.

Here we see why students feel more comfortable interacting with coethnics. The first woman views shyness as a cultural attribute that other Chinese people share, making it easier to connect with other Chinese. The similarity in background makes relating easier. The second woman echoes this sentiment, but adds the dynamic of empathy and implies that communicating in one's native language allows for deeper understanding of personal challenges that may be difficult to understand when expressed in a different language. Although most of the Asian American students mentioned the role coethnics played in the development or maintenance of their ethnicity, most also saw the ways they and their ethnic groups were changing as a result of becoming part of American culture.

Transforming Culture: Becoming American

"I'm definitely Americanized, definitely Westernized." Nearly every Asian American student made this statement in one way or another. Like this Indian American student, most were either first- or second-generation Americans, giving them immediate connections to home countries and the process of assimilation or acculturation their families and/or communities were undergoing at the time of the interviews. There were three primary ways students talked about culture being transformed and ways in which they were becoming American. The first explains how students felt their families, and thus cultural values, were changing as a result of living in the United States. The second explains the ways they felt they were changing as a result of coming in contact with peers outside their ethnic groups. In the third, students spoke more generally about changes in the importance of relationships that were causing them to consider themselves hyphenated Americans.

Familial Changes

Almost half of the students felt their families were changing primarily in the relationship between parents and children. In general, more Americanized families had less of a focus on the communal nature of the family and more of one on children's independence. Students perceived this as a positive development. They embraced the emerging opportunity to achieve greater independence, as evident in this Korean student's account of a change in his friends and family.

> Some of my Korean friends are more Americanized, their values are more underlined by individuation, they focus more on the needs of their children. Whereas for me, it's more like, not what's best for you, but what's best for the family. Seeing that other side or attitude, you know, made a big impact on me, where I wanted to be associated with my friends in being able to do what's best for me and not what's best for the family.

When the interviewer asked if the student felt he was being more individualistic now, he responded:

> I still feel that the family is important to me. But I also think that growing up I'm trying to be more focused on myself rather than my family, because I know that in the future I have to develop a life for myself, too. That becomes my main focus now.

It is not evident that the student's family is changing, but it obvious that his relationship to his family is beginning to change. He wants to place his needs before the family's—a highly uncommon practice in his culture. Another student expressed a similar point of view about the change in the family, the motivation for which is not necessarily the students' desire to Americanize the relationship, but parental behavior becoming Americanized:

> I think it's partly because, first, they used to be really strict on how we had to be and how we had to act. But then they realized that we're in a different culture, and they can't treat us the way they used to treat us back in Vietnam. And they saw that we're grown up and we know how to think. They know that they raised us well. We can think on our own and we can make the right decision, so they just let us go and do what we feel is right. And so I think that's different from like when some other parents that might still have the idea that they can force their kids to do what they want, and they're still back in like the olden days.

The way this student described his parents' trusting their children's decisions rather than trying to exert greater control over their children sounded very American, indeed. Conventional beliefs about parenting in the United States rely on the assumption that raising children well will result in appropriate adult behavior when the children become independent.

Whatever the source of change (American culture's impact on child or parent) in the nature of the parent-child relationship, students felt generally positive about the change. Sentiments ranged from subdued longing for independence, "If I was raised by American parents, maybe I would have more independence," to more specific accounts of the change:

> Adults are dominating figures in the household where the children have to keep quiet, whereas in America, everybody is an individual and everybody is independent of one another. Whether you are in a family or you are on your own, everybody has their space and their privacy. In the Vietnamese culture everything is in the community. Everybody knows everything about everyone.

Here the student seems to have come to value both independence and privacy, two belief patterns that are antithetical to his culture. Another Vietnamese student considered this type of change in the family as the primary way he was becoming Asian American.

> I think I consider myself to be Asian American, because even though I still keep my culture, I assimilate the American culture. I'm more open and I learned to be more independent than if I were still back in Vietnam. There, you have to do everything that your parents say you have to do.

These are reminiscent of some of the students' experiences described earlier in the chapter, when they spoke of family and how they pictured the evolution of that family.

Asian American women also experienced changes in their families that were more associated with their gender. These changes involved expectations for modest dress and proper female behavior, about the ethnicity of dating partners, and about the women's relationship to their parents after marriage. Many women spoke about being more Americanized in these regards, but often hid their behavior from parents:

[My boyfriend's] parents are divorced and they're accepting of me, whereas my parents aren't accepting of him, because of his nationality and because he went into the Air Force after high school and not college. Because he's not really studious, I guess, in a sense. And so, my parents don't like that. And plus, they don't even know. My parents don't know that we're together.

A strategy for changing relationships with the family, such as this woman hiding the fact that she has a boyfriend, actually is a sign of changing elements of a culture where deference and loyalty to family are so highly valued. Like this student, many other women spoke of the difficulty they had with their parents when they dated outside their ethnic group. And like this woman, most women kept these relationships secret from their parents. Related to this was the notion that daughters were expected to remain close to the family in adulthood and marriage (as discussed earlier in the chapter). When women talked about their desire and expectation for a change in this pattern, they felt that they were becoming more American or Westernized. One student explained, "I guess, well, my mom would call it Americanized you know, that part about leaving home before you're married. She's not too keen on that, but I've adopted more of those Western values."

Changes in child-parent relationships were indicative of adoption of new cultural values. Immigration status can have a strong impact on intergenerational conflict, as younger immigrants tend to have an easier time acculturating than do older immigrants (Nghe, Mahalik, & Lowe, 2003), making subsequent generations more likely to morph cultural values to reflect acculturation to more American values. The forces that cause assimilation or acculturation are strong and come from many sources, such as the media, popular culture, and education, but the most significant source of change in cultural values stems from contact with peers from other ethnic groups.

Influence of Peers

The literature that attributes strong socialization to peers is vast and spans the years of early adolescence to early adulthood. Many higher education researchers note that the strongest influence in college is, indeed, students' peers (Astin, 1993; Kuh, 1996; Pascarella & Terenzini, 1991, 2005). However, over a fifth of students noted that peer pressure to become American began much earlier than college. In fact, a common theme among Asian Americans,

Latinos/as, and African Americans was that high school was a time of assimilation and a time of stepping away from ethnicity. This student observes:

> The children of Vietnamese immigrants, being raised in American culture, are more assimilated. I know peer pressure in high school has a lot to do with how you are, but [the Vietnamese kids] are totally assimilated into this culture by the time they hit high school. Even within the first two years of arriving, I see them wearing the trendiest clothes. We had next-door neighbors that just came from Vietnam, and within two years those kids were wearing the most popular clothes, the trendiest clothes, they were all in style. They had the cars. They lived in a rundown house, but you better believe they got the car, they got the clothes, they got the money. Their parents gave them whatever they wanted, as long as they held up the grades.

One way non-White Americans, who may be perceived as having less of a claim to an "American" identity than do European Americans, try to assert their "Americanness" by attempting to adopt cultural norms as quickly and completely as possible (Cheryan & Monin, 2005). The intersection of adolescence and recent immigration status may increase this urgent need to belong. Another Vietnamese student supports this account and discerns that the motivation was to be accepted quickly in a culture where new arrivals felt conspicuous.

> I think new immigrants just really want to be accepted into the culture. When you first come here, you hear, "There's the fresh off the boats," and they want to lose that stigma. They don't want people looking at them as retarded people. They don't look like Americans, so they try as fast as they can to be accepted by wearing the clothes, by getting the car, and their English might not be that good, but they learn fast.

Again, given the recent immigration of many of these students, the pull to assimilate and become American was quite strong and often supported by the ethnic enclaves in which they lived. These students were referring to the influence of peers in high school. In terms of the growth and maintenance of ethnic identity, high school peers appeared to be the greatest threat.

Many of the students in this study were high achieving and found themselves in honors and advanced placement courses that were predominantly

White. Like Asian American students, African American and Latino/a students reported that ethnic identity was deemphasized in high school, with an active suppression of the expression and importance of culture.

> [Ethnicity] is an up-and-down thing. Like when you were little, you were really into it, then it kind of went down. I wasn't very proud of being Indian. I thought it was kind of freaky, you know when I was [ages] eleven to sixteen. All of my friends were Christian; none of them were Hindu. Now I'm very proud of it.

This student appeared to experience a recovery of ethnic identity in college. In fact, later in the interview, she reported:

> Now some of my friends went to sororities like those who weren't into their ethnic background. We've all pursued some kind of club or organization. They've all gone to theirs, like the Korean Student Association, Chicano ones, Latino ones, Indian, whatever. When they all did that, it supported me: like, I can do this. This is cool. I didn't feel like they thought I was abandoning them. In that way, we all kind of mutually supported each other and we can all come together still.

Her peers from other ethnic groups motivated this student to reconnect to her culture. When her peers joined ethnic student organizations, they served as role models, and their ability to remain connected to each other while building relationships with coethnics gave her the confidence that she could manage both social systems.

At times, influence of peers, even those who were coethnics, influenced students in ways that pulled them away from their cultural background. One student who primarily interacted with friends from her own ethnic group reported that she learned to be more independent with her family from her Vietnamese peers:

> I've learned to be independent, I guess. When you're a teenager you learn to rebel like everybody else is rebelling. That would never happen if I was in Vietnam. I would never learn to talk back. I could never dare talk back, or else they'll hit me or something, you know? Over here, I guess, I've learned to be braver. I guess I kind of follow the way other people are doing it, instead of like following what my parents are saying. There's a time when you don't want the parent authority. You're young, you don't want the

parent authority to tell you what to do. In that period, I pushed myself away from them. I just wanted to be on my own. I wanted to follow the way my friends did, what they would say and do. I guess in a way, it was disrespectful . . . I would argue with them a lot. I would talk back in a really, really bad tone . . . I behaved, well I see it on TV, people are doing it. I see my friends are being disrespectful. I guess I acquired it, I learned it.

Not all students felt that interaction with peers had altered their ties to their own culture, but there was the sense that they felt the change was coming. One student did not think she had changed as a result of interacting with those outside her culture, but she finished her response with, "I'm still in the process of assimilation; in that sense I will become more Americanized, but not now." As discussed earlier, family supports and maintains culture and ethnic identity. This was especially important for students who lived in predominantly White environments. Like for the student below, the family established the cultural values that balanced the Americanization of social interactions and relationships.

When I say I was brought up with the culture, I'm mainly talking about the cultural values my parents have imbedded in me. I think their strong beliefs in family values and all kinds of old world thinking is still going on in the Philippines. I think that they are my morals, and my values were set by that. But in terms of social interactions, I think I was brought up more American.

A Japanese American student who had made several visits to Japan throughout her life was beginning to see how she was changing, becoming less Japanese.

[My parents] wanted to instill a lot of Japanese values in me, but all my friends were all White . . . I never had any close friends that were Japanese, except the ones from school. . . . When I was younger, [my parents] spoke [Japanese] to me. They wanted me to learn English because we live in America and we weren't going back to Japan. So they sent me to Japanese school [because] they wanted me to pick up Japanese somewhere. I understand almost everything, but my talking, when I start to talk, I just get by.

Then when asked if she was starting to associate with the dominant culture, she said:

I'm not reserved, they always say that [Americans] are self-expressing and Japan is a lot more quiet and reserved. I'm not quiet and reserved. So I guess my personality has changed, well, because most of my friends are Caucasian . . . when I went to Japan I noticed a huge difference.

She demonstrates that living in contemporary U.S. communities and interacting with assimilated coethnics and American peers causes students to experience acculturation, where the student's ethnic culture changes into something unique—that is, the student's culture is transformed. This new culture is one that is not quite American, yet it is distinct from the more unitary ethnic culture. Research on Asian Americans has found that Asian American college students are able to embrace American cultural identity without feeling as if they must deny their Asian heritage (Yeh, Carter, & Pieterse, 2004), or in other words, that "it was possible to be both 100% Asian and 100% American" (Cheryan & Monin, 2005, p. 726). Like those who talked about assimilation, these students felt that the drive to acculturate was precipitated by the peer culture and peer groups with which they were in contact in both high school and college. By and large, students felt generally positive about these changes. There may have been a sense of loss, but they appreciated what they gained in terms of a broad appreciation for multiple cultures.

In contrast, a Filipina student who grew up in a predominantly White environment compared her college experience to that of her sister, who attended another university.

I was living in a Caucasian community and they accepted me and that was all good, and then, when I came here, it was all different because there are so many Asians everywhere. I thought, oh my god, I'm not the only one. I kind of went through a guilty stage because my friends were still Caucasian, and I joined a sorority and it wasn't an Asian sorority and I started to feel guilty. I felt guilty if I was wearing my letters for my sorority, and like Asians would look at me, like, what kind of Asian are you? My sister had gone to [another public university] four years before me and she joined an Asian sorority and I remember watching her through all that and she was so proud of being Asian and for me I loved seeing that in her because in high school she was very superficial. When she got to college she was very proud about who she was and stuff, and I thought that was very cool and she had all these new Asian friends that she never had in high school. For me, I tended to be friends with Caucasians. I just felt guilty because I wasn't part of an Asian community as much as I could have been here. I feel like I'm in between, I feel like an Asian token, but when I see an Asian group, I think how it might feel to be part of that group, because to me it seems like two different cultures.

This woman sees the opportunity in college to connect with her Asian peers and even admires her sister for accomplishing that at her university. However, there is a sense that something is holding her back from these groups. She's aware of feeling like a token in the predominantly Caucasian groups in which she is a part and wonders what it might be like to join with other Asians. Coethnic peers also served a social comparison function that brought inner conflict to students who struggled with guilt associated with "not being Asian enough," as expressed by the Japanese American student below.

When I joined a sorority I was constantly around all of these Asian people. It really hurt me because people were like, "Yeah, have you met Tina? She acts so White! I can't believe she joined an Asian sorority!" My cousin was even saying that to me. I didn't take it badly from my cousin, but it hurt when someone else says, "Yeah, she's really whitewashed." I'll joke about it, but it hurts when it is someone that is supposedly your own race saying that about you. It hurt a lot because they don't know. I'm trying, you know. I joined an Asian sorority because I wanted to become more culturally aware.

Crossing Ethnic Boundaries

Students who felt negatively about the change in their ethnicity, and ultimately about the changes in their culture in the United States, were the exception. Students felt comfortable with the changes and saw them as evidence of their ability to live more fluid and inclusive lives, with over a third of them highlighting the importance of crossing ethnic boundaries. One woman, who compared herself to her sister, who was an activist for the Japanese American student population in college said, "I don't think I'm as Asian as my sister was in college, but I still feel Asian. I still have Asian friends, but I don't exclusively hang out with them. You know I still do cultural things that have to do with my ethnicity."

There is the sense that this woman traverses ethnic groups easily and does not feel that peers from other ethnic groups are a threat to her being

Asian. Other students could articulate the process of acculturation they were experiencing more descriptively. The following student describes what it means to be Korean American.

> All of my siblings were born in Korea, so we still actually follow their teachings and their way of life, and at the same time, we are trying to integrate into Western culture as well. It's creating Korean-Americanism. It's appropriate because you do have both cultures. In order to live here in the U.S., having a Korean ethnic background, you've got to actually accept other cultures and views and so forth, not only the American culture, but other cultures as well.

In his experience, being Korean American was not only a process of selecting elements of American culture, but it also encompassed the inclusion of other cultures. To him, a part of becoming American is accepting the country's multiple cultures. In fact, Korean Americans largely consider themselves to be bicultural, meaning they are able to retain their cultural heritage while incorporating some aspects of dominant culture into their lifestyles (Lee, Falbo, Doh, & Park, 2001). This student, and the one below, does not feel he is becoming something "less than," but something unique and necessary.

> When we walk into a culture, we see things and pick them up and then we throw out the things we don't like. Given the opportunity of any individual to come to the U.S., to come here and experience the many varieties and experiences that this country has to offer, then I think they would do the same things I would. But there are things we can't throw away that makes us, us. There are things that are the foundation.

Another student admired qualities she saw in Americans: "I see Americans as being really open-minded and stuff. I think that's an admirable trait, you know. I think because if you're able to accept different things and differences among people, I think that's good, that's a plus."

Cultures are transformed when they come in contact with other cultures, and elements of them all are valued enough to be integrated into new identities and cultures. This occurs more strikingly for students who come from bicultural or biracial backgrounds. Only a very small number of students in this study were biracial (only one identified as so), with all using labels of single ethnic groups. However, during the interview, this student articulated what it was like to grow up with two cultures in the home.

> I'm not just one ethnicity, I'm mixed with two. My father is Caucasian, so he is American. I feel like I get more of a variety of what the world is like, a broader view of things as far as being Vietnamese [is concerned]. I see the differences being raised up in a bicultural household. I get a lot of the training up and honor and respect of the elders and how to treat people. There is a lot of respect in Asian culture. Not to say that the American culture is not the same; it's just that they show it differently. I just think that I'm at an advantage because I get to see more of the world. A broader horizon of the way I think and the way I look at things. It's not just narrow-minded as far as one way of doing things. There are several ways of doing things, and there's no right or wrong.

A Filipina talked about the bicultural nature of her experiences growing up in a mixed community and emphasized the benefit of multiculturalism.

> I consider myself a very mixed person. It's kind of unusual, too, since I grew up with Mexicans and Filipinos. Sometimes it's hard for me to distinguish which culture is which, but in a way I think it's very good to know that there are other cultures and that to be educated means knowing other cultures. Even now, I don't really fully understand my culture. I went to the Philippines over the summer, I was hoping to go to school there. . . . But when I went, it was more of a visit than learning, but I'm glad I did go and I know where my relatives are. I really wish I could go back there and live there for at least one year or two.

The ability to assume a broader worldview and to retain what is best about each culture is a benefit of being raised in a multicultural environment. This student's experience foreshadows what may be the experience of successive generations of Asian American students as the individual ethnic groups move further away from the immigration experience, making intentional efforts to maintain ethnicity and culture more important. Despite the increasingly multicultural nature of our communities and the likelihood of intermarriage in subsequent generations, the distinct possibility remains that ethnic groups can be maintained in areas where there are large enough populations to sustain monoethnic churches, community organizations, and youth activities.

Summary and Conclusions

Asian American students in the study came from specific ethnic backgrounds that were more important to their ethnicity than the pan-ethnic term typically used to identify students and the group. All students were clear about their preference for their specific ethnic group label and were adept at discerning differences among Asian ethnic groups. They expressed their ethnicity through language, food, customs, religion, and family structure. Students also demonstrated the impact generational status has on ethnicity. When students were closer to the time of immigration, or actually part of the immigrating family group, their ethnicity was stronger through the fluency of language, the ability to traverse both the culture of origin and American culture, and through connections with family members who continue to live abroad.

Family played a critical role in both the transfer and maintenance of ethnicity and how students experienced college and young adulthood. Nearly all students, regardless of their specific Asian ethnic background, thought that enmeshed family structures were unique to their ethnic group. They felt that close family systems caused students to remain closer to their families by their continuing to live with family in and after college and by allowing family norms and expectations to determine life decisions and lifestyles. For instance, women in the study saw themselves replicating the male-dominated family structure in their own families. Many students also anticipated being in close physical proximity to their families as adults, even when raising their own families. They saw these actions as a characteristic of their culture and identified the obedience implied in these decisions as another cultural characteristic. In fact, many felt their respect for their families and the respectful deference shown to elders primarily distinguished them from their "American" peers. Close proximity of family members had a significant impact on maintaining ethnicity since practicing the language and culture was easy when supported by so many. Some saw this as a form of protection against assimilation into American culture.

Asian American students felt that family had an impact on many of the typical tasks of the college years. Residence during college emphasized close proximity to the family. Therefore, many students attended colleges close to home, and more than half of the sample actually lived at home while attending college. Students also felt incredible support and high expectations for their educational success. There was a sense of obligation because many family members had made sacrifices to enable these students to attend college.

This obligation ranged from serving in more traditional gender roles in the home to needing to take time off from college to support the family business. There was the strong perception that strong family endorsement of education was another characteristic of Asian families. Some of the women felt that choice of dating partners and, ultimately, life partners, was influenced by family pressure to marry within their ethnic group. At times the pressure was so prevalent that women hid their interracial dating from their parents. Although no students in the study reported pressure from parents to pursue specific careers, some noted this was the experience of coethnic peers.

Students were also very aware of the acculturation process they were undergoing as they grew up in the United States. Some looked forward to taking on "American" characteristics, especially as they related to changes in gender roles and the family system—primarily adherence to strict parenting and discipline. They were also aware that language, a primary external marker of a strong ethnic identity, was slowly being lost as they participated more fully in American culture. Peers both sustained ethnicity and challenged ethnicity. Many students in the study seemed to be highly self-conscious when they felt that coethnic peers were evaluating the ethnic identity of others. In many interviews, we heard statements such as, "She acts White" or "He's not Asian enough," which made students feel a sense of shame and guilt from not having placed more importance on language and culture. Peers supported ethnicity when they modeled involvement in ethnic student organizations or ethnic studies classes. They also provided avenues for speaking native languages regularly and for engaging in other cultural activities.

Despite an acculturation process that many students reported as positive, nearly all took great pride in their ethnic group. This pride came from knowledge of historic pasts, but also from current challenges as immigrants in a new society. This level of pride, associated with supports for ethnicity in universities and communities, seemed to allow students to look forward to an acculturation process that included the best attributes of two cultures. We sensed a confidence that, although their language may subside, their ethnicity would remain strong, and they would try to pass that pride and ethnicity on to the next generation.

4

AFRICAN AMERICANS
Pride Through Legacy and Action

African American students demonstrate both their ethnic and racial identities in ways that differ from those of other groups. The historical racialization of African Americans in the United States has led to the development of racial identities grounded in discrimination, exclusion, and oppression. The racial and ethnic identity literature has largely neglected the cultural and ethnic aspects of this group; however, the students in this study spoke quite strongly and consistently about the ethnic aspects of their identities—that is, identities composed of a sense of shared history and destinies with other members of their group, traditions, and customs (Allen, 1992; Ryan & Deci, 2003). Opportunities in higher education to take African American studies courses and to connect with other students through African American student organizations have helped to promote this sense of ethnicity in African American students, rather than the sole development of racial identities. The strength students developed as a result of group empowerment and collectivity and individual explorations in and commitments to ethnic identity have resulted in students' feeling optimistic about the group's future. Thus the themes for this chapter focus on Forming Racial and Ethnic Identities; Expressions of Ethnicity; The Complex Relationships Among Racism, Oppression, and Ethnic Identity; and Prospects for the Future.

Ethnic labels for African Americans were primarily just that, African Americans. Of the 21 African American students interviewed, 17 used "African American" to describe their ethnic identity. Three students preferred to use "Black," and one student preferred "Afro-American." Two students, although primarily identifying as African American, also noted they were of mixed ethnicity. One student talked about labels, and in his explanation demonstrated the flexibility in using these labels.

> I think there are so many different classifications and groups within the African American communities. You have your very well-off African Americans, you have your poor African Americans, middle class, whatever. And I feel whenever I'm in a Black community I's fine. I'm around my people. I just feel like I'm not rich, I come from a middle-class home, and I didn't live in a Black community. I lived in a mixed White-type community. But when I got to like, let's say, visit my cousins that live in a Black community, it feels more like home.

He uses "Black" and "African American" interchangeably and then highlights his ability to enter and interact in communities that vary in terms of socioeconomic status and racial composition. He's clear that home is in the Black community. African Americans in the study generally lived in communities that were predominantly African American. In fact, compared to other students in the study, African Americans lived in neighborhoods with the highest proportion of African Americans (81.33%). However, their high schools were more diverse, but remained predominantly African American, with 56.66% being African American, 24.25% White, 16.58% Latino/a, and 7.9% Asian American. African Americans were also the group that generally had the longest history in the United States, with nearly all students being either fourth- or fifth-generation in this country.

Forming Racial and Ethnic Identities

The final question of the interview asked students to reflect on the importance of ethnic identity in the development of their personalities. In the responses to this question, more than a quarter of the students were able to demonstrate distinctions between ethnic and racial identities. For example, one student explained the development of her ethnic identity as reflecting both ethnic and racial identity as separate constructs:

> I think that most African Americans living in our country go through stages. We first enter that stage where we don't identify or see that differentiation. We don't see Black or White; we say, "Okay, if I achieve or if I go through the mainstream I will be accepted." Then there comes the point

where we realize that's not going to happen. You will only be accepted to a certain degree because, regardless of what you achieve academically or economically, when someone looks at you, you will always be still African first and American second. That is my perception. And then you enter the stage where I am in, where you are actively seeking out your African heritage; you are actively seeking out the positive things about being a black American so that you can have a shield on this negative thing that you are constantly being bombarded with. So I think I'm in the militant stage now.

Those familiar with Cross's (1991) model of the development of Nigresence in adults see the sequence she describes in this student's account of her development. In fact, we assert that Cross's third stage, *Immersion/Emersion*, illustrates the intersection of racial and ethnic identity for African Americans. In this stage, the exploration of culture, history, traditions, language—the "positive" things she describes—are closely associated with definitions of ethnic identity discussed in chapter 2. This stage provides a venue for unlearning the negative effects of racism on the creation of ethnic identities. Another student demonstrated more clearly the interplay between racial and ethnic identity and the overall sense of self.

So ethnicity plays a pretty good role because you know your makeup is based on how you look at yourself and how others look at you. So if you're getting positive or negative feedback, then it's going to determine how you're going to be.

Here we might distinguish racial identity as the way others "see me" and ethnic identity as "how I see myself." These are both connected to how this student sees herself. A significant element of developing identity is the role others play in helping the individual develop an identity. The "mirror" Erikson (1968) describes enables the individual to see herself the way others see her. The negative evaluation the woman above speaks about strongly influences "how you're going to be." Thus racial identity has the potential to have a strong effect on ethnic identity and, ultimately, on self-concept. The ethnic identity measure used in this study revealed that African Americans had the highest identity score (role of group membership in the self-concept) of all the groups. Conversely, their public acceptance score (how individuals believe others evaluate the group) was the lowest of all the groups, an acknowledgment on their part of their lower status within a racial hierarchy.

A male student focused more directly on ethnic identity in the response to the question:

> I think it's healthy for society, for people, for different groups to have strong ethnic identities and strong cultural identities, and I think for personality development, ethnicity is important because it gives you a strong foundation. If you know your history, and if you know your ethnic groups' customs and traditions, if you understand them, not only know them, but know why they came about or what circumstances caused them to come about—I think that it makes for a well-rounded person. I think that you have to know it, love it, and believe in your foundation before you can cross over and share some of the other groups' ethnicity or culture or tradition. You have to be well grounded in yours, and one thing that happens is that prejudice and that stupid racism will be alleviated because people will know where they are and who they are.

This student emphasized not only the importance of ethnic identity for the individual, but also its importance for improved intergroup relationships. He has "used" this well-developed ethnic identity to do two things: provide a buffer against the negative effects of prejudice and racism and build a bridge to reach out to other groups. Cross and Strauss (1998) outline five functions of Black identity that help people in everyday life. *Buffering* acts as a psychological shield against racism and discrimination. *Bridging* allows for strong relationships with out-group members without a threat to one's Black identity. The remaining functions of a Black identity are instructive, though this student did not delineate them. *Code switching* allows individuals to move easily between Black and White cultural situations, and through *Bonding*, individuals are able to connect with other African Americans to build the community necessary to support them when ethnic identity is threatened. Finally, a function of Black identity also encourages *individualism* of that identity and calls for support by coethnics to nurture that unique identity. Earlier work by Phinney and colleagues (Phinney, 1995; Phinney & Kohatsu, 1997; Phinney, Madden, & Santos, 1996) shows the positive effects of having a strong ethnic identity on buffering the adverse effects of racial discrimination.

Students were fairly consistent in their evaluation of the role of ethnic identity in their own personal development, with discussion and descriptions of ethnic identity consistent with definitions found in the literature, such as the connection between ethnic identity and pride. One student explained:

> I feel good. [My ethnicity] means a lot to me. It's something I take a lot of pride in and it's very important in my life and it's something I have to deal with every day. So it has to be important and it has to be special to me in order for me to deal with [living here].

Again, we see the utility of ethnicity as a buffer for living in our society. Another student stated simply, "I am proud to be Black and I wouldn't want to be any other race." Both these exemplars note the connection between pride and ethnicity, and both illustrate African Americans' use of ethnicity and race as interchangeable terms.

Ethnic Practices and Expressions

The majority of African American college students in the sample noted ethnic practices and expressions consistent with the other groups in the sample. However, unique to this group, as mentioned earlier, is the impact of living in a society that has systematically oppressed and discriminated against the group. This is seen through the purposeful nature of many of the practices and expressions the African American students describe; the fact that, for some, resisting assimilation is an expression of ethnicity; and that many of the students learned or acquired the expressions and practices after childhood. This stands in stark contrast to the groups who were less removed from the time of immigration where expressions of ethnicity and culture are maintained through family and community systems that regularly practice traditions and customs. Due in part to the length of time African Americans have been in the United States (fourth and fifth generations), and their forced "emigration" to the United States where their culture, language, and customs were intentionally stripped upon arrival through the dynamics of slavery, ethnicity based on country of origin for African Americans is usually difficult to reclaim. Specifically, students were able to identify practices that indicated religion and spirituality, family, active cultural learning, and resistance to racialization processes.

Religion and Spirituality

The most frequently cited ethnic practice and expression for African Americans was spirituality, with two-thirds of the students identifying religion or spirituality as a characteristic of being African American. This took several forms. Some had a general perspective on spirituality such as, "I don't want to say religion is important to me, but being spiritual is important." Many highlighted the importance of church in the lives of African Americans. One woman said, "I would say that going to church is an ethnic thing. I grew up with a strong church background. My mom and dad always went to church, and my brother, we had to go. And you know there was no saying no. You didn't stay home on Sundays." Others made much stronger generalizations, such as "Black people get their foundation in the church" or "All Black people are religious." One man reminded us that there are many forms of spirituality and religion in the Black community, some of which were dictated by regional cultures. Others saw religion as blended with culture. One man spoke of religion as connected to cultural habits: "I'm thinking my religious beliefs are pretty much tied to my cultural habits, dress, the way I see the world." Another offered a unique perspective on spirituality and "regionality" when he spoke of the experiences of his relatives in Louisiana:

> I feel that Blacks, let's say, that live in Southern Louisiana, are different than, let's say, Blacks that live in Harlem, New York. Okay, I guess you can say they were raised in two different cultures. [In Southern Louisiana there's] a lot of superstitions. I don't know if that has to do with ethnic background or maybe it does. I know my relatives are very superstitious people and that's where my parents are from. [They do things like], you might say, voodoo practices, keeping ammonia underneath their bathroom sinks open to keep evil spirits away, keeping blessed soap, not regular soap. It's a mixture, you know what I mean? I think it's more African than anything. I think the people in Louisiana had to convert to Catholicism to some extent to cover up their African religion because they would have been crucified.

His explanation offers another example of how the legacy of racism interacts with cultural expression. The inability to practice African religion prompted this group to develop hybrid religions. African American religious denominations today, such as the Baptist and African Methodist Episcopal (AME) churches, evolved out of a blending of Christian teachings with African oral traditions (Boyd-Franklin, 2003).

Another perspective on spirituality offered by students was tied to ethnicity and other values they consider to be important. The following student best expressed this blending of values:

What is important? It gives me something to hold on to. It gives me something to reach that is intangible. Something, that is, of spirituality and not of something that can be taken away. It is sort of like the old saying that education can never be taken away and learning about your identity and your ethnicity is something that can never be taken away.

Not only does this student illustrate the connection between spirituality and ethnicity, but he also demonstrates how closely his ethnicity is intertwined with his sense of self. In total, nearly half the sample identified elements of spirituality as being an ethnic practice or expression. Historically, religion and spirituality play key roles as indicators of African American cultural identity (Boyd-Franklin, 2003). Furthermore, negotiating between religious and racial values has been found to be an integral component of identity development among African American college students (Sanchez & Carter, 2005).

Family as a Cultural Attribute

Family was also mentioned as an ethnic practice, with half of the students describing the role of the family in ethnicity. One student said she recently learned that her outlook on her family was a cultural tradition.

Well, from what I've just recently learned, the way I react with my family and my outlook toward family units is something that is a cultural tradition. Because, like I feel like everything I do, I can never be just me . . . I have to go to work, but my mom needs a ride here, so I have to go. . . . That's something that is maybe traditional of Black people, African Americans, their beliefs in the family unit.

To stress that this is common to African Americans, she cited her boyfriend's family as another example:

He has his own business and he has another job, and a lot of times he just wants to be able not to worry about his family's problems and just concentrate on what he's doing, but he can't. You know, if his mom needs something he has to help her out. He has to give her money. You know, it's important for him to be there for his mother, for his little sister, for his grandmother. I just see that in a lot of people. Their families are important, and no matter what you're doing, no matter what you're trying to accomplish, you still have to stop and consider what's going on in your family and what you need to do to help them out or be supportive or be there for your family.

In fact, duty to help out family members was a definite commonality among the students. The man below extrapolates the phenomenon to the group in general.

> Unity of family is a great part of being an African American to me. It's more of a family group-oriented type of ethnicity or race. Sticking together, although we have periods of time when we don't stick together, still, the basics of being African American is the family and sticking together and helping those in your family and those not in your family.

The success and functioning of the family is reliant on the ability and will of group members to contribute and, at times, suspend their own needs to the betterment of the family. Likewise, that sense of obligation is often transferred to the group in general with the sense that the success of the group depends on the collective actions of group members.

Family and extended family members not only came up in connection with the obligation students felt toward them, but family members also offered them something in return. One woman talked about the role her grandmother played in filling in the historical gaps in her heritage.

> Even though being Black, you can only go so far back into your heritage, and that kind of bothers me because I don't know more about my heritage and where I came from. But I guess, like growing up and being around my grandmother and having her in my life and my other family. I guess that was a big factor in me just knowing who I am because when I'd go to school, like I said I'd be around White people. I still feel, you know, well I'm Black, they're White.

The sense of history in her own family has contributed to her self-concept in a way that allows her Black identity to remain intact despite her contact with Whites she encounters in school. Another woman spoke in terms of extended family and family celebrations and noted that she felt this was characteristic of African Americans.

> My family is really big. My external family, my grandmother, my cousins and aunts, like every holiday we always get together and have dinner. I

don't know if that's common or not for most people. For most Black families, I would think it's common. Like for birthdays we do the same thing. We all pitch in and fix dinner and have cake and ice cream and also have family reunions every three years.

For many African American families family reunions are regular occurrences and well attended, despite how dispersed across the country the family might be. Extended family networks, which are common in ethnic minority communities, are sources of support in a potentially hostile environment and have a positive effect on ethnic identity development (Harrison, Wilson, Pine, Chan, & Buriel, 1990).

Active Cultural Learning

Although spirituality and religion were the most frequently expressed elements of ethnicity, slightly less than half the students spoke more passionately about their involvement with activities where they learned more about African American history and African history and culture. One student made the distinction between these two genres:

I'm very much into African American history. In fact, that's my minor. But, even before it was my minor, I was always into discovering more about African American history because it's the truth. The history had been distorted so much so [that] you have to sift through all of the untruths to get to what's real. But, as far as events like that, I pretty much enjoy African art. I enjoy African history. I'm not talking African-American. I'm talking about African. I got a son who was just born in September. He's got an African name. People ask me, "Why didn't you name him Kevin Jr.?" Because that's my name and they figure you'd name your first son after you. But, I wanted him to have an African name. So that's ethnic identity to me.

He makes it clear that there is a difference between African American and African history and culture and that it is important to learn both to enhance development and pride. This student used both personal explorations into these areas and his minor in African American history to enhance his ethnic identity. Other students used these methods as well. One man was encouraged by his mother: "At the age of sixteen I got in touch with my ethnicity by my mom introducing me to a lot of poems and a lot of information that had been written between the years of 1910 and 1960." That encouragement helped him to "[get] in touch with who [I am] as an African American." Parental encouragement was also experienced by the following woman who has taken practices taught to her as a child into adulthood. She said:

> We were encouraged to get into, to have African American Studies to do something for our future, for our people. To read books or try to get into certain classes and groups and clubs so that we can learn more about our race.

African American parents often inculcate their children in culture and history as a way of buffering them from discrimination and racism, and this is an example of Cross and Fhagen-Smith's (2001): high race salience pattern of child rearing. Students also explored their culture and history on their own, such as the woman below who has turned learning about African history into a daily ritual that sustains her ethnicity and grounds her sense of self:

> Over the last six months, every night before I go to bed I read something about my history, something that has to do with African history and why our people were displaced. It kind of keeps you grounded and helps me when I go to sleep and those are the things that I dream about and think about. I think for me that is important.

One woman found that through learning the history of non-White groups, she would not only be able to deal better with living in a racist society, but she also would learn valuable information about other groups.

> All we learned is . . . White history . . . you know, we learned that Columbus sailed around the world. I don't know why we need to learn everybody's history or we can't cover all history, but we need to learn a wider scope of history and social studies. We need to learn about our society and other societies. And if you start to learn about it young, then you'll be more comfortable as you grow up in dealing with stuff like that.

The phenomenon of learning more about one's ethnic group history and societal experiences is a hallmark of Cross's (1991) *Immersion/Emersion* stage.

In his theory this pride and confidence built through these lessons help the African American individual to survive and thrive in contemporary society. This is seen through the words of the man above who minors in African American history, in the woman above who uses reading about the African Diaspora as a way to "ground" herself, and in the words of the woman below who draws a direct connection between learning about "true" history and the development of ethnic identity, pride, and, ultimately, her own academic achievement.

> I was never taught true history. All I was ever taught was that Black people were brought over here as slaves and it was a good thing that happened, too, because we weren't very civilized. Once I came to college I became interested in African American history and African history. It really changed me, changed everything about my life because then I was proud of my identity. I'm proud to be Black. I'm proud to be African. I didn't realize the transformation at first, but as I look back and saw how my thinking started to change and as soon as I started taking African American history classes, I probably would have done better in school. Maybe I would have had a 4.0 and got[ten] a scholarship to a better school or a different school. Like when I graduated, I went to Howard and maybe if I had those better grades, I would have had a scholarship at Howard instead of trying to struggle and pay tuition with my own money and then having to leave and come finish school at home.

Indirect support for this finding is evident in the strong correlation observed between students' ethnic identity and their college academic self-efficacy (see Table 1.3). This student was adamant about the positive effects she would have experienced had she been introduced to "true" history earlier in her academic experience. It is notable that she is able to connect educational opportunity and economic reward. Another student also emphasized the importance of knowing "true" history.

> I saw my identity change in a matter of just a few years by first being told that, after not knowing true history, not knowing about true African history, that not all Africans were brought over here as slaves. Not knowing where our forefathers came from and what they've accomplished. Knowing that, I didn't feel, "Oh, gosh, I wish I was White," but I just didn't feel a great amount of pride in the fact that I was Black. But as I learned more about being Black and Black people and Black history, I really changed. It

has really made me proud of being who I am. It has really made me proud of being Black, we have accomplished a lot, we have overcome a lot. I have a really good self-identity and I'm really proud of my identity. There are some things about being a part of my ethnic group that I feel are negative. The lack of morals in a lot of Black people and the lack of motivation all boils down to that, so many people have not learned their true history. They are not proud of being Black and this has a negative effect on them.

She has acknowledged that knowing history has helped her to take pride in herself and in being Black. She even hypothesizes that lack of knowledge about "true" history is associated with some of the problems African Americans, as a group, experience in our society. In her words we can observe a more integrated identity, where she has gone through the immersion stage and is now in a place where she can evaluate her own group in a more objective way that does not have to result in the negative in-group attitudes that represent the early stages in Cross's developmental model (Cross, 1991).

To offer a different perspective on the role of history in the African American community, one student even associated rap music with history; he said:

I also like to listen to rap music because I feel like in a sense it's a . . . it records history. Some rappers record history. Some of them deal with realities of life, seeing from their perspective. I think their perspective is representative of, in a sense, their culture and their place in society.

This student's sense that rap records history also positions what is sometimes seen as controversial and a vehicle for erecting barriers to group progress in a more positive light. Research indicates that African American adolescents may be more likely than their White peers to view rap music as life-affirming even though both groups enjoy listening to the music equally (Sullivan, 2003). Scholars suggest that rap music may be considered an oppositional cultural product that could promote an empowering, Afrocentric cultural identity for African Americans (Henderson, 1996; Martinez, 1997).

Resistance as an Ethnic Practice

A smaller number (about a third) of students spoke about aspects of culture or their behavior that resisted assimilation into mainstream culture. Although there is little obvious commonality among the content of the data presented in this section, there is an underlying feeling of preserving elements of culture, of acknowledging the multifaceted relationship African Americans have with society and the defense mechanisms necessary to survive despite racism. The woman whose words are below is an example of this resistance.

> Just the way I am is an expression of my ethnic identity. I don't purposefully try to become part of the mainstream society, or I don't try really hard to assimilate and act White, or I'm just myself: I'm Black. You know, that's an everyday expression, being Black.

Although she does not delineate specific behaviors in which she participates to "be Black," she tries hard to not act White, which would be a sign of assimilation to her. For other students they find spaces where they can "act Black" and distinguish those spaces from those where they find that they need to change their behavior. For example, one of the woman talks differently in the classroom from how she does with her friends: "We use slang words, we may use words that come up in hip hop, we use this all the time, it's just like a culture thing. I may not use it in the classrooms, but just around my friends." For her, her language is a part of expressing her culture, but that expression is confined to places where this behavior is accepted. This is also example of code switching—a function of Black identity discussed earlier in the chapter: students know where they can comfortably express elements of Black culture and how to act in a way that is more compatible with mainstream culture. One man has a similar perspective, but finds the closeting of speaking "Black English" problematic.

> The one thing that troubles me with Black people, is that this, this shame that we have in speaking Black English, or hanging out with Black people. I mean, that's a release mechanism. When I'm hanging out with the fellas, it's just, you know, we've got guys that went to law school and guys that might be a doctor somewhere and that's all fine and good. But right now, all we're talking about is who's going to win the [basketball] game. You know what I mean? So, come on off all that. You can be Dr. Jones tomorrow. Right now, you just Leroy.

This student seems to expect that professionals bring their culture, through language, into their professional settings rather than limiting that to social situations. In his remarks there is also a critique concerning the perception that professional African Americans define their social spaces to limit contact with other African Americans, thereby making social contact with coethnics an ethnic expression.

Racial identity had an influence on what students defined as ethnic practices and expressions. One woman said that violence, drugs, and gangs are a part of African American life that affects the group's culture.

> The Americans are dealing with very comfortable situations for them. It seems to me they deal with more personal issues of who they want to be and, I don't know, more character types of things, Whereas the African Americans are dealing with violent situations such as drug issues and the high intensity of gang violence. All these things are very much a part of the culture you're in, and what's outside is going to assume that this thing is all a part of you. So, you know, you still have to be a certain type of person that can go with the hardships.

She does not speak specifically to the practices and expressions here, but rather, she connects a worldview that is influenced by urban realities to culture and to individuals' identity. Another student touched on this reality through his assessment of rap and what it has meant to him.

> I didn't know how to interpret [rap's] school of thought so I took them out of context. It's sort of listening to Ice Cube or listening to Snoop Dogg or listening to some of the other entertainers and interpreting the information the way it should be interpreted. I misinterpreted the information, and it caused me to kind of stay bottled up in a lot of bad ideas, and I went through a process where I had to learn about myself between the age of sixteen and twenty-seven years old. It was a very, very, very hard journey. My main problem was I didn't know about deferred gratification and I didn't understand the system the way I understand it today.

Multiple understandings of the effects of rap, a cultural expression inherent in this exemplar, are striking. This student seems to have been influenced by the kind of culture the woman above describes. The music he listened to reinforced anger he felt about the "system." However, in retrospect, he concludes that his interpretations of that music may have been incorrect, and through reflection, he has a better understanding of what is needed to survive in the system. Although we might interpret his remarks as a sign of assimilation (rejecting elements of pop Black culture), it would be a simplistic evaluation of his point, which speaks more directly to the challenges African American youth face in constructing positive identities where pride also translates to care for the self. It also demonstrates the complex nature of and the role rap plays in the development of identity, especially for men, where they find an external community of support and a lifestyle worthy of adolescent aspiration. However, this student's experience calls for caution in using rap as a culture identifier and a tool to develop ethnic pride and suggests that rap can be used as a tool for identity development as long as it is accompanied by cautious discussion of its underlying messages.

It is important to remember that, in large part, expressions of African American ethnicity are a blend of what has been passed down through five or more generations and what has been created through centuries of constructing a parallel and often separate culture. The following student explains:

> 'Cause we were brought over here as slaves and our cultural background was stripped from us. You know, we weren't allowed to converse in our language, so our language was lost. Also, whatever cultural things we do, as far as like dances and whatever, we wouldn't know. Like Asians and Latinos/as do, they know theirs because they still have some traces, even though those were almost destroyed, too. I think we probably suffered the most from it.

The development of a culture parallel to dominant U. S. culture, where the culture is separate and unique, is a constant challenge for African Americans, as outlined by the students' narratives in this section. Students appeared deliberate and persistent in their ability to contribute personally to the ongoing development of a collective culture.

Complex Relationships Among Racism, Oppression, and Ethnic Identity

One of the remarkable findings of the study was how readily every African American student converted the negative effects of racism, oppression, and discrimination into positive outcomes for themselves as individuals and for African Americans as a group. In interview after interview, students spoke of the injustices levied against African Americans, but in no case did this appear to dampen their assessment of their abilities and contributions, nor did they seem to be pessimistic about the strength of their group or its contributions to our society. As will be seen, they spoke of overcoming obstacles as a vehicle of empowerment and pride. Students gave several examples of how they observed racism, discrimination, and oppression as a part of their realities. These were expressed in terms of experiences with covert racism, institutionalized racism, and stereotype threat, and each of these they ultimately use to redefine positively what it means to be Black. In a way, they have transformed the negative effects of racialization into catalysts for pride and achievement.

According to The Cooperative Institutional Research Program, White students have consistently perceived a decrease in discrimination in society over the last 30 years (Pryor, Hurtado, Saenz, Santos, & Korn, 2007). However, this was not the case for the African American students in this study. One student explained that, although discrimination has changed and taken on a different character from the discrimination of the past, it still exists.

> Discrimination is not, as you know, out in the open as it used to be, like the fire department coming out and spraying us with water and stuff like that, but there's still prejudice that goes on. The people just wait for the lights to go down at night and then they start just wreaking havoc on whatever minority groups there are, you know.

This student implies that the discrimination she has experienced is the covert kind of discrimination that goes unspoken in attitudes and beliefs and permeates societal institutions, but out of the eyes of the seeing public. Others echoed her concern about racism and discrimination being alive and well in contemporary U.S. society. One man said:

> There are many racist people still lingering about, and there have been several occasions where people aren't shy about expressing their views they have about African Americans. . . . Sometimes it makes me laugh that we are still dealing with this. Other times, it really, I don't want to say it, depresses me because I know that what they're saying is from pure ignorance. But it kind of stresses me out that there are people like that you just can't change, and their children are going to think the same thing. In

today's country, racism still exists on a higher level, and there are people in power who agree with that.

Although he acknowledges that he does not experience the psychological distress of depression over racism, it does cause him stress. He also expressed concern that intergenerational effects will persist, which is similar to the assessment of another student, who asked, "There's a whole lot of racism, so it's like it's still going on, you know. When does it end?"

Understanding Limited Educational Opportunities

Over half of the students gave examples of prejudice and discrimination they experienced in their K–12 education that was initiated by schools, personnel, and fellow students. A student who experienced the prejudice of his classmates said, "When I went to high school, most of my friends other than African Americans told me they were afraid of me before they even had verbal contact with me or any type of contact, physically or anything. But when they heard me speak, they all say that fear just went away." Educational institutions often carried out discrimination. The student below reflected on his elementary school experience:

> As I got older, they told us that, during my elementary school, the school district intentionally placed the black kids in a lower level—meaning level one was for highest, for kids who were very smart. Level two was for those who knew little or in the middle range, and level three was for the dumb kids, which were for the Black kids (emphasis, high-pitched voice). We were automatically put in level three to hold you back, and that was one of the things that we protested about.

His knowledge about this institutional discrimination in education was revealed to him in an African American studies class, and it motivated students in his class to become involved that semester in a public protest in the community to bring to light discriminatory practice in the K–12 system. Another student witnessed educational disparity:

> Asians and Caucasians probably get the best educational advantages because they're expected to perform well, so they're pushed to do well. But, then, like Latinos and African Americans, they're thought to be less intelligent in some people's minds so they're not expected to perform as well, so they're not treated the same.

Again, students were able to see and understand the important connection between teachers' beliefs in their students and those students' academic performance. Although Rosenthal and Jacobson's (1968) *Pygmalion in the Classroom* study, which is widely cited as evidence that teacher expectations in the classroom can lead to self-fulfilling prophecies for academic achievement or failure, has been criticized for both its methodology and conclusions (Elshoff & Snow, 1971), more recent studies have demonstrated that teachers perceive African American students' abilities as below those of their White or Hispanic peers (Elhoweris, Mutua, Alsheikh, & Holloway, 2005; Hughes, Gleason, & Zhang, 2005). Furthermore, low teacher expectations may have more of an effect on self-fulfilling prophesies for students from stigmatized groups, including African Americans (Jussim & Harber, 2005).

Students also spoke specifically about the educational advantage conferred by exposure to superior college counseling.

> I remember in high school not getting a lot of counseling about college and the counselors' not really stressing college or really preparing you for college or preparing for your career, as opposed to Caucasians' being really prepared and counselors telling them to make sure you start applying and really letting them know, and gearing them toward college . . . society has had this idea that Black people don't really have the desire to go to college and they don't have the grades or they're not college material.

While high school counselors can be strong institutional agents for channeling students into a college-preparatory track, African American students report feeling little support from school personnel that would encourage college aspirations (Freeman, 1997).

What students learned about the effects of racism on their educational experiences was prompted by the courses they took in college. Through discussions in African American studies, sociology, and psychology courses, they were able to pull their collective experiences and use them as foundations to examine course material. In many cases the course material supported students' experiences, giving them better lenses through which to analyze their own experiences. This process is similar to Freire's (1970, 1993, 1999) concept of *conscientizacao*, where through examination of negative societal effects on individuals, individuals can be empowered to overcome those effects. This consciousness also promoted one student to note that she not only experienced educational barriers, but also saw limited career opportunities and was already feeling constricted in her career because of her ethnicity.

> [The barriers that arise from racism] put a restriction on my career; they want to choose my career. Because of this restriction, getting to my goal is a struggle. Sometimes I think of these obstacles as a ball and chain around my neck. I see discrimination in my job, how I am treated in interviews, and all kinds of things.

Unfortunately, the experiences of K–12 education, which students saw as barriers to their success, continued to arise in new contexts as they worked to achieve their goals. From a sociological perspective, the hidden curriculum that African American students encounter in public schools—namely, the class, racial, and gender biases that dictate who is and who is not supposed to achieve—follows them as they try to make their way in American society (Baker, 2005; Fleming, 1984).

Living With and Conquering Stereotypes

Almost three-quarters of the students explained the covert nature of societal and individual attitudes and beliefs about African Americans. Students found they were consistently judged on the basis of racist stereotypes—both historical and contemporary. One student felt that images of the past influenced how he is perceived today.

> Other people seem to have this image of a long time ago. A lot of people deemed African Americans as, I guess, lazy or whatever, and a lot of people put that off on you when they don't even know who you are.

Attitudes from long ago are compounded when students encounter Whites who have had little contact with African Americans other than what is portrayed through media and popular culture outlets.

> Let's say a White person looks at you, and they haven't had a lot of contact with Black people. All they know is what they see on TV or on the news, the negative images, then they're going to associate that with you. And so you're coming into a situation where a person may already have a negative judgment of you or a negative [evaluation], negative image of you being Black.

This student knows that, at times, she does not have the opportunity to make a first impression based on her own attributes and personality and needs to overcome these prejudices on a regular basis. The concept of stereotype threat (Steele, 1997) describes how the stereotypes others have of African Americans convert to forces that actually become internalized to the extent that the stereotypes actually limit the performance or success of African Americans. The student below talks about what she would like to do about the stereotypes she experiences.

> I wish I could just tell them that we're not like that or all of us aren't like that. So that's the only disadvantage I see, as like when they see one person of my culture do it, then they think all of us do it, they judge us all that way. So I think that's the only disadvantage in the whole world. Like on TV, most of the gangs are either Latino or Black, and they're violent or always doing something. So sometimes, when people come around me or any other Black person, that doesn't even do those things, they judge us, saying that we do that.

She sees this as the "only disadvantage" she experiences. A common experience students reported was that others would tell them how unlike most African Americans they were. A male African American student was more pointed in his response to these stereotypes and how they affect him.

> People have this preconceived idea of how you're supposed to act, and it really pisses me off when they say, "Oh, you're a different Black." What the hell do you mean a different Black? It just ticks me off. It just rubs me the wrong way, being a different Black. I guess they watch too much television and they see a stereotypical Black on television. Well, that stereotypical Black is bad or good. I don't know how they're looking at it, but they assume I'm going to act the same way.

It can be assumed that, when others judge a person as being a "different Black," it should be a welcome compliment. However, this type of comment proves that the stereotype holds, and it is up to individuals to demonstrate that they are unworthy of those characterizations while under the scrutiny of others. This type of judgment also resulted in the following common belief among students in the study:

> My thinking is that I have to work maybe two or three times harder than
> Whites or Caucasians to accomplish what we need to accomplish or to
> succeed. Whatever my standards of success are, to reach that, I have to
> work twice as hard.

This position, having to work twice as hard to achieve success, is reinforced
continuously by encounters students had with members of other groups.
Because they must prove themselves in virtually every new encounter, they
believe they have to work twice as hard, a message that is often passed on
from generation to generation.

Students also used their knowledge of African American contributions
to the country as a defense against the negative feelings associated with these
stereotypes. One said:

> We're stereotyped as dumb, basically. And, you know, they try to say that
> we're savages and all that, but we, we were the first ones to start civilization.
> We brought civilization to the Europeans and to the Asians, basically.

Another noted that, despite the continuous struggle, "We've done a lot in
this country and for this country." So again, the importance of knowing
African American history is reinforced. Knowledge of African American history and African Americans' contributions was used as a buffer to discrimination and racism, much like ethnic identity was used as a buffer as noted
in the previous section of this chapter.

Even as students spoke of their frustrations in being stereotypically
labeled and ascribed stereotypical characteristics, they were able to covert
that frustration into action to help to correct stereotypes whenever possible.

> I try to act opposite the stereotype. A stereotypical African American
> woman would probably, in general, be loud, ignorant, talking loud, pro-
> miscuous. If you were to hear me on the phone, you wouldn't think I was
> Black. A lot of people would say that, unless you know me, by my voice
> and I guess the way I talk and the way I express myself, most people would
> look at me with a surprised look on their face, like, "You said that? That
> came out of your mouth?" I guess they wouldn't think an African Ameri-
> can woman, especially since I'm only twenty, can articulate as well as I
> do. . . . Many other people say, she's doing something good. She's a young
> black woman, she's not a stereotypical woman. She doesn't look like this,

she doesn't look like that; she's totally the opposite. And they would look at me and notice the difference.

This student took a personal approach to deconstructing stereotypes, and she consciously works to develop and present a persona that confronts the stereotype. Unlike some of the sentiments of others in the study, she seems to welcome the comparison of her own attributes to those of the stereotype's. This was her way of dispelling stereotypes of African Americans—not just for her benefit, but for the benefit of the group. Other students also talked about becoming personally stronger as a result of discrimination against the group, its history, and the stereotypes others hold of their group.

> I'm one of those people who think that pressure will either kill you or make you strong. So I don't mind a good fight, and being African American has made me, has placed me in a position where I have to stay sharp all the time, you know. It has placed me in a position where I feel this sense of having to complete things that I might not have to complete if I was White.

He has converted a negative factor—the pressure of being African American—to a force that makes him better, sharper, and stronger, attributes that are a result of being a member of his group. Another man took this same idea and generalized it to the group as a collective.

> Because of all of the pain and hardship and struggle that the group has been forced to deal with, I think that generations have learned to adapt to certain oppression and stereotypes and discrimination to the point where the people as a whole have certain creative skills to overcome obstacles. And I think that that's passed on traditionally from city to city, generation to generation, all across the United States. There's a certain uniqueness about the African American experience.

This social creativity, which is also described by Tajfel (1978), occurs when someone takes the effects of oppression and converts them to a strength. The language of both these students demonstrates this conversion. The same young man talks of the call to reverse stereotypes through his individual action. His positive feeling about being a part of the group helps to motivate him to take on the struggle.

I feel good about being African American or part of the culture. I feel like it's a daily challenge, a daily struggle. I feel like it's always a daily struggle for me because of society's stigmatizing of my group. So, I feel it's a challenge. I, for one, don't mind taking it because it corrects a lot of the false stereotypes. It's the responsibility of all people from the group to disprove the negative or the untruth. Although there are some negative characteristics, which we can't deny, the untruths and prejudices and stereotypes aren't true.

This student best exemplified the complex relationship among racism, oppression, and racial identity. He takes pride in the struggle, and he sees a collective responsibility of the group to change the negative behavior that fuels the stereotypes. He sees the power in the distribution of adaptive skills to overcome the obstacles to successive generations and to communities across the United States. For him, the combination of these forces makes for a unique African American experience.

Pride in Overcoming Obstacles

Two-thirds of the students spoke extensively about the pride they had in their ethnic group because of its ability to overcome obstacles. Like the student above, who took pride in the struggle of African Americans, other students agreed that one of the sources of group pride comes from the struggle the group endures, in both historical and contemporary perspectives.

With the [Jim Crow] laws not being in effect, that's an advantage of being Afro-American today. You don't have to really deal with what happened back then, and you can stand up and be proud that it happened, but we got over it as a people. Politically, I see the advantages. We're moving up, we have a lot of advantages, we're able to do a lot of things we couldn't do and to be a part of things. That makes me really happy. I know my people struggled to get me here, and I'm proud of it. I hate that they had to go through it, but I'm just proud to be here to see that, be a part of the people that see what happened, still standing, still here.

Another student makes the connection to the past and her present and sees the impact of history for African Americans reflected in the change of the preferred label for the ethnic group.

Well, it means a lot to me. Even more now because, well, just the other day we were called Black and now we're African American. Actually, I really don't care about what name we get, but it means a lot because we've been through a lot of struggle and I'm just striving for success.

When one student was asked if he was proud of his ethnic group, he answered emphatically:

They have struggled and endured. It makes me very proud that we have struggled and endured and still been able to stand our ground and reach our goal. So, it makes me proud to be, you know, of African American race because we have been through so much and, still, we managed to succeed in certain areas.

Another student echoed this sentiment:

You get to feel good that you are strong, that you are a strong man and that you are a strong woman. You get to feel good that, despite all the obstacles, you continue to persevere and stay determined, and when you accomplished something and when you are given, not necessarily respect— when people are happy to see you doing what you are supposed to be doing is a good feeling. So it's an advantage that no other race could ever have. No other race has been through what we've been through, not even the Jews. . . . I still stand, even though I am an African American and I am in a racist society and the racism that exists, I truly believe that one can overcome.

Whereas others spoke specifically about their own struggles in relation to the group as a whole, this student stepped away from his own experiences and reflected on the group's past and its ability to reach collective goals. This is also made evident by another student, who said:

I'm African American. And, well, what's important to me is just to know that I do have a background that I can look into because, well, not me, but my ancestors had been through like a lot. And for me, just to be in this world today is a little bit better for us than it was for them. It's a little bit easier for us to kind of get jobs and so forth because they did fight for our freedom, and I'm proud to be in a culture that has something to look back on, even though it was bad.

In each of these exemplars are examples of the conversion of the negative effects of racism and struggle to positive outcomes for students in the study.

To this point, data presented have referred to the student in connection to the group. The group's history and struggle was personalized for students in their sense of pride in self and in the group. However, students also spoke of their own personal development related to being African American. Their ethnic identity or positive feelings regarding affiliation with the group have had positive outcomes for students.

> For me, finding my ethnic identity has been enlightening. I have become stronger and I feel beautiful for the first time inside and out. I am secure with myself. I feel empowered because I have my ethnic identity because I know where I am going. I am changed.

This student highlights three distinct outcomes—becoming stronger, feeling beautiful, and being secure. She sees herself as beautiful, debunking the sociocultural norms related to beauty. Schooler and colleagues (2004) view these as outcomes of a strong ethnic identity. Black women with affiliations with African American communities or with strong ethnic identities have been found to have healthier body images than do Black women with low ethnic identities. One of the men in the study spoke of a similar outcome associated with the strength of his ethnicity: "Being able to accept that your hair is not straight and being able to accept that your features may be different from what is accepted in society, but that is okay, you are still a beautiful person." He noted more explicitly the need to accept self in spite of dominant cultural norms and echoed the connection between inner and outer beauty. These students and others distinguished a positive self-concept as another outcome—one reported most frequently in the literature. In fact, self-esteem as an outcome was reported by most of the African American students in the sample, even by the student below, who, despite acknowledging ethnicity, had not acted as a catalyst for change.

> Ethnicity hasn't changed me that much. The only thing it has done is I've gone from low self-esteem to having higher self-esteem by finding more positive things to look at within my culture and to make me feel better about myself.

This is corroborated by the survey data showing that African Americans scored the highest of all groups on the self-esteem measure (see Table 1.2). Strong racial identity has been linked to higher self-esteem and among both Black males and females (Okech & Harrington, 2002). Crocker (1999) argues that self-esteem is a situation-specific construct that emerges in response to the meaning individuals assign to events in their lives. It makes sense, then, that students with higher levels of African American ethnic identity salience, who may have achieved a higher level of self-authorship, are able to evaluate negative messages about their ethnicity without feeling negated personally. Like their evaluation of the group itself, the students in this study also felt that their ethnic identity and group affiliation helped them to move ahead in their lives. As one of the women reported, by having a strong ethnic identity, "I am stronger and nothing will stop me from achieving my goals." Overcoming their own obstacles, and taking the lead from the group overcoming obstacles, has helped these students to achieve their goals in life, as the students below exemplify.

> Being African American, I think, has influenced my identity because, as I talked about earlier, because of the struggles, and it gives me more strength to keep going on and to endure whatever comes my way, to overcome the obstacles.

And:

> I, as a Black male, have experienced a lot of, you know, harsh experiences that I have to endure and to deal with. So, being a Black male taught me to endure some situations, you know, to overcome and to get to the goal at the same time. To overcome my struggle and get to my goal by enduring whatever I had to endure to get to that goal.

Psychological theory suggests that African American students may be expected to perform poorly in academic settings because of the effects of negative stereotypes that predict low academic achievement among Blacks (Steele, 1997). In contrast, the students in the study support the hypothesis that strong ethnic salience could act as a mitigating factor, thus enabling African American students to overcome the stereotypical threat and to succeed in higher education (Smith & Hopkins, 2004).

Prospects for the Future

Just as the students in the study reflected on the impact of African American history on both the status of the group and their own constructions of ethnicity and associated outcomes, they proclaimed what they intended to do for the future success of the group and also on the work the group itself needed to do to succeed. Over half of the students definitely felt they played a direct role in the destiny of their families and communities. The role generativity played in how they constructed their futures was evident in this student's description of what he hoped to contribute:

> I would hope to be in a position to relay that information to generations to come, to the children, and give them something to hold on to, a strong sense of identity, something they can be, something they really can feel good about, something they can strive for. Something that will make them feel good as a group because I think a lot of problems with our young people is that they have a low sense of pride and identity in a positive sense.

This man focuses on the work that needs to be done with youth. He has taken lessons from his own experiences with developing his African American ethnic identity and found ways to use them with others. He knows the connection among a strong sense of identity, pride, and goal setting. He was not alone in these goals for the future. The woman quoted below saw her work with her family, specifically, and then her race, as venues through which she could change the perceptions of African Americans in society, similar to the process Cross (1991) describes in his final stage of Nigresence, Internalization:

> Being an African American has helped me to achieve more because I want more for my family and want my race to be looked up at as great. I don't want us to be perceived as bad and ignorant because that's what a lot of people perceive us as, and I don't think that's right because there are so many of us that do so much good. I want us to be perceived as if we're intelligent and are good individuals.

The strength of family as a value that African Americans hold was related to this sense of common destiny and that, despite within-group struggles and differences, the group could progress by coming together. Like the following student, students saw how choices they make in living their lives continue their good work and endeavor to correct persistent problems within the African American community.

> So it happens so often in the African American community, where the fathers are absent from the home. So family's important to me, and when I raise a family, that both parents are in the home. It's really important to me that African Americans are aware of their history and their background and the younger generations coming up are aware of what's happened in the past because I don't think too many . . . I know things aren't being taught in the schools. So it's kind of really important to me that people are aware of what happened and the negativity that stemmed from this country and the interaction of African American and Caucasian people. It's important that younger people know these things.

Here it was important that he not only live his life to address perpetual issues within the ethnic group, but that he also extend those efforts to young African Americans in general. Like the man earlier in this section, this student recognized the importance of youth's learning history to provide what is typically not taught in schools.

Although the student above directly references ongoing racial conflict between Africans and Caucasians, others (more than a third) also drew attention to conflict within African Americans that needed to be addressed for the group to make progress. One student summed up this dynamic by saying, "I feel that every ethnicity has their type of inner turmoil within that group." Others spoke more specifically about that inner turmoil and identified that most of the conflict revolved around competition within the group.

> I think we as Black people have strived so long for acceptance, and we've strived so long to be treated fairly and to have a better life. I think that in order for us to ever get that, then we have to be willing to give what we're so eager to get. How can you say to me that you want a better life, yet you condemn that man to a worse life? Is that not the same thing that's been done to you? Am I to measure my success by your failure? Or am I to measure my success by our successful efforts together? I choose to measure by our successful efforts together. I have paperwork, and all my notes and everything and people need notes, anybody can have my notes. I'll help anybody because I want us all to pass the class. You know what I mean? I can accomplish nothing by myself. There's absolutely nothing I can

accomplish by myself. It has no meaning to me to be by myself. I don't want it!

The competition comes through quite clearly in the words of this student. Although he initially speaks in broad terms regarding the notion of measuring one's success by another's failure, he brings it down to his life as a student by saying that he will help anyone—everyone can pass the class. His collectivist value goes as far as to provide meaning for his own accomplishments, as his accomplishments have no meaning without the success of others. Another student echoes this evaluation of the African American community, yet is more biting in her criticism of the group, and she contrasts this with what she observes in the White and Latino/a communities:

Well, I guess really in the Black community is, it's like having a big barrel of crawfish, and once one of the crawfish crawls up to the top and is almost out of the barrel, another crawfish pulls him back down. And that's what I feel like in the Black community. Once another Black person sees another Black person like rising to the top, they dig up whatever dirt they can find on them to try and like mess up whatever they had going for them, and that I think is a disadvantage. I don't like all that. Whereas Whites or Latinos will get together and interact and help each other, you know. . . . When Black people were slaves, they learned from the slave master that if you turn on your brother and tell the slave master that he did something wrong, then you reap the reward because you just ruined it for your brother and then he gets beaten or killed. Then I look today, and it's almost the same in a sense. Black people really don't stick together the way they should.

She draws a historical connection using the slave/master narrative, but also speaks specifically about what she sees in contemporary times. The competition she observes involves members of the Black community purposely putting others down to elevate their own positions. Another student summed this up by saying, "For some reason, African Americans tend to treat their own people worse than they do other cultures, other races. I don't know why. I'm still trying to figure it out. It's still bothering me." There is this sense that her plans for the future involve trying to better understand this behavior and what might be done to curb it. Another verifies this dynamic— African Americans holding each other back—when she compared Whites to

African Americans in her assessment of how other ethnic groups promote one another.

> I guess Caucasian people seem to be more approachable. I guess it seems like, for the Caucasian people, the networking is really there for them. They network back and forth. If a person of their ethnicity makes it, they reach back and pull the others that haven't made it yet to make it, and they tell them how to make it. Like in the Black culture, sometimes it's like I got mine, you get yours. So you get yours the best way you know how.

Students were astute at drawing connections between the willingness and ability of individual members to perceive themselves as part of a collective where everyone has responsibility for the future success of the group. Because collective destiny is a characteristic of ethnic groups, we may conclude that African Americans, as they move from a racial identity group experience (encounters with and coping with racism and discrimination) to an ethnic identity group experience (based on shared cultural attributes, pride in group achievements, etc.), will begin to build attitudes and skills needed to form a collective destiny.

Summary and Conclusions

Although several students in the study critiqued the behavior of the group, most group members expressed a general sense of pride in the group, including those critics. The experiences of overcoming the struggles of the past and the discriminatory experiences of the present helped African American students to develop pride in the accomplishments of the group and to set goals for themselves and the group as a whole. The woman below spoke of her own immersion activities and how she can take that energy and education and begin to change the ethnic group:

> I'm very militant, very into the readings and writings of the Black Power movement that occurred in the sixties, and seeing where that is going now and how I can be a part of the change that I would want to see occur in my community as far as what our values are, as far as being able to accept delayed gratification and not wanting things now, now, now.

African American students also experienced ethnic practices and expressions as contributors to their positive feelings about being African American.

Many, like the man below, connected other facets of the ethnic experience to their ability to overcome obstacles they experience.

> God is the main importance in my life. I believe that without him, I would just be Jell-O, no spine. Family is very important to me. They also have structured, you know, my life and who I am, you know, today. Being African American, I think, has influenced my identity because, as I talked about earlier, because of the struggles, and it gives me more strength to keep going on and to endure whatever comes my way, to overcome the obstacles.

Here he takes his connection to family and the strength of his faith and uses them as tools and supports to achieve his goals, thus demonstrating the interplay among several findings in this chapter.

The consistency of African American students to construct identities carefully that were strong and filled with pride, and their ability to identify specific efforts and experiences that brought them to this point, was an encouraging finding. More than the other groups in the study, African Americans were able to connect the anti-Black attitudes or tendencies toward self-hatred (both characteristic of Cross's [1991] *Preencounter* stage) and the discoveries they made and realizations they came to during their immersion experiences, that ultimately led to the development of ethnic pride. The discoveries related to relearning history and to uncovering the sociopolitical forces in this country that have more covertly limited opportunities for African Americans were direct catalysts to attaining healthier and stronger ethnic identities.

There was also the sense that collective group identity would strengthen if more people, and these students spoke of themselves as being a part of that "people," would learn about African American history and those limiting sociopolitical forces. The following student perhaps best exemplified what others felt regarding this conclusion:

> Black people tend to feel like a kinship with each other, whether you know a person or not. If I go somewhere, and there are five hundred people there, and there's very few Black people, and I do finally see a black person, I feel more comfortable being around that Black person. There's like a special kinship and it can put you at ease. Now that I have learned my history, I feel that is a great advantage to me, because I'm very proud of where we

came from. I'm very proud of how far we've come since slavery. I have a lot of pride in being Black.

Shared experiences of miseducation and struggles that included the slavery experience have caused African Americans to reconstruct a culture while confronting contemporary racism and discrimination. Students felt empowered when they realized that, as a group, they have accomplished a great deal despite great odds. The ongoing development of a culture that includes reconstruction of African identities, the unique expression of religion and spirituality, the role of extended and inclusive families, and the formation of a unique dialect, all demonstrate that African American ethnicity and culture continue to retain a fluid characteristic, that its members feel that they make significant contributions to their ethnicity and culture's development. When individuals believe they can make those contributions, they are much more likely to see that their own individual actions and achievements affect the destiny of the ethnic group as a whole. These students definitely saw themselves as capable and active participants in achieving that destiny.

5

LATINO/A AMERICANS

Bringing the Family Along

If people ask me what ethnicity I am, unless they ask me what country, I will just say Hispanic or Latino depending on who I'm talking to. If I know that the word "Hispanic" bothers people, then I'll say Latino. But if they ask me from what country, then I'll say Dominican Republic. I see being Dominican Republic more as my culture than my ethnicity. . . . If they're asking about my ethnicity, I would say Hispanic. If they were asking me about my culture, I would say Dominican.

L atino/a students are the fastest-growing ethnic group on college campuses in California. Like many of the Asian American students in the study, Latino/a students remain close to the immigration experience, and like African American and Asian American students, Latino/a students have also been subject to racialized experiences from being a target group of political activity and negative social attitudes. Most Latinos/as in this study were residents of Southern California and some transferred to the university from neighboring states. The vast majority, 84%, were the first in their families to attend college. Generational status, in terms of immigration, was also notable for Latinos/as. Nearly a quarter of Latinos/as in the study were born in another country; more than half were the children of immigrants, representing the second generation of their family to be in the country; and the remaining represented three or more generations in this country.

In this chapter we present the elements of ethnicity that were important to Latino/a students in developing their ethnic identity. These include how self-designated ethnic labels reflect and challenge ethnic identity, expressions of ethnicity, the collectivist nature of family, ethnic identity processes, emerging political awareness and consciousness, and acculturation in becoming *Americanized.*

Ethnic Labels and Issue of Ethnic Self-Designation

There were 26 Latinos/as interviewed; 18 Latinas, 8 Latinos. It is interesting that none of the students identified as Latino/a on the demographic form each was asked to complete during the interview. We have chosen to use the pan-ethnic term, Latino/a, because students used a number of labels, and not all students traced their origins to Mexico. Ten of these students identified themselves as Mexican American; 6 identified as Mexican; 3 identified as Chicano/a; 2 identified as Hispanic; and 1 student each identified as Latin, Mexicano, American, Ecuadorian American, and Puerto Rican. The varied terms the students used overly simplified the issue. In the interview, when students were asked about their ethnic background, answers like the following were typical:

> Latino/a includes everybody. It includes Mexicans, it includes Central Americans, and South Americans. That's how I see it. Since I'm not from Central America or South America, I feel that I'm more Mexican American. Also, [what does it] means to be a Chicana? I think it is more political. I think that it is a political term. I know about different issues that they advocate, but I don't participate, so I don't feel comfortable in calling myself Chicana. I always thought of myself as Mexican American. But there have been times that I have said that I am something else because of the environment, you know, the moment that I was in. One time that I went to a [Chicano] conference, I was helping out, and everybody called themselves Chicano, so I did. But I have to say that I can't identify myself as one. I see myself as Mexican American, that's how I feel.

She sees Latino/a as a more inclusive term, prefers Mexican American, but uses Chicana in some situations. In fact, these students saw college as a new context that called for consideration of self-identification terms.

> I consider myself a Mexican first of all [and] foremost. I've never had to deal with such terms until I got to college pretty much. All my life I've been a Mexican, and I got here and I'm Chicano but I'm foremost a Mexican, a Latino.

When I got here, you see more mixes [of Latinos/as]. And it's a big issue: Are you Chicana, Chicano, Latino, Mexican, American, or what? I think that I identify more with Mexican American. I don't know, I guess that's because I have been told that since I was young. [Despite] the fact that I am registered as a Chicana or Latina, but I see myself more as a Mexican American and that's my heritage.

Again, we see three terms used by the above students, who had not considered the significance of their choice of ethnic label before attending college. We note how ethnic/racial classifications used by university admissions forced students to make a choice for registration, and some chose ethnic self-designations that were not entirely congruent with how they perceived themselves. Nonetheless, the process sensitized students to the diverse meanings that ethnic labels carry and the potential implications of embracing any given one. One student, a woman from the Dominican Republic, shared the problems that surround her self-identification:

I consider myself Hispanic. Although the way the things are now, a lot of people disagree with the term, but I consider myself Hispanic. I was raised to think of myself as Hispanic. If people refer to me as Latino, I have no problem with it. If people refer to me as Hispanic, I have no problem with it [either]. If people refer to me as Chicano, I correct them because I'm not Mexican . . . I let them know I'm Dominican, so they can refer to me either as Hispanic or Dominican, however they wish. Actually, living here and not knowing any Dominicans outside of my own family, it's easier to feel [part] of a larger group. I'm Dominican, but I feel when I [see] myself part of a group, I consider myself more part of the Hispanic or Latino group than I do to the Dominican group.

She is from an island called Hispaniola, which makes *Hispanic* a logical choice for her, but she knows whenever she uses it she might have to defend that use. She also appreciates the pan-ethnic terms as they help her to connect with a group larger than her own, whose numbers on the West Coast are limited.

Conflict over ethnic labels arose when students were in different situations or when they were with their more politicized peers. One student saw intragroup conflicts among students as a result.

I think too many people are too caught up with the ethnic label. They pit each other against each other, meaning [that] you'll have people within the same culture fighting against each other over a simple little label. A name of what they want to be called.

Because of the varied political, ancestral, and cultural meanings attached to ethnic labels, intragroup conflicts and discord regarding the appropriate naming of ethnic group do occur (Comas-Diaz, 2001). On university campuses, ethnic labels and the correct naming of ethnic groups can be a controversial topic among Latino/a students.

Accordingly, students were cognizant of the intraethnic politics associated with ethnic label designations and the fact that Latino/a subgroups were also stratified in the United States by status (Santiago-Rivera, Arredondo, & Gallardo-Cooper, 2002). For instance, students knew what the favored Latino/a groups were and how important precision in the ethnic label ascribed by others was to individuals who were not Mexican American.

> So in high school, I mean we knew very few Mexican students in the APs and that selective line of students. Like I told you earlier, I had a friend who was Latin. He was Spanish mostly, and so he was different. He definitely would not associate at all [with the label Mexican]. I called him Mexican one time by accident and he nearly bit my head off. I'm like, "Whoa, sorry, I forgot you're Spanish." [For him] it was a very negative stigma. So automatically when I came here, I had a very negative view. I'm Puerto Rican, and if you call us Mexican, it's a huge insult, just like if you call a Spanish person Mexican. It's a very awful thing.

This finding is consistent with Ferdman & Gallegos's (2001) model of Latino Racial Identity Orientation. In their model they describe the Latino/a subgroup-identified persons as those who embrace a specific ethnic identification (e.g., Salvadorian, Puerto Rican) that is positive, but these persons do not necessarily view other Latino/a ethnicities favorably and may have negative and disparaging attitudes about them. Hence, such persons do not adopt a wide lens when framing ethnic identification, such as accepting a pan-ethnic descriptor that would unify all Latino/a subethnicities as one community (Ferdman & Gallegos, 2001).

In the case of students who were unsure of their ethnic identification, external forces influenced their choice of ethnic self-designation.

> It's just, a long time ago, me and Andrea (friend who attended CU with the participant) were talking: "Okay, so what are we? Are we Mexican or

Mexican American? Are we Hispanic? Are we Latino?" We were asking ourselves [this] and then we saw in one of our classes this MEChA [Movimiento Estudiantil Chicano de Aztlán] poster [which said you are] Mexican. "[I said] like, does that answer your question, Andrea?" She started laughing and she said, "Yeah."

Other students also discussed the conflicts they experienced when considering their ethnic self-designation, especially when others question the legitimacy of their credentials to assume a given identification. As one student explained:

> Sometimes it's weird because if you say you are Mexican, people who are from Mexico say, "No you're not; you were not born here. Just because your parents were born in Mexico doesn't mean you're Mexican." But you can't say American either. I don't really consider myself American because America is so diverse and has so many cultures. I don't see [the] American [ethnic label] as an ethnicity.

In line with the notion of marginality and identity confusion discussed by Stonequist (1937) and DuBois (1990), the above student described the experience of living in between two spaces (i.e., neither this nor that) in terms of who he was ethnically and sought a defined ethnic self-designation. Most interesting is that we see once again how emerging adulthood brought issues of ethnic identity to the foreground for students as well as the complexity of ethnic self-designation for some, which forced them to consider ethnogeographical and sociohistorical factors.

Some students experienced cases of mistaken identity. Because of the racial heterogeneity that encompasses the Latino/a group, errors by others when identifying Latinos/as is not uncommon. The Latino/a racial spectrum can range from White to Black (e.g., Puerto Ricans) or White to indigenous (e.g., Mexicans), with many people falling somewhere in between (Ferdman & Gallegos, 2001). Hence the experience of being mistaken for someone of another ethnicity may be a common one for some Latinos/as, as one woman explained:

> It's funny because a lot of people don't even see that I'm Mexican. A lot of people don't think that I look Mexican, so a lot of people ask me, "Oh, what are you?" They'll say [that] I'm Filipino sometimes. It's like, I don't

even look Filipino. But that's some people. So I make sure they know, oh no, I'm Mexican. I feel really proud about [being] Mexican, because I'm comfortable with it. It's all I've known really.

Or another, who is Puerto Rican, said:

I've actually had someone going, "You're French." And I'm like, "No, I'm not." But I've had people go, "Oh, maybe Greek." I've had someone think I'm Portuguese. I had many people actually speak to me in Spanish. But I say, "You better stop right there." I've had many speak to me in French. I've had many people speak to me in, I'm not sure what it's called, but Middle Eastern languages like Hindi and stuff like that.

These findings illustrated how the continuous system of racial classification among Latinos/as does not fit neatly into the binary classifications predominantly used in the United States (Ferdman & Gallegos, 2001), resulting in errors in ethnic identification. They demonstrate further how other-identification plays an influential role in how persons experience their ethnic identity and whether they are forced to "claim" a given ethnic self-identification frequently.

In all, 40% of the students had something to say about their ethnic label or the importance of ethnic labels in general. Many of these students used multiple terms that were largely determined by the spaces they inhabited. It was clear that they personally preferred more specific terms, such as Mexican American or Dominican, but most were also fine with the pan-ethnic term, Latino/a. Chicano/a was reserved for situations when they felt their identity was more politicized, such as when they were on campus or interacting with peers. Some struggled with finding the right ethnic self-designation and sought external vehicles for informing this process; others felt ambivalent and conflicted about their ethnic identification, especially when questioned about their qualifications (i.e., birthplace) for assuming a specific ethnic label. Students did not appreciate instances of mistaken identity when Latinos/as or others thought they were of another ethnicity. Some who assumed a subethnic identification were offended when others mistook them to be Mexican, for instance. The findings described here illustrate how external pressures (i.e., sociocultural, ethnopolitical, and geopolitical dynamics), along with psychosocial developmental forces, strongly influenced the process and framing of ethnic labels for these students in their construction of a Latino/a ethnic identification (Comas-Diaz, 2001).

Expressions of Ethnicity

The proximity of Mexico, the country of origin for most of the Latinos/as in the study, enables a retention of culture that may not be possible in other settings. Buriel and De Ment (1997) have discussed the importance of geographical proximity to country of origin as a critical factor in transmitting and maintaining a cultural identity for Latinos/as residing in the United States. The cyclical nature of migration patterns, where citizens—American and Mexican—frequently travel from one country to the other, as documented by Portes and Bach (1985), allows for repeated participation in traditional Mexican culture and the transformation of Mexican American culture in the United States. The positive influence of visits to the so-called home country for students' developing cultural identity is described by two students:

> [My family] went to Mexico City and we learned about [cultural and historical] things and it's just really beautiful. [Because of that] I started reading more Mexican authors, [Mexican] stories, and stuff. I'm proud to have a heritage that has these things and to learn more about the history of Mexico.

> It was fun [going to Mexico to visit relatives]. It was fun getting away from this atmosphere over here. Over there, there's more liberty. You get to see real life, what the hard life [is like]. My grandma lives in a little *pueblito* (little town), in a *ranchito* (little ranch). [She has] all these animals and everything. You have to do [things] like the old fashioned way. It was fun.

Of course, Latino/a students in the study varied in terms of the degree to which they embraced or enacted a Latino/a cultural identity. Nonetheless, for a great number of students, this cultural identification was a source of pride and strength that afforded them a sense of groundedness within a society where their ethnicity/culture was not dominant. Almost half of the students reported that being a member of their group brought them pride.

> I really like our culture. I mean, I think that's one thing we [Latinos/as] really have going for us. It's really beautiful. A lot of our values are, I think, good. I know a lot of people who say, "Well, I don't have a culture" or "I don't know what my background is about." I really like the fact that I am into my culture.

The beauty of the culture was also described by this student:

> Well, the community, the people that I'm around, have made it seem like Mexican [culture] is beautiful. It is very beautiful and I love it. It gives me pride. If you're proud of who you are, in a lot of things you do, you're just going to be a happy person. So I'm proud of being Mexican, and if I'm proud then I'm happy, you know.

Many students mentioned that pride in their culture brought them happiness and prompted them to retain their culture. Pride in ethnicity also made students eager to learn more about their culture.

> I feel proud of being a Mexicano. Understanding the background of how the Mexicanos came about is important to me and to realize who and what I am today. That's the mixture of the two groups that created the Mestizo or the Mexicano. In our culture, we have a mixture of the Mexican culture and the Spanish culture, it's important to both. Many people believe that Spain came and conquered and that Spain should be eliminated. However, we must understand and accept that, because of both, we are who we are [today].
>
> It means everything about who I am, what I want to do, where I come from, and where I'm trying to head to. It's really important. I am proud of who I am. I mean I [still have] a lot more to learn about who I am and what my background is about, but I'm proud of it.

These reflections highlight how explorations into ethnicity infused students with a sense of collective pride regarding their ethnicity and cultural heritage. Ethnic group esteem, expressed in terms of developing ethnic pride, gave students added strength for embarking on adult challenges and tasks that spoke to a more coherent identity for these students. Having ethnic pride helped define for these students their place in the larger society. Even in the case of one student who specifically stated that he did not feel that his ethnicity meant a great deal to him, he still found a sense of pride in that affiliation that grounded him.

> Ethnic identity? Uh, it doesn't mean much to me. I'm more of a humanist; I believe in myself. I'd like to see everybody equal. Ethnic identity would mean keeping my cultural customs and having pride in where my cultural background comes from, being Mexican and a quarter Chinese, and that's

what I take pride in. I don't look down on other people's cultures. So I do take pride in my background.

In sum, students mentioned a number of outcomes as related to pride in their culture and ethnicity. Some connected pride in their own culture to how they perceived and interacted with other cultures in a positive manner. Many spoke of deriving a sense of strength from having ethnic pride that was grounded in their knowledge of culture and history. Most significant, students found that pride in culture/ethnicity gave them a sense of self-confidence and self-efficacy for the future; as one student noted, "Having pride in my culture gives me a sense of security."

Ethnic Activities and Traditions

Each student was asked how they practiced their ethnicity. Forty-four percent of students mentioned food as an ethnic practice, either eaten on a daily basis and/or as a central feature of weekly family gatherings. That same number of students found music and dance to be a common ethnic practice. Over half of the students reported that speaking Spanish was a daily practice. A third of the students mentioned family as a daily ethnic practice. Nearly a third described traditional Mexican holidays or celebrations, such as *quinceaneras, Las Posadas, Cinco de Mayo*, and Mexican Independence Day, as ethnic practices. A quarter of the students mentioned that going to church was an ethnic practice, and 22% reported that they considered home country visits as an ethnic practice: as one student reflected, "I have two places to call home." Five students reported taking ethnic studies courses or participating in ethnic-based student organizations as ethnic practices. Although we note that many students simply saw these ethnic activities and traditions as expressions of ethnicity, they failed to expand on their meaning. Nevertheless, we believe these were, indeed, significant practices that defined for students their sense of cultural self and ethnicity. The following quotes illustrate how students spoke of the ethnic traditions, practices, and behaviors that defined their cultural identity.

> We are a typical Mexican family that celebrates Christmas in the traditional Mexican way, *Cinco de Mayo*, Independence Day, all the traditional holidays Mexicans celebrate. We celebrate Mother's Day on the day that it would be in Mexico as compared to the day that it would be over here in the United States.

Pretty much we have *frijoles* (beans) every day if not every other day. On special occasions or on the weekends, we have *nopales* (cactus) whether it be with *picadillo* (meat) or *huevos* (eggs) in the morning. Other things that we have [are] special holidays, like for example Christmas. We have *Las Posadas* (religious festivities) which begin on the sixteenth of December, and we also have *El Dia de Los Reyes Magos* (Day of the Wise Men, a biblical religious celebration) on the sixth of January. One of the most important things about culture is the language that we speak at home, which is Spanish, and that's what spoken mainly at home. My parents don't speak any English, so Spanish is spoken for the most part.

She [grandmother] always makes *menudo* or the *posole*. Those are like the two [main] things and that's what everyone comes for. Well, my parents and aunts, they know how to make it but it's not [like] grandmother's. You know how that is? It's not your *abuelita*'s. So they have to come over for the menu, [which] mostly it's *menudo* that she has every week. She makes it every week, and then, like on special occasions, she'll make *posole* or *tamales* or something. So, yeah, definitely it's food.

For us, it's the dance. It's you know, you learn to dance when you're two years old. The minute you can stand on your feet you're on the dance floor. I've salsa'ed [Latino/a dance style] since I was a baby and there's little [children] dancing songs. They [family members] bounce you around and they talk about rhythm and that's another association. The music. That's what we like. That's where I would say my identity is coming from.

I dance [a] Mexican traditional dance, called [*Ballet Folklorico*]. So that's a big part of my life here at RU. I'm very involved in the Mexican folklore dancing. I guess that's a way for me to identify with my culture.

Although ethnic practices were supported through various community entities (i.e., church and religious Catholic schools) and participation in ethnic-based activities and academic programs, family members emerged as the primary vehicle for maintaining ethnic and cultural expression. The student below highlighted the importance of her grandmother—as the matriarch of the family—in maintaining Latino/a cultural traditions and bringing her extended family together.

We (family) do a lot of the culture, a lot of the traditions because of my grandmother. She's the big source [for passing on cultural traditions]. She's the main person that we do almost everything for. I feel that if she were to pass away, our family would fall apart almost. I mean, of course they have fights—my mother and my uncles—but no matter what, we always seem to come together when it comes to my grandma. So she tries to keep the traditions going. She's like the center of everything. Do you know what I mean? So we do everything [because of her], me and any [of my] cousins. That's where I see a lot of the culture and the traditions, like the *Posadas* that they have over there [in Mexico].

This finding is consistent with a previous study that examined the role of the grandmother as a significant agent in the socialization of ethnic culture and heritage among second-generation Latino/a youth (as reported in Padilla, 2006). By and large, students credited *la familia* for teaching the traditions and customs they valued so much. Students viewed family as a place where culture was transmitted and important values and beliefs were passed down. As one student reflected, "My family, my parents, their way of thinking, almost everything, it goes back to what their parents taught them. So I'm going back generations and we've kept the customs." When asked if he felt having these customs passed down through generations was an advantage, he was quick to agree. These findings underscore the importance of the family as an ongoing influence for young Latinos/as as key transmitters of ethnic culture, practices, and traditions.

Language

I usually speak a lot of English with my sister, but my mom doesn't speak English you know. She uses a lot of Spanish. She tells us, "Learn first the [Spanish] language and then learn your second one [English]." My mom tells us [all the time], practice Spanish, practice Spanish.

Over half the students mentioned that speaking Spanish was an ethnic practice. Language is considered one of the most important expressions of ethnicity and is a powerful ethnic and cultural marker among groups (Giles, Bourhis, & Taylor, 1977; Phinney, 2000b). Language is used as a means of achieving positive ethnic distinctiveness and group esteem in contexts where ethnicity and culture matter. Furthermore, as an ethnic practice, language provides the mechanism for persons to forge connections with coethnics and create supportive linguistic communities in a society where one's ethnicity is accorded a minority status and the threat of cultural/ethnic loss is real. In this study, 85% of Latino/a students reported being able to speak Spanish fluently; only 2 Latino/a students in the sample said they spoke some Spanish, and one did not know or speak the language at all. These findings reinforce the significance of language in transmitting culture among Latinos/as and are consistent with those of previous studies (e.g., Santiago-Rivera et al., 2002), indicating that the Spanish language is being maintained in the United States, and there is a sizeable and growing bilingual (Spanish and English) population.

Students saw knowing two languages as a benefit of being Latino/a. Many recognized the significance of mastering both English and Spanish as a unique opportunity that was not as readily available to other ethnic groups or in parts of the country outside of California. "I think there's a lot of advantages of being our culture. You get to learn two different languages, especially in California, which is remarkable," said one student. Others remarked how knowledge of both languages gave them the flexibility to negotiate a Spanish- and English-speaking world. Hence, those knowing two languages had the added advantage of being familiar with two cultures where the ability to relate to members of each group was seen as a valuable attribute, the essence of being bicultural (Padilla, 2006). Researchers have identified language mastery as a key factor in gaining competence in a second culture that is fundamental to the process of becoming a truly biculturally competent individual (LaFramboise, Coleman, & Gerton, 1995). Students were aware of the benefits of knowing the official dominant language of the United States (i.e., English) and welcomed the opportunity to act as cultural mediators or brokers between their native Spanish-speaking community and the White community (Morales & Hanson, 2005).

> I have two cultures that I'm familiar with; that would be an advantage. I can speak Spanish and English and that helps in a lot of jobs. I can relate with Hispanic people and also with White people.

Furthermore, as illustrated in the quote below, students commented on the psychosocial gains of bilingualism to them personally on the potential monetary rewards in being bilingual and bicultural.

> I think here in Southern California, in particular, there's an advantage to being bilingual. First of all, you either get a stipend or pay increase because

of speaking two languages. Along with speaking two languages, there is [greater] sensitivity to another culture.

Finally, students were indeed aware that language was tied to a system of institutional power, status, and ethnopolitics. They reflected that being bilingual had not always been perceived positively and knew people who still hid from others their ability to speak Spanish: "Before, if you [spoke Spanish], they [larger society] put speaking Spanish down." Hence, we observe that students were not completely ignorant of the dynamics of language, power, and ethnicity in terms of race relations in American society.

Students also spoke of a blended language of code-switching that they practiced when they felt English was not sufficient to express what they truly meant, as demonstrated by the following:

> When I can't express myself well in English, I usually come out speaking both languages at the same time. I think that the big advantage of being able to know another language, and being able to use [both] to communicate with other people is important.

This finding is consistent with Ardilla's (2005) argument that Spanglish has emerged as one of the most "important contemporary linguistic phenomena in the United States," and it represents a form of code-switching among Latinos/as that is a cultural expression among persons who live on linguistic borders (p. 60). It reflects the blending of two languages in conversation that enables its speakers to integrate into the larger society while still expressing loyalty to their native ethnic langue. As one student reflected, "With friends that I have that are Latinos/as, we do speak Spanish and sometimes we switch off and on [between Spanish and English], and [with] my parents, it's all Spanish because they hardly know any English."

On the other hand, students also spoke of the Spanish language as an ethnic practice they wished to strengthen and master. This perspective is from a young man who knew Spanish but wished to learn the language better:

> You are one up by knowing two languages and I feel kind of proud of that. I try to develop more of the language because I was taught the language, but in a more streetwise way, by my parents, not grammatical Spanish. . . . I want to know it better. If you don't know it well and you go to Mexico

and you're talking to people, they will say, "No, this is how you say it." So I want to learn how to write it better. I knew how to speak it, but I didn't know how to write it.

He is seeking to be literate in his first language by speaking and writing it properly. This is an important issue for college students who may have learned to speak Spanish fluently, though colloquially, because their only formal education has been in English. The university context provided such individuals with a formal course curriculum for achieving Spanish fluency that enhanced their positive ethnic distinctiveness as future Latino/a professionals who would also be fluent Spanish speakers. In sum, this finding is in line with previous research identifying language proficiency and language use as an important dimension of ethnic identity for cultural groups that is closely tied to their ethnic self-definition (Giles et al., 1977; Phinney, 2000a).

Religion as a Cultural Value and Practice

> Religion and family come first. . . . Ever since we were small we've always gone to church and it's really important. We'll go with my grandma because it's really important. Like my cousins, we'll go to retreats, religious retreats, those are really good just to relax and open up about yourself and problems—kind of like a therapy type thing. Even the traditional things, like the *quinceanera* it's not supposed to be [about] the party [but] it's supposed to be [the young girl] making a commitment to God.
>
> When my mom's worried or something, she's like always turning her little *veladoras* [religious candles]. She's all into San Martin de Porras (a saint) and she does the rosary, we do rosary in the neighborhood. The older women and men do it like almost daily. Yeah, my mom does it daily. There's this thing called a *Novena* (praying for nine days). I do that often also.

Previous researchers have noted the importance of religion as a core value of Latino/a culture (e.g., Ramirez & Castaneda, 1974; Santiago-Rivera et al., 2002). As such, we find that religious beliefs and practices are intertwined into many aspects of daily life, and religious ceremony is used to mark major life events—baptisms, First Holy Communion, *quinceaneras*, weddings, and funerals. This was certainly the experience of many Latino/a students in the study, as illustrated by the above quotes. The importance of religious ideologies, practices, and beliefs in the lives of Latinos/as is punctuated by the fact that religion reinforces many of the core traditional Latino/a values that center on "identification with family, ethnicity and community; personalization of interpersonal relationships, and status and role definition in family and community" (Ramirez & Castaneda, 1974, p. 41).

Being a member of a religious group, usually Catholic, was an important ethnic practice for students in the study, and it shaped their definition of the Latino/a identity. As one student reflected, "I mean I'm a Catholic, so I guess that's one aspect that incorporates being Mexican." Likewise, another student noted that being Catholic has endured through multiple generations: "You could say my background, my religious traditions, they're Catholic. I'm Catholic you know, it just goes back to the family, two, three, generations ago." In addition, one student commented, "I went to a Catholic school since I was in elementary school [through high school]. That's part of my parents' religion, they want to instill that religious value in me." Although students differed in terms of the significance religion played in their lives, many who saw themselves as not very religious nonetheless said they participated regularly in religious activities. "Well, I'm Catholic but I'm not [really] into it. I go to church every Sunday, but it doesn't rule my life. It doesn't rule my mom's life, either, but she is a very strong believer." Students also spoke of religion as being important in helping them make life decisions and cope with stressful situations. It also served as a source of strength in times of difficulties.

> I'm Catholic, so like most Catholics, well, I should say some, I do go to mass. I think most of my friends go, too. They don't take it so [seriously but] they go and they listen. They're there. Afterwards it [supports] you, you know. It's what they think about when they make decisions or when they're stressed out and they don't know what to do.

Most significant is that, throughout students' commentaries, we see again and again the connection of religion and family. As one student reflected, "Going to church is an [ethnic] tradition that we have. [My] family, we believe in religion and [in] God." Another stressed the importance of values imparted by the family as stemming from religious beliefs: "My values were set by my parents. They instilled very strict religious values on us. In my family, family has always been very important." Likewise, another student offered a similar perspective: "I was raised with my grandparents growing up. So a lot of [my] values I got from church and from home because my grandparents raised me going to church and doing all those things." Another student saw churchgoing as both a family and a religious activity.

> A typical American, I won't generalize, but they are more like [into] appearances, and with Latinos/as it's more like a family. That's something that I learned. That was the first thing that was taught to me when I started going to church. I was not just going to church, but being with my family.

He generalized that the typical American only went to church for appearance, but Latinos/as go to church for both religious purposes and to be with their families, thus signifying the many ways family and religion mediated so many of life's activities for Latinos/as. Finally, the Dominican woman, who had not been raised Catholic but chose the religion when she was older, described the interplay among religion, family, and ethnicity for her. She explains:

> My parents were very lenient with me. They waited 'til I was old enough to decide what religion I would choose to be, and I chose [Catholicism]. I don't think I would do that with my children. I think I would want my children baptized in my religion when they were babies. I mean, it's just, and I've seen, like the rest of my family has done it that way. My parents were very lenient; they thought it would be better for us. So they just never even thought about religion, my brothers weren't even baptized. But I mean, for my sake, I think just the Hispanic in me would want my children baptized.

For her, being Catholic and following Catholic traditions was an important part of her cultural and ethnic identity.

In sum, although students varied in terms of what made religion important for them, religion did emerge as central theme of a Latino/a identity. In the case of some, the importance of religion stemmed from the values that it instilled, for others it was the celebrations or traditions that came with it, and for most it was significant to them because it was one way the family congregated and shared valued traditions.

Family as a Collectivist Entity

There is no question that the most frequent contributor to or outcome of ethnic identity for Latino/a college students is the role family played in their lives and the centrality of family. The overarching influence of *la familia* on its members is considered the defining characteristic of Latino/a culture that is associated with the development of a *familial self* (Falicov, 1998; Santiago-Rivera et al., 2002). One of the students described this connection among self, ethnic identity, and family:

> I think my ethnic identity created who I am. I keep talking about my family, my parents, but I think it created who I am because of my parents' being Mexican, growing up in the traditional Mexican home, in Mexico, and learning the value of hard work, eventually education. The importance of family—that's shaped who I am now in that those are my beliefs.

Nearly every student in the study talked about the importance of family, with only one reporting negative feelings toward her family. Families were key sources of support, comfort, and pride. Students felt a strong desire to respect and please their families, and it is was this dynamic interplay between their own actions and their impact on the family that led students to have a collectivist experience with family, that everything they do as individuals is influenced by the family and, ultimately, affects the family. As seen later in the chapter, this collectivist orientation, which began in the family, also extended to the broader community. Being a part of a family helped students to realize their priorities.

> Values such as my family are very important to me. Above everything is my family, above everything. And then after, close after, comes school, and then work. It's helped me to establish my priorities.

It is important to note that for many Latino/a students, family takes precedence over everything, including school. Therefore, if a family emergency or need arises, school is often set aside until the family crisis subsides, even if it means stepping out for a semester or more. The student below also identifies the family as vital:

> My family definitely, definitely takes precedence. I would choose my family over anything except God. But in my mind, that's because my family is

twenty minutes away, so I don't always get to see them or talk to them. So then it's like spirituality, then my education.

What is instructive about this student is that in her mind she lives far away from her family, but they are only 20 minutes away.

This notion of proximity and extended family, similar to the Asian Americans', was a factor for Latinos/as. The woman below is close with her family members and also has a grandparent in the home:

> I'm very close to my older brother, tight, I mean, to a point where [for] most of my life he was my best friend. I get along extremely well with my mother. . . . I practically raised my little sister for her, her first one or two years. And my little brother, I get along with him now as well as I did with my older brother a few years ago. So, I mean we're close, and now my grandfather is living with us.

Another student attributes the unity she feels in the family to her grandmother. When asked where the importance of family came from for her, she said:

> I think, basically, probably from my grandmother, and because they've always been so united. My uncles and my aunts, they've always been united, but I think it has to do a lot with my grandmother because she plays a big part in all our lives.

Grandmothers were important to maintaining the family, as echoed by this woman:

> Every week on Sundays, we all get together at my grandma's house. . . . It's my, my whole family, as many as can [come], because I have a few cousins, a few uncles that live out of state. So they can't come on every Sunday. But the ones that do live around the area, which are about four of my aunts plus their kids, my cousins, we all get together at my grandma's house. Not like a formal thing, we don't all wait for everybody to get there and then sit down. Everyone is just kind of in and out and doing their own thing. We'll have food there and everyone's eating constantly. My grandma's trying to feed you all the time.

Once again we hear the importance of the grandmother: a key figure in the lives of young Latinos/as whose influence extends into emerging adulthood

(Ramirez & Castaneda, 1974). When one student mentioned family multiple times during the interview, she was finally asked if she felt family was an advantage to being Mexican. She said:

> Oh, definitely! 'Cause we're so close. That's definitely an advantage because a lot of my friends don't even know their aunts and uncles. [Not that] I know exactly what [family] line order they come, but I know uncles of cousins of third cousins . . .

Another student contrasts her experiences with her family with those of her friends.

> Most families don't eat together, but for us dinner is always a family thing. Now that I'm working it's a little harder, but when we can, we all eat together, all of us at the dinner table. I find that it's not common anymore. My friends say, "I eat in front of the TV or go to my room." I always thought it was very important that we [family] set the table, we eat, and we talk.

One student thought family values were so strong that she remarked, "Mexican Americans go home every weekend, and they are required to go home every weekend."

The collectivist orientation of the family was evident in how students explained the importance of family and how the family worked together to overcome obstacles:

> I was ill a little while ago, and throughout the whole illness my whole family was just there for me, like, I was never alone, you know. Because of my illness I broke down really bad, and there were times when I didn't really feel like you know, like going on and they've always been there for me. They've always brought me up.

She went on to say:

> I just feel that without my family I don't think I would have gotten quite as far, especially without my mother, because she's always been there for me. She's always pushed me to do, you know, my best and everything. My family, especially in crisis, they've always been there you know. They're always there. Always support us [in] everything, no matter what.

Students were realistic in reporting family problems, but with the exception of one student, they noted that families also knew how to resolve their disputes within the family.

> I think Mexican people are really like that. I think they really value their family, and that they're close with them. Of course, there's always exceptions to it, but I think that Mexican families are really close. Since they're really big, everybody usually gets along, and if there's any problems, there's definitely solutions to them.

And another offered:

> I guess 'cause I have everything. At least for me, in my culture, [everything] centers around family, you know. You deal with the family. You work out problems with the family, and I guess, ultimately, whatever I'm doing in my education, in my career, in my future, includes my family.

Here she not only emphasizes that family deals with each other to work out problems, but she also considers her family when planning for the future. Students, again, compared their own family experiences with coethnics' and then with other groups.

> The family values that we have, umm, from what I have seen, and not just in my own friendly group, but a lot of Mexicans are very close. They tend to stick together through a lot of things. Whereas, from what I've seen, some other ethnic groups think, "Oh, you know, I can't count on my family."

Here a student shares her mother's expectations for keeping the family together through whatever might happen in the future:

> She's always told me, you know, "Whatever happens with your father, if we have problems, get divorced, or if we die before our time, you're the oldest. You gotta make sure you and your brother and your sister stay together, whatever happens."

Many other authors agree that the importance of the family and the collectivist orientation that generates from that unit is a defining characteristic of the Latino/a family (e.g., Ramirez & Castaneda, 1974; Santiago-Rivera et al.,

2002). We see this in the students' accounts of the importance the family. Although the students in the study are primarily Mexican in origin, this finding also held for the Dominicana and the Puerto Rican in the study.

Respect for and Within Family

Because family is so important to these students, we would expect there to be a great deal of respect for and influence in the family unit. Indeed, in line with previous conceptualizations of the Latino/a culture, students spoke extensively about the respect (*respeto*) they had for family, especially elders, and how that translated to behavioral expectations (Falicov, 1998; Halgunseth, Ispa, & Rudy, 2006; Ramirez & Castaneda, 1974; Santiago-Rivera et al., 2002). Again, students used their other-ethnic peers as the comparison group when evaluating the characteristics of their families.

> I'm glad that I'm Mexican because it teaches you to respect . . . your parents, and the love for your family, that's very important to me. I don't see that in a lot of my friends of any culture and I think that's really sad that they don't have that family unit there, 'cause [in Mexicans] it's very strong. I think [that] it helps throughout all, all of college.

This woman saw that the respect, love, and value for her family and parents was unique and acknowledged how it helped her in her college years.

> Where I was living, that's where the Caucasians, a lot of them that I knew, they just couldn't get along with their families, sometimes. Sometimes they would get along with them and they would be all great, and the next thing you know, they're just like bad-mouthing their parents and everything. And, umm, if I have differences, like I know that when I have differences with my mom, I don't go out and bad-mouth her in front of everybody. If I have a difference with her, I keep it inside of me.

Of course, it may not be best for the student to subvert the differences she has with her mother; however, her analysis highlights the importance of *personalismo*[1] and deference to parental figures as signs of respect for Latinos/as

---

1. *Personalismo* refers to a Latino cultural script that emphasizes behaviors that promote smooth, pleasant, and harmonious interpersonal relationships. The expectation is that interpersonal relationships will be characterized by openness, warmth, and commitment for mutual help.

(Marin & Marin, 1991; Ramirez & Castaneda, 1974). Another student outlined what she believed to be the consequences of having strictly defined respect for elders:

> I think the way I was raised, the way my parents [set] those beliefs [in me]. [Also] religion I would say has a lot to do with my values. I think it's good to have respect for older members of a family or society, but sometimes it can be negative in the way that I never really feel comfortable confronting that authority. And that's really what you truly want [to do]. You confront and analyze everything thoroughly, and that's always been hard for me.

As this student has come to think independently and question what authorities tell her, she's frustrated by her socialization, which has taught her not to confront elders or authorities. Family expectations stress students in different ways—whether it is the pressure always to be on one's best behavior or to contribute to the welfare of the family. Other researchers have addressed the intergenerational stress that can occur within families whose members are acculturating at different levels. This is especially difficult for daughters in the parent-child relationship (Buriel & De Ment, 1997). One student summarized that family "can also be a disadvantage, because if anything or everything you do is related to your family, sometimes it brings stress and problems, too. [There are] people that can't handle that." This points to the importance of student services personnel's understanding the enmeshed family systems that influence many Latino/a college students (Santiago-Rivera et al., 2002).

The respect students had for families and elders transferred to their acceptance of strict rules and limits set by parents, which also typified their experiences. Previous cross-cultural research indicates that Latino parents do tend to be more protective and enforce greater control over their children than do non-Latino parents (see Durrett, O'Bryan, & Pennebaker, 1975; Okagaki & Frensch, 1998). As one young woman said:

> When you have a family, oh, God this is so broad, umm, it all comes from my mother. My mother is so responsible. So like I said before, her beliefs influence me so much, and even if I'm against them, I would do what she thinks is right before what I think is right. It's just, I don't know, I think I'm so responsible and I think it's because my mother. . . . I think, I don't know, that just being Mexican I'm so responsible, I don't know why. I

never really thought about this. . . . Everything has to do with my family, and what they mean to me is important. It's like I'd rather choose what they feel than what I'm feeling.

Here she describes the ethos of responsibility that has been instilled in her by her mother and her ethnicity, and she would even subjugate her own beliefs to those of her mother's. The students generally appreciated the strict parenting.

Like my parents are very strict, and they're always saying don't do that or do that, or like they always base it on your reputation. They're always saying, you can't do this and you can't do that, so in a way it's made me be more of a person. I think more about the things that I do before I do them. I'm more cautious, that's based on my parents, on how they treat me, how they raised me. I think that my grandmother has to do with it, too. She's very old-fashioned, like, "Oh, you can't do this, you can't do that." I think more about things that I'm going to do and how probably it could affect me later on in my life.

Because her parents stressed that actions affect reputation, and because she was consistently told that she could not do things, this student developed a pattern of thinking about her actions and their long-term effects. Likewise, another woman explained how she had to defend her compliance to her parents' rules with her non-Mexican friends:

And a lot of my other friends are like, "God, why do you even do that? God, my parents don't do that to me, [I'm on my own]." I think it's because we're Mexican, it's very strong; they did the same thing with their parents, so that's just the way things are. I don't question them. . . . My friends say, "How come you come in at twelve and you do what your parents say?" and I'll explain to them. But I don't feel isolated from them for that, I'm just trying to explain to them that this is my family, this is the way they are. I think this is kind of the way it is in the Mexican tradition, and they'll be like, "Oh, okay."

Although her friends question her obedience, she did not feel that it threatened their friendships and felt comfortable explaining herself and, ultimately, she connected the value of obedience to her culture. Strict parenting was also connected with religion, as illustrated below:

A big part of [my values] has to do with my religion. . . . My parents would never let me watch movies with a guy or something, and I would never do that either. . . . I'm pretty sure it's against my religion, but [they never really] say anything about that. Female sex is a big "no" in our religion. My parents always taught me to be respectful of adults and that they're the authority and to listen to them.

Religious values and parental rules were pivotal in how this student experienced her options in dating and relationships with men. The expectation of obedience, especially by girls, is apparent here and is similar to the experiences Asian American women shared. Gender roles were instrumental in how students experienced parental expectations.

Obedience with family rules and expectations was closely connected with a desire to avoid bringing shame to the family. For students, this was also connected to the responsibility they felt toward the group. One woman said, "It's important that I don't go doing something that would make me feel bad or my family or that would reflect badly on who my ancestors were." This is tied to collectivistic values where appearances truly matter (what people might say—*el que diran*), in that one's actions reflect not only on the individual but the family, community, and, ultimately, the group as well (Ramirez & Castaneda, 1974). A similar sentiment was articulated by another woman:

Just trying to change to something higher than what your parents had. I guess my mom has always stayed at home and my dad has always worked, you know, blue-collar work. He worked with his hands, and now they struggle for their children to get educations, to get educated as much as possible, and achieve goals that they have for you. That's the reason that they came over here, [left] their home country. . . . The motivation, again, is that you represent the Mexicans, you represent a lot of what your family is. You just don't want to bring shame to your family, just as you do something right it brings pride to the family. Just my family motivation keeps me pushing.

She avoids bringing shame to her family as a form of respect for the sacrifices they made by coming to this country, but also out of respect for the future they want for her. She also feels that she represents not only her own family, but Mexicans in general.

Although women predominantly expressed this trait, men also had their experiences with behavioral expectations. One man who had a baby outside of marriage reported:

> My dad is saying, 'cause I have a girlfriend and we just had a baby, and he was saying, "Oh, yeah, this is gonna look bad on the family," and I was thinking, wait a minute, I have no problem with it.

A gender difference may be that, although he recognized that he was bringing shame to his family, he did not feel his actions conflicted with his own set of values. This sharply contrasts with how women generally felt responsibility to their families for being role models, as expressed here:

> My values? With my family, it's being a role model for my family. Being a role model for my brothers and sisters. Making sure I do what's right for my family. That's really high, and God. . . . Family, God, are the basis for everything else, and all my actions and behaviors, everything that I do, [is based] on that. I mean because my family is really, extremely important to me and also God. . . . I want them to be proud of me being here, both my parents and my brothers and sisters.

The fact that grandmothers were often the sources of strength and connections for families, and that women in this study considered their behavior as a direct reflection of the family, along with their strong desire to support their families, demonstrates a gender difference. This difference in how families are maintained and supported is important, especially when considering the inevitable acculturation students speak of later in the chapter—especially women, who could see how their higher education and career goals were changing the roles they would assume in their present and future families.

Gendered Roles

Respect for the family has an uneven influence on the behavior of women and the expectations held for them. In this section we continue to explore how the heightened gender roles women experienced in their families resulted in the family's desire to protect them from outside influences and to have a say in their lives, education, and career plans. We also see how Latinas were working actively to reconstruct gender roles that reflect modern times and goals for their futures.

Women experienced restrictions as a result of their families' need to protect them from outside influences, especially as they related to dating and socializing with friends. One woman noted stark differences in rules in her family for her and for her brother:

> My parents are more, um, liberal. They gave him [my brother] more freedom, as opposed to where I always stayed at home, studied, went to school, and was home before dark. All through high school, I'd be home by 10:30 p.m. My brother, he could be out all hours of the night, and so it was just different for me and my brother.

The double standard women experienced was frustrating in many ways, especially as they were beginning to see themselves as independent college women. As Olsen (1997) notes, immigrant or second-generation Latinas often experience more pressure to conform to the native culture of their parents than do males. Clashes between the two cultures tend to revolve around issues related to gender role expectations and typical teenage behaviors "such as dating," where "girls are often caught in a double bind and forced to conform—and many feel a certain degree of resentment against their parents who immigrated to the United States" (Padilla, 2006, p. 476). This theme is articulated by a young woman who speculated about what she might have missed because of culturally based parental restrictions:

> With male-female relationships and experiences at home, my parents have been too protective of me. They haven't really allowed me to get to know how I am [to know my sense of self], to really do a lot more for myself. They just kept me as close as they can. "You just go to school, you go to work"; that's basically it.

This woman felt that the restrictions her parents placed on her behavior inhibited her ability to take care of normal, adolescent developmental tasks, where experiences help young people to test their values and boundaries. She shows great insight in her evaluation of those restrictions, restricting her ability to discover more about herself. A Dominicana also explained how, in her culture, dating is a closely guarded activity: "Women are accustomed to going out with chaperones, no matter the age . . . in the Dominican Republic, it's a lot more serious to have a boyfriend or girlfriend than it is here." Protecting the purity of Latinas is important to many families, with women

reporting hearing messages from a young age about the value of virginity
and how vigorously they must protect it from alternatively motivated men.
Sanchez (1997) notes that "sexual activity prior to marriage" is prohibited in
many Latino/a cultural groups, although it is a common practice among the
younger generation (p. 70). A woman explained how she received these messages from her grandmother.

> She usually tells [us] when she was [our] age [she] did this and that and
> got married with the white dress and the big party and everything, and
> that's nice. You know, I would like to get married with the white dress, big
> party, and everything. But she, of course, she tells us nowadays, "Guys just
> want that" you know, and she doesn't use the "s" word; supposedly that
> is "sex." She's like, "Respect yourself, you know, before you do anything."
> I really do follow that. If you don't have respect for yourself, then what's
> the use?

This student learned her lessons well, as she went later to say, "I want to
wear the white dress that really signifies purity and, you know, you're giving
everything to your husband there, like my mom told us . . . I mean. I'm an
old fashioned girl!"

Families' desire to exert control over their daughter's lives was not only
directed at their dating and social behavior, but extended to their life plans
and educational opportunities as well. Most Latinas in the study lived in
close proximity to their families, as was the expectation. This is illustrated
best by this student:

> Let's say that my mother is really into living at home until you get married.
> I've been wanting to go to Santa Barbara, UCSB, and move away. When
> I graduated, I was seventeen, and she wouldn't sign the papers for me to
> go. Now I'm eighteen and I want to leave, and she's like totally against
> that. So I'm caught in the middle. I don't want to feel like I'm choosing
> my career over my family, but it's coming to a point where I'm gonna have
> to. . . . My mom is really not into it. My sister's married; she lives right
> next door. You see what I'm saying? My brother's married; he's at the
> house every day with his family. And it's like moving away, it's going to,
> like, really affect her.

She is planning to break the family pattern and make the choice to attend
the college of her choice rather than her mother's choice. Several women,

when visualizing and planning for their futures, saw themselves as purposefully being different from their mothers. When asked where her value for education came from, one woman explained:

> I see my parents and they tried. They went to school but they weren't very successful. My mom was gonna be a secretary in Mexico but she got married. I guess I learned from her mistakes. I want to do something for myself.

She does not respect her mother less or reject her as a role model, but she wants something different for herself. Another woman had a similar experience:

> There were a lot of things that my mom had to go through because she's Latin American. Once my mom had us, she wanted to go back to school, and my dad didn't want her to do that. He disagreed with it, and they were constantly at war with that. I didn't see how that's wrong . . . I've watched my mom work really hard, work really hard in life to come up. She got married at a really young age and she had to struggle with us. That's basically what motivated me. I don't want to have to go through that. I want to make that change.

These changing gender roles often were precipitated by what students saw happening in their homes. They saw themselves as changing family patterns. While some found resistance from family members to some of their decisions, family members generally supported their decision to pursue higher education. There was more of a sense that the larger ethnic group felt the traditional family structure may be in jeopardy if more and more women made these decisions. One woman shared:

> Well, basically, Mexican-Americans have big families, usually big families. Some of them, you know, think, well she's the oldest you know, she finished high school, she doesn't need to go to college, she doesn't need to go to work, you know. She can stay home and take care of the kids and take care of the house and cook. I mean, you can see that very much, and you know that's crazy. I mean, why deny values or education or anything to anybody?

This finding mirrors previous research indicating that some Latino parents see pursuing higher education as important for their sons as *a vehicle for upward economic mobility*, but not really necessary for their daughters (Gandara, 1995). Another also felt that the general ethos of the ethnic group supported keeping women in their traditional spaces.

> I do believe that there are a lot of Latin women who want to get a good education, who want to work. But the tradition says that they have to stay home, take care of the children. That a woman isn't supposed to speak out loud, or that the woman isn't supposed to be into her work too much, or she's not giving enough time to the home or to the family. We need to project that this is important, that you need to concentrate on education, you need to teach your kids that education is important, and that they need to speak up for what they believe in. We need to project that more.

This student calls on other members of her group to join her in changing these traditional gender roles that have limited women and Latinos/as in general. There was also one man in the study who was attempting to do this within his own family:

> My family gets mad. My girlfriend and I have a deal where if I cook, she'll wash the dishes, or if she cooks, I'll wash the dishes. And for me that works perfect, but in my house it seems like my mom's like the slave, which is kind of sad. She'll have to cook. I guess that's what's expected of her. . . . But she tends to do it, and then later on she'll say stuff about it, she'll talk about it. She doesn't like to do it but she feels like she's kind of forced to do it. . . . And they got mad at me once, not mad, but they're saying, "Oh, yeah, Ramona she has control over you." And I'm like, "Well, what do you mean?" And what it was, they brought it back to when they were sitting in the living room when Ramona was visiting, and she asked me, "Can you wash my car?" And I said, "Yeah, no problem." It's our little thing, so I said, yeah no problem, and then later on my, my dad said, "Yeah, she just bosses you around." I'm like, "What are [you] talking about?" And he said, "Yeah, like the other day she just made you wash her car, like a little *mandeloncito* (effeminate male)."

To his father, he was not acting like a man, head of his household, in a position superior to his girlfriend. The student's attempts to build a more egalitarian relationship that avoids the pitfalls he sees in his parents' has not been well received. He continued:

Through a lot of history classes we studied about women's rights, and I consider myself to be a feminist. They kind of put me down because of that, maybe not put me down, but they'll say stuff about it, and they'll joke around.

He demonstrates that women are not the only ones who have a difficult time transforming gender roles in Latino/a households. In fact, it may even be more difficult for men as, like this man, coethnics may have a difficult time understanding why they would want to change a facet of the culture that clearly benefits them. This finding is consistent with Niemann's (2001) analysis regarding changes in gender role beliefs among young Latinos/as, which often clash with their parents' more traditional gender-based expectations for men and women.

Family as a Support for Education

There is often a misunderstanding about the role of Latino/a parents in supporting or valuing their children's educations. Deficit model perspectives frame the Latino/a family as being a deterrent to children's academic achievement and, coupled with expectations to contribute financially to the family, can erect a barrier to college attainment. What we heard from students in this study is quite different. They did not see their parents as actively supportive of education, but that was because they did not know how to be effective in that support, and they lacked the tools to help their children achieve a college education. Students' reflections indicate an analytic comparison between what they experienced and what they assumed to be the experience of their non-Latino/a peers. But the support they did feel from their families was instrumental and, coupled with the knowledge that parents lacked the tools to show them the way, they made it a personal responsibility to assume that role with younger siblings.

Students definitely felt their parents supported them in attaining higher education. This finding is supported by previous research by Portes and Rumbaut (1996), who report that children of immigrant parents are more likely to attend college and come from family households where education is highly valued. Only one student reported that family members discouraged her attendance or saw her efforts to become educated rather as taking away from the family's financial welfare. For the vast majority of students, support for education was linked to the immigrant experience and sacrifices parents had made to provide better lives for their families. One student explained:

The value of family is part of the culture where Mexicanos or Latinos are very family-oriented, group-oriented. That's the way we are. Coming from such a big family, it's difficult not be group–oriented, and being immigrants from Mexico, we had to maintain a very close-knit family because we were the support for each other. One of the reasons why we immigrated to the U.S. was because of the education that we're allowed here. So, basically, we came because of the education, and my mother, my parents, wanted us to have [an education] and we have succeeded so far.

Through the immigrant experience and collectivist orientation that developed as the family worked to succeed as a unit, the student felt that his role in his family's destiny was to achieve a higher education. Another shared:

My parents and family, my uncles, aunts, everyone, ever since I can remember, they've stressed education, education. I think all my life, [all] I've known is school. It was never a question of will I go to college or not, it was more of a question of what college do I want to go to. I think that for the most part because, like my parents, my friends' parents also came from Mexico and they understand the value of hard work and the value of education. All my friends either they came from Mexico as small children, or they're like myself, first generation here. And, uh, we've just been pushed by our parents that education is everything. That's what makes us all share that goal. . . . The value of an education I mean. The mere fact that my parents didn't even go through what we consider junior high in the U.S. in Mexico, they never achieved higher education, and being the first generation here, I'll be the first in my immediate family to finish college, you know. They've always stressed education. They've put our educations above everything. Anything we might have needed, they've been there for us, whether it be taking us to school, activities. My household is very important. I'm the oldest of three in my family and I'm here in college now. My second brother, he's also in a community college. My younger brother, he's doing extremely well for being in junior high. He got accepted to a science and math academy, which is a pretty good accomplishment. So [education], it's very important in my family.

Here the power of the collective group experience of immigration has provided this student with a web of support for pursuing education that he and his brothers have enjoyed. Extended family, friends, and their families reinforced the message that a college education was expected.

Other students experienced the same support, but it tended to be more general in nature. They also critiqued the kind of support that was available in their own families. One man said:

> The disadvantages for us growing up is that nobody ever gave us the top structure. Nobody gave us any guidance on how to get a proper education. We knew mom wanted us to get a high school diploma, maybe a college degree, and dad said that when we turn eighteen, "You either go to college or you go to work." That was your option.

He felt his parents wanted him to have an education, but that desire was not clearly defined, nor did his parents have the knowledge necessary to guide him to higher education. This experience is common to first-generation college students, who frequently have to pave their own way with little knowledge and guidance. Despite having parents who strongly stressed education, one woman also found their instrumental support to be lacking:

> In our home, even though our parents really, really enforced education, they never did anything in the home to increase it. They never really pushed us intellectually at home. They would only rely on the school. So I think that's, that's a big thing. If they would have pushed us more at home, asking questions . . . it would really have increased precision in our work.

She found that her parents did not provide the intellectual rigor she felt she needed to make her a better student, nor did the environment provide the tools she needed. Likewise, a man who was also a first-generation college student said, "In my home, we didn't really, my parents really couldn't help us with the stuff. So we had to basically learn it on our own, or through someone else." A lack of role models who actually had experienced college and had inside information to help students navigate their way to college made students look elsewhere for that guidance. One said:

> I haven't had any role models in my ethnic group, in my family. I really have to depend on my own, on myself, and what I've learned from other people. My parents have been there for moral support and security, but that's basically it. I haven't been able to learn a lot from them.

Moral support and providing a secure existence are important, but this student needed more. He was able to take what he learned from others, however, and he relied on his own capacity and resources. One woman found this guidance and role modeling in another family that was not Latino:

> My friend's older sister went to college, and I am the first to ever go to college in my family. My dad didn't graduate from high school, [but] my mom did. My grandparents didn't graduate from high school, either. I was the first one to even really pursue an education. I think [that value] happened to come from Mindy's family. They're wealthy. They're well off. They live in a really nice neighborhood and drive nice cars and everything. They've always treated me as part of their family . . . I'd say it had to be from her family 'cause her sisters went to college, so we both wanted to go to college. But I think I got it from her and I brought it over to my family, and now my sister wants to go to college and get an education as well.

This student got the knowledge and motivation for higher education from her friend's family, but she transferred these to her own family when she took home what she learned to help to motivate her sister to be college-bound.

The effect of the "sibling college attendance" was important to students—either in their own college-going or in the college aspirations of their siblings. One student saw his brother make sacrifices for him, which has motivated him to complete his college education:

> When we lived in Tijuana, my brother was about to receive his BA, he was a year from receiving his BA. Knowing that there were many other kids following him, he decided, he along with my parents decided, to immigrate to the United States. So he sacrificed his education for us. So, in return, I feel like I'm doing him justice for his sacrifice of his education.

Sacrifices were not only the purview of parents making the immigration decision, but of siblings as well. Another student explained the benefit she felt her brothers conferred on her: "School has always been important to me, I've always liked it. I guess it has to do with my brothers also, because they've gone on with their lives and are pretty much successful. That motivates me." Like this woman's brothers, students in the study saw themselves as role models, but also as transmitters of college knowledge and catalysts for the college aspirations of their younger siblings—essentially saving them from the difficult experiences of being first-generation college students. The first-generation Latino/a college student in a family plays a key role in the college aspirations of younger siblings (Hurtado-Ortiz & Guavain, 2007). One woman illustrates how she is doing this:

> My sister, now that she's going to high school and everything, she's chosen the route that I've chosen. She's like, "I'd rather be like Susana, I'd rather go to school, be a participant in sports." . . . I still keep in touch with [my teachers] and I go back and see them every so often—and I just say how I'm doing and I just tell them, "Watch my sister, she's going to your school." I watch out for my sister. . . . I feel good 'cause I want my sister to have all the benefits that I had. I think she's excelled a little bit more because, you know, I've helped her out a little bit, eased her into school and helped her to get to know the teachers. Since they know me, although we're two different people, they still see her as an individual, but they remember, "Okay, Susana wants me to help her out." They like her, too, because she wants to excel, too.

Susana is doing what many college-educated parents do: she is becoming actively involved in her "children's" education. What makes this particularly effective is that Susana knows just what her sister will need to get to college and uses her own resources to help her get there. Another student used a different strategy to get her sister to college:

> I'm the oldest and nobody in my family has ever come to college, nobody. . . . Well, my sister really didn't want to go to college. She was like too laid back. She didn't want to go 'cause she's like, "Well it's another two years, gotta take all these general education classes." I just told her, "You know, use your life, what's another two years you know? It's not gonna be a waste, it's gonna be a gain. Once you go to place that on a job application, it's like, wow, you know, at least she has some college, you know. Nobody wants to work for $4.25 a job. I'm telling you nobody wants to work for that." It worked. She's really gotten into it. I also have two younger ones, they're like ten and eight, and they're at the age where they're like, "Gosh, look at what my big sister did, look at what she's doing." They will go places based on what you're doing.

She goes on to express the pride she feels not only in helping her sisters, but also in representing Mexican Americans.

The pride, gosh, the pride I feel is like, you know, I could just yell it everywhere. It's like, "Oh, you know, I'm Mexican American, I'm proud of it,
you know." I'm the first generation of all of them going to college, you
know. Putting examples for younger kids, 'cause, you know, there's a lot
of gangsters, there's a lot of young girls getting pregnant, who don't have
any ideas about what to do. When they see like a Mexican role model or
something, they have some idea. Like, "Gosh, she did it and look where
she came from. I can do it, too!" I tell them, "It's more like an incentive
for doing it, you just wait."

The enthusiasm with which these students acknowledged their responsibility, not only for raising up their families, but also for their own groups gives
credence to the strength of the family and group and the collectivist value
they instilled in their members. They did not wait to have their own children
to pass on the benefits of their college experience, but saw their siblings and
other members of their communities as their protégés in achieving this
important goal.

Family is so central to the Latino/a ethnic experience, in college or out,
that it appears in different ways throughout this chapter. Here we saw the
important place families had in the hearts and identity of nearly all the La-
tinos/as in the study, and how family influenced so many different aspects
of their lives. Whether it was the comfort or support offered by what was
often a wide circle that included extended family members, or the challenges
that being in such a tightly enmeshed group presented to students as they
navigated their way to and through college and young adulthood, it was clear
that family was the ultimate group in the students' lives. They embraced the
teachings of their families and worked to change those parts of the family
and cultural dynamic that did not resonate with the adults they wished to
become. They saw themselves as collaborators in the family journey that, for
many, began in another country, and as contributors to the success of the
family in this country by taking on leadership and modeling roles for
younger family members. They also considered themselves to be transmitters
of family and cultural values that would sustain their own future families.
Without a doubt, family was integral to their ethnic experience.

Ethnic Identity Processes

Students were able to articulate how their ethnic identity changed over the
years and what either challenged that identity or supported it. They could

also see the positive outcomes associated with having a stronger sense of self as a Latina/o (or whatever specific label they used), especially a sense of confidence that enabled them to tackle life's challenges. Although they saw elements in the college environment that helped them to develop ethnic identity and to learn more about their ethnic groups, they also experienced challenges from society (and the university campus) that threatened the positive sense of self they were attempting to achieve. This section of the chapter highlights these elements that are often considered part of the ethnic identity process. We do not present them in terms of a stage-like process (e.g. encounter, immersion, etc.), but, rather, as the students presented them: as contributors and challenges to themselves as ethnic people.

College Influences

Like students from other ethnic groups, Latinos/as also experienced college as providing opportunities for them to explore, learn, and engage in practices that expressed and strengthened their ethnic identity. For some, college provided the freedom to explore that was not present in their high schools or communities of origin.

> Before coming to L.A., and it could also be that I lived in a small town, but you were not exposed to different types of music. I wouldn't listen to Mexican music. I wouldn't, I would try not to talk Spanish because of the fact that my friends wouldn't be familiar with it. But now, here, it's like my friends celebrate it, my friends listen to that music and they speak Spanish. So I guess that I've changed a lot.

This student found an open environment where she could safely share ethnic practices with others. Being in an urban setting enabled her to access more cultural resources. For others, the expectation that, in college students "find themselves," allowed for purposeful exploration, as illustrated by this woman, who sought and found methods for learning more about her culture:

> I started looking around and going, "I'm going to find myself." Some people were just like, you don't know anything about your culture and you need to learn about your culture. . . . So that was a fair question. You know, that's right. I think I need to learn more about who I am ethnically. I knew

who I was in character. That was very easy. But ethnically, I think [laughing] granny's this, and grandpa's that. And that's what I did. I started asking my grandparents a lot of questions, talking a lot more to my family, learning a lot more. And when I started studying some history, I focused on Native American history and found some similarities within those cultures and my own, and how my feelings came out in a lot of these topics. And it was like, these things I understand. And so it sort of defined me that way. And then, as I was looking more into the indigenous side of being Puerto Rican and realized I had a lot in common, historically. And I defined myself. . . . Last year I was doing my history side, and this year I'm doing my art history side. When I was doing that, I was very pleased in finding [that] the Polynesian culture is very much like my own and I'm going to study it. And now people are like, "Oh." I think it helped to make me more confident in myself.

After being challenged by other students to learn more about her culture, this student went on a quest to learn what she could through courses and through her grandparents. Her academic exploration involved more of a comparative study that allowed her to see connections between the experiences of her ethnic group and others. She seemed to gain confidence in herself through the steps she took to meet a challenge and the feelings she had as she learned more about her group. Another student also found that ethnic studies courses were important in the development of her ethnic identity, though she studied her own group rather than make comparisons to others.

In high school you have your GATE (Gifted and Talented Education) students in every class and they take different courses. So it was mainly White students. So being Mexican-American, I didn't, I didn't want to, I wouldn't say that I was Mexican-American. I would just say that I was American, and when I got here it changed a lot. I became more familiar with my identity. I was taking Chicano Studies courses and the Mexican-American experience. I became like, more in tune with my identity. And I feel that now, it means a lot to me and my family. I feel my family, both my parents' being Mexican, and I mean kind of like being very, like, culturally aware, they are always telling us, you know, about our culture and stuff. I think that now it is starting to be significant in my life. And I want to pass it on to my kids.

In her predominantly White courses, she did not feel she could acknowledge that she was different from her peers. In college, she had the opportunity to embrace her ethnicity more fully and actually develop it more fully by taking courses, ultimately making ethnicity and her family more meaningful.

This social comparison was a method other Latinos/as used as they learned more about their ethnicity and its importance to them. Two students were motivated to learn and explore by observing their peers from other ethnic groups:

> Actually, because most of my [non-Latino friends] know more about their cultural background and traditions, it's made me go and ask questions about my cultural background. 'Cause they are always sharing with me, and I'm really a little ignorant, I've never really been taught. So, I have to go to the library and check it out, or ask aunts and uncles, or mom and dad, and then I can share information too. So it's helped me, because when I was hanging around high school with just my own culture, we never asked these questions, curiosity was never there. By them asking me these questions, I go and I ask and I find out and then they find out. So we share information, so it's made me grow.

For this student the social comparison was important because in her monoethnic experience, she and her friends did not have the opportunity to compare and contrast. They may have just assumed that they all knew where traditions and practices originated, taking meaning and history for granted. For another student, the social comparison with her friend allowed her to value elements of her culture more.

> I could see what her culture was, and, I guess, kinda compare 'em and see mine and appreciate mine more, because I really didn't see too much in hers. Maybe it was just from the way she practices her ethnicity or whatnot, not like in general . . . . To me there's so many things from a family function, religion, family. With her, she didn't have really a lot of family, it was mostly her and her mother. . . . From my viewpoint, I thought mine has more, more togetherness.

The social comparison allowed this student to see that things that were a "normal" part of her life were, indeed, cultural in nature. She was able to learn more about what she had by learning what her friend did not have, almost the opposite of the White students who learned about what they did not have, culturally, by observing the cultural traditions and experiences of others. Another student had a similar experience, but this one was due to the general diversity of the campus:

> I guess school has made me a difference also. Just, just being exposed to different cultures, I guess, different people, different ideas. Then, that again, also has allowed me to just feel different. It's allowed me to feel Mexican and identify myself as Mexican.

Related to this social comparison was the motivation Latinos/as provided each other to learn more about their own culture. When the woman below was asked to pick one experience where pride in her ethnicity was solidified, she said:

> Think with my roommate. I think that living my with my roommate, a Mexican-American, especially in my first year here, was important. She was very active. Umm . . . she was very aware of her culture. And when I got here they would laugh at me because of the fact that I wasn't sure I was being teased and they listened to different music. I didn't know about the music. They read different authors, I didn't know about. . . . Because of that, I changed a lot. 'Cause I did live in this one suite for like two months and I had White roommates. And I know that if I would have stayed with them, I probably would not have changed. I would not have emerged, like I did when I lived with my roommates which were all, you know Mexican Americans.

Having those Mexican American roommates was pivotal for this student. They acted as models for her and educators about her own culture. She was fortunate that, instead of being judged by them, she was embraced, and, ultimately, they served as catalysts for her change. While peers were not always as kind as some students experienced, their impact was generally positive, even for the woman below, who earlier talked about peers' challenging her to learn more about her culture. Here she discusses what it has been like for her to be Puerto Rican on a campus where the dominant Latino/a population is Mexican in origin.

> I get called "whitewashed" and get dirty looks. Even on this campus, I'm shunned. I'm a [special program] student and I'm not accepted by what I see as the traditional Latin [special program] students. . . . So, oftentimes I find myself having to explain myself. And that's sometimes positive

because I can explain to people. But when people don't know something, they automatically will give an attribute. . . . I think if I go to New York, it would be different. But here, nobody really understands and it's negative. It kind of makes sense because I'll say I'm Puerto Rican and a lot of people associate it with Latin American, and I say don't do that because it's not. And like I said, I always feel like I can say I'm Latin American because of my father's side of the family is, but I would never call my mom's grandmother side of the family Latin American. . . . I used to think, what used to be my idea is that Puerto Rico is Mexican. As I've gotten older, I've realized that I'm not Mexican really, all that much. But that's where I used to associate being Puerto Rican, under the Mexican thing. I used to say, "Oh my dad's Mexican." That became really negative for me, so I started to say I was Puerto Rican.

Although this is largely a negative experience, as it would be anytime a student is called "whitewashed," these experiences of peers' questioning and challenging ethnicity has caused this student to clarify her ethnic identity. Through having been questioned and asked to explain her ethnicity, she had come to a more precise definition of what it meant to be Puerto Rican and how important that distinction was to her.

Additional students reported age-related changes, but did not necessarily cite the college influence specifically in those changes. Students noted how long it took to develop an ethnic identity, how much change they saw in themselves over time, and how much of this evolution was a learning process. For instance, one man said, "It's a learning process that when you know your ethnic background you get to know it little by little as you grow older, by your parents [and] by your grandparents." The student below concurred, but offered a more specific time frame for herself.

I'd like to say that it took a long time to even create an ethnic identity for myself. It's like, everything I've told you has only developed within the last couple of years and it's my fourth year now. The last couple of years, I've determined where I stand.

For this student, this change happened during college, which could have indeed contributed to the change. The man below also has experienced change, which not only was limited to his sense of identity, but also altered his ethnic practices.

> I guess, for example, my culture, you know, I try to learn as much as I can. Before I didn't really know that much about it, you know, while I was growing up. In my early teen years I never really did anything with my family, [but] I would always do something with friends. So now is when I'm trying to find out about my culture and improve my Spanish.

It almost seems as if the student had a plan that he followed to enhance his ethnicity. Embracing the language, a critical ethnic practice and marker of ethnicity, was also noted in the following student's observations about what she has seen in others.

> I don't know what happened, but as people grow older, they become more proud of what they are. If you were Mexican, you were proud. When I was younger it wasn't that way. If you knew Spanish, you didn't really speak it unless you were with your friends that spoke Spanish. I knew people who pretended they didn't know Spanish, but they did. It really got to me. I was like, what's wrong with it? There is nothing wrong with it. When I got older, I thought, this is great. You know two languages and you can communicate better with people. It is easier, I don't know why people used to hide it, but I noticed that something happened. People became proud that they were Mexican and there was no more of this "I'm from here and I don't know any Spanish." People want to know more about their ethnicity.

College was a significant location for many students to develop their ethnic identity, as was the time frame of late adolescence or young adulthood. Students' commentaries are consistent with the vast amount of literature delineating this time in life as important to the development or solidification of ethnic identity (see Phinney, 2006).

Role of Language Competence in Ethnic Identity

As was the case for Asian Americans regarding their ability to speak their specific language, knowing and speaking Spanish was often a marker for others' judgment of students' ethnicity. Since 85% of the Latino/a students in the study spoke fluent Spanish, the three students who did not speak Spanish at all discussed the difficulty they experienced with acknowledging that, indeed, they did not.

I didn't feel as though I was really a part of Latin American culture because a lot of people somehow had rejected me because I couldn't speak the language. . . . A lot of people would approach me and, just like I explained earlier how they would say to me, "You're Mexican American and you don't speak Spanish?" And the environment that I live in, in my high school, about eighty-five percent of it was Mexican American. So you can understand kind of what I was feeling and what I was going through, although I really wanted to be a part of that. I considered myself a part of that, but they looked at me as if, "Well, you don't speak our language. Then how could you consider yourself that way?" and that I was more Americanized. In some ways my Caucasian friends made me feel comfortable with that, but yet I was still not part of them or like them. So it was, I was kind of like in the middle.

This middle space was an uncomfortable space, not fully a part of her Caucasian friends who appeared to accept her, but also not a part of the predominant group on her high school campus. The interviewer asked whether she felt rejected by her Latino/a peers in high school, and she acknowledged that she did. When asked if she felt people were making judgments of her when she said she could not speak Spanish, she admitted that she felt they were. However, she did go on to say:

Yet I feel very proud about being a Mexican American woman, and this is something you feel positive about. And now that I've gotten older, I'm dealing with a lot of that, a lot of those issues. Like when people [are] constantly coming up to me, speaking to me in Spanish, and that seems to be a major problem, although I feel it's very important, and I do, I'm working hard to pick it up. It is a big problem, and it's frustrating sometimes, because I am Latin American, or Mexican American, and yet I don't speak the language. It's somewhat embarrassing, and a lot of people are like, "You're Mexican American and you don't speak Spanish?" I think it's important that we, we have a role model of someone that represents us, represents where we come from, someone that we can look up to and say, "If they can do it, we can do it." And it's important that we have somebody that represents us, come[s] from where we come from, speak[s] the same language. I don't think there's enough of, enough of Mexican American, Latin American people that are like that.

Despite being proud of being Mexican American, she continued to deal with her inability to speak the language. She also discussed how important it was to have role models that represent "us." We sensed that she would like to be one of those role models, but, again, she felt limited because she considered the language to be such an integral part of being Mexican.

A second student had similar experiences with a lack of language and the challenge she received from peers. When the interviewer asked her why she was not in a Latino/a-based student organization, she replied:

> Well, I guess since I don't know Spanish very well, I'm kind of ashamed of that. But I feel like when I try to speak Spanish with people who know it and stuff, who are Mexican, I get uncomfortable. I jump over the grammar, so because I'm so concerned with that, and I feel like they're judging me or something, like oh, my God, they probably think I'm a lousy excuse for a Mexican, or something. Also, just on this campus, those people tend to be kind of radical and stuff like that and I'm not really into the whole "Go people!" or something. I mean, of course, I'm for everybody to have equal rights, not just the Mexican people.

She was a bit more expressive about her feelings that she was a "lousy excuse for a Mexican" and she felt a sense of shame about the fact that she did not have the language. The last of the students, who was not fluent in Spanish, shared the experience:

> Like one of my best friends says, "You're not really Puerto Rican because you don't speak Spanish." It's just a joke. Sometimes she says it and it gets kind of personal, but it's never like I feel like I'm not accepted as being Puerto Rican.

Although she knew her friend was joking, it at times felt more personal, but she has been able to maintain a sense of acceptance by her group. The differences here may be slight, but the experiences of these three women point to the significant role speaking Spanish plays in students' construction of their ethnic identity, especially when the skill is not well developed.

Racism and Negative Images of the Group Impact Identity

As Latino/a students entered young adulthood, they became increasingly more cognizant of negative societal views of their ethnic group and recognized that they lived in a racially stratified society where certain groups— namely Latinos/as—were disparaged and viewed unfavorably. These findings are consistent with Niemann's (2001), who reports that negative stereotypes of Latinos/as still abound in the United States and there is a potential stigma of these images for young Latinos/as. Students spoke pointedly and passionately to how derogatory portrayals of the ethnic group through the media reinforce and perpetuate the low status of Latinos/as in American society as violent, uneducated, and in the country illegally. Students did not report that these portrayals launched them into cycles of self-hate, but they did challenge their positive group self-esteem. Quite a number of students commented on media portrayal of the group:

> You'll have other ethnic groups looking down on others because of a stereotype of a culture. I can give you a perfect example: a lot of Anglos believe that Latinos are stupid and they're gangbangers. Why? Because the news only portrays those gangbangers who drop out of school and are in trouble. So that's the image that they think that most Latinos are, they don't promote the educated ones.

> Um, well, I guess when some people have views of Mexicans, they always have the derogatory things. And I'm like, well that's not the way all Mexicans are . . . I just don't like the films, too, or the way TV shows portray Mexicans. I don't like that very much either because they always, like, make it like all we do is speak Spanish. Many people living in one house and all we want to do is be destructive. That's all negative, and I don't like that.

These negative images, though not directed at students, caused them to analyze critically how Latinos/as are portrayed and also caused them a certain amount of stress. Other students experienced more direct affronts:

> I hear a lot of comments like, "Oh, a bunch of wetbacks. We have enough," or whatever, and that makes me feel uncomfortable. I guess the situation right now, the political and social situation right now, is the biggest negative thing that I see.

> We feel that we can be discriminated against, and that we can be intimidated by a lot of factors at work and in school. It can be a professor, or at work, it can be a boss or another employee. They might tell you something in a loud voice or something, you might just get intimidated, or you might feel offended.

> People think that, you know, I only speak Spanish and I can't compre-
> hend. Some people tell me I look Hispanic so they confront me. They
> confront me in Spanish. And I'm all, "No, I speak English you know, you
> can talk to me in English." The [stereotype] that Mexican people are
> dumb, I think it's negative.

With these kinds of incidents, students' only choice is to respond, either to
the offending person or to themselves, through comforting themselves or
through reconstructing the experience. The notion that a person must always
be ready to battle an onslaught of racial slurs takes up valuable mental and
psychological energy that could likely be used in far more productive ways.
Additionally, as Araujo and Borrell (2006) discuss, continuously needing to
protect one's sense of self from these negative images interferes with what
normally might be a positive process of self-development.

Growth in Confidence

Models of ethnic identity development almost uniformly end with a stage of
integration, where ethnicity is incorporated into an overall identity and helps
the individual to live a psychologically healthy, productive life where conflict
around ethnicity has ceased. Although we do not pretend to report that students in the study achieved that pinnacle of identity, many did report knowing who they were as ethnic people, as Latinos/as, had provided them with
a sense of confidence that enabled them to do a variety of things. For example, the student below felt that her desire for intercultural learning stemmed
from the confidence she felt in herself as an ethnic person.

> I would say that ethnic identity helps me by kind of like knowing who I
> am. I have a confidence, I'm not really like, like a real quiet person who
> just lets things go by, especially when it comes to other cultures. I like to
> experience other cultures and be friends with people from those cultures.
> Therefore, I have to feel very confident about myself.

Another student connected knowing and accepting ethnic identity as important to the development of self-efficacy and associated that with a comfort
with self that allowed for experiencing a variety of environments in ways
consistent with his identity.

> Once you understand who you are and accept who you are and have self-
> efficacy, then I believe you're able to live with yourself wherever you're at,

because if there's some discrepancy with who you are, where you live, or where you're at, then that creates friction not only with you but with your environment. . . . I think the most important thing is, first of all, understanding who you are, whether it's your culture, your traditions, or your language, and accepting who you are regardless if you don't have much of this but as long as you understand it.

He also implies that individuals may have varying levels of ethnic identity or practices and that it is important to achieve self-acceptance in that regard. Finally, a young woman offers perhaps the best of all outcomes associated with a positive identity when she says, "I know who I am and where I come from, where my family comes from, what our values and morals are. It makes you ready for the world, I guess." These findings are in line with earlier research that links a positive and coherent ethnic identity to better functioning in persons across a range of psychological domains (see Phinney, Cantu, & Kurtz, 1997; Roberts et al., 1999; Walsh & McGrath, 2000).

Emerging Political Awareness and Consciousness

The White man is still the government, and until we have different faces in the government, then it'll be unequal, but right now they have more power than us. The White man and Asians I would say would be taking over jobs from Hispanics and Blacks 'cause that's the way they're looked upon.

More than two-thirds of the Latinos/as said they were beginning to develop political awareness and an accompanying political consciousness that was collectivist in nature and prompted them to see their actions and plans as benefiting their group. When students acknowledged the low status of Latinos/as in American society and analyzed why that was the case, they noted the importance of rectifying ethnic inequalities through engagement in social change as a means of reversing a low-status social identity. Students referred to the importance of increasing the representation of Latinos/as in positions of leadership and power, so that changes to better the group would be enacted. There was the perception that Latino/a leaders were needed to pave the way for younger generations, and some of these students saw themselves assuming this role.

Understanding the Need to Represent

It was quite obvious to students that it was important for Latinos/as to have better and more representation in the media and in the various power structures in society, whether in government or in the business world.

> We want to show that being Mexicans we can also excel. We are not going to be in the lower position jobs. We need to see more Latinos, Mexicans being out there in the workforce that are in higher [positions]. There are some, but I feel we need more in higher places so that they could help not only Mexicans but other minority groups [as well]. I think this has motivated me because I think, if I could do this, then maybe my sisters and other people would do it as well.

This woman sees the need for representation at higher levels of society. The lack of representation helps to motivate her, and she sees herself as someone who can contribute to the betterment of the group and serve as a role model to others. Several students then talked about their responsibility to improve representation and constructed this as an opportunity to act and get involved.

> We're still not as [well] represented as we could be, and we're lacking, I guess, representation. But again, from my point of view it turns into an advantage in that there's room to grow. There's a lot of possibilities for me to go out there and do something about that.

Students had heard the message that the workplace and society in general were seeking greater inclusion of Latinos/as. One student mentioned that Latinos/as who made it through college to graduation were valued,

> I would say, by society in general. Just because there are so few out in professional fields that we have become valuable. I guess, in the sense that if [we] wanted to go into professions, they would really look highly upon us [because we] have the credentials.

Another felt that society in general was looking for more diversity and that Latinos/as would be well positioned to offer that diversity.

> Well, there are a lot of opportunities for Latin Americans here. I think being that we are minorities, as far as education, there are lot more opportunities for us. . . . People are looking for more, they want more diversity.

The notion that students would be valued in workplaces that wanted to enhance diversity helped students to see that their individual choices ultimately would improve the status of the group. Their education would enable them to make inroads into areas that seriously lack the skills, talents, and knowledge they would contribute to those environments.

Individual and Group Upward Mobility

Like African Americans, Latinos/as also felt that hardships the group and individuals encountered helped to motivate them to succeed so they could contribute to the improvement of themselves and the larger group. For example, one student explained how the perception of discrimination, actual or not, served as motivation for group improvement:

> I think that sometimes, when you go into a company, they look at your last name, they look at the color of your skin, and, sometimes, there have been times where you can be rejected because of where you come from. I know a few people that have been. I can say that I have been, I mean there's no proof of it, but I can say that might have entered into their mind as the reason. I think everybody wants to work towards improving and bringing up their own kind, as well as others.

Discrimination was seen as a motivator, though an unfortunate one. Students wanted to prove they could succeed and even found that success in the face of discrimination was a noble event.

> We do keep getting discriminated [against], so that's a disadvantage. I mean, I don't use it as a crutch or an excuse. I never use it as an excuse. You can never say, "Oh, so and so, that's what happened to me." I like to believe you didn't get the job because you weren't qualified. So, if anything, it just makes you work harder to prove yourself.

Another student talked about the importance of early messages and gave an example of how she saw the status of the group improving.

> My motivation is that, when I was young, if I had someone tell me that "You can't make it," it would make me want to make it! Well, I do feel I can make it, but there are some people who feel they don't want me here, so what's the point? They go through thinking that they are not wanted in society and they don't do anything to improve themselves. I think we are

making some improvement this year. For instance, they are starting to make more movies with Hispanic directors, and I think there is a lot of pride in that because you see these people trying to get into positions where we can be noticed. Before you never saw Latinos/as. But now, we have these movies that are coming out dealing with Hispanics. So more Hispanics are entering the [film industry] and that is positive.

She considers that the better representation of Latinos/as in film will help to contribute to children's having more positive images to counter negative messages they receive from others. The notion of pride in overcoming obstacles, a common theme among several of the groups in the study, did help students to keep their goals in focus, as the students expressed below.

Just knowing what Mexicans are and how much they've come through all along, [all that] they've been through. Knowing that, I can achieve whatever I want to achieve.

I think that because of the fact that I am Mexican-American, and I know that I am going to have to try a little bit harder. I'm very motivated. I am very determined to do what I am going to do. And I also see my friends struggle, you know? That adds to my determination that I need to really do what I set out to do.

Education was seen as a vehicle to improve the status of Latinos/as. The low representation of Latinos/as in college was a concern for students, even as they saw their own presence in higher education as motivating other Latinos/as, as noted by the following student.

I've had experiences such as being here in school, being the only one in my family to go to school. I can look back, not just in my family, but also Mexicans, my Mexican background, [and] I can see that a lot of them go on, but in very low numbers. That's another thing that keeps me going, just knowing that I can, that we can do it. Mexicans can do it.

One of the women called on the group to emphasize education more than it had in the past as a way to improve the status of the group more permanently.

I think that we need to project, as a Latin culture, we need to project focusing on education and thinking about the future so that later on in life we can give something [back]. We can [give] something to our kids, and our kids can give something to their kids.

Education makes it possible for Latinos/as to access influence, as outlined by this student.

Education, the advantage is that you're able to acquire positions of influence. You're able to provide assistance to your community [and other groups], whether it be minorities or low-income people. So the education is a plus, along with the language.

The stories of struggle prompted one man to consider how other groups are treated and include them in a more collective commitment to guide his own behavior:

I've talked a lot to the elderly that are Mexican and they all have stories of how hard their lives have been, and it gives me the sense that those things were because of some type of discrimination. So I guess that's why that influences a lot in me not to be like that, not only with my own group but with everybody else as well. Because I'm sure there are other people that are elderly from other ethnicities and they have similar stories.

The collectivist nature of considering groups as partners in a common struggle was expressed by others as they considered career choices they planned to make.

Most people want to feel as though they've made their life here worth living, or they've contributed something. With the kind of support, the career opportunity that I want, I want a job where I can say that I've contributed something. And I'd like to go back and contribute something to my own kind of people, as well as others who are worthy and deserve it. . . . I have a background working with Mexican Americans and in speaking the language and knowing about it, so that I can work towards bringing my own kind up.

[It's important] to have an education. You need an education so that you can better yourself, better yourself so that you can help other people that need it. I want to be a child psychologist. I think this is very important because children need to be placed at a young age so that they don't grow up to be a bad example.

Both students see their work as benefiting the group and others whom they encounter. While it is quite common for college students to have goals like these, to contribute to the lives of others, for these students there was also a politicized element that involved bringing up their own group. Students saw education as the primary vehicle for social mobility.

Becoming Societal Critics

As a result of a number of factors, courses taken, proposed legislation, and current events, students recognized discrimination and racism at a societal level. Their raised consciousness allowed them to analyze everyday occurrences and current events critically with new knowledge and vigor.

Structured activities such as courses and organizations were often places where students gained the information they needed to begin questioning the status quo. Students began to consider a political consciousness, as was the case for a man who took a class studying the Chicano movement. He thought, "Well, I don't want to be involved in a radical group, but now I'm just not really sure." At first he rejected the radicalism he saw in the readings and the movies shown in class, but in the end he thought that he might actually consider joining such a movement or group. A woman found that participation in a high school *Movimiento Estudiantil Chicano de Aztlán* (MEChA), told her "stuff we didn't know. . . . I wanted to know more, but I just didn't know which way to go and learn more." In both of these cases, students learned enough to pique their interest in more knowledge. An example of the connection between what was learned in class and then enacted in students' lives is offered by a woman who took the public bus to school each day.

> I feel that a lot [of people] are faced with racism and discrimination, in a general sense. . . . I see the people in the bus and I think that, to me, that is discrimination because they aren't given assistance in any way . . . I've taken a class that compares the transportation system, the way in which, umm . . . the Amtrak [train system] is subsidized by, I don't know, like [more] dollars per passenger. And you know, like the MTA [bus system] subsidizes like, I don't know how many [exactly], like forty cents or something. [Now] the rates were going to go up, and I think that I am going to be affected by that. I'm faced with that. I feel like that something [needs to] happen to the structure and the way that it is run or we're always going to be affected by that.

The class she took taught her to analyze how transportation funding benefits socioeconomic groups differently, giving the most money to the trains that service the suburbs. This knowledge subsequently affected her behavior, as seen in the continuation of her story:

> Specifically, I remember this lady once, this White lady. She looked like she was, I don't know, she looked not like a working-class woman. She was White, forty, late forties, middle-aged. I was sitting in the front of the bus when she got there. That day I had my backpack with like tons of books and I didn't want to stand up in the bus; it was pretty crowded. So I wasn't going to give her my seat because I thought she wasn't old enough [for me] to do that. She wanted me to move and I just looked at her, and I did not want to move. First of all, it was her tone of voice and then she said, "You're just a Mexican, a wetback." . . . So what I did, at the next stop, these other ladies, Mexicans, like working-class women, came in. So I got up and I let one of them sit. Oh, she got so mad! She just got so mad! She started cussing at me and saying I should go back to my country and this and that. That affected me for a while. It bothered me, I mean, I guess [I was] not hurt by her comments, but I [have] never actually been faced with that.

The incident accelerated this student's reaction, and the consciousness-raising experience of learning about transportation funding helped her to have a more layered construction of the incident that prompted her to give up her seat selectively, making that act a political one.

Multiple external sociohistorical and political forces paved the way for Latino/a students to gain greater political consciousness and develop a politicized ethnic identity. As a result of these forces, Latino/a students considered discrimination and racism and how groups' accorded minority status played a role in their ascribed social identity as ethnic/racial people living in an unequal society. One Latina student in particular reflected on how moving to Los Angeles had contributed to her expanding views of race/ethnicity and to question what role she would play in improving the status of her group.

> There are a lot of current events that have influenced me. Affirmative Action and Proposition 187, and also just being in L.A., where the majority of people that live here, who are Latinos are working class. It has really been an experience. I see the problems out in the streets when I go to places

like East L.A. That has motivated me to get an education and get a sense of my identity and say, "I need to do something about this."

Affirmative action and immigrant rights were clearly two highly charged and controversial political issues at the forefront of the national agenda at the time of the study. Because such policies affected students and their families and communities, students questioned the legitimacy of the status hierarchy. They interpreted race-based initiatives being enacted as formidable barriers to the advancement of the ethnic group. There was the perception among students that their group was being targeted unfairly for discrimination.

> Affirmative action, they want to take it out. But why? That [would] just give minority students less of a chance to get a good job, a good education. They (Whites) have opportunities, more so than we do. You don't see Blacks or Mexicans [living] in Pacific Beach or Malibu. It's all White.

> What's happening right now with the immigration, immigrants' rights now [is a big disadvantage]. I think it's harder for them to get jobs because they don't have an education. Politically we are still a minority. I think it is a disadvantage because that's what overcomes everything, is the political system, so minorities are minorities.

> If you are Mexican American they are like, "Oh, you got here on affirmative action." Not knowing that, you know, I think that I did pretty good, you know? Maybe I did get here on affirmative action, but I did try hard in high school to do well, and that is what I think is another negative factor. That kind of makes me feel like, makes you doubt yourself. Maybe I don't deserve to be here.

Another student offered a similar perspective: "Proposition 187 is an indirect form of discrimination, I believe. It's brought the Mexican American community [together and made it] a lot stronger. [It has] made me more motivated to try to succeed [in my education] and help the community." Yet, the following Latina student spoke deliberately of the negative impact of Proposition 187 on her immigrant peers on campus, which politicized her ethnic identity further.

> Proposition 187, the [law that abolished financial aid to nonresident immigrants] and that new one that just got out that is charging the [undocumented] students here, people that are from Mexico, or further, from El

Salvador, South America. They're charging them an enormous amount of money to come here, like four thousand dollars, and some of them are dropping out [from college] and that's sad. Even though this doesn't affect me because I was born here, but I still feel for the plight of other people, you know. People here on campus that you know that were not born here, you can sympathize with them.

Political consciousness and ethnic awareness paved the way for expression of collective activism in some college students, which has been associated with greater ethnic pride and esteem (Kuo & Roysircar-Sodowsky, 1999).

I am proud of being Mexican. . . . I have participated in marches and protests to support the Mexican community. I have been involved. Just the other day my girlfriend and I went to a rally and marched. It's not right. It's not right because it's not just going to affect Mexicans, but it's going to affect all other races.

The call to action was precipitated by external events and students' raised awareness. They said that, working together, the group could fight political currents that threatened its future. The need to unite was expressed clearly as the way to accomplish these goals:

I just feel like more of the Mexicans, *La Raza*, should be more united. Rather, we see the ones that are successful and not coming back, [helping those] that are trying to go up the ladder. With the ones that are going up the ladder, we see too many that are at the bottom trying to pull [down] those that trying to go to the top. So there should be more of a unity. We should be more like other ethnicities, like the Japanese, Chinese, they work as a group and they push each other, I see a lot of that. But in the Mexican American [people], you don't see that. I think we should work more as a group than as individuals.

As students became critics of the social order, that critique turned inward as well, exploring the dynamic of members of the group pulling other members down, or that successful members who do succeed neglect to reach back to help others. Students' emerging political consciousness tended to be fragile, in that it was easy for them to become discouraged by the gravity of the changes that needed to be made or by their experiences with coethnics who may not have met students' expectations. This is summarized well by this student's foray into the political arena. He became disillusioned with the political process after interning with a prominent Latina political official.

> I used to think that if I go into politics I can help the Latino community. And I got to do an internship locally, and I got to do it at the state capitol. I went through there, and you get sucked into the game, and it's a whole different society. You don't even know who voted you in, you just show up. So that changed my philosophy. There are a lot of Latinos, don't take me wrong, who want to make a difference. But I know that none of them will ever be able to make a difference. They might make a little niche into the system, but they'll get discouraged and disillusioned, and they'll go on to a different thing in life. [It's good to get] a lot of that disillusion and discouragement at a very young age, I'm glad I wasn't forty-five or fifty and found out that what I was doing wasn't worthwhile.

Although he was happy to have realized early in life how difficult societal change is and how easy it is to fall into political traps, this young person who was so eager to get involved has found that it is not worth spending his life working to make change happen. The students who were represented in this section were all at different points on a continuum of developing political awareness and political consciousness. It is important to remember that higher education can act as a starting point for this process, but it is one that should be guided carefully and should support students as they encounter tests of this nascent component of their ethnic identity.

Acculturation: Becoming Americanized

Half of the Latino/a students reported taking elements of other cultures and integrating them into their own. This acculturation process involved participating in activities associated with other groups, losing language, transforming traditional cultural values, and, in the end, creating a hybridized culture that students found to be satisfying and beneficial. A woman who viewed the activities she enjoyed such as playing volleyball and going to the beach as American and who watched "American" shows and movies said,

> I would say that if I watch a Spanish show once a week, then that would be a miracle. But like I said earlier, I do listen to Spanish music at least

once a day. I would say I have picked up on other habits. . . . People that
I think that matter that are in my culture I still communicate with. The
people who have the tendency to call me a sellout, or a coconut, or white-
wash, I don't pay too much attention to them. The reason I say that is that
I feel I know who I am. I'm comfortable and I don't feel insecure, and I
don't have to sit there and justify the way I am.

She understood that cultural practices were changing for her, but was adamant that she should not have to defend or justify herself to those who might
criticize her. Furthermore, there was a sense among students that ethnic loyalty was expected, and failing to embrace it would be seen as negative.
Another student said:

> [Other Latinos/as] tend to stay within their culture. They feel that if they
> get out, if they get involved with another culture or another tradition, that
> they're gonna, I guess, betray their ethnic group.

Retaining and participating in Latino/a cultural traditions was important to
Latino/a students' sense of ethnic loyalty. Other than speaking Spanish, only
a few students talked about having incorporated cultural practices of other
ethnic groups. Students had so many Latino/a-oriented practices that they
engaged in regularly, as seen at the start of this chapter, that when they were
asked about actual practices they learned from other groups, they could offer
few examples. Transformation in the self, as a result of acculturative experiences, tended to center on language and the acquisition of new cultural values that embraced the best of multiple worlds.

Changes in Language

Some students felt that the loss of their own language, or blending it with
English, was a sign of changing culture. Although students here did not feel
that it interfered with their ethnic identity, as did those presented earlier in
the chapter, they did note the change:

> For me to be sent back to Dominican Republic now, I would be lost. I
> would be completely lost. I speak Spanish fluently, but they'd probably
> think it was a little funny. I mean, I've got Dominican slurs, and Mexican
> slurs, and Guatemalan slurs, and Salvadoran slurs, all coming out of my
> voice, out of my mouth. I have my Central American friends saying that I
> have a Dominican accent, and I have my Dominican family telling me that

> I have a Mexican accent, and my family from New York saying I have an accent from California. I would be so lost . . . I am, for the most part, not totally, but quite a bit Spanish illiterate. I can read. Ask me to write you a paragraph, and unless you want to put the accents in there by yourself, unless you want to figure out what I'm writing, and put in the accents yourself, you're not going to understand it. . . . I do not understand where accents go, so I would have a really hard time living there.

Blending so many linguistic differences that came from exposure of Spanish spoken by friends from different Latin American and Caribbean countries created a unique linguistic cultural expression for this woman, but failed to result in a barrier to her feelings of belonging and acceptance. Other students felt their language was changing, primarily because their peers did not speak Spanish, as a woman explains:

> So a lot of my friends haven't really been Mexican, like full-on speaking the language all the time. Like my other Mexican friends also grew up in the same neighborhood that I did. They don't really speak too much Spanish either. They know it, but it's not like they know it very well.

She and her friends shared a process of acculturation in which the language wanes, but no one criticized them because of it. Another student who only knew limited Spanish phrases and who did feel devalued by other "Mexican girls" was planning to raise her own family differently; she said:

> I guess when I have children down the line I plan to teach them to make the food as well. And I, um, I can't really speak to them in Spanish but maybe, you know, [I could] teach them. They'll probably still learn words or phrases. I think it's to their advantage to learn two languages, to keep their [Latino/a] culture. I think that's good. I mean if it's really important to you, then I think you should hold to it.

She is actually planning a reverse acculturation experience with her own family, by teaching them more of the culture than she acquired. Language, because it is such a marker of ethnicity for Latinos/as, was a charged issue for students and caused them considerable angst as language and other parts of their ethnicity were being transformed.

Changing Cultural Values

Students were able to identify several cultural values that were changing as a result of their becoming more "Americanized." In nearly all cases, students regarded these changes as positive, especially as many of them had to do with becoming more assertive within the family and changing gender roles and elements of the parent-child relationship. When one student said he thought more like an American than a Mexican, he explained, "Personally, I think I would rather be more independent." Perhaps this student thought that, in thinking more independently, rather than considering the collective, others in his family, and group, he was exhibiting more "American" traits.

Changes in the family and in parent-child relationships were common ways in which students saw their culture changing; one student explained:

> Actually, any person that was born here in the United States, they act different from your traditional Hispanic family, and [my parents] are always saying things like I'm not respectful. I do whatever I want, just different things like that. I guess they see I'm changing.

Respect within the family is valued highly, and deviations from this behavior were often key indicators that students were moving away from their families. Another student offered:

> None of my friends call their parents, and if I call my parents to tell them, "Hey, I'm not gonna come in," my friends will think, "Hey, what a wuss." I don't know; I guess because of that, now I don't think of it twice. I don't come home, I don't call, and they don't really say much any more because they got used to it, I guess.

Peer pressure to disobey parents was strong for this man, so much so that it caused him to change what had been a polite, respectful attitude toward his parents. There was the sense that his behavior disappointed his parents, but they had no choice but to learn to accept it. On the other hand, the sense of independence that becoming "American" afforded Latinos/as was welcomed in that this independence also offered opportunities that were nonexistent in Mexico. A woman explains:

> I think I get benefits from both cultures. I get a little bit from Mexico and a little bit from here and I bring them together. That's the benefit from

having two different cultures in my family. . . . If you live here you get more independence. In Mexico, you're not really allowed to be independent unless you're a man, and here in the U.S. women have more chances to become you know, get a higher education. If they want to not get married, do whatever they want. And I get that from both worlds, like I tell my dad. My dad comes down and tells me, umm, "Now, I don't think you should be in school, you know, because you should be married by now." I'm all like, "Dad, I don't live in Mexico. I live here." And you know we gotta move with the times here. So far, I think it's been helpful in my life.

The independence she feels in the United States has allowed this student to consider accomplishments such as higher education, options that were not readily available in Mexico. When another woman was explaining why she did not consider herself "truly Mexican," she also mentioned changing gender roles: "When you're at home you have to serve the men, or it can be my father, I have to serve him. I know from what I've learned here, now, it doesn't have to be that way, you see?" Women also considered actions they took, such as moving away from home before marriage, as indicative of changing gender roles and, ultimately, the culture:

My mom says that I'm different from everybody else. She says that I'm too independent, that she doesn't know why I'm not like my sisters. It always comes back to this moving away thing. It's like, "Oh, your sister would have never thought of this when she was your age"; you know, things like that. I like to go out and my sister doesn't. She's like, "Oh, why can't you be like your sister? Your sister doesn't want to go here and there like you do." But I don't see coming to school as something I have to do to please my parents and my family; I just want to do [that] for me. It's something that I'm doing for myself.

Although compared to her sister and despite pressure from her mother to conform to family expectations, this student was able to express her unique personality and hold firm to her goals. This liberation from traditional gender roles in the home was echoed when a different woman spoke of the liberalized values she was gaining when she was asked what made her Mexican and what made her American. She said:

Okay, [I have a] sense of [being] American, you know. I was born here. I was raised with the traditions, roles, and everything. I go, you know, mostly with their [American] ideas of going to college, but not the free liberalism and free sex in the world.

She appreciated taking on the American value of college, but stopped short of assuming the "free liberalism" she saw in her American peers. Given how strongly women felt the gendered roles in their families were enacted, as discussed earlier, it is not surprising that liberalizing these roles is something they strongly valued.

Students also determined that, to be Latino/a, especially Mexican, limited their ability to be independent and encouraged soft-spokenness and a level of compliance with authorities they felt was changing as a result of living in the United States. One student explained:

> I think that it's important to be an assertive person. It's important to be open-minded and, what is the other word I'd use, outspoken. I mean, I can guarantee you that if I think something, you will find out. It's true that I picked [up those traits] from my African American friends in high school. Like I said, I can do nothing but thank them, because I think those are just as important as being nurturing and friendly.

Through her friendships with her more outspoken African American friends, she learned that she could express herself, her opinions, and her needs. Other students mentioned assertiveness when they discussed how they have changed since being in the college environment. One said, "Thus far in school, I've come this far and have gotten more and more assertive."

In sum, consistent with previous acculturation research, we see students engaged in selective acculturation in specific life domains that they believed would benefit from incorporating more Americanized ways of thinking and behaving. However, in other areas, students expressed ethnic loyalty and commitment by retaining valued elements of their native culture (Buriel & De Ment, 1997). Most interesting were individual differences in acculturation observed in family members, even among siblings close in age, illustrating wide variations in adaptation strategies that may exist within a given family in regard to how its members chose to adapt to American society.

Reaping the Benefits of Two Cultures

The students who talked about acculturation did so in a highly favorable way. They were constructing new selves in a new culture and welcomed the opportunity to take the best of their "home" culture and blend it with the best of "American" culture. Like other students who felt that being more outspoken was a positive "American" cultural trait, this woman described her "partnered culture":

> I'm Mexican, but being born here has helped me be more [outspoken] instead of being quiet, which is how you think of being Mexican: quiet and shy. I think I'm more outgoing and independent than I would be if I were living in Mexico. But I'm also conscientious, hard-working, willing to learn. So it's like making me culturally aware. I've put both things together and made them together as partners, you know. Some parts I just leave behind and I just take the best parts. I don't know, it just makes me a more well-rounded person. It gives more of a creativity to [live a unique life] and be more open.

She understands that there are positive parts of her Mexican culture that make her a better person and that she needs to retain, but she also sees that being more outgoing and independent enhances her ability to succeed. The notion of success as an "American" value was important in building a culture that reflects the best. One student stated it simply: "Mexicans [give you] morals, Americans [give you] the dream to accomplish what you want." Assuming traditional "American" values of independence, achievement, and equality was important to these students, but not so important that they would reject the culture of their parents and their country of origin. At times the need to take on American cultural attributes was necessary, as stated by one of the men: "I have adopted some of the Anglo ways, not having sacrificed mine, but yet maintained mine. And I have to adopt the Anglo way in order to survive in society." The acculturation process was one where students embraced what they could to make themselves better people and to take advantage of living in a resource-rich country that, as the student delineates below, allows for the maximization of opportunity.

> I would say that people should always take pride in who they are. Not to forget your past, always try to teach it and hand it down. I mean, you've got to teach it, you've got to learn it, you should learn it, but don't dwell on it. Enjoy life, enjoy the riches that we have living in a nation, well, at least a state that's very diverse. You go to other parts of the country or the world, and you won't have that diversity. People learn from others. [Some]

other cultures know how to organize, others are clever thinkers, and [still] others have better morals that you may be able to pick up, or just basically they know right from wrong, and how to fix the situation without hurting anybody. So basically, I would say it's good to know your identity and it's great to have friends of different mixtures, it makes you a person of well-rounded intellect, and that's my goal. I want to be as well-rounded as possible.

Indeed, a bicultural orientation "is seen as the wave of the future and a strength to be embraced" by many young Latinos/as who serve today as the "bridge" generation between the new American culture and the native culture of their parents' homeland (Padilla, 2006, p. 492).

Summary and Conclusions

Latinos/as' ethnic identity was influenced by a number of forces, some direct in nature, such as the choice of ethnic labels, and others as complex as "family," which intersected most of the themes and data presented in this chapter. The Latino/a participants in the study were primarily Mexican in origin and were very close to the immigrant experience, with a vast majority being either immigrants themselves or children of immigrants. Additionally, a vast majority of them were the first in their families to attend college. These similarities—a common country of origin, a recent immigrant experience, and a collective experience of first-generation college students—resulted in the remarkable consistency with which Latinos/as, or specifically Mexican Americans, experienced their ethnicity in college. Those who were not Mexican in origin did share common cultural values, such as a family orientation, religiosity, and acculturation, but they had the unique experience of being Latino/a in an environment accustomed to Latinos/as' being primarily from Mexico.

Latino/a college students in this study constructed ethnic/racial and cultural identities that were the result of intersecting developmental processes and sociohistorical and political forces. To illustrate, ethnic self-designations tended to be flexible and contingent on the social context, with specific ethnic labels chosen with the intent of conferring an explicit cultural, ancestral, or political connotation (e.g., Mexicano, Mexican American, or Chicana). The process of naming the ethnic group was not always easy, and some students struggled with finding the "right" ethnic self-designation, especially when others questioned the legitimacy of an assumed ethnic-identification (i.e., the phenomenon of in-between spaces). Furthermore, encounters of mistaken identity (e.g., other-identified as White, for instance) forced some students to have to "claim" a Latino/a ethnic identification frequently.

Like Asian Americans, there were resources in communities, in families, and on campus—ethnic-based organizations, ethnic and language courses— to promote maintenance of Latino/a ethnic practices and expressions, with language being one of the most important cultural markers. Most Latinos/as could identify several ethnic practices and expressions in which they partici- pated regularly. These practices and expressions were often mediated through the family or through the Catholic Church—two prominent insti- tutions for Latinos/as. In addition to speaking Spanish, these practices included home country visits and large, weekly family gatherings around food, religious holidays, and age-related rituals such as weddings and *quince- aneras*. Students reported that participation in these activities gave them opportunities to develop pride in themselves and their ethnic group. In fact, a repeated message from students was pride, in what many termed, their "beautiful" culture. Students also took great pride in being both bilingual and bicultural, which they viewed as one of the inherent strengths of their ethnic group. Some who had lost the Spanish language expressed embarrass- ment and shame (i.e., I'm a "lousy excuse for a Mexican") and spoke of working to reclaim that element of cultural identity through formal study.

Family was a major influence on the ethnic identity of Latinos/as. It was through the family that the culture was sustained and, with the support of or confrontation with family, that ethnic identity was constructed. The family orientation laid the groundwork for the collectivist values that typically char- acterize Latinos/as. Family as a collectivistic entity was clearly a defining and fundamental aspect of students' ethnic self-concept. This familial self-con- cept was articulated through students' reflections of their values regarding *respeto* for and within the family, *personalismo*, and deference to authority, especially parents and elders—values that were reinforced through religious beliefs regarding morality and proper behavior. Hence, students felt they had a common destiny with their families that caused them to highly respect family and elders and monitor their own behavior so shame would not be brought to the family and, ultimately, the ethnic group and ethnic commu- nity. A common feeling among students was that family was the most impor- tant thing in their lives, with many of them prioritizing family above God and school. This, coupled with a sense of collective destiny, also prompted students to consider the political status and position of their ethnic group in the United States. Through encounters with various sociohistorical and political forces, Latino/a students spoke of gaining greater political consciousness and awareness that was collectivist in nature. As such, political consciousness prompted students to see their actions and plans as important to improving the overall status and power of their ethnic group. Education was seen as a primary vehicle for achieving this aim, and many saw themselves as future leaders of and role models for the Latino/a community who would enact changes for the group's success.

For many students, the importance of education was at the heart of the immigrant experience and the sacrifices family had made to ensure the success of the younger generation. Students felt strongly supported by their families to pursue a higher education. Many who were first-generation college students felt a great sense of responsibility in guiding their younger siblings through the educational process that would ultimately ensure their family's success in this country.

Students articulated how their ethnic identity had changed over the years and what things either challenged that identity or supported it. They spoke of elements in the college environment—the presence of coethnics, taking ethnic study courses, and participation in ethnic organizations—that helped them strengthen their ethnic identity and learn about their group. Likewise, students experienced challenges from society (i.e., racism and negative images of the group) and within the university context that tested their ethnic identity and presented barriers to achieving a positive ethnic self-concept. Ultimately, Latino/a students associated a strong ethnic identity with having a sense of confidence that enabled them to tackle life's challenges and struggles.

As in the case of Asian Americans, experience with acculturation strongly shaped and transformed students' ethnic identity and views about how they would enact their futures. Changes in values regarding gender roles were not uncommon, especially among young Latinas, who were more likely to experience parental pressure to conform to traditional expectations of womanhood. Young Latinas' more liberalized views of gender, education, social behavior, dating, and life plans often clashed with the more traditional expectations of their parents' native culture. Nonetheless, many saw themselves as different from their mothers, and through higher education, they were redefining the roles they would assume in the future as Latina professionals, wives, and mothers. In all, Latinos/as spoke of becoming Americanized and of forging a new hybrid culture they found to be personally and collectively beneficial—one that did not entail sacrificing valued and treasured elements of their Latino/a culture and heritage.

6

WHITE AMERICANS
Trying to Make Sense of It All

I remember one time when I was little and I asked my mother, "Mommy, what am I?" She goes, "You're White, that's it, you're White." You kind of go, well, what's my culture, you know? What kind? I know that I'm European. Okay, but what kind am I? From England, from France? A lot of it gets mixed over when you come over here, you're White. I don't have any ethnic culture. I don't have any real ethnicity as some people [do]. So I'm just an ordinary person doing my own thing. I don't take time to worry about, "Well, what am I going to do [that's] White today?" "What can I do towards my culture today?" I don't, and sometimes I think that's good and bad. I don't have any culture really to stand up and fight for.

I worked in a funeral house over the summer, and I started thinking what they would put on my death certificate when I die. Well I have Scottish, English, Cherokee, and who knows what else. There is probably slave in me because I grew up in the Tennessee-Kentucky border. So I'm affiliated with all things White. So I guess that is who I am.

Of the 30 White American students, 3 were born in another country—Poland, England, and Australia, respectively—2 of whom had immigrated to the United States as young children. The remaining 27 participants were native to the United States, and their families had lived in this country for 3 or more generations. The vast majority of these students (76.3%) had lived in predominantly White neighborhoods and attended predominantly White high schools (67%) before attending college. Hence, with the exception of a few individuals, most White students came from ethnically segregated upbringings, marking their arrival at the university as their first exposure to a truly ethnically diverse environment.

Unlike many other Whites, these students were attending university campuses where they were not the numerical majority.

This chapter focuses on how this unique group of students constructed their ethnic and racial identity as White individuals within the context of attending multiethnic universities and through their contact and association with diverse others. More specifically, we explore in this chapter the labels White students use when describing their ethnic/racial group membership; the meaning of a White identity for such students and their personal views and attitudes regarding Whiteness; the implicit expressions of Whiteness as articulated by students in terms of behavioral practices, values, and beliefs; and the diverse and problematic meanings associated with Whiteness when framed within the context of interethnic/interracial relations. Our analysis of White identity revealed the struggles and contradictions students face when framing Whiteness in reference to its cultural/ethnic meanings versus Whiteness as a racial identification in relation to other ethnic minority groups.

In attempting to balance their identity in terms of its cultural/ethnic meanings *and* its racialized connotations, we note that White students lagged behind their ethnic minority peers in this process of ethnic and racial identity development. That is, White students struggled more to negotiate their cultural/ethnic and racial identity within a context of diversity where ethnic/racial discourse was frequent and often at the forefront within the university and the larger society. More specifically, as an ethnic/cultural identification, students varied in terms of the meaning they associated with being White and the psychological significance they attached to that social identity. Some articulated feelings of dissonance related to having a weak ethnic identity compared to what they saw in ethnic minorities. As a racialized identification, students spoke of Whiteness as a privileged status and the conflicts and dissonance engendered with an identity that has been linked to racial oppression. Whiteness as a racial construction within the university environment was difficult to negotiate at times and left some students feeling victimized. Nonetheless, we see an attempt by some students to reinvent and reconstruct Whiteness as a positive, nonracist racial identity. Individual differences in how students spoke of Whiteness as a cultural/ethnic *and* racial construction not only point to distinctions in ethnic and racial identity development (Hardiman, 2001; Helms, 1990, 1995; Phinney, 1990), but also highlight the importance of the intergroup context and social comparison processes in shaping current notions of a White identity (McDermott & Samson, 2005;

Tajfel & Turner, 1986). That is, Whiteness signified different things to different persons and acquired varied meanings for individuals when cast within an interracial framework.

Who Am I? Labels Used to Define a White Ethnic/Racial Identity

When asked to discuss their ethnic background, White students described this identity in one of two ways: by referring to a symbolic identification based on White European ancestry and heritage, and/or by simply labeling themselves as "White" or "Caucasian." In the end, 37% of students in these two groups favored an *"American White"* identity as their cultural identification, one they believed implicitly captured who they were as individuals in ethnic and racial terms.

Symbolic Identification

Many participants (well over half of the sample) chose to answer the question concerning their ethnic background by describing their family heritage as stemming from European ancestry. Typical descriptions of their European heritage were made by the following two students:

> Well, I'm White. . . . My mom's parents are from Germany, so I am fourth-generation German. . . . My dad's side . . . his mother and father were born here and have a French base.

> My ethnic background? I am a mutt! I am half Czechoslovakian, my father's whole family was Czech. My mother's side is just about everything: European . . . Irish, French. We're mutts. [What I consider myself above all?] It would be Caucasian.

Although aware of their familial ethnic background, many of these students spoke of their ancestral heritage with some detachment and voiced little psychological connection to their European roots. For many students, this appeared to be more of a *symbolic identification*, one they acknowledged on a cognitive level but were not highly invested in affectively. In the end, 41 percent of the students who spoke of their mixed European heritage defaulted to "White" or "Caucasian" as their preferred ethnic/racial label. It is interesting to note that this finding held true even among those students who did voice a strong identification to a specific ethnic European heritage. For instance, as one student commented: "Even though I'm just as much German and English as I am Italian, I tend to identify more with the Italian part of me . . . I have more of that to cling to." Nonetheless, when asked which ethnic label she preferred, this student replied, "I would not say I'm not proud to be European or anything like that. I would just call myself White." Likewise, one woman who was a mixture of several European heritages but who claimed to identify more closely with her Spanish ancestry identified herself in the end as White. Only a handful of students in this study laid claim solely to a specific European ethnicity and used that heritage as their ethnic identification.

Conversely, approximately half of the students (47%) who spoke of a symbolic identification stemming from European ancestry ultimately labeled themselves as "*American*" or "*White American*" and viewed this as representing their true ethnic identification. For such students the term "White American" emerged as a pan-ethnic descriptor that appeared to capture and embrace their mixed European heritage. This is evident in the following students' remarks: "Most Americans are blends of something or other. Sicilian, Irish, Hungarian. . . . It's the American way." "I'm three-quarters German and one-quarter Mohican, and I don't think it plays that big of a role. I am American, White." "I have very little connection to the American Italian community here in Los Angeles, so I would define my ethnicity as an American." A similar perspective was voiced by another student, who said, "My mom's Italian, her parents are first generation coming here. My dad's Irish . . . but I don't really identify myself as anything other than American." Finally, a woman who spoke extensively about her Italian ancestry and was proud of this cultural heritage noted: "I think it's all somewhat a joke . . . Italian American, Mexican American, African American. . . . It's bullshit as far as I'm concerned, you know. I'm American, more American than I'll ever be Italian." It is apparent that students in this subgroup, by virtue of their mixed European heritage and other cultural/ethnic blends, claimed an American identity that was somewhat removed from their ancestral European cultural past but clearly a meaningful and relevant social identification (Perry, 2001). Therefore, although these students spoke in some detail about their European lineage, it did not mean as much to them personally as did being an American. Hence, their primary social identity as ethnic individuals lay within the core society (McDermott & Samson, 2005). These findings are in line with those reported by Phinney and colleagues (Phinney, Cantu, & Kurtz, 1997), who found that among White youth, embracing an American identification correlated positively with having a positive ethnic identity and a strong sense of nationalism.

Racial Identification

The remaining group of students (approximately 30% of the sample) simply labeled themselves White/Caucasian or White American but did not link these labels to ethnicity or to having European ancestry. There was a greater tendency for these students to see themselves in racial terms and not as having ethnicity. As one student noted, "My ethnic background? I am just White. My whole family's White, so we don't have much ethnicity." Furthermore, a young woman who was more introspective about who she was and its larger social significance said: "I am Caucasian and I am American. It's clearly a part of my identity, like how people perceive me. Like when someone first sees you. It says a lot about you . . . I am in the majority or my ethnicity [is]." Similarly, another student noted, "I am White . . . [that means] I'm a member of the majority." Most evident in these students' narratives is that, although they did not think of being White as having ethnicity, they did think of it as a "social category, as a group position with respect to other racial/ethnic groups" (Perry, 2001, p. 73).

Accordingly, about a third of the students in this subgroup tended to equate "White" with "American." As voiced by one student, to be an American was implicitly synonymous with being White: "I think that White people are in the American category." Likewise, the following student reflected on this issue, saying:

> Well I guess I am American because I was born here, my parents were born here, and my grandparents were born here, so I don't really have a strong ethnic identity. I don't consciously think of myself as being attached to a specific ethnicity. So when people ask me, I'm just, like, well I guess I'm American and my skin's white, so I guess I'm White American.

This *White = American* effect has been documented recently by other researchers as well. In line with the findings reported by Devos and Banaji (2005), there was a tendency among White and non-White students in this study to see "the cultural 'default' value for American as White" (p. 464). Whites students were more likely to see themselves, and to be viewed by ethnic others, as the prototypical representative of the category "American." In her research of White high school students, Perry (2001) proposed that this perspective is consistent with the "dominant constructions of White as the 'unhyphenated' American standard" (p. 79).

The Meaning of a White Identity

In this section we discuss how participants created meaning about what being White meant to them through constructing a cultureless identity and reflections of Whiteness as the norm. Evident from students' commentaries was that some perceived a cultureless identity to be more favorable; however, for others, such an identification was more problematic and conflicting and left them with a sense of cultural vacuum. Students also seemed to have a contextual construction of Whiteness that was variable and, at times, contradictory.

Cultureless Identity

The construction of Whiteness as a cultureless identity was a salient theme that emerged from participants' narratives (over half of the students alluded directly and indirectly to having a cultureless identity). For many White students, ethnicity and culture were something minorities had, and they defined White to mean that one was a nonethnic, without culture and ethnicity (Eichstedt, 2001; Perry, 2001). This notion of Whiteness as nonethnic and cultureless was heard from the following student: "I am not sure that I have an ethnic identity. I've gone to school with White people my entire life. I don't think about it [being White] as an ethnic identity." Likewise, another student said: "I'm just White, my whole family is White. So we don't have much ethnicity. You know how [other] people [of color] have traditions and their culture. . . . My family is just easygoing." Further, another student commented: "I don't really feel that I have one [ethnic identity] but I'm in the leftover category, like 'other,' the White. . . . Probably if I was member of a minority group, I would feel I had an ethnicity identity." Similarly, another student noted: "I grew up in a White community that you really didn't think about like cultural [identification]." She states further that an ethnic/cultural identification is something that one mostly sees in other "ethnic groups." This "us-them" construction revolved around majority-minority comparisons for these students in defining what it meant to be White (Perry, 2001).

There was also a tendency among some White participants to articulate a cultureless construction of Whiteness that implied that one was beyond having ethnicity and culture. More specifically, to be cultureless meant that one was simply an individual, a person. As Eichstedt (2001) noted, Whites tend to see themselves as being racially/ethnically *neutral*, consequently *just human*. This cultureless construction of Whiteness can be heard in the statements offered by the following students:

> So my ethnicity and my race wasn't something that was stressed when I was growing up. It wasn't like . . . you are White and you should do this . . . so it didn't really play a big role. The thing that played more of a role in my personality was more ethics and things like that, I suppose. I was always taught morally and ethically that my race should be kind to all others, but I wasn't hugely ethnically brought up.

> The role ethnicity has played hasn't been too big or too great in my life. In a way, I like it that way, because I can appreciate people for who they really are, and I don't go around stereotyping or prejudicing or thinking I am better or worse than anyone.

> Like I said earlier, being exposed to other groups has led to an understanding, at least in my life, to not care about [ethnicity], to not regard it or consider it. So it has probably benefited me that I don't know about me culturally, because I don't want to identify with [a specific] culture.

> I don't know if my ethnicity really shapes my personality. I guess it's because I don't tie very many things to being American, you know. I wouldn't say I do go to church because I am American, and if I was another culture I wouldn't do that. I think because I am White I try to make an effort to understand other cultures. I've tried to, a lot. I am really open-minded and helpful to anybody who would need it.

The ideological viewpoint expressed by some of the students was that to be cultureless could be viewed as personally advantageous in that one was able to operate from a more rational, ethical, and open-minded perspective. For some of these students, having a high level of ethnic identity was seen as potentially interfering with a person's ability to appreciate others without stereotyping or bias. There was a belief that if one were too identified with an ethnic group, this could potentially cloud one's judgment and affect interactions with other groups (i.e., ethnocentrism). This rationalist construction of Whiteness was heard by a student who felt that ethnicity had little to do with her personality, yet she identified strongly as being a White ethnic and an American: "I am proud of being Italian. I am proud of being American, but I'm not so proud that I like to rub it in on other people's faces." What underlies this student's differentiation is the color-blind perspective that many Americans believe that being too ethnic may be construed as racist and that ethnicity should be deemphasized (Sellers, Rowley, Chavous, Shelton, & Smith, 1997; Wolsko, Park, Judd, & Wittenbrink, 2000). The following students offer their perspectives:

> What does my ethnicity mean to me? Any special meaning? Not really. I just think we are all people and that it shouldn't really matter, we all have red blood. When people make such a big deal out of ethnicity, and you know I understand that people grew up in different cultures, but it should not make us pit each other against each other.

> It is my overall belief of ethnicity and race is that it exists but it shouldn't be an issue. It should be acknowledged—I mean you can't ignore it that some people have different skin colors . . . but you don't focus on it as an everyday issue. . . . You just move past it and take people on an individual level. And you try not to force it to the front, because it shouldn't be a daily issue in our lives.

Taken together, these findings shed light on important ideological perspectives associated with White identity that include viewpoints regarding the significance of ethnicity/race in living one's life and how Whites ought to view, relate, and behave toward non-Whites (Sellers et al., 1997). That is, that as members of the majority group, these students felt a responsibility to be open-minded and to behave ethically and morally when it came to the treatment of minorities. In doing so they embraced a positive nonracist and race-neutral White identity (Silvestri & Richardson, 2001).

> I just think it's like our generation. You know, I see most people around here aren't like prejudiced against whoever and I just think it's the generation. And I mean my brothers are like open. They've always traveled and stuff and told me about different cultures, like down in Costa Rica and stuff and they met like all these cool people. You know they're not like bad people if they are from somewhere else.

Arguably, part of these students' thoughts regarding Whiteness was articulating and defining what it was to be a *good White person*. Being a good White person meant one abided by certain ethical and moral standards associated with tolerance of, openness to, and sensitivity toward diverse cultural groups. Yet, also heard in some of these students' narratives was that other personal meanings of Whiteness remained unexamined and that they have not reflected on the role ethnicity has played in shaping their lives.

Finally, also associated with a rationalist construction of Whiteness was the tendency among some students to dismiss the significance of having a cultural past and to articulate a more individualistic and present-/future-oriented definition of the self (Perry, 2001). As one student stated, "I basically think that where I came from, where the people that preceded me genetically came from, doesn't seem to be for me as important as maybe other aspects of my life." This perspective was also heard in the words offered by another student.

> It hasn't so much affected me in that way because I've never identified myself primarily as being Caucasian. I mean, the way I feel about myself is based upon my own experience and my own beliefs about myself. I don't look to something that happened with a Caucasian man four hundred years ago and say, "It's great that he did that, and I can really identify with him because he's Caucasian." I don't think that way. Anything that happened in history could have impacted how I got here but not who I am.

Whiteness Is Not Salient, Therefore Seen as Normal

White identity also differed from other ethnic/racial identities in that it is often experienced as the norm and, hence, is invisible to many Whites (McDermott & Samson, 2005; Perry, 2001). Perry argues that as a member of the dominant status, White persons tend to construct White identities defined as normal or ordinary. When asked to discuss what their ethnicity meant to them, approximately one-third of the White students made references to having a normalized identity. This perspective of Whiteness as normal and culturally invisible was pointed out by the following students:

> I don't know. It's just, I never thought about it. Never, never crossed my mind. That's who I am and that's it. I mean nothing to it. Thinking about it, I guess I feel indifferent.

I don't know how to summarize it. Maybe it's so hard because I don't really think about it, consciously on a day-to-day basis. I don't . . . I really don't think I can do that. Like I said in the beginning, I don't think being White gives me my values. I think it's an extremely broad group. I don't see that it's the fact that I'm White that it does that. I haven't really thought about it too much, and it's not a huge factor in my life.

You know, honestly though, the only time I ever think about it is when I have to fill out a form that makes you fill in your race and check off one box, and the one I check off is Caucasian. How I feel about it, I guess I (pause) don't have feelings about it. I mean, it's just something that is. It's not like a car, where I feel okay with what I have, but I want something better. It's just (pause), I don't know.

I don't have any ethnic culture. . . . I don't have any real ethnicity as some people. So I'm just an ordinary person doing my own thing. I don't take time to worry about, "Well, what am I going to do White today?"

The viewpoint these students offered was that to be White was to be ordinary, not something to ponder or reflect on in living one's day-to-day life. It just was. This naturalized construction of Whiteness "is grounded in and validated by the normal way of things in the present therefore does not seek meaning in culture and in the past" (Perry, 2001, p. 73). As one student said, "I'm just going through everyday life like everybody else." (p. 56) Likewise, in line with previous research (Phinney, 1995; Phinney & Kohatsu, 1997), it was evident from the White students' interviews that ethnicity was not a salient aspect of their identities and that it had played an "invisible" role in shaping whom they had become as individuals. Perceiving Whiteness as invisible and therefore *not* psychologically salient among those who possess it is consistent with Helms's (1990) theory of White racial development. Helms (1990) proposes that many White individuals, because of their privileged status, are seldom forced to consider the meaning and implications of their ethnicity. When asked to reflect on his ethnicity, one student exemplified this finding:

Doesn't really have any specific meaning to me. It's the ethnicity that labels me, I guess. No feelings really. I've never thought about it in that way. I've never really thought about it like that—Who I am? . . . If someone asks, "Who are you?" I would not say, "I'm Caucasian." I would say, "I'm John, it's nice to meet you." And if you said, "But who are you?" I wouldn't say I'm a Caucasian. Anyone asking in reference to who I am, my answer would never be that I am Caucasian. I don't now if that clarifies it a little bit. I don't really identify myself—I mean I've been labeled Caucasian, this is the race you are, but I don't walk around saying I'm a Caucasian. Everything I do relates to that, everything I am relates to that. That's not the view that I have. . . . Ethnic identity really hasn't had an effect on me because it's never been an issue in my life. My identity is rarely brought up, if ever, [or] discussed. So it probably has had no impact on my beliefs and experiences. It's never really impacted me on a level that I'm aware of.

Students' narratives point to an unexamined and unexplored ethnic identity associated with having a weak ethnic/racial identity (Phinney, 2005). These qualitative findings are corroborated by the survey data in that White students scored significantly lower than did African American, Asian, and Latino/a students on the ethnic identity measures. Scores on these measures indicated that ethnicity was neither as crucial to Whites' definition of their self-concept (i.e., personal ethnic identity) as it was for ethnic minority students, nor did it appear to afford White students a strong basis for self-worth and pride (i.e., private acceptance of ethnic identity).

A Sense of Culture Vacuum

Close to one-third of the sample "defined Whiteness as empty, bland and without traditions" (Perry, 2001, p. 79) and to be devoid of culture, which engendered in them a sense of cultural vacuum. One student who grappled with this question said: "It is so boring to be White. Sometimes I wish that I was mixed. I know that sounds strange." For these students, White culture lacked continuity with some shared past and connection with other group members, unlike what they saw inherent in ethnic minority cultures or even in other White ethnicities such as Italians or Jews (Giroux, 1997). This construction of Whiteness as cultureless was more negative for participants and left them with a sense of cultural vacuum: an identity that had been stripped of something essential and fundamental.

> I mean, it seems to me that other ethnic groups tend to have stronger traditions and a more defined culture. An example, the Jewish have a lot of traditions. The whole slavery thing and America's past. And you have a lot of rich—you can look back and see people from Africa and say this is where

this man's history came from and this is what they did and they're still doing it now. There's a definite scene you can identify as being part of your past.

I don't [have culture]. I don't because, maybe it['s] just from me looking on the outside, but to be Mexican, you have Mexican traditions and you are family-oriented and there is certain things. But when you are considered White American, you are just White American. I mean there's no real strong sense of identity or passages that you do or go through, you know. . . . I think that [there is] the lack of culture. Everyone's like, well, you are American, you are just American, and there's nothing really tied to that, there's no real [meaning].

Well, I think it [ethnicity/culture] gives you confidence if you have something to tie yourself into. If you can always look back on the fact that you are Hispanic and you are very tied in with that culture and you eat this type of food or you do this type of thing on this holiday or that holiday. . . . I think that if you ever feel unsure about something, you always have a tie-in with that particular culture. So, I think that that's important. I think it is important for people to be tied in with their culture, even though I also think that we should mix, too. But I think it's important for confidence, for self-esteem, and for security within yourself. I think that's very important.

Unlike the previous group of students, these students acknowledged the significance of culture in one's identity, and in seeing themselves as cultureless, these students felt deprived of a vital part of their social identity. Hence, being "normal" and "ordinary" had consequences for these White students. The price was paid in terms of loss of culture and ethnic identity and desire for what they lacked yet saw in other ethnicities. A student who had recently discovered he was part Native American Indian expressed a clear interest in that heritage he hoped would satisfy a cultural void he felt in being White:

You know, what I like was the Indian part of it. I just found that out recently in the last year and it was interesting. Because being White for me, it just didn't feel special in any way. It was kind of like, well, I'm White. Maybe that's because nowadays there is more emphasis on ethnic groups and minorities and things like that. Where it is almost you know, bland to be White, or something like that. So to find out that I actually had some Indian in me, it was intriguing. I liked it.

Similarly, another White student also spoke at some length and with mixed emotions about having Native American ethnic lineage and the importance of that discovery for her social identity as an ethnic individual.

> I had no idea what my roots were. I tried to dig into that about a year and a half ago when we had one lady speak to our whale watch group in San Pedro. Her dad was Chumash. He was a full-blooded Indian, he died several years ago. In his last couple of years, she started tape recording all his stories because Indians don't really have a written history. It's all verbal. So she is writing them a book. I think she's at CSULB (California State University, Long Beach). She is in their Indian Studies or their Native American Studies [program]. It blew me away because I think one of my grandfathers was Indian. I have a cousin who goes to Long Beach, he recently searched it out and there is a great grandfather that we share. We're distant cousins, but it's the one we share. He was a Cherokee chief. I don't know that for a fact, but [my cousin] says it is so. So after I listened to their stories that this lady was telling, that her dad had related and what she tape recorded, it really made me sad that I don't know more about the Indian heritage in my family. Probably why I don't is because it was the White people who married into the Indian family who were shunned, and the Indian may have been shunned as well for marrying into the White community. So a lot of the history was cut off there because of the interracial [marriage].

Implied in students' commentaries is their belief that the ethnic minority culture is somehow superior. Previous theorists (Helms, 1990; Kincheloe, 1999; Rowe, Behrens, & Leach, 1995) have discussed that one reaction among Whites who struggle with their ethnic/racial identity is to romanticize a more visible minority culture and conceptualize it as being superior. By not knowing their own culture, the minority cultures appear to be all that more visible and tangible, thus sought out and explored as an alternative cultural identification.

It is important to note that students were often contradictory in articulating the meaning of their ethnicity. For instance, an Armenian White student who had discussed the benefits of not being too ethnic earlier, later said he regretted having lost parts of his ethnic heritage and expressed a need to reclaim that aspect of his identity:

> With the Armenians, I speak Armenian with them instead of speaking English. I try to make more of an effort to seem like I know more about my own race, about Armenians, when I'm around Armenians. Sometimes I'm afraid of being looked down upon 'cuz I used to know how to read and write Armenian. I can only speak it now. I forgot how to read and write. I don't know as much as I should about my own culture. I wish I knew more. It's just that I used to go to an Armenian school until the third grade, and then my parents took me to American school. So I was kind of deprived of the knowledge I should have known. It doesn't make me feel good. Some people get on me for that. I'll get on myself for that, too.

Likewise, others who had described themselves previously as nonethnic and cultureless later said they wanted to learn more about their cultural roots and explore their ethnicity as White individuals. Such contradictory expressions of Whiteness as cultureless are offered by the following students, who felt conflicted about having lost part of their social identity:

> Sometimes it's almost as though . . . your ethnicity is lost in a way. So you are the majority, and that is just who you are. But the feelings of the minorities, it is like there is something stronger. They're like, they come from African groups or [have specific] group affiliations, in other words. So a negative aspect is that you lose a strong identity, which is okay, because you want to be open to all kinds of different things.

> I think like there are positive aspects in having something to feel more proud about. There's like a rising-up type mentality. You're a minority and you can feel like you can identify with something different from the norm and feel proud of that.

Finally, this sense of cultural loss was heard even among some of the few individuals in the sample who laid claim to a specific White ethnic identity.

> Well, I'm German. German was not spoken or taught actually in the house, so I feel I kind of lost touch with that, and I would like to explore and learn more about my heritage and where I actually came from. So I mean to me, being German is important.

Expressions of White Identity

Many students found it quite difficult to describe specific cultural practices or behaviors they engage in regularly that expressed their ethnic identity as White individuals. A common finding was students stating, "I have no specific traditions" that are specifically linked to ethnicity. This finding is in line with the notion of a normalized and cultureless identity discussed earlier in this chapter. According to White studies scholars, the visibility of culture varies according to a group's social status, and cultural invisibility is a privileged status that characterizes those who have institutional and political power (Frankenberg, 1993; Helms & Cook, 1999). The experience of White cultural practices and behaviors as being invisible was heard from the following students:

> Not that I can think of. I just do normal college student things. I have family reunions with my family, but that's nothing that shows anything about my background other than that my family is Caucasian. But no, nothing like that.

> To be honest with you, I cannot name any specific Caucasian cultural practices. Some people would say general American culture is Caucasian culture. I think it's a little bit of everybody's culture mixed in. So, I can't honestly pick out specific practices that I engage in. . . . Part of my culture? Nah, just sports, family, work, school. I don't see any of it as being part of my culture per se. I couldn't pick anything out.

> We have, like, holidays but those are the ones everyone in the country celebrates: like Thanksgiving, Easter, Christmas . . . I see I can't even give you an example. I'm thinking, well, it's not like Great Portugal Day, because I don't even know if that exists (laughs). But there's nothing like special days like some other cultures have. I would think African Americans celebrate Martin Luther King [Jr.] Day. Actually, don't we do [so], too? I'm confused. I don't know.

Because White Americans are the majority (i.e., in status and power) in the United States, their cultural traditions and practices predominate; as such Whites frequently view "their customs and traditions as normal rather than cultural" (Tsai, Mortensen, & Wong, 2002, p. 259). Hence, for many youth today, a White identity seems cultureless because many of their cultural practices are taken for granted, so they have not been explicitly defined or reflected on. Therefore, they find it difficult to articulate in words that which comes natural or is ordinary (Perry, 2001). In attempting to demarcate expressions of White culture, we heard students referring to special ethnic celebrations of minorities that are visible because they deviate from the norm or what is typical. When discussing these ethnic celebrations, the self-identified White Americans saw themselves more as spectators at these ethnic events.

> In Western Kentucky obviously it's a big day [August 8] for the Black community in the whole area. I call it emancipation day. The day when the word that the Blacks were free reached that area of the country, August the eighth, because there was no radio or newspapers. It was all word of mouth, and they have a big festival and it centers pretty much in Paducah. We watched a lot of that on TV and read about it on the newspapers and radio. But there is not a lot of that for us.

Nonetheless, well over half of the White sample was able to identify at least one practice they considered to be tied to their culture. Here we see a difference between those who embraced a European symbolic identification and those who embraced a White racial identification. Students who had acknowledged earlier an ethnic heritage based on European ancestry were able to identify more easily explicit cultural expressions in their lives. The most common of these were specific foods that they connected to family and cultural celebrations and holidays. One Italian woman said, "It's like the food we eat and the way our family looks when we're together . . . we pretty much are the normal Italian family. Whenever we get together, we always eat Italian food." Likewise another student stated, "Saint Patrick's Day when we were younger . . . big dinners and beer . . ." Also, religion was seen as an implicit expression of ethnicity for some of these individuals. As one student noted, "We do Christmas, Thanksgiving, and Easter, but that has to do more with religion than it has to do with ethnicity." These perspectives can also be heard in the following:

> A lot of the foods we eat are Italian. My parents, they did a lot of, like, traditional holidays. Like New Year's we'd eat certain foods, they mean certain things. Like green means money and black-eyed peas is prosperity.

There's like, for each dish you eat on New Year's, it's supposed to mean that you would have that throughout the year and it rarely worked. They're pretty superstitious. I don't know if it is an Italian thing or if it's just my family. We are also Catholic. That's Italian, I think.

I would say just the family gets together from the Irish side. The Irish, we actually got together and went to Ireland and had the family reunion there. . . . Of course, St. Patrick's Day. We usually get together just about every holiday—Easter, Memorial Day, or something. Don't remember marching in any parades or anything like that though. The Italian side don't really do anything that is specifically for the culture or anything, just go to the Italian restaurants. Nothing specific. But my family can't just go to any Italian restaurant; it has to be a very traditional restaurant or otherwise . . .

Unlike the other ethnic minority groups studied, evident in many of White students' narratives was a lack of knowledge or clarity regarding the practice of specific cultural traditions. These students sounded somewhat uncertain when they spoke of cultural expressions and were not as confident in that ethnic knowledge. It was clear that these cultural expressions of ethnicity had had a more subtle influence on the lives of these White ethnic students than they did on their peers of color. This was heard from the following student: "Okay, I'm Eastern European, so that would make me probably third-generation American. I personally enjoy the culture; well, just like the music and that kind of thing." One woman who described her ethnic heritage as being of French and German descent also shared this perspective:

Right. Yeah, I guess if there were things that I can look at and see if I did, it would be more subliminal or it would be under . . . it wouldn't be something I would set out to do. Okay, I do this because I'm German, and I do this because I have this part French in me. It would be more underlying things that I would do naturally. That culturally I was raised doing. . . . The only thing, I don't do it now, but the only thing I can think of would be church. Because my dad was real big on that and grew up in the South and was Baptist. On my mom, I think Christmas was a big thing. We celebrated it with her parents, and I consider that a heritage thing because we shared it with her parents, and there were certain foods that were eaten at that time, which I could not name but I know they were German.

This student was quite insightful in recognizing that culture may have influenced her life in ways she was not consciously aware of or that she would regularly link specifically to her ethnicity, but she could not name specifically what these might be. Finally, some students discussed how much easier it was to see White culture outside of California and other parts of the country that are less diverse. A woman of Irish descent shared this perspective when speaking of cultural practices:

> I have one of these rings . . . (she explains about an Irish wedding band she is wearing). I think that even in different states there's more of a tie to being Irish because in Chicago there's more Irish people and they are more into being Irish and that kind of thing. I don't think it's as much practiced here. . . . My sister lives there and they have a lot of ties to the Irish [community]. . . . I don't particularly listen to that type of music, but there is a definite Irish music. It sounds different, and they have a language in Ireland. Gaelic I believe is what it is called. I don't listen to the music [or identify with anything else Irish] other than [eat] corned beef and hash.

There was a tendency among these individuals, when reflecting on their cultural practices, to express a desire to visit their European ancestral homelands and recapture, to some extent, an ethnic heritage that was somewhat elusive. This was expressed with a positive sense of curiosity and interest in further examining one's cultural identity:

> That's something I'd actually like to look up, or find out more about that. Because, for me, my Hungarian side was more just my grandfather. He has no more relatives or anything and he died when I was very young. Of the Hungarian lifestyle, I don't know too much culture or anything like that, but it is something that I find interesting. I've looked up some things. It would be something I'd kind of like to do—go visit that part of my ancestry—go visit Hungary.

As Gallagher (1995) noted, for many individuals "this fuzzy connection to the European 'old country' provides the historical backdrop and cultural space for the construction of a White identity" (p. 181), which is embedded within a positive American identification. It served a purpose for these students in that it gave them a sense of direction where an exploration into their ethnic identity may begin and what they may want to learn.

A few students in the sample reflected on and defined White culture by alluding to specific interests, use of language, taste in leisure activities, and travel. For instance, one woman said, "definitely the way that I talk or the way that . . . I say 'like' a lot . . . and [my choice of] reading materials are definitely" examples of cultural practices. Two other White students noted participation in leisure activities such as "sports" and "football" and "having barbecues in summer" as cultural practices. Likewise, some students discussed family vacations and other travel as a cultural practice. We heard this perspective more clearly in one student's description of her childhood family experiences: "It's like the things we did for fun. You know, we'd go to like concerts outside or like museums or we'd go to Boston, the city, on the weekend and . . . walk around the churches." These findings are in line with Perry's (2001) study on ethnic identity among high school students in which she reports that White culture is not altogether invisible or nonexistent among these youth. It may be taken for granted, but it is real and articulated in the discourse of taste and leisure and the belief that different life experiences are more defining and common among Whites. What was implied here was not so much that other groups do not do these things, but that they were primarily observed among Whites and potentially alluded to distinctions based on class and race (i.e., travel and vacations).

Unlike the previous students, immigrant White participants in the sample were able to discuss at greater length specific cultural behaviors and practices. For instance, the Polish student noted that when the family celebrated Christmas and Easter it did so in the Polish way, rather than following American traditions:

> I would say just on the holidays. I know that it is very different, like Catholic holidays in Poland. There's different customs than there are in the United States. There are certain things that you do differently. For example, during Christmas, instead of having Santa Claus come in the morning or over the night, he comes in the evening when the first star appears. There's also Easter, I think that it is underplayed here. Like there is no Easter Bunny or anything like that. Most festivities are done on Easter Day, and you are supposed to spend it with your family. You are not supposed to go Easter egg hunting.

He also associated his affinity for outdoor activities with his Polish background: "I would say, like, being outdoors kind of ties in with my ethnicity, because almost everyone that is Polish enjoys the outdoors and just enjoys the countryside and going out to the woods and so forth." He goes on to say how in Poland people work hard for 11 months out of the year so they "can take a month off on vacation and go into the woods or skiing somewhere. . . . So that would be a way that I emulate my culture." Furthermore, he discussed how his participation in Polish Boy Scouts had helped him maintain his Polish background and history:

> In the past I was part of the Polish Boy Scouts, which is pretty much the same as American Boy Scouts except it is a bunch of Polish people. It tries to maintain like Polish background and history . . . so I am pretty fluent in the history, language and so forth.

This man was able to talk more extensively about his ethnicity in this part of the interview than when he was asked about the meaning and importance of his ethnicity, to which he responded that it did not mean a lot to him. An Armenian student said he did not practice his culture on a regular basis: "I don't go to a church on a certain day. I don't celebrate certain things. . . . I don't take a day off for, let's say, Armenian genocide. I still come to school, even though it is a day of mourning." What was interesting about this individual was that in other parts of the interview he did mention cultural practices. When asked about his interactions with other Armenians compared to other Whites, he noted that with Armenians he spoke Armenian. Both the Polish and Armenian students seemed to have a compartmentalized approach to their ethnicity in that they did not feel they had a strong ethnic identity, yet they participated in their respective ethnic communities.

Expressions of Ethnic Pride

Unlike the other ethnic groups in the sample, we saw a discrepancy among White participants in voicing explicit expressions of ethnic pride (approximately a quarter of the sample referred to having ethnic pride). Ethnic pride was stated indirectly and more ambiguously when compared to the narratives of ethnic minority students:

> I'm proud of myself as a person. As I said, I think I have a lot of integrity and I think that I am fair. I am what I am and what I was born into. I'm not out to hang anybody or do anything like that. So I'm comfortable with whom I am and White being part of my characteristics.

There was a clear sense that expressions of ethnic pride were not permissible and were frowned on socially, especially among students who embraced a racialized White identity. Although not always articulated explicitly, students' reluctance to claim ethnic pride stemmed from recognizing that Whiteness signified a social location in relation to other groups of color, and that Whiteness had historically been linked to power and racial dominance. Hence, students' reticence in claiming ethnic pride stemmed from concerns that it would be construed as racist and that one had White-supremacist inclinations (Phoenix, 1997). As one student noted, "Only a few individuals would in a positive sense say, I am proud to be White." Arguably then, because "American" was viewed as being synonymous with White, claiming to be a proud American could be seen as a safe proxy for saying proud to be White. This speaks to the intersections among race/ethnicity, power, and class in American society.

On the other hand, expressions of ethnic pride were easier to articulate among students who voiced an attachment to a specific White ethnicity and/ or made references to being a White ethnic and a proud American also. This perspective was heard from a handful of students:

> Well, probably like with every other race, you're proud of where you come from and proud of everything else about your culture and history. You know how you go back to World War I and World War II and people look back and frown a little bit on everything that happened then, but I'm proud to be German, and you know nothing can take that away.

> I feel good about it. I'm proud, you know. When people ask me [if] I'm proud, I don't know. I'm proud of being Italian. I'm proud of being an American. . . . I don't think it would be different. I don't think it would be different if I hadn't been raised here all my life. I think I would still consider myself more American than anything [else]. But I would still be proud of where my parents came from.

Stated Values

When asked to speak of their values and what was important in living their lives, some White students alluded to abstract concepts and principles associated with American political ideologies. For instance, one student discussed her core values by stating, "I believe in humanity, fairness, and equality."

Others spoke of the importance of having "freedom" to pursue one's "happiness," of "egalitarianism," and of being "nonprejudicial." Still another student reflected on values learned as a child that included the importance of being a patriot and believing in "your country." This articulation of ideological values associated with freedom, equality, and justice, as well as having pride in one's country and patriotism, are central aspects associated with embracing an American identity (Tsai et al., 2002). Furthermore, linked to American ideals of democracy and freedom, several students noted the importance of living in a society where one feels "safe" and is able to achieve "security" in life through "ownership of property" and the accumulation of material wealth—that is, "having a nice house, nice cars." Arguably this is the American dream of many, White or not, that continues to draw many immigrants to this country. Taken together, the values these White students voice are in line with their self-identification as American and their psychological attachment to that identity.

Also in line with embracing an American identity, some students explicitly referred to values associated with the development of an individualistic and autonomous self-concept. This independent definition of self-concept differed, to some extent, from other groups in the study, whose conceptualization of the self, in terms of expressed values, was more collectivistic and interdependent. For instance, related to individualism, students noted the importance of being "independent" and "taking care of oneself first" and being able to pursue their personal ambitions, which for many included "achieving personal success" in various spheres of life but, in particular, in one's education and career path. A number of students also spoke of the importance of maximizing their individual potential by "doing everything to my fullest" and always "striving to get ahead in my own mind and body and soul without hurting anyone in the process." Success could be achieved through individual "hard work," by making "conscious, educated decisions," and by having a "clear purpose" in life. Students also spoke of "being happy" and "doing whatever it takes to be fulfilled" as an individual. The following student commentaries illustrate these values associated with individualism and the importance of self-actualization and achieving personal happiness:

> I think people should feel freedom. I think it's important for people to be able to make their own decisions. They should be able to do what they

think is best and not worry about what other people are thinking . . . but without doing things that are going to hurt other people.

Being what I want to be. Being comfortable [with myself]. Setting goals for myself and then trying to achieve those goals . . . trying not just to make money for myself, but trying to achieve something in life, to achieve a goal, or to be able to, at the end of my life, to look back and say that I was happy with what I did.

Well I think it is important to try and do your best and not just for the idea of getting money or being successful. That's not important to me. What's the point of going through life with just reaching a goal and missing all the things that you could have been doing along the way? Trying to enjoy life and trying to do well. I think people need to define what success is and not the typical American idea of money and success.

White students spoke of the importance of family and friends as one of their core values, though to a lesser extent than other groups. These relationships were viewed as important influences in their lives and sources of support. As one student stated, "[N]umber one is school; I mean graduating from here would be a big plus. Then, after that, it would be my family, you know. Whatever affects them affects me." Likewise, another student said, "There is a sense of protection, security, unity, knowing that you are part of a support network. There are all these people rooting for you." The importance of family and friendships is heard in the following student's reflection:

The most important thing in my life is my family. Definitely my friends play a big role in that. Yeah, I think it all centers around the people I love. School is important to me . . . getting through school. But getting through school and doing what I want to do and go[ing] to graduate school all play a part in what I want to do in life. It's not centered on how much money I want to make or the kind of car I want to drive. I'm very happy living a metamorphic life. I just want to someday have enough that is going to make me happy. I want friends and family around me.

Finally, the students indicated the significance of key moral values in their lives, such as "honesty," "hard work," "loyalty," "trust," "respect," "integrity," "honor," "kindness," and "helping others," which also included family and friends.

I'm very honest. I like to believe that I have a lot of integrity. Those are probably the most important things to me . . . are honesty and integrity. Everything kind of falls in line from there. You know.

Definitely loyalty. Loyalty is very important to me. Trust as well. . . . My family is very important to me. We're real tight after my dad died. Yeah, I think those are the main things.

Family. Values like honesty, respect, love, supporting one another, and really know[ing] your aunties, uncles, and cousins and spending time with them. . . . Dad always says, "Don't lie, cheat, or steal." And there was this phrase he used, "You always have your word. They can take everything away from you, but they can't take away your word."

What was most striking about these students' stated values is that they contradicted previous studies that found White college students to have a predominantly individualistic orientation, that is, highly independent and autonomous self-concepts (Baron, Byrne, & Branscombe, 2006). The findings illustrate the complexity of students' self-concept, which included a view of the self that was not only individualistic, as seen earlier in this section, but also collectivistic in nature. White students spoke of the self in *connection* to family and friends, and their definition of self was most meaningful when cast in terms of such relationships. Hence, our findings challenge the predominant viewpoint in the literature that family does not matter as much to Whites as it does to ethnic minorities, and demonstrates that ethnic differences in value systems—that is, familialism and interdependence—between Whites and other ethnic groups are more a matter of degree than of absolutes (Ramirez & Castaneda, 1974). Unfortunately, such differences in value systems often tend to be exaggerated in the psychological and sociological literature (Arminio, 2001) where individualism in White Americans and collectivism in American ethnic minorities become almost stereotypical characterizations.

Sources of Values

Most students said their values came from their parents and family, and they reflected "a way of living, a way of behaving" that they linked to familial upbringing:

They might have come from my parents, 'cause no matter what I chose to do, my parents may not have supported it, but they always had my back. They gave me a lot of independence. So most of my values came from my parents.

My parents had a lot to do with values [when I was] growing up. They were always telling me how important school was, how important the future was, how important it was to do better than they did, you know. Because they don't have better than a high school education and they're middle class and they, like, make good money, but they want their kids to be more. That always stressed me out. I always tripped on school. I had to do good and wanted to do that. But, yeah, they had a big part in my life and they still do.

I think to me preserving a certain honor and dignity that comes more from my father's side. There we do have a strong family code. You have strong loyalty to the family and not wanting to dishonor the family. So that's fairly important to me. Also, getting good grades and not screwing around too much. So family in that respect is important. You consider yourself a representative. I kinda want to say money. I think anyone would say that. I want to go out and make a living, get ahead a little bit. Though it's not . . . specifically important to be a money machine. It's important to be a success. . . . So there's always been a kind of a push [in my family] to be successful.

Even individuals who were immigrants or second- or third-generation White ethnics in this country described their values as stemming from family and explicitly stated that they believed their values were not directly related to their ethnicity:

Pretty much my parents. It's not an Armenian thing, you know, or anything I've learned from race or ethnicity. It is pretty much what my parents taught me.

I would say from my background. It's basically from my upbringing, my immediate upbringing through my parents. I wouldn't say that other German people have the same values, and I wouldn't say that they didn't, but, basically, I think it stems from the immediate family.

Likewise, students who embraced a more racialized White identification found it difficult to say whether their values were a reflection of ethnicity and/or cultural background:

> It comes from my parents, and I don't know if it's because they were White Anglo and because something was passed down for years and years. In my rose-colored view of the world, hundreds of years ago, more families appeared to be closer and more responsible for each other, so maybe somewhere along the line some families didn't get that passed down.

> I am really honest. I don't lie about things that I don't have to lie about. I don't know if that is a White trait or a Black trait or where I picked that up along the way, but I've always been that way. Sure, I think people shape you, but I don't think that you can really classify it as where it comes from.

Conversely, a few students specifically mentioned religion as an important source of their values. One woman felt that her values came from her Christian beliefs and friends from church. She described herself as having strong Christian and traditional values: "I think abortion isn't right and you shouldn't live in sin." She said her parents were "wishy-washy about values like these," which was why her friends and her church have been more influential. Furthermore, another student discussed the role of church in combination with her family upbringing as shaping her present-day values and beliefs:

> From my church, from my parents, from my grandparents, aunts, and uncles. I am really fortunate to have grown up in the Bible belt, and I got the best of it. . . . I grew up in a fundamentalist atmosphere. My parents and both sets of grandparents . . . lived by Christian principles, and I think you can identify Christian principles to everybody. Christian principles are a way of acting, a way of behaving that puts yourself last and others first, and they live that. You know what I mean. I am so lucky to have had some of these examples.

Another student felt that her values regarding equality and being "nonprejudicial" differed from her parents because she was more open-minded: "My mom would refer to them as like 'the Black people' or 'the Hispanics.' It's like they're just totally prejudiced against them." Finally, one student noted that her values came from identifying with the Seminole Indians because of their beliefs regarding the interaction between man and the environment:

> I identify with Seminole Indians because I like how Indians believe. I'm a vegetarian, not necessarily saying that Indians were vegetarian; some were, but they were more of, like, if you eat meat you were aware of the cost. You were aware of the environment. You were aware of the price that it took on the earth and conscious of that in an environmental way and I live my life that way. I recycle, I don't eat meat.

When asked whether others of their ethnic group shared their values, some students said "sometimes." It is interesting to note that many of their responses had a somewhat skeptical tone. An example comes from a woman who listed her values as honesty and doing the best she can without hurting people: "I'd like to say, everyone shares those values, but then I get suckered and then I realize that's not how everybody is. So, maybe I would hope eighty percent, but I think that's high." Likewise, a Catholic woman who noted that her values stemmed primarily from attending Catholic school stated, "I learned how to treat people with respect. I learned how to treat myself with respect, and that's a lot . . . something that a lot of my generation doesn't know about." Finally, one of the students who considered freedom a value said, "Most Americans would say this is a value that they have, but they don't act that way because there are so many prejudices and because everybody wants everyone to believe what they believe." One student noted insightfully that she probably had more in common with those of her economic class (other upper-middle-class Whites). Still, the largest group felt their values were not associated with their ethnicity or shared by others of their ethnic group.

To conclude, only a few students felt their values could be considered cultural values that stem directly from their ethnicity. One man felt that his staunch conservatism was a cultural value because of Poland's history of being under military reign for a long time. Likewise, another man felt his values regarding family loyalty, having a strong work ethic, and behaving ethically stemmed from being both Irish-Italian and Catholic. Three other students considered their Catholicism a cultural value, and these individuals were of Italian and Spanish heritages. One of these students specifically noted that her strong sense of morality had to do with "having been raised Spaniard and being [both] Spaniard and Catholic." Another stated:

Most Italians are raised in the Catholic church. They are raised with religion in their lives, and I think that makes them different. So the ones that I've come into contact with, I'd have to say, yeah, they probably share a lot of the same values.

Whiteness Framed Within an Interethnic/Interracial Context

I never thought about it [being White] before. It didn't matter to me. But now that I go to [this university], I've had some thoughts and experiences, and it's made me think of my ethnicity.

I never really thought about what it meant to me [to be White] until the last few years. I went to a little school out in the country. There were eight hundred students from grades one through twelve, and there were two Black families. So what did it mean to me? It meant that I was like all my peers. That I wasn't different. I was like them. I didn't think about it (being White) until I came to California. It means a lot more. It's just that then I felt like I was like everyone else, and I guess that was the majority. Now I am not, I am different from a lot of people.

Most White students discussed their racial/ethnic identity most deliberately when framing it within an interethnic and interracial sociopolitical and historical context. Prior to their arrival at the university, the majority of the White participants seldom had to negotiate their Whiteness on a daily basis. As a consequence of their exposure to a multicultural environment, and through interactions with diverse ethnic/racial peers, White students' racial consciousness was raised, and they began to ponder issues regarding racial identity (Gallagher, 1995; Kincheloe, 1999; McDermott & Samson, 2005). Likewise, adolescence and young adulthood also marked for many of these students a time when race and class issues became a significant part of their immediate landscape, not only within the university academic context, but outside this arena as well, where the media, pop music, and interracial dynamics played out within the larger society, all influenced their identity formation as White persons. In this section of the interview, Whiteness was not as easily denied by participants or seen as invisible, but was constructed as an explicit, visible, and meaningful social identification that centered on race (Gallagher, 1995; McDermott & Samson, 1995). Race clearly mattered for these students, and through the discourse of racial and ethnic politics that unfolded within and outside the university walls, Whiteness became a racial identity marker based on color. Here students spoke of their identity in one of five ways:

- they recognized Whiteness as a privileged status;
- they framed Whiteness in terms of having a conflictive racial history;
- they encountered White racism firsthand;
- they dismissed White racism and privilege; and, finally,
- some positioned Whiteness as the new victim in race relations.

In this part of the chapter, it is easier to see varied levels of racial conscious-ness and racial identity development as expressed in students' attitudes and viewpoints (Helms, 1995; Rowe et al., 1995). It should be noted that these themes are not meant to reflect a stage-wise progression of racial identity development, as not all students expressed them.

Acknowledgment of Group's Privileged Status

One of the most frequently mentioned themes the students discussed was that being White had had an impact on them through the privilege it imparts (over half of the sample noted this theme). Students felt they had an easier time in life because of their White ethnic identity. One student described the influences of her ethnicity on her personality development as, "I don't have to deal with a lot of prejudice that others have to deal with, and it's made me a lot more confident . . . I have the strength to be outgoing. I don't have to worry about the pressures of being a minority." Another said, "It's easy for me because I'm White, so I'm accepted readily by the major portion of society. I don't know if that is good or bad." Others said they had not thought of their ethnicity before going to college, where they encoun-tered people from other ethnicities. In comparing their lives with others', they realized that, by virtue of being White, important life opportunities were more accessible to them:

I'm glad I'm not a Black woman growing up because I know it's difficult for a woman, let alone being Black. It's still a White world run by White people for the most part, which is really hard to acknowledge and admit, but that's what it is unfortunately. I've probably had a better education and a better upbringing just because of the opportunities I've received from being White.

I would like to think that it wouldn't be different, that I'd just be the same that I am now. But I think that if I were of a different ethnicity, there are different things that I would have to deal with, and maybe my life wouldn't have been as privileged or as easy as it has been up to this point.

I guess it makes you realize how naïve you are without realizing it. When you wake up, jump in the shower, come home. When you talk to people . . . an African American whose culture (background) made it difficult for him to go to the university. I see how lucky I am to have the opportunities I got. I guess it makes you appreciate then how difficult it must have been for that African American guy—that I am really good friends with—to have gotten in here.

These students had a fairly clear understanding of how they benefited from being White in a White-dominated society on both a cognitive and affective level. They realized the random nature of their fortune and expressed an empathetic perspective in trying to understand what it was like for other ethnic groups in this country. This perspective was offered by the following students:

I think that definitely I have had more advantages. I think I've definitely been able to walk through more doors. But I honestly and wholeheartedly believe that, if anybody educates themselves and goes for it, they can do it. They can make the best out of themselves. I am sure that if there was some-body that mirrored me that was Black, I probably could walk through more doors than they could because of my ethnicity . . . and I am aware of that. I can't help that I was born White. I am sensitive to other ethnicities.

An advantage, although I don't love it, is the color of my skin. I think it's a shame that people take advantage of that. I'm sure I've taken advantage of it and not even known it. . . . I just see that they (ethnic minorities) don't have the same opportunities. People like to toot their horn and say that they do give them the same opportunities, but I don't see that. I still think we are far from that. It's gotten much better since the sixties, but there is still a long way to go. I think that they (ethnic minorities) struggle a lot, are still struggling. . . . I think we are extraordinarily narrow-minded, in a lot of ways selfish and threatened by any kind of movement by any minority. I think in a lot of ways our ethnic group is threatened by them (ethnic minorities), that we try to push them down. Even talking to you, I have to say "us" and "them." It's so bad. I don't like that at all. I'd love to get to a place where we didn't have to differentiate. We could just say "us" as a whole and maybe just distinguish between the length of our toes. I don't know. . . . It just seems so ridiculous . . . so I think that's a huge disadvantage . . . our narrow-mindedness and stubbornness and resistance to change.

As a social identity marker, being White had sensitized students to the ways in which their current social status and implicit power was tied to that of their racial group. This finding lends support to Knowles and Peng's (2005) notion of a power-cognizant identity, in that students were acutely aware of their unearned privilege and recognized that Whiteness was implicitly linked to a "system which restricted the allocation of resources in a stratified society" (p. 239). As stated by the above student, "I think we [Whites] are threatened by any kind of movement by any minority. . . . In a lot of ways our ethnic group is threatened . . . that we try to push them down." Likewise, another student noted, "I have had certain advantages because I am White, but it wasn't stated because you are White you get this. So, maybe it's helped my self-esteem because I've gotten this [unearned privilege]." Yet another student reflected:

I was part of the chosen ones, the blessed. I never thought about that. But growing up, yeah, I had it easier than a lot of people because I was White. I guess moving to California has had a big impact because the world didn't revolve around my group anymore because there is so much diversity here. But I never thought about it before I came here. It's just what it was.

These students realized that, in addition to having benefited from White privilege in terms of having access to important society resources and educational opportunities, they had gained from "living in a culture that delineates one's worldview as correct" and from having had "a sense of entitlement" (Spanierman & Heppner, 2004, p. 249).

In summary, by acknowledging White privilege we hear from students reactive attitudes associated with higher levels of White racial consciousness as well as the pseudoindependence and immersion-emersion statuses of racial identity development (Helms, 1995; Rowe et al., 1995). More specifically, these students were clearly not oblivious to race and White privilege, and as a consequence had adopted a more intellectualized stance regarding racial issues by attempting to understand the meaning of racism and how they benefited from it. Likewise, such students articulated a sense of discomfort with the White status quo and personal meanings of Whiteness.

> White men have always been the standard by which to measure everybody else. So it's not so hard to meet that standard when they're measuring against you. So conformity comes real easy. It's when I don't conform that I am perceived negatively. So, yeah, there are advantages to being White because Whites have been the standard for so long. Doesn't mean it is right, but that's the way it is. Yeah, it's an advantage because it gets you in sometimes when you don't have a chance another way. But it's a disadvantage because it can keep you out of other things. It can keep you out of knowing other ethnic groups and cultures.

What was interesting about this student's reflection was that she not only recognized the meaning of White privilege, but she was able to articulate explicitly that these gains came with a social and psychological cost (Spanierman & Heppner, 2004). In the next section, students speak more pointedly about the personal and psychological costs of White privilege.

Whiteness Defined Within the Context of Personal Encounters With Racism

Close to one-third of the sample made specific references to having *personally* encountered acts of discrimination by other Whites against minority individuals. The *event* of witnessing discrimination, for some perhaps for the first time in their lives, had a strong conscious-raising effect on students. Such experiences clashed with their values of fairness, justice, and equality, and students voiced frustration, irritation, and anger toward other in-group members, whose discriminatory actions damage the group's chances of developing a positive White identity. These students could not deny prejudice as a thing of the past; they had personally encountered White racism and observed the insidious nature of discrimination firsthand.

> I guess it (discrimination) does affect the way I feel about my ethnic group because I hear all the ethnic slurs and that makes me so angry. All that stereotypical stuff makes me really angry. . . . So that has affected the way

I treat other groups in terms of racism. . . . I'm more disappointed in my culture [because] I see other White people treating ethnic [minority] groups poorly. Seeing the stereotypes that people put on [ethnic minority groups]. Now I'm more sensitive to that.

Yeah, discrimination. It's definitely a disadvantage. I mean, you assume that it doesn't go on that often today, but I still see it. I mean, my old boss that I used to work with was an extreme racist. Wouldn't hire people based on race. I think it's still around and still prevalent. Yeah, it's sad.

One of my friends went shopping and she tried to write a check, and the owner decided that he wasn't going to take a check from her because she didn't look like she had the money in her account. She's African American. That has never happened to me.

I see that there's still prejudice there. I feel bad for my Panamanian friend because he does look African American, and I've seen that he was discriminated against in getting housing by two wealthy White women in the real estate firm. I see that at work sometimes. People assume that they [ethnic minorities] might be stealing so people will watch the Hispanics or African Americans to make sure that they are not going to steal something.

These students articulated feelings of empathy and understanding for the experiences of minorities in this country, in particular for ethnic-other friends who they see are victims of racial/ethnic discrimination. These students observed discrimination happening in everyday situations and were cognizant that they were, for the most part, exempt from these types of experiences by virtue of their race. The following student discussed his discontent and anger with a system that targets certain individuals for racial profiling and harassment based on skin color and the blatant unfairness of it:

Mostly a lot of minorities tend to get the short end of the stick when it comes to the law just based on prejudices. For example, a friend of mine has gotten pulled over so many more times than any of us and he's Black. The police will pull him over because [they say] he's got a taillight out and won't let him out of the car to check, and when he gets home, it's all right. They pull[ed] him over the other day and he was wearing blue and they told him that he looked like a Crip (gang member).

And some of us who look different (are not Black) haven't gotten that same treatment. It makes me angry that someone would just automatically, would mark someone. I am not sure that's an actual conscious decision or whether it's sort of [unconscious]. I don't know. It doesn't make me happy.

This student clearly acknowledged the realities of racial oppression and understood that racism occurred not only on an individual basis but at an institutional level as well. For some students, personal encounters with racism triggered a more serious consideration of the meaning of Whiteness, which was associated with having a more mature racial identity (Helms & Cook, 1999). This finding is consistent with Arminio's (2001) qualitative study of White graduate students who reported that race-related experience "stimulates learning, growth, and change" through multiple-perspective integration, which can then position young Whites to take action and work to eliminate racism on a personal, individual, or group level (p. 246).

Accordingly, in acknowledging prejudice and racism, we hear from some White students about attempts to reinvent "Whiteness" as a nonracist identity (Kincheloe & Steinberg, 1998; McDermott & Samson, 2005). The following students offered this view as they struggled to deconstruct negative images of Whiteness and create a new racial identity that was less problematic and reactive. Unlike their view of some other subgroups of White individuals, in particular the "older generation," these White students saw themselves as nonracist.

I was brought up in a very White neighborhood and I was sheltered. Even nowadays, where my parents are concerned. Like you go uptown and you see a Black person, it's like, "Oh!" So I think I've moved away from that. I've just become more opened . . . I don't know how to explain it besides what I've been saying. It's through my own education and my own experiences outside of my parents. Because when I was dating a Black person, I had no idea that they (parents) would have a problem with it. And my mother still insists to this day, it's not because they were Black. . . . My grandmother was like . . . she said the word "colored" . . . and I went, "Grandma!" I was clueless. I didn't even think that it would be a problem. Maybe I am just naïve.

So the riots affected me. . . . Historical events, and the civil rights movement, Martin Luther King. It fills me with mostly joy but sadness as well that that even happened. Just the main historical things as far as freedom and rights. Even though its not totally there one hundred percent, but it still feels good that there is an attempt for that to exist and that, for the most part, a lot of people know and want to acknowledge that everybody should be equal.

I think what impacted me most when I was little were my parents, you know. They grew up in the Midwest, mainly White. They held [negative] stereotypes and, you know, when me and my sister were born, whether they knew it or not, they instilled them in us. Fortunately I've had other people with broader experiences and teachers. Coming to this school helped me open up my eyes to that, you know. People live different styles no matter what ethnicity they are. But everyone's still a person . . . . You['ve] got to look at them as individuals.

I think that White people in general should educate themselves more about what it's like to be Black in the United States. I think that we should do that. Just like taking Women's Studies classes and the Development of Black Child classes. It has helped me a lot to understand another culture's point of view. I think that everybody needs to do that. Other cultures are forced to understand how to get along in mainstream White America, and White people are never forced to do that.

These students' reflections are representative of Helms's (1995) immersion-emersion and autonomy statuses of racial identity development and point to a more mature level of racial consciousness. Students expressed a more flexible and integrative analysis and awareness of race-related issues and have striven through their personal reeducation and experiences to abandon racism (Helms, 1990, 1995). Unfortunately, current forms of multiculturalism within university settings do not do enough to provide White students with the narrative tools needed to reinvent Whiteness as a positive, antiracist social identity (Kincheloe, 1999).

A Dismissal of White Racism and White Privilege

Another, albeit less prominent, theme to emerge from some students' narratives was the tendency to minimize the existence of racial and ethnic disparities in American society. Less than a handful of White respondents voiced this theme when they spoke of Whiteness in connection to other racial/ethnic groups. Consistent with Rowe and colleagues' (1995) model of racial consciousness and Helms's (1995) contact stage (immature and/or unexamined identity status) of racial identity development, students who articulated

Whiteness in this manner were more likely to espouse avoidance-type attitudes when it came to race and interethnic relations.

> I don't think racism is an issue. I think pretty much each group has its own equality and their own rights. American is pretty much an equal country.

> In the past, there were [disadvantages to being a minority]. Throughout history, but right now, the experience that I've had, and the things that I've seen, I have not noticed any advantages or disadvantages or positive or negative aspects. Like I said before, I mean, with every race, different races have enslaved other races. Other races have gone to war with other races and religions and all of it. In the past, every ethnic group has suffered at one time or another. But not based on experiences or what I . . . can think of right now, or what I've observed going on in society right now. . . . I mean, of course discrimination is a bad thing, but I think it happens on an individual level. Certain people in the world hold certain views and they might discriminate against others based on these views, but I don't think society is discriminating.

These students denied present-day structural racism and tended to trivialize racial and ethnic inequalities in American society by viewing them as a thing of the past. Such students believed that ethnic minorities today generally experience little discrimination and that ethnic relations in America had changed and were now fine. Characteristic of individuals in lower levels of racial/ethnic identity development (e.g., avoidant status of racial consciousness and contact stage of racial identity), students tended to negate White privilege selectively and adopt a distorted view of reality when it came to race-related experiences of people of color. This finding is consistent with research concerning the negative affective cost of White privilege for White individuals; that is, some Whites express a general sense of apathy regarding White racism and a lack of consideration for issues affecting minorities in this country (D'Andrea & Daniels, 2001; Spanierman & Heppner, 2004). When asked whether there is still discrimination against African Americans today, one student said,

> Sometimes. I think a lot of it is really their perception or maybe just because I'm not that ethnic group I can't see it the way they can. But I think a lot of it they make up to get what they want and how they want it. They can sit there and do a discrimination lawsuit. I think they push

that a lot, and sometimes it can be to their advantage or to their disadvantage. They put a lot of pressure on ethnicity and a lot of stake on ethnicity, where I think it's just another one of those things, like men-women issues.

Accordingly, another avoidant defense mechanism among some Whites who had a distorted view of other groups was to adopt a color-blind perspective (Spanierman & Heppner, 2004). Some students minimized and negated the importance of race and ethnicity by embracing a color-blind ideology that espouses that individuals are all human beings regardless of color, yet form opinions of others based on race (Knowles & Peng, 2005):

> I think that it will all come down to the person. I believe that if a person wants something in this country, regardless of what's put in front of you, if you push hard enough and long enough, you are going to get it. You may be on your own stumbling block. So if a person of color is going to let their color get in their way, that's their problem. . . . I believe everybody deserves the best that this country has to offer them. I don't care who you are. I think surveys and things that deal with ethnicity are bullshit. Any time that I have to write down on a piece of paper on this campus what my ethnicity is I get angry, because it is used for something that I don't know, and I don't think that my ethnicity or anyone else's should have anything to do with education. I'm a person. That's it.

> I don't believe in making race an issue. I don't like that term "minority status." I hear that a lot up here. I think it makes irrelevant all the issues of a person's individuality by saying—it's so hard to explain, but I just don't think that you focus on one minority group and say that the status of this group—I don't think you should focus on an ethnicity, first of all. So it's hard to say, there could be studies that say maybe a lot of Hispanics live in poverty and so they'll publish something that says that the Hispanic group status is in a bad situation. But that's not speaking on an individual level. It's a tough issue.

By embracing a color-blind perspective, these students could avoid more easily any sense of accountability for past or present ethnic/racial inequalities. They adhered to the belief that ethnic and racial differences should be disregarded in favor of individual, personal, and pan-human characteristics (Knowles & Peng, 2005). Knowles and Peng note that a color-blind ideology appeals to many young Whites because it "spares them the discomfort of considering the many unearned advantages conferred by Whiteness" (2005, p. 225).

A History of Conflictive Interracial Relations

White students spoke most frequently of their Whiteness in the context of past and present racial history and conflictive interracial relations (approximately three-quarters of the sample made references to this theme at some point in the interview). While some students noted this as merely reflecting a factual reality, for others it carried a more negative connotation. Specifically, in discussions of interracial history—in particular White-Black inter-ethnic relations—we heard from some students a real sense of collective guilt when confronted with the wrongdoings committed by members of their own group (Arminio, 2001; Baron et al., 2006). The sense of guilt for past/present injustices was perhaps one of the strongest feelings reported among White students. This finding is consistent with previous research concerning the concept of "White guilt" that points directly to the psychological cost of White racism for White persons (Arminio, 2001; Spanierman & Heppner, 2004). One student said that at times he found it "really upsetting to be classified as White. Okay, you're responsible for this form of prejudice . . . [for instance] the two hundred years of Black slavery." Another student offered a similar perspective:

> I used to live in, like, Manhattan Beach. There is this beautiful park in Manhattan Beach and everyone looks at it and they say, "Oh, it's really pretty. It's nice." But the true story behind that park is that a long time ago there were these Black families that lived in that neighborhood, and what they (the community) did was pretty much ran them out of town . . . I don't know if someone actually torched one of their houses or something like that and they burned them down (houses). And then they made the park [where the Black people used to live]. So there aren't that many Black families or any other minorities [in Manhattan Beach]. Just a bunch of different things I've seen as far as racial things like that in the different areas that I lived in. . . . Sometimes I think that being White automatically puts you into that category, and I don't like that.

She elaborated further:

> Well, I think that we all have to deal with the fact that our ancestors enslaved people. I think that there is always going to be tension because of

the fact that we, as White people, thought that they weren't even human beings and that's always going to be there. There's always going to be unwritten rules that we think we are superior, and maybe we even act like we are. I don't know. It's just something that's there. I mean it's just funny when you think about it. It wasn't even that long ago that Black people couldn't even sit in a movie theater with us or sit in the front of the bus. That is embarrassing. And the Ku Klux Klan and the whole Oklahoma thing, that is embarrassing. It's frustrating, and it makes me not want to be White.

Through academic and nonacademic public discourse of U.S. racial history and racial politics, students entering young adulthood gain greater racial consciousness and an understanding of the social-political implications of their identities as White individuals (Kincheloe, 1999). As a result, some experienced a sense of guilt and shame from being linked to a group that has perpetuated ethnic/racial oppression. Guilt in this case was an emotional response to experiencing a decrease in group esteem and positive identity because of the behavior of the group. It stemmed from a violation in students' personal belief systems regarding core American values of humanity, equality, and fairness and the existence of race-based discrimination (Arminio, 2001). This finding is consistent with those reported by Swim and Miller (1999), who found that college students who experienced White guilt also reported feeling less positive about their race and had stronger beliefs about White privilege. This was also linked to having fewer personal prejudices concerning people of color. For example:

It makes me sad when I think that people who are members of minority groups feel that White people assume that they are superior, or people of ethnic groups feel less advantage than White people. I feel that it's true in many, many external ways, that our society sees us differently. It makes me sad to feel a part of the privileged when I would like it to be equal. . . . I hope for better opportunities and chances for people in the minority group that feel there is prejudice against them. I feel sad that people have to live with the reality that just because they're born a certain color there is prejudice against them.

So how does it make me feel [when I see discrimination by Whites]? Does it change my opinion of other Whites? Yes. I don't necessarily want to identify with that. That is one way in which I have changed. I really started, especially since I moved out here to California, I really started taking people on a person-to-person basis. I don't think that [most] Whites do that. . . . It irritates me when I see White people typically not taking people on a person-to-person basis.

A number of students spoke more deliberately about the stigma attached to current constructions of Whiteness as the *oppressor* of minorities: "I don't know how to change that. It makes me personally feel bad that I'm associated with the oppressing group, so I feel not guilty, but ashamed that people would do that." Likewise, the following students offered their perspectives on Whites as oppressors:

> Over the years there have been a lot of negative images attached to it [Whiteness]. I guess I'd rather not be associated with that. The racism, the hatred-type deal. It is often associated with the White European descendents. The whole concept of Western domination. . . . [Like I said] Again, there's a lot of stigma attached [to Whiteness]. There's always a stereotype attached. Again, it's something like an oppressor type. There's a lot of White Anglos, a lot of them in power, and there's always a question: are they discriminating? are they doing something that's harmful to one certain group? It makes me wonder every time I meet someone new, just in the back of my mind. Do they think I am that way?

> I think historically just the whole slavery thing. At the time that it was going on White people thought it was okay. I think that people assume that White people still think it's okay. And because historically White people held that position, now it's affecting us negatively.

These students plainly echo the feeling that Whiteness has become demonized as a racial category, particularly when framed within the context of American racial history. As a consequence, these students found it difficult to identify in a meaningful and positive manner with a racial category they viewed as being explicitly linked to prejudice and discrimination. Hence, as a defense mechanism some White students choose to distance themselves from their group membership by avoiding that social identification (Eichstedt, 2001). Students also felt threatened by the perception that other groups viewed them in a negative light, and as a consequence, some students felt the experience and/or feared being stereotyped negatively—"All Whites are racist." The following students illustrate this fear when discussing what they perceived to be the negative aspects associated with being White:

> I think it's getting tougher to be considered White because everyone seems to be putting White people down a lot. There're so many stereotypes that I don't think people recognize—a lot of people say, "Well, White people are racist," you know, "White people are prejudiced." I think it is almost getting to be embarrassing to be White. I am afraid to say, well, I am White because people kind of have that way of thinking that maybe you are racist or prejudiced or you get benefits that other people don't, which I don't think is necessarily true all the time. I don't know. I guess . . . I think there's a lot of stereotypes, just a lot of negative stereotypes about White people.

> As far as negative aspects, we have to take on the responsibility of keeping relationships good with other ethnic groups. It's the White man's fault, in a way. I just think there's a bad rap. It's like just in being White, you have taken something away from some ethnic group when I know I haven't taken something away from a Black person. Feeling a little bit shaky all the time that anything I say could be misconstrued. Since then I've dealt with that better. Now I'm just going to say what I'm going to say, and if it's taken as prejudiced, then I'm sorry but it wasn't meant that way.

Students also discussed how other groups blame and discriminate against Whites because of what their ancestors did:

> Like I was mentioning before, how White people have made a lot of mistakes, like big mistakes. That affects me in the sense that it has strained some ethnic relationships these days. I don't think that it was totally White people who made mistakes in the past, but they made the major ones. Even the establishment of the United States—White people—came and swept through. Now it causes a bitter, bad relationship among people. And I think that on both ends we feel like, why do we have to pay for that? But then again, you feel like it was bad.

> I think a lot of things historically impact how we are now. I mean, I remember being in the mall when I was little and having an African American come up to me and say they hated me because my great, great, great grandparents might have had slaves, you know. It's like, wait a minute;

why are you saying that to me, you know. I'm thirteen years old, I had nothing to do with it.

Likewise another student said, "Whites are discriminated against" because

> Blacks and other cultures look back on history and they say they were jerks, they didn't treat us right and that's why we're in the situation we are in now. Our parents' parents' parents were not able to get jobs. . . . It goes down from generation to generation.

The interviewer asked if this last student thought that was fair to other groups, to which the student replied, "I don't look at it like that because it's true they were discriminated against, although it wasn't me." Others were not as forgiving in their interpretation of their responsibility in past events. One student noted,

> I guess the way I look at it is, we're here and now, and I personally did not do that to you and so you know, let's sort of start over. I have a difficult time with people focusing a lot on history because that was not you and that was not me and it is now.

One woman saw it as a struggle: "What was done [a] hundred years ago, people are trying so hard to improve, and sometimes I feel that, rather than working toward that, some people are against it."

Taken together, these findings reveal that White racism affects not only its victims but Whites as well. Students communicated this in terms of a loss of group esteem and positive group identity stemming from feelings of guilt and shame concerning their race (Spanierman & Heppner, 2004). Students conveyed other negative emotional reactions related to White guilt, including sadness, frustration, and racial anxiety. More specifically, approximately half the students in the sample expressed some form of negative affection-reaction when discussing White racism. Students noted that they are now burdened with the legacies of White racism that are manifest in terms of present-day conflictive interracial relations and discrimination. It is important to note that, for some of these students, such negative emotional reactions were also associated with expressing higher levels of White racial consciousness (reactive-type attitudes) and racial identity development (pseudoindependent and immersion-emersion type statuses) (Helms, 1995;

Rowe et al., 1995). More specifically, those voicing a deeper understanding of racism also tended to express more empathy for the plight of ethnic/racial minorities and a sense of responsibility and indebtedness toward such groups (Spanierman & Heppner, 2004; Swim & Miller, 1999).

This sense of accountability toward racial minority groups was heard in the following student's statement, "that it's the White man's fault," hence, "we have to take on the responsibility of keeping relationships good with other ethnic groups." Finally, although Helms and Cook (1999) discuss guilt and shame as an aspect of the process of developing a nonracist positive identity when faced with the moral dilemma of White privilege, there is a danger that persons can become paralyzed by such feelings. Spanierman and Heppner (2004) note that "sometimes Whites become 'stuck' in guilt and shame, which consequently may inhibit them from increasing their racial awareness beyond their current levels and further prevent them from taking action to challenge racism" (p. 260).

Whites Positioned as the New Victim—A Sense of Ethnic Victimization

Another theme that emerged from students when they spoke of Whiteness in relation to other racial groups was that, at times, they experienced a sense of ethnic victimization (43% of the White students in the sample voiced this sentiment at some point during the interview). This finding of White ethnic victimization is consistent with survey research (Sidanius, Van Laar, Levin, & Sinclair, 2004) of White students attending ethnically diverse universities as well as earlier qualitative research (Gallagher, 1995) of White college students from working-class backgrounds. Here students reconstructed Whiteness as an identity of uniform privilege that is also a victim of race-based discrimination, current forms of multicultural discourse, and campus racial politics.

One way in which students explained White ethnic victimization was by saying that being White now came with a social cost in the form of "reverse discrimination" (Gallagher, 1995). Some students stated that racial double standards existed on campus that favored minorities and positioned Whites as the "new losers" in race relations (p. 175). One student discussed evidence of discrimination on campus because minorities "get better treatment" in terms of programs (i.e., tutoring) that are available to them and said, "I would get rid of every special group or ethnic advantage there is, first of all."

Likewise, another student stated: "You are treated as a minority. You get prejudice like with respect to graduation and graduate school." When students spoke of reverse discrimination in terms of professional and occupational opportunities, they evidenced a real sense of anxiety and insecurity about the future. "It makes me bitter sometimes, like in applying for school. Right now, I'm thinking of that and I think that we're all the same qualified, so why does it even have to be an issue?" asked one student. Others thought that if minorities were being granted certain opportunities, this implied that something (e.g., job and career opportunities) was being taken away from them as Whites, which put in jeopardy Whites' future (Kincheloe, 1999). One student explained, "I cite my friend as an example whose wife couldn't get a job as a fireman because she was White. They needed to fill their quotas for the minorities because of that law." Likewise, another noted:

> Well it depends, like, I kind of wonder about quotas sometimes. If they (ethnic minorities) will not be hired on the basis of merit, will I not get the job because I am White and if there is anything I can do about that. But I just figure, on the other hand, that I'll just try my hardest to do whatever I can to get by.

Heard in these students' narratives were attitudes that resemble the conflictive-type status of White racial consciousness in that they struggled with competing values regarding justice, fairness, and equality versus individual achievement and merit (Richardson & Silvestri, 1999). Although these students did not endorse any form of discrimination toward minorities, they had mixed feelings about educational and employment initiatives aimed directly at redressing the long-term negative effects of past discriminatory practices. For example:

> Affirmative action, that's something that upset me. I agree why we have it, but then, on the other hand, I think it's kind of become reverse discrimination in some respects. It's kind of sad to me that it might impede my happiness in life. I mean, other people definitely need an advantage. African Americans and women all have been stepped on. They do need to get some respect. Then again, I think maybe that I don't want to pay for other people's mistakes when I had nothing to do with it.

> A disadvantage is just being White. With all the affirmative action and everything for minorities, I kind of like being a minority. I feel like that

when I'm turning in stuff for grad school. I am trying to get accepted into the program that only accepts eighteen students per year, and the person at the office told me, "You're a White male; well, good luck." When it's put to me like that way, it's kind of discouraging. It's not the kind of advantage it used to be, like in the sixties when, if you were White, you weren't a minority. You were treated better and had privilege. I think it still shows itself now, but it's not as prevalent.

I guess maybe . . . before, more people used to hire White people, I guess. I don't know; I guess White people were considered at one time they had more, were offered more, had more access to things, but now I kind of feel, I have mixed feelings. I do have a lot of minority friends. Now it's almost like, well, "Now that you are White, well, you know, we really need to hire more people that are minority so—you know" [not more Whites]. I don't feel like there are very many disadvantages [with being a minority] . . . to me it seems there's almost more advantages. Especially, I guess, in L.A. where we have so many cultures.

Students also felt uneasy about multicultural and racial discourse they viewed as an explicit attack on White people. "Right now, it's popular to bash Caucasian men. That's not a good thing." Likewise, another student noted her displeasure and unease with multicultural curriculum:

I've taken some classes that have . . . like this one [cultural pluralism course], and I had an idiotic teacher that was White but thought he was Black, and he really made a point to demean the upper middle class White people and how they are responsible for repressing Black people. I just thought, you can't open your mouth because there is some tension, and I never really thought of it that way and I don't really see why there needs to be . . . I'm uncomfortable because I don't know how they feel. To me, it's like I'm a human being, you're a human being, so what. You have a better tan than I have. But I don't know how the other person is going to react.

Classroom discussions regarding race-related issues engendered feelings of discomfort and racial anxiety among White students because they did not know how to handle such situations, especially with ethnic-minority peers. As Kincheloe (1999) notes, White students often perceive "multicultural requirements as Anti-White restrictions that subject them to charges of racism merely because they are White" (p. 176). Hence they view multiculturalism and race-related discourses as an unfair assault on Whiteness. As one student noted:

> I'm taking U.S. history, and all I hear about is the typical slave history and how the White race is responsible for a lot of oppression. I know there's a lot of damage but after a while, you know. I hate feeling that there is animosity just because of color. If someone has animosity towards me, I would like to know what it is, how I can fix it, and how we get past it. So sometimes I feel it's just because I'm White they're thinking that, as a whole, White people really hurt them and are they putting me in that category without knowing me.

Furthermore, the perception of White victimization from multiple directions was pointedly heard in the words of the following students as they discussed the disadvantages Whiteness confers:

> Yeah, I would say positive and negative in the same category in terms of, like, how people view you and discrimination-type things. In the past, it has been a White person's world. So it probably makes stuff easier that I don't even notice, but then, it would make things easier than if I were from a different ethnic background. But also, sometimes I feel discriminated [against] for stuff I didn't do. And I don't think it's a good because it makes me bitter sometimes, like in applying for school. Right now, I'm thinking of that and I think, we're all the same qualified, so why does it even have to be an issue? I also think that sometimes, not just in applying to schools but in general, like, I feel a little blamed.

> A disadvantage [in being White] is that people put a lot of pressure on what color you are and that people are, like, "White people are prejudice[d]," and it's like sometimes I feel they're more prejudice[d] against me because I'm White and it's like, you know, I don't care. I can't see any advantage to it [being White]. You know, I think the disadvantage is that I can't get all kinds of scholarships and everything because I'm not ethnic. It's just, like, I'm not Hispanic. I'm not Asian. I don't have any Indian. I'm not anything. They got all these scholarships.

> The slave days are over, and if we don't get past that and move on, none of us are going to be able to function together. I know that I may sound

so naïve. I know that there is a lot of anger and a lot of pain there. But I really believe wholeheartedly that we all have the power within us to make ourselves better. To say that you can't get a job because you are Black or because you are this or that, you know. I'm busting my butt to go to school. I'm managing to do it. Yeah, I'm White, but I'm angry that I can't get loans or aid because there are people ahead of me. We all have our hardships, and to blame the White race is not constructive. It doesn't help anything.

Not to undermine students' real sense of victimization, but arguably much of their resentment stemmed from espousing color-blind ideologies and the desire to embrace the belief in an egalitarian and merit-based society (Gallagher, 1995; McDermott & Samson, 2005), where minorities are now granted every opportunity and advantage (if not more) as are Whites. There was the perspective that past government and legal initiatives have leveled the playing field between ethnic minorities and Whites; hence, race-based organizations and/or student aid programs are seen as discriminating against Whites because they are exclusionary. The students seemed to perceive a loss of power as Whites stemming from unwarranted liberal concerns over past racial/ethnic injustices that are no longer relevant. This perception is coupled with their recognition that America's racial population is undergoing major demographic changes, and that Whites are becoming a racial minority (Kincheloe, 1999; McDermott & Samson, 2005; Wong & Cho, 2005). Although they did not always articulate this explicitly, students saw these forces as threatening the status of Whiteness. As one student noted, "In the past it was a White man's world."

Also linked to this sense of ethnic victimization was the perspective that Whites were not allowed to express their ethnicity, and that multiculturalism and campus racial politics repress White identity (Gallagher, 1995; Ingram, 2005; Kincheloe, 1999). Students also spoke of racial double standards in that minorities were free to explore their ethnic and racial identities, whereas Whiteness as a cultural identity was suppressed within the university walls.

I am not sure what it means to be White really. There are so many functions, like Black History Month, the *Cinco de Mayo* celebration, and there's not really a White celebration. I don't really see anything on this campus for my culture. I kind of feel left out.

> You're really not allowed to express your ethnic identity unless you are a minority group. I'm in a sorority, but I don't think that people allow you to express your ethnic identity even if you think you have one, because people start screaming racism.

These students fail to recognize that White culture is dominant within most university institutions and permeates major aspects of campus life and learning. It is seen through curriculum content and ideological perspectives taught (White Eurocentric paradigms predominate in academia), as well as in dominant campus organizations such as the Greek fraternities and sororities and events, which continue to be a part of the university landscape (Kincheloe, 1999; Sidanius et al., 2004). Nonetheless, this perspective is consistent with many White students' view of Whiteness as a normalized identity; hence, its symbols and ideologies are invisible to them.

Students also spoke of how campus racial politics prohibited expressions of White pride, and they expressed resentment that such actions were denied to them and not to ethnic minorities. More specifically, there was resentment that if one were to open a White club on campus or claim White pride, others would construe it as racist.

> You got the African American Club, you got the Mexican American club, you got the Japanese American club and you got all these cultures and you're going, you know, "Where's the White Club?" You know, and you see all these cultures and you kind of go . . . you know. Yea, and it's the kind of people who make such a big deal out of it. But if you open something like a White club or a Caucasian club, people start screaming discrimination.

> Those that say that they are proud to be White are negative people thinking bad things, you know. So if I was to wear a shirt that said, "Proud to Be White," as opposed to a Black person wearing, "Proud to Be Black," I couldn't do that. I couldn't wear a "Proud to Be White" shirt because it would be, "Well, you are a racist. Well, you hate African Americans. Anyone who's not White." You are just not allowed to be positive. . . . I think where we are right now it is okay for people of other ethnic groups to be proud of what they are, but it is difficult to be White nowadays and be proud of that.

Because of the obscured legacy of structural privilege, young White students frequently ignore or overlook the power differential that exists between Whites and non-Whites (McDermott & Samson, 2005). Hence, current iterations of racism that continue to affect ethnic minorities in this country go unseen. In denying White privilege and how they benefit indirectly or directly by their skin color, these students reconstructed Whiteness as the new victim. Other scholars have argued that this perspective of White victimization would be valid if it were, indeed, true that being White is no different from being Black, Latino/a, or Asian in American society (Gallagher, 1995; Ingram, 2005). Only within such a social context of racial parity would the creation of a White club or White pride not potentially be misconstrued or questioned as an attempt to reaffirm and reestablish a threatened and illegitimate privileged status (Ingram, 2005; Tajfel & Turner, 1986). Students either naively or selectively denied this power dynamic that links race to class in our society; consequently, they failed to recognize "race-neutrality as a way of maintaining an unjust status quo" (Kincheloe, 1999, p. 176).

In light of the above discussion, it is clear that some White students have reacted negatively to the multicultural movement in academic discourse. It has engendered in some feelings of resentment and racial anxiety and triggered a somewhat defensive approach in others, as seen through the construction of White victimization. These outcomes belie a central goal of multicultural pedagogy, which is to provide a more inclusive pedagogy grounded in social justice (Kincheloe, 1999). If multiculturalism and, more specifically, multicultural pedagogy is to reach such students effectively, we must consider the sociopolitical context that creates the selective denial of White privilege among such students, while at the same time takes into consideration the viewpoints of those who do "genuinely feel victimized" (p. 176). This point is underscored by the fact that some of the students who voiced feelings of ethnic victimization in this section were also some of the same students who earlier had grappled with the issue of a conflicted racial history, how to construct a better racial environment, and the importance of developing a nonracist identity. These findings point to how problematic a White racial/ethnic identity was for such students as they struggled to reconcile their experiences as White individuals within the larger sociopolitical and historical context of race relations.

Summary and Conclusions

In this chapter we attempted to provide a comprehensive analysis of the discourse of White identity as articulated by young White students attending ethnically and racially diverse universities. Whiteness in these university environments was salient by the mere fact that White students were numerically in the minority relative to students of color. Hence, these individuals were forced to negotiate Whiteness and consider, perhaps for the first time, the meaning of their ethnic and racial identities. What emerged from students' narratives was not a unified description of White identity, but rather one that was varied and at times expressed in contradictions.

In describing their ethnic backgrounds, students either made reference to an elusive European symbolic identification or simply labeled themselves racially as White or Caucasian. There were many, however, among these two groups of students who in the end favored an "American" or "White American" identity as being most descriptive of their cultural and ethnic/racial identification. That is, to be White was seen as a cultural default for an American. Worldviews associated with an American identity were implicitly and explicitly heard throughout students' commentaries, in particular when they were describing their values. Likewise, American political ideologies related to equality, justice, and humanity also shaped students' reflections regarding Whiteness, especially when framed within the context of interracial relations.

White students' construction of Whiteness and the meaning of this racial/ethnic identity differed from other ethnic groups' primarily in that Whiteness was defined as cultureless. Minorities were viewed as having ethnicity, and to be White meant that one was a nonethnic, without culture and/or ethnicity (Perry, 2001). Other expressions of Whiteness as a cultureless identity were reflected in students' seeing themselves beyond ethnicity/culture to be racially/ethnically *neutral* and, consequently, just a person, an individual, a human being. Heard in this rationalistic and cultureless construction of Whiteness were also ideological views regarding how Whites—as the dominant group—should treat and relate to other ethnic minority groups in an ethical, moral, and open-minded capacity (i.e., what was meant by being a good, nonracist White person). To be too ethnic, however, could cloud one's ability to be rational and nonprejudiced (i.e., the fear that one would become ethnocentric). In this sense Whiteness signified a social location in relation to other groups with ethnicity. Furthermore, the tendency among some students to dismiss the importance of having a cultural past in favor of a more present- or future-oriented definition of the self was linked to notions of a cultureless identity.

A White identity also differed from that of other ethnic groups in that it was seen as normal, ordinary, and therefore invisible and not psychologically salient to one's definition of the social self. This was indicative of attitudes that resemble an unexplored and unexamined ethnic identity (Phinney, 1995). As illustrated in the section concerning expressions of White identity, for many students, Whiteness was not a tangible social identity with clear cultural demarcations and sense of connectedness to a group and an ancestral cultural past. Expressions of White identity were elusive and difficult to articulate, especially among students who demonstrated a racialized White identification. For some, this "normalized" and "cultureless" construction of Whiteness left them with a sense of cultural vacuum and envy of what they saw as an inherent strength in other ethnic minority groups.

Whiteness was discussed most explicitly when framed within an interracial context. Exposure to multiculturalism and diverse peers made it impossible for students to deny Whiteness or see it as invisible and transparent within that social milieu. Within this context, Whiteness was clearly a racial marker that was psychologically salient and significant within students' social identities. Inside the discourse of multiculturalism and racial politics, race mattered for White students, and personal meanings attributed to Whiteness were clearly more problematic, reactionary, defensive, and conflictive. In this section of the chapter, it is easier to identify varied levels of racial consciousness and racial identity development, as expressed by students' attitudes (Helms, 1995; Rowe et al., 1995).

Some students acknowledged Whites' privileged status on a more factual level, and others understood more clearly that privileges conferred by Whiteness are linked to a system of ethnic/racial stratification. For many, acknowledging White privilege engendered negative affective reactions (i.e., White guilt) that were associated with a loss of group esteem and positivity regarding one's racial group. Students felt blamed and discriminated against for their ancestors' transgressions, and, consequently, they now bear the stigma conferred by Whiteness as the "oppressor" of racial minorities. The experience of being negatively stereotyped (i.e., that others will see me as racist because I am White) was felt acutely and provoked feelings of racial anxiety in some. Encounter experiences with White racism directed at ethnic minority individuals—especially friends—had a powerful conscious-raising effect on White students. These students understood that racism occurs not only on an individual basis but exists at cultural and institutional levels as well. Some of these students grappled with deconstructing the negative images attached to Whiteness and attempted to construct a new positive, nonracist racial identity characteristic of Helms's (1995) immersion-emersion and autonomy statuses.

There were also a few students who chose to deny or selectively ignore White privilege and racism. Such students tended to trivialize racial and ethnic disparities in American society as a historical phenomenon and, consequently, felt little sense of accountability or indebtedness to people of color or responsibility for dismantling racism. Of more serious concern was the somewhat defensive approach some students took in reconstructing Whiteness as the new victim of discrimination (Kincheloe, 1999; McDermott & Samson, 2005). Students described issues related to reverse discrimination and the existence of racial double standards that make Whites the new loser in race relations. Likewise, students spoke with resentment about current forms of multiculturalism that they viewed as an explicit and unfair attack on Whiteness. Some of these students also felt campus racial politics such as "political correctness" repressed White identity and expressions of White pride. Unfortunately what was implied (although never directly stated) was that those responsible for repressing Whiteness are ethnic minorities (Kincheloe, 1999). As other researchers have noted, this can only exacerbate students' resentment toward these groups and accentuate ethnic/racial divisions and tensions.

In conclusion, other scholars have spoken of Whiteness as being in a state of crisis and transition (Giroux, 1997; Ingram, 2005; Kincheloe, 1999; McDermott & Samson, 2005) triggered by the multicultural movement and recent changes in U.S. racial/ethnic demography. Although current forms of multiculturalism in university settings have succeeded in raising White racial consciousness, they have not provided White students with the space or narrative discourse needed to "rethink their identity around a new, progressive, assertive, counter-hegemonic, antiracist identity" (Kincheloe & Steinberg, 1998, p.20). Clearly, students need to be afforded the space within multiculturalism to articulate a new White identity in which Whiteness is not demonized as a racial category or, in a defensive response, reconstructed as a victimized identity. Many young Whites have responded negatively to multi-culturalism, "not so much out of disbelief or rejection but out of frustration as to what to do with their new knowledge. . . . Without a vision of racial reinvention and support for the difficulties it entails [Kincheloe & Steinberg, 1998, p. 21]," such students feel lost, alienated, and victimized by multicultural and race-related discourse. Furthermore, according to Arminio (2001), what adds to many young Whites' negative feelings and guilt regarding their race is the failure of multicultural pedagogy to highlight positive contemporary White role models who work to dismantle and eliminate racism and whose actions could serve as a template for healthy racial/ethnic development. Based on the findings reported in this study, we agree with previous scholars' arguments that a central pedagogical goal of future White studies must be the articulation of a "positive, proud, attractive, antiracist White identity that is empowered to travel in and out of various racial/ethnic circles with confidence and empathy" (Kincheloe, 1999, p. 174). Accordingly, Kincheloe proposes that:

> The reinvention of Whiteness must operate outside any notion of racial superiority and inferiority, as it seeks to transverse the terrain of transitional identity. While it confronts White tyranny directly, it avoids projecting guilt onto White students. In the process, it generates a sense of pride in the possibility that White people can help transform the reality of social inequality and reinvent themselves around notions of justice, community, social creativity, and economic/political democracy (p. 187).

7

INFLUENCES OF DIVERSE UNIVERSITY CONTEXTS ON STUDENTS' ETHNIC IDENTITY AND COLLEGE ADJUSTMENT

There is so much diversity at RU, it helps me to feel comfortable, and if people do look at me differently, I do not notice it. At RU there is so much racial diversity, I do not think people look at me and say, "Look, there is a Korean girl." No, it's just another RU student. (Asian/American)

On this campus . . . I don't feel any discrimination or nothing like that. You know, you go do your work to get the grade, that's just the bottom line. And I feel like I'm just a normal girl on campus. I don't feel I'm narrowed out or singled out or anything like that. I just blend in. (African American)

During the course of the past decade, America's ethnic minority population has increased dramatically. This has brought about major shifts in the ethnic and racial composition of universities and colleges across the nation, which has important implications for higher education and the preparation of young individuals for life in an increasingly pluralistic society. Moreover, these changes in the ethnic and racial demography of universities have significant consequences for campus climate, which bear on important psychological processes related to students' ethnic identity as well as their adjustment and success in college. With the greater diversification of university campuses, ethnic identity issues have become more salient for persons and interethnic relations a more central focal point of college life. As noted by French and colleagues, the college context and its associated interethnic dynamics is most likely to be an "ethnicity conscious-ness-raising experience that makes students begin to think about who they are and what it means to be a member of their racial/ethnic group" (French, Seidman, Allen, & Aber, 2000, p. 598). Hence, this phenomenon of ethnic diversification and the experiences of students who live and study in structur-ally diverse university settings are the focus of this chapter.[1] Therefore, we deviate in this chapter from discussing the ethnic identity development of specific ethnic groups of students, to an examination of the role that cultur-ally diverse university environments play in this process, and the challenges and difficulties that role presents for students and their adjustment to college as ethnic persons.

Campus Climate and Ethnic Identity

Upon entering college, many students find themselves in the middle of a process that embodies their own psychological development as well as the demands of two or more environments—home and college. Most students will encounter university environments that are different from those from which they came, in both experience and expectation. More important, stu-dents entering universities today are more likely to come from "highly segre-gated high school environments across the nation" and to confront ethnic and social differences for the first time in college (Hurtado, Engberg, Pon-juan, & Landreman, 2002, p. 166). As they struggle to fit in the worlds of their past and present, ethnically diverse institutions will need to create cam-pus cultures that support and respect students' past, acknowledge their dif-ferent experiences, and support their development as they prepare to enter an increasingly diverse future.

Campus climate refers to the judgments and evaluations students make of the university institution (Reid & Radhakrishnan, 2003). This concept has been used to explain how structural, sociohistorical, and political factors can impinge on students' perceptions of an institution, which can, in turn,

---

1. The qualitative findings reported in this chapter were first published in *Cultural Diversity and Ethnic Minority Psychology* (Santos, Ortiz, Morales, & Rosales, 2007). The findings reported in this chapter pro-vide a more extensive analysis of the entire interview protocol where the college experience emerged as significant to students' development.

profoundly affect their college experience. Key factors known to influence campus climate are: (1) the structural diversity of a university in terms of the numerical representation of various ethnic/racial groups; (2) interethnic attitudes and relations among various groups; and (3) an institution's history of inclusion/exclusion of various ethnic groups (Hurtado, Milem, Clayton-Pedersen, & Allen, 1999). Taken together, these factors can contribute to the perception of a "hostile" or "chilly" campus climate for some ethnicities or one that is "friendly" and promotes a sense of belonging and inclusion (Ancis, Sedlacek, & Mohr, 2000; Reid & Radhakrishnan, 2003). Hence, the college environment, and its associated experiences, has the potential to positively and/or negatively influence students' academic success and psychological well-being (Cabrera & Nora, 1994; Cabrera, Nora, Terenzini, Pascarella, & Hagedorn, 1999; Hurtado et al., 1999; Reid & Radhakrishnan, 2003).

Accordingly, the nature of an institution's climate of diversity can play a critical role in students' development and psychological adjustment to college. The diversification of universities has necessitated that institutions now place a much greater emphasis on multiculturalism and divert resources to the development of support services for ethnically distinct students and ethnic studies (general or specific) programs and departments (Hurtado, 2001). A great deal of political pressure and controversy has surrounded the push to diversify and, with it, the importance of showing explicitly how such multicultural learning environments benefit and/or potentially hinder students' development and success (Hurtado et al., 1999). More specifically, considering that a climate of diversity in higher education is likely to affect students' ethnic identity and their personal growth and adjustment to college, it is central that we understand how such processes can prepare individuals for life in a pluralistic society.

This chapter examines the shared and unique experiences of African American, Asian, Latino/a, and White students attending ethnically diverse universities as well as the different obstacles they face on the basis of ethnic background. The two university sites we selected for this study have been characterized as having two of the most ethnically diverse student bodies in the country; hence, they provided an ideal context for asking research questions. One of the universities is considered a major research institution (high prestige, high resource, and high student preparation) that awards doctoral degrees, and the other is a smaller, comprehensive state university that awards bachelor's and master's degrees across a broad range of disciplines. Both are public institutions. At the time of the study, the student population of the comprehensive university (CU) was 32% White, 30% African American, 26% Latino/a, 11% Asian, and 1% other. The average age of undergraduates was 29, and 52% of all students attended school part time. The student population at the research university (RU) was 37% White, 35% Asian, 16% Latino/a, 6% African American, and 6% other. It is a traditional student body, with most undergraduate students ages 18–24 and attending school full time. Of the students who participated in this study, 59% were enrolled in the comprehensive university (CU), and the remaining 41% attended the research university (RU). Twenty-nine percent of the interviewed student participants were White, 25% Latino/a, 23% African American, and 23% Asian. In line with earlier research (Hurtado et al., 2002), most of the sample participants transitioned to the university from relatively segregated high schools and homes in ethnically homogeneous neighborhoods. This was particularly the case for White and African American students. On the other hand, a greater percentage of Latino/a and African American students (especially those raised in the greater Los Angeles metropolitan area) came from integrated communities and high schools where Whites were not the predominant group (see Table 1.1).

Findings Related to Multicultural Contexts: Positive and Negative Outcomes

In the interview, participants were asked about their experiences of ethnicity within the university context, their interactions with coethnics and diverse others and their influence on ethnic identity development, and sociopolitical forces that have impinged on their ethnic identities. The findings of qualitative interview data provided insight into students' ethnic identity in terms of specific university contexts and how interactions with multiethnic peers are important to this development. More specifically, the qualitative findings revealed 10 themes as relevant to students' university experience within a multicultural context. These themes fell logically into two broader dimensions, reflecting both the positive and negative facets of cultural diversity. Table 7.1 presents the themes under each dimension—positive versus negative—along with the percentages obtained on each theme for the total sample, by ethnic group and type of institution attended. For the sake of clarity,

TABLE 7.1
Positive and Negative Dimensions of Campus Diversity: Total Percentages of Themes for the Entire Sample, by Ethnicity and Type of Institution

Themes	Ethnic Group				Type of Institution		Total
	White (%)	African (%)	Latino/a (%)	Asian (%)	RU (%)	CU (%)	Percent
Positive Elements							
1. Sense of belonging	81	67	37	68	82	53	73
2. Multicultural competence	58	62	71	52	65	63	62
3. Evolving ethnic identity	50	39	32	39	35	52	31
4. Interethnic connectedness	5	14	11	13	7	15	13
5. Ethnic political consciousness	50	28	21	26	13	36	22
6. Courses/campus organizations	38	32	18	35	39	39	28
Negative Elements							
7. Ethnic inadequacy	31	29	57	04	22	36	22
8. Perceived discrimination	31	31	43	26	22	42	25
9. Interethnic tension	23	26	43	23	13	30	24
10. Ethnic segregation	19	23	32	22	17	33	18

we discuss the positive and negative themes related to cultural diversity separately. When appropriate, we highlight theme differences based on ethnic group and type of institution. Furthermore, before we begin, it is important to put these findings into perspective and note that, although some students spoke of their diversity college experiences as being solely positive or negative, others experienced both facets of diversity during their college tenure. Hence, the positive and negative themes related to campus diversity to be discussed should not be interpreted as being mutually exclusive experiences. For example, a Latina student who voiced a sense of ethnic belonging and inclusion on campus because of the presence of coethnics also discussed having encountered racial discrimination by White peers. Therefore, as one would expect, some students had mixed campus experiences that point to the complex dynamics associated with living and studying in an ethnically diverse context.

Positive Elements of a Multicultural University Context

As illustrated in Table 7.1, themes 1 through 6 exemplify the positive aspects of campus diversity in relation to a student's ethnic identity and personal development. Students mentioned most frequently that attending an ethnically diverse university engendered a sense of belonging and acceptance and fostered multicultural competence and favorable attitudes toward multiculturalism. Other consistent themes to emerge from students' commentaries were that campus diversity encouraged exploration of ethnicity and promoted political ethnic consciousness and opportunities for experiencing a sense of connectedness with different ethnic groups. Finally, campus ethnic organizations and taking ethnic studies courses were contextual features of the university that catalyzed ethnic identity development. What follows is a discussion of these themes highlighted by students' own personal experiences.

Campus Diversity and the Presence of Coethnics Engender Feelings of Inclusion in Students

Campus diversity proved to be a positive and enriching experience that fostered a sense of belonging, feelings of inclusion, and acceptance in a large number of students. This theme was particularly salient in the reflections of ethnic minority students—African American, 68%; Asian, 82%; and Latino/a, 81%—who expressed this sentiment with greater frequency than did Whites

(37%). The following commentaries are representative of how ethnic minority students spoke of being a member of their ethnic group on campus:

> There are a lot of Blacks here. It feels kind of good to be around my own race compared to high school where it was only about twenty-five of us versus a hundred Latinos. Not that I had a problem with it, but it just feels good to have somebody else around right there, so if something, maybe, if something goes wrong in the news, you just know that there is support here. Even just going through the education, "Oh, there's another Black person that's going to try to make it like I'm trying to make it." We will be up there (referring to graduation) together. (African American)

> On this campus it is great because I always see African Americans. There's a lot of minorities, and I am sure that has helped me in my success because you look around and you don't see that you are the only one. You feel like you belong. It helps my success, I think. (African American)

> Coming here was a really big step and I['m] glad that I did because I'm in an environment where people are really working to get up in life, and I see that a lot. It keeps me going to see people from my own background coming up and succeeding. That keeps me going. (Latino/a)

> I see more Latinos than I thought I would have seen here at RU, so that's very empowering for me. I go to class where I know I will see other Latinos there. I mean it's positive. I don't feel isolated. (Latino/a)

> I feel comfortable on campus because there are a lot of other Filipinos, so I don't feel like I'm in the minority. I feel like I am part of the crowd. I don't feel like I'm stereotyped on campus . . . but that I have as many rights as the next student. (Asian American)

Likewise, other students noted, "It's so diverse here [at RU]. There are so many Koreans and Asians around here. That makes me feel more secure on campus than I would feel if I were on the East Coast" (Asian American); "I feel like I'm just a normal girl on campus. I don't feel like I'm singled out or anything like that. I just blend in" (African American). Finally, one student explicitly stated that she purposely chose to attend the comprehensive university "because there are a lot of African Americans . . . I like that, and I feel positive and proud to be here" (African American).

It is clear from the above comments that a positive factor that related to minority students' identity as ethnic individuals was the visible presence of coethnics on the campus. Ethnic congruence speaks directly to the extent that individuals are ethnically and racially similar to other people attending the school. Having a sufficient "critical mass" of students from one's ethnic group, and from other ethnicities, gave students an important base of support that enhanced their sense of belonging at the institution. More specifically, the presence of coethnics afforded ethnic minority students a sense of pride and belonging within the college environment (Murguia, Padilla, & Pavel, 1991). For these students, the campus environment felt safe and non-threatening, which allowed them to communicate and socialize comfortably with both coethnic and diverse peers (Wright & Littleford, 2002). Hence, a climate of campus diversity appeared to ease minority students' transition from high school to college by facilitating their integration into a community of learning where they felt welcomed and accepted. It is important to note that students associated this ethnic diversity with their success in college.

This sense of ethnic inclusion and acceptance resulting from campus diversity was voiced less frequently by White students (37%). One possible explanation for this finding is that, in the case of White students, who were more likely to come from predominantly White communities, campus diversity presented more of a challenge, which may have influenced their sense of belonging and acceptance within the university. Another explanation is that, unlike their ethnic minority peers, for these students, being White on a college campus was not something they considered or pondered, which is consistent with having a normalized ethnic identity. Some said there was nothing "positive or negative about it" or "it doesn't mean much" to be White on campus. Hence, we should not assume that a large percentage of White participants did not feel a sense of belonging. They may very well have, but not because of their ethnicity or something they would relate to being White. White students scored lower on the measures of ethnic identity than did students of color, meaning their ethnic identity was not as salient in their definition of self-concept. Nonetheless, among those White students who did voice sentiments consistent with this theme, campus diversity was perceived as a positive and enriching experience and their first exposure to a truly multicultural community. The following students discussed the differences they observed in the ethnic demography of the college campuses they now attended compared to their earlier experiences and explained how they had adapted well to this type of context.

> On this campus, it's not like I'm in the majority as much as I was back home, because there are a lot of African Americans and a lot of Hispanics. So I feel that I'm just another person that is part of this tremendous diversity. On this campus, it's a little bit of everything. (White American)

> My mom worked here, and I remember when I was a kid coming to visit here and it seemed like predominantly teen types walking around with the tan, blond, blue-eyed look. It's really interesting because, now that I am here, there are more minority groups represented and it is very different than what it used to be. For me, this is fine and I feel fine walking around here. I don't feel like the majority or the minority. I just feel like one of many. (White American)

> At first it just feels like you are in the minority. But it's really not something that I even think about anymore. I don't really think of it any more because I don't feel like I get treated as though I am White, or that people don't say hi to me because I am White. I notice the differences. I actually like it. It's nice to have it here. (White American)

Likewise, another White student noted: "I like it. I think there is a good blend. It's a place where you can learn about everyone you know. I like being here." Although most of these students came from relatively segregated high schools where Whites were the numerical majority, they are intrigued by the diversity of the college context and find a sense of inclusion within a campus culture that embraces and supports a climate of diversity. As is evident in the next section, White students spoke most frequently of the benefits of campus diversity in terms of their becoming more multiculturally competent.

In all, campus ethnic diversity proved to be vital to many students' attachment to and integration into the campus culture, especially students of color. As a result of campus diversity, many students said they did not feel singled out or isolated by their ethnic background. Students belonging to the four ethnic groups studied expressed feelings of integration and inclusion related to ethnicity. As indicated by the survey data, ethnic identity correlated positively with college self-efficacy, suggesting that students' ethnic identity was related to having a positive adjustment to college and being able to find membership and a sense of ethnic belonging on campus (Hurtado &

Carter, 1997; Tinto, 1993). Likewise, a high level of social and academic self-efficacy were reported by African American, Asian, Latino/a, and White students in this sample.

Acculturated Experiences, the Development of Multicultural
Interpersonal Competence, and Multiple Perspective Taking

The second most frequently discussed theme was that campus diversity was associated with (a) acculturative experiences in terms of second culture acquisition, (b) development of multicultural interpersonal competence, and (c) higher-order thinking in terms of multiple perspective taking. This theme, which relates to the development of multicultural competence in students, was heard among the four ethnic groups studied (African Americans, 52%; Asians, 65%; and Latinos, 58%), but most frequently by White (71%) students. Hence, for many students, encountering a truly diverse community of peers was a salient learning experience in their development and growth as individuals. Perhaps this was particularly true in the case of White students who came from ethnically homogeneous communities. The college setting afforded minority students with additional opportunities to integrate aspects of American culture into their definition of the self as ethnic individuals.[2]

> I have one male White friend, and I guess the reason that drew us together was that he was really more into my culture and he was really interested in what I like to do, so I had no problem sharing these things. Like, what I like to do and how it felt being African American. He was trying to learn about my culture so I learned about his. (African American)

Although students from the four ethnic groups referred to ongoing acculturative experiences, these were most germane in the stories of immigrant students, in particular Asians. For instance, one Korean student discussed his acculturation experiences while in college: "I see some negative aspects to mainstream culture, but there are a lot of positive points, which Asian culture lacks . . . like being independent, being open-minded and assertive." Acculturative experiences enabled such students to incorporate values and

---

2. Most immigrant students' discussions of acculturation in regard to becoming more Americanized were in reference to their high school and junior high school experiences, hence they are not discussed here.

customs of the mainstream culture into their self-concept that were seen as assets for their personal growth and development. However, most noteworthy is that ethnic minority students' acculturative experiences were not solely in reference to the dominant group; they also viewed other ethnic/cultural groups as important sources of influence in this process. Two Asian students noted:

> I find my Black friends to be very interesting because they are very independent, very strong. There is just a confidence about them. I find that to be something I would like to be. I find that very admirable about them. It draws me to them. [Hence] I have adopted not just White culture but minority culture, too. (Asian American)

> My Colombian friend has helped me a lot with my self-esteem. . . . Just her outlook on life I have adopted. She is very individualistic and that is a good thing. She has definitely helped me change for the better. (Asian American)

These students interweaved into their cultural identity what they believed reflected the best qualities they observed in other minority cultural groups as well as those that American culture had to offer. A Korean American student reflected on this issue by stating, "In order to live here in the United States having a Korean background, you've got to actually accept other cultures and views . . . not only the American culture, but others as well." In a similar vein, two Latina students commented on the influences of diverse peers on their acculturative experiences in college: "I see the positive thing that they have. [My] Asian [peers] value education, I've really tried to reinforce that in myself and really try for achieving in school" (Latina–Mexican American).

> Having the urge to be more than what you are, to always achieve more [I have adopted from] Chinese friends. I've seen how persistent they are and I think about that . . . and that's what's driven me to go on. I kind of see them as role models in the sense that in being persistent you can achieve a lot. (Latina–Mexican American)

Students were also careful not to detach themselves completely from their cultural roots during this process and were quick to stress the importance of retaining valued elements of their native cultural identity. One student offered this perspective: "I get really close to people [ethnic others], I'll interact with them and respect their beliefs and, yeah, get different perspectives . . . but still hold on to what I am" (Latino/a). Likewise, a Filipino student who had immigrated to the United States as a teenager stated a similar viewpoint:

> When we walk into a culture, we see things we like and pick it up and then we throw out things we don't like. I think, given the opportunity of any individual to come to the United States and experience the variety this country has to offer, I think they would do the same things I do. But there are things we can't throw away that make us. There are things that are the foundation. But my American [peers] did change me. About seventy-five percent of the time I'm interacting with White Americans and Blacks because of the nature of the science classes that I take.

In sum, for these students, acculturative experiences related to exposure to diverse cultural groups influenced their ethnic identity development, their view of self, and their orientation toward ethnic-others. This finding is in line with those reported by Phinney (1995), who found that a strong ethnic identity, when accompanied by a positive mainstream and ethnic-other orientation, is linked to healthy self-esteem in ethnic minority college students. Arguably, such experiences better situate students to embrace a multicultural interpersonal orientation. What follows is a discussion of the benefits of multicultural interpersonal competence for students' adjustment to college and their ability to negotiate the challenges that come from interacting with diverse groups.

Most salient in students' commentaries was how an ethnically diverse learning community catalyzed the development of multicultural interpersonal competence. Confirming the research conducted by Chang (1999), many students' commentaries reflected that campus diversity enabled them to engage in meaningful cross-ethnic socialization and establish personally significant cross-ethnic friendships. For such students, increased interethnic contact encouraged them to see ethnic-other peers as individuals and not solely as members of specific ethnicities. To say this more explicitly, encountering others from diverse ethnicities and cultural perspectives was associated with interactions among students that promoted a type of learning that is essential for bridging social differences among ethnic groups. As one African American student noted, "It just made me realize that I don't have to limit myself to having just Black friends. It's okay to have friends that are White, Chinese, and Indian." These students expressed similar sentiments:

> I guess it makes me feel like I can associate with anyone, you know. I'm not just stuck with my culture. I can take it elsewhere and talk about it and learn easily from other people. I can accept other people's cultures. (African American)

> I feel like I always gain something from someone, the [diverse] people I interact with. I feel it gives me an open mind. You know, I'm not narrow in my vision. I am able to see someone else's culture. (African American)

Most important, diversity experiences were associated with students' greater confidence in being able to negotiate cross-ethnic relationships comfortably. As one African American student noted, "Attending a diverse campus and becoming friends with a White student and a Hispanic student has made me more sure of myself."

Likewise these two students commented:

> It made me feel good that I can deal with people of different ethnic backgrounds than my own. You know, just knowing that I can do that, it just makes me a better person for being able to do that. And it makes me feel good that I know I can do that. I know I didn't let any biases or prejudices that I might have had in the past affect things now or stop me from talking or working with other people. If anything, those friendships have made me stronger. (Latina/o)

> I thought I would be intimidated and I am not. I like it because I learn a lot. I'm a psychology major so I love it. I am a people watcher, too, so I like to watch and pay attention to different people interacting and things like that and just the way different cultures behave. I like that a lot. So I feel that I've learned a lot. It makes me more broad-minded. (White American)

Accordingly, many students spoke of the relevance of a multicultural context for their personal, social, and intellectual development. To illustrate more specifically, the following ethnic minority students reflected on the benefits they garnered from attending a diverse learning community:

> I didn't start to look at different cultures until I came to CU, and then I began to learn new things about other groups. During my first semester I

lived with a Chinese girl, a Japanese girl, and an Anglo girl, and this was a very enriching experience for me. It taught me never to underestimate someone, never belittle someone's beliefs. Other people have different values they go by, and just because they are not what you think, that doesn't mean that they are wrong. (Latina/o)

In general it's very positive. I'm sure that there is conflict here and there, but I think that this is a wonderful campus. It is so diverse and we have representatives from various ethnic groups and I think that's good. Me, personally, I get along with everyone. They all (other ethnic groups) have their own values and so forth. I think those things are very interesting and it is important to me. It's different and yet it's all the same. I think that's the beauty of this campus and you could really share that. Not many outside of California have the opportunity to do that, so it's very unique and I think people in general get along fine. (Asian American)

I'm staying on campus. My first roommates were White, and I was the only Black girl there . . . we enjoyed doing the same things so we became kind of close. Ever since then, it's been different in how I've proceeded [in terms of how I view ethnic others] or how you hear other people saying White people are this way or White people are that way. You never know until you actually interact with them. It feels good to me. (African American)

[Campus diversity] has affected me. I learned about other people's culture and the way other people are. So when you are looking at those other people, you have a different attitude, you know. If you're Black and you don't know anything about Hispanic culture, then you might have one point of view or one outlook toward the Hispanic people. Just hanging around with different people and learning a little bit [of] their train of thought, then you start to look at them differently. (African American)

Similarly, White students also considered how cross-cultural interactions and friendships with ethnic-others had strongly influenced their worldview of other ethnicities and their interpersonal development and growth as individuals.

My best friend is from Panama, and my other best friend is from Thailand. Several of my good friends are Filipino. I think it's made me aware of the variation, and not just the Filipino friends. I'm more aware of the differences in different people and the way that they think. . . . I do have an understanding of why they think the way they do.

I'm friends with Asian people, including my roommate here and a lot of people on my floor. When you come to RU, you have to get along with Asian people because they're, like, sixty percent or something. . . . I'm friends with three African Americans here. It's good because they represent a manifestation of something I don't have. I don't know what it's like to be African American or to be Asian at RU. It's good to talk to them about who they are, and I do. So that's good to talk to people outside your own ethnicity. You get a sense of different experiences.

I think diversity is what made me who I am, just being grown up. . . . So I think in a way that has made me smarter than some people, all those people who go to those fancy private schools. I think it taught me something. I feel like socially that gives me, like, something that other people won't have. I think it's been positive that I've had such diversity and I value that.

Indeed, like their ethnic minority peers, White students said that just being exposed to members of other ethnic groups had made them more open and accepting of ethnic differences. As one student commented, "If I was surrounded by White people all the time, whether it was intentional or not, it might make me a little more close-minded towards other ethnic groups."

Related to greater multicultural ethnic awareness, many students also mentioned how campus diversity made dialogues regarding racial and ethnic issues salient and meaningful. More specifically, interactions with diverse peers encouraged students to consider complex social issues surrounding human rights, equality, and justice. This viewpoint was shared by the following students.

I like the diversity, there's a good blend here. If you go back to some Midwestern town, it might be all White and you don't learn about others. You don't understand how people are unless you're in contact with them and talk to them. I think being here has helped me understand the plight of different ethnic groups. (White American)

In terms of treating people equally . . . I've adopted that from the people that I've known in college from hanging around [with] those kinds of people. Not really any certain behaviors, but attitudes towards others. Just being open-minded. I was really narrow-minded when I first started school. (White American)

I understand a lot of where ethnic groups are coming from. Like, I wouldn't have understood why they had certain attitudes or why they felt oppressed or prejudiced against. Definitely [being more open-minded], it's exposed me to the prejudices that some people go through because they are Hispanic or Asian. . . . I think that in that way it's helped a lot. (Asian American)

I had a history class and there were a lot of White people in there. Like, for the first time it seemed to me, it was their first time interacting with a lot of Black people. We would have good discussions and we learned more about them and they learned about us. They bring their own perception into it and we do, too. (African American)

Furthermore, students also expressed a willingness to challenge and change their beliefs when exposed to diverse perspectives, which reflected positively on their desire to achieve greater ethnic understanding. Here students spoke more pointedly about how diversity experiences were associated with fewer racial biases, which fostered a greater openness to diversity and pluralism (Baron, Byrne, & Branscombe, 2006).

How has [interacting with diverse peers] changed me? I guess the main thing I can say is that I'm not so self-centered about my own culture. Maybe less prejudiced and not stereotype people based on their ethnic background. I find that I am more tolerant of other races and ethnicities. I guess around the Korean community I see a sense of arrogance and a sense of prejudice in their attitudes about other cultures. (Asian American)

I think that [becoming close to people from different ethnic backgrounds has] made me a lot more open-minded. My family is not exactly open-minded, you know. They are very right wing and sort of racist in a way. Since I've met different kinds of people, I have come to realize that people are people. (White American)

I think really knowing people does away with a lot of prejudice, because you hear a lot, even here on campus, like jokes about lazy Mexicans. If you know people, like a friend of mine, her father works twelve to fourteen hours a day, literally has a hard time getting a job because he's more a first-generation Mexican. That's why she is in college, he wants her to do better. I mean, you really recognize that the prejudices are not based on reality. It's the same way with the Blacks. (White American)

I grew up in a predominantly White area. After I came to CU, I met a lot of different people. It changed a lot of the way that I looked at people. You know, people hold those views that they (ethnic minorities) are all lazy, and you find out that they're not. And if you've never seen it before, you go by what your parents say and what your community says. So I was very happy to come here and wipe those views out of my head because I just think that they're not right. So it's broadened my knowledge and [helped me] overcome some stereotypes. (White American)

If it wasn't for this [diversity experience] I think I'd be more narrow and close-minded. I think I would have a tendency to blame one specific group. I wouldn't want to see the whole picture in general. I would only want to see the surface and not go into the core of a situation. I learned you can't judge people for their color. That's the biggest thing I've learned. I was taught that I can't just speak my mind and not have anything to back it up. They've (diverse peers) taught me to be more intellectual, meaning do your research before you [speak]. I was taught that by other cultures. Other things they taught me is to enjoy having friends of other cultures. You can learn from them. It's great to have friends of a different mixture. It makes you a person of well-rounded intellect, and that's my goal. I want to be as well rounded as possible. (Latino/a)

It is clear from students' comments that this ability to assert a multicultural perspective was acquired through interactions with diverse others and related college learning experiences. Such students demonstrated greater flexibility in cognitive perspective-taking-related higher-order critical thinking (Hurtado, 2001; Ramirez & Castaneda, 1974; Tracey & Sedlacek, 1987). This finding is consistent with Gurin and colleagues' (Gurin, Dey, Hurtado, & Gurin, 2002) longitudinal study on multiculturalism, which reported that diversity experiences consistently and meaningfully affected learning and civic outcomes in students, such as seeing the world from another's perspective and valuing the importance of pluralism and ethnic tolerance.

In all, students' comments highlighted how campus diversity gave them a unique context for learning interpersonal skills that involved more tolerance toward ethnic-others and a greater understanding and acceptance of cultural and ethnic differences. Students talked about having incorporated the values and beliefs of other cultural groups, which they saw as an asset to their personal development. Increased ethnic contact with diverse peers was related to a greater sense of multicultural self-efficacy in students in terms of feeling more confident in negotiating and establishing positive interpersonal relationships with ethnic-others (LaFrambroise, Coleman, & Gerton, 1995). This is an important human-relational skill that prepares students for effective social and civic engagement in a diverse and complex democracy. Likewise, students' also discussed how greater knowledge and understanding of ethnic others made them more aware of social justice and ethnic inequalities in American society and taught them to value pluralism as an ideal to strive for. This form of multiple perspective-taking was a theme voiced by students belonging to the four ethnic groups, which argues in favor of current university initiatives that support a climate of diversity by promoting ethnic and racial understanding through formal and informal curricular and extracurricular activities.

Diversity Prompts Examinations Into Ethnic Identity and Transformation in the Self

Another common theme among students was that a diverse campus environment encouraged exploration of one's ethnicity and an evolution of one's self-concept as an ethnic person. Students belonging to the four ethnic groups (group percentages ranged from 32% to 50%) studied spoke of the relevance of diversity in their personal growth and ethnic identity development.

One way in which students voiced this theme was by reflecting on how exposure to multiethnic peers had caused them to consider their own ethnicity. Such peers, as explorers of their own identity, served as role models in the process of ethnic identity development. Especially when such interactions were positive, diverse peers helped to make students feel more comfortable about their ethnicity, giving them the confidence to explore their own ethnic identity in a relatively safe and nonthreatening environment.

The people who I have met who have become my friends, I mean. I've talked to them about my culture, for example. So it lets them see who I am, what my culture's about and erase some of the negative stereotypes they might have had. If anything, it's a plus. They've made me want to learn more about my own culture. I mean, you know, and other cultures, too. . . . Learning more about other people's cultures makes you question, "Do I do that? Do I have something similar in my own culture that I may not know [about]?" It's just made me want to find out more about my own culture. (Latino/a)

My roommate is Chinese and we talk a lot about culture [and ethnicity]. Like, I always compare Japanese and Chinese history with him. A lot of times when we talk, [it feels] I guess, like we are stimulating the mind. . . . [Just being Japanese] on this campus allows you to research the roots of your culture. There are a lot of people that know about it, and we just talk about it. And from them I learn, and sometimes they will recommend a book. (Asian American)

Two of my really good friends are Jewish. I've met Indian friends now, Asian friends and White friends. It's like we talk about our cultures all the time. I guess we are all Americans, but I definitely think [ethnicity] is really a good thing to have. We all have our own identities, separate, but we come together. We're not carbon copies of each other. (Asian–Indian American)

I'm friends with Asian people, including my roommate here and a lot of people on my floor. . . . I'm friends with three African Americans. It's good because they represent a manifestation of something I don't have. So that's good to talk to people outside your own ethnicity. You get a sense of different experiences. . . . When I came here, it really did put questions in my head about "who you are" and "where you came from." (White American)

Another common thread among students was that encountering multiethnic peers who had stronger ethnic identities, or who knew more about their cultures, prompted them to begin or strengthen their own exploration. "You hang out with a group of people who are really strong about their culture, and they want to learn about you and you want to learn about them. And that's real positive. . . . It's made me realize how important it is to have a cultural identity" (Latino/a).

I would say that [I have become] more aware of the things that I like, in particular about my ethnic background. I'm more aware of the values. Irish people and Welsh people traditionally tend to be Catholic. I've become aware of things that are identified with people who come from those cultures, the values they have [that are a part of my ethnic heritage]. (White American)

I don't know if it was my own ethnicity that really had more of an impact [on my personality development], or the fact that I know that people have other ethnicities than me. The fact that they do have different ethnicities has made me see that there's a lot to learn [about ethnicity]. (White American)

Being Mexican [before coming to college] was a different story, [I felt insecure]. But now I guess college has made a difference. Just being exposed to different cultures, different people, and different ideas, it has allowed me feel Mexican and to identify as Mexican. (Latina/o)

This process of ethnic identity exploration was described more pointedly by a student who said that he came to know himself better by being in a study group with multiethnic peers who were more closely connected to their ethnic background than he was.

Most of my study group knows more about their cultural background and traditions. It has made me go and ask questions about my cultural background. They are always sharing with me, and I'm really a little ignorant. I've never really been taught, so I have to go to the library and check it out or ask aunts, uncles, mom, or dad. Then I can share that information, too. It's helped me because when I was hanging around in high school with just my own culture, we never asked these questions. The curiosity was never there. I became, like, proud of saying I'm Mexican American and doing things that, you know, . . . Mexican Americans do. It has made me grow. I feel I know who I am. I'm comfortable and I don't feel insecure [about my ethnicity]. I don't have to justify the way I am. (Latina/o)

Also to emerge from students' narratives was the knowledge that attending a university context where there was a strong presence of coethnics facilitated their exploration into ethnic identity and positively affirmed their identity as ethnic individuals. As one student put it, "I feel I can explore my ethnicity, my cultural feelings and traditions on this campus. The fact that there are other Latinos/as with whom I can share this with here makes me feel good and proud" (Mexican American). Making friends with coethnics often strengthened ethnic identity in students because peers who were actively exploring their own ethnicity encouraged them to do the same. A Latina student who felt she was somewhat naïve about her ethnicity discussed the positive influence of coethnic friends: "The roommate that I had last year, she was very active, very aware of her culture. When I got here, she would laugh at me because of the fact that I just wasn't experienced. Because of that [experience with roommate] I have changed a lot." This influence of coethnics on ethnic identity development was also described by a young woman whose friendships in high school had been mostly with Whites. She reflected on how attending a university where there was a significant number of coethnics had affected her ethnic identity:

> In high school I wouldn't listen to Mexican music. I would try not to talk Spanish. I would not listen to the music. I would not, you know, for example, on a holiday I wouldn't even mention it or anything because of the fact that my friends wouldn't be familiar with it. But now, here, it's like my friends celebrate it, my friends listen to that music and they speak Spanish. So I guess that I've changed a lot. (Latino/a)

A diverse campus environment also encouraged greater maturity in how students thought about their ethnic identity. Students evaluated their identities as ethnic individuals critically and made decisions regarding the role ethnicity would play in their lives and how they would express that identity. This spoke to the development of more-integrated identities for students, which reflects higher levels of ethnic identity status (i.e., internalized status or achieved identity) or those that are undergoing a process of exploration.

> My ethnic background? I never thought about ethnicity [before coming here]. I did a lot in the last semester with Dr. Martinez. She talks about ethnicity a lot as far as when she gives examples on the board, and I never really thought much about ethnicity [before]. [Now] it means a lot more. (White American)

> I really do not have like a strong religion or strong ethnicity like some Blacks or Italians. So I think, like, me not having a [strong] set of views of what I am [ethnically], everybody has been able to influence me in some

way. So you can see the differences, and I have been able to adopt my [personal] beliefs [about ethnicity] from that. (White American)

As a kid I didn't really think about it [ethnic identity] at all, you know. Once you're in high school, you start considering it. But once you enter college, it is on your mind constantly and you think about, "Are there ways that I can improve my culture?" Or "Are there ways that I can learn from another culture?" (Latina/o)

I can honestly say that my ethnicity, "Who I am" [has changed since starting college]. I think college changed a lot of who I am because I made a lot of interesting friends, like different ethnicities. I think of college and my ethnicity together. I'm really happy now. I've been through these exploration phases [during] the first two years. Now I am pretty solid in "who I am." I'm American. I'm definitely Westernized, but I [also] have a lot of Indian things. (Asian American)

I didn't have a strong ethnic identity at all. It wasn't until I got into situations as a young adult entering college where I realized, for a lot of non-Black people, the bottom line was that I would always be Black, regardless of whether you're my "best friend" or "you're my girlfriend." It is because of those experiences that I began to seek out my culture identity. I needed to accept my identity and accept the beauty of my African qualities and explore those. And so it was from there that I went in search of my ethnic identity. I mean, truly, truly in search. That was the best thing that could happen to me because had those things not happened, I would still be confused. (African American)

This process of exploration into one's ethnicity was articulated most explicitly by the following young women:

Some people were just, like, you don't know anything about your culture and you need to learn about your culture. So it was a fair question. That's right. I think I need to learn more about who I am ethnically. I knew who I was in character. And that's what I did. I started studying some history. I focused on Native American history and found some similarities within those things and how my feelings came out in a lot of these topics. It was, like, these things I understand. And so it sort of defined me. And then, as I was looking more into the indigenous side of being Puerto Rican, I realized we had a lot in common historically. And that defined myself. When

I was done doing that, I took last year doing my history side and this year I'm doing my art history side. When I was done doing that, I was very pleased in finding [that] the Polynesian culture is very much like my own and I'm going to study it. I did a lot, a lot of searching, defined a lot of things, and now I'm perfectly fine. I have an identity. I'm happy with myself. (Latina/o)

Taken together, students' commentaries highlight how a diverse college environment served as a catalyst for examining and exploring their identity as ethnic individuals. Theorists on identity development have noted repeatedly that ethnicity becomes central to one's definition of self during late adolescence and young adulthood (Phinney, 1990, 1993). Hence, the college years are a time when individuals are likely to question the meaning of their ethnicity, which is often associated with an active search for knowledge and understanding. As centers of learning, ethnically diverse university campuses provide students with the ideal context for exploring these issues, which can facilitate their journey toward greater ethnic awareness and achieving positive and healthy ethnic identities.

Campus Diversity Provides Opportunity for Connectedness

A relevant, albeit less prominent, theme to emerge from students' narratives was that campus diversity provided opportunities for connectedness with ethnic others. A small percentage of students from the four ethnic groups (percentages ranged between 11%–17%) spoke of notions of inclusion that went beyond their own ethnic group.

I lived in an apartment-style dorm, and there were eight of us. I lived with a Japanese girl for a while, and there were several Black people. In broadcasting communications, when we got to be juniors and seniors, we were having all the same classes. There were so many of us who were rarely apart except at sleep it seemed. We were alike because we were in broadcast communication. We were talking communication law and theory and all of the hard stuff. We were together all of the time. We didn't look at skin color or ethnicity as a difference, we looked at what was the same. (White American)

[Being Latino on this campus] I don't think it's much different from being Black, Asian, or White. I mean, we are all striving for the same things, you know. We all want the good things in life . . . we are basically the same, we have the same goals. I don't think that I am different than someone else, just in a superficial level. (Latino/a)

When I'm in the weight room, everyone talks to me. You know, it's not like, "I'm not going to talk to you because you are different." It is like, "Hey, how are you doing?" I wouldn't feel that way out there. Because you see them [other ethnic peers] around so much, maybe you don't even know their name[s], but you have seen their faces before and that helps. (Asian American)

Last year, when I came to college, my floor was extremely diverse. There weren't any other Indian people except my roommate, who was totally randomly selected. We had every ethnicity. One of my best friends is Colombian. I think the floor experiences are the best. I learned so much from living with people. We ate together, slept together, showered, brushed our teeth, we were close. (Asian American)

I moved on campus, so I had one Hispanic roommate [and] we became really close. We just did a lot of things together, went to the mall or whatever, just hung out . . . I feel accepted [by Hispanics]. I don't feel strange or anything. I don't think we even see each other as a color; we just see each other as people. Sometimes we do have questions about each other, like, they ask me something, because we have a different texture of hair. They wonder, "How do you get your hair straight and stuff?" I just explain, and we laugh about the things that are different between us, that some things are the same and some things are so different. (African American)

These individuals spoke of coming together and connecting as students in their endeavor to achieve a higher education. Some sound almost surprised by having had these experiences with diverse ethnic peers where ethnicity was not the focal point of their interpersonal relationship. Student reflections underscore how universities provide unique opportunities and social contexts for diverse groups of individuals to come together and nurture positive and harmonious interethnic relationships. As Mack and colleagues note, the open and informal exchanges that occur among university students within various contexts such as in the classroom, the gym, and residential halls, and during campus events (sport games, dances, student meetings) "contribute to a type of interchange found nowhere else in society" (Mack et al., 1997, p. 256). Arguably, this type of frequent and informal interpersonal interactions is key for learning and fostering greater tolerance for diverse ethnic others (Baron et al., 2006). One student reflected this viewpoint: "I've never really seen them (African Americans) as different people, they're just friends. They're not different, because they enjoy the same things I do" (Latino/a).

A Politicized View of One's Ethnic Identity and Political Interethnic Consciousness

The college years have often been associated with the development of greater ethnic consciousness and political awareness in young adults (French et al., 2000). Indeed, political consciousness was a salient aspect of many students' ethnic identity; however, compared to other ethnic groups (African Americans, 26%; Whites, 21%; and Asians, 13%) a greater number of Latinos/as students (50%) voiced a politicized and activist view of their ethnicity.[3] We attribute this difference in part to the state political climate at the time of the study, when several anti-immigrant initiatives were on the state ballot, which appeared to target Latinos/as for discrimination.

The findings described in this section encompass not only the influences of campus political discourse on students' growing ethnic and racial consciousness but also how external political/historical forces that affect race relations in American society come to bear on students' ethnic identities. Hence, it was through an intersection of these processes that students pondered their place as ethnic individuals within the larger society and/or considered the sociopolitical and historical conditions that influence past and present minority-majority interethnic relations. This perspective was evident in the voices of the following students:

> This institution was created for the White man, and to be here and see other Black people, Latino people, Asian people here, you know, just walking around school makes my heart feel good. And being here makes me feel good because I feel like I beat the odds and won. (African American)

> I have entered a stage where I am actively seeking out my African heritage. Actively seeking out the positive things about being a Black American so

---

3. These percentages include four students (three Latinos and one White American) whose political activism within the community may or may not have been directly related to their campus experience. However, they were included because, while in college, they continued to manifest deep political consciousness.

that you have a shield for the negative things that you are constantly being bombarded with. I am in a militant stage where I am very militant, very [much] into the readings and writings of the Black Power movement and seeing where that is going and how I can be a part of the change that I want to see in my community. (African American)

I have always been very [politically] active, and at the end of the day I ask myself the hard questions. . . . I am interested in anything where the focus is on multiethnic (political) pluralism. I have a multicultural class, and I know where he (the professor) is coming from and I really appreciate the approach, but he's basically teaching me Black history and talking about the Black movement. When you go to the Hispanic teachers, they're talking about Hispanic culture. If you go to the Asian [teacher], they're talking about Asian culture. But the reality is that this world keeps on turning, and these [ethnic] divisions are driving us farther and farther apart, and at some point you have to start thinking about what is good for us collectively as a group of people. Not as a group of Asians, Africans, [and] Eurasians, but as a group of people. No [ethnic] borders. I am interested in anything . . . where the focus is on multiethnic [political] pluralism. (African American)

I remember when Jesse Jackson ran for president and there was such a fear in the air, and I don't think that should be. Maybe we all would be a little bit more informed if there were more politically speaking minority people. Maybe we wouldn't have this problem [of racial conflicts]. As far as culturally, I think it would be very important to have a bigger mix rather than just White men ruling the world. (White American)

Accordingly, students' increased political ethnic consciousness was also strongly influenced by the political circumstances of the times. Affirmative action and immigrant rights (i.e., Proposition 187) were two highly controversial political issues at the forefront of the national agenda at the time and, certainly, a part of the university political discourse. Because these political initiatives affected students and/or their ethnic communities directly and indirectly, they served as the catalyst for the development of greater ethnic consciousness and political awareness.

Well, I have a lot of misgivings about affirmative action in that just what they are trying to accomplish. I mean, I know what it's really supposed to be, that everyone is in the same level playing field, but nowadays I wonder if it's outlived its usefulness or needs to be modified. (White American)

I think [it's important] to give more access [in terms of political and economic rights], especially to Latin Americans, African Americans, and even Asian Americans. [However a] major thing I can't stand is affirmative action when it's just based solely on race. I think it should be done on a socioeconomic base. . . . I would love to have it looked at more [in terms of] where you were placed socioeconomically. (Asian American)

Similarly, a Latina student described how she became more politically aware when she moved to Los Angeles to attend the university:

Proposition 187 is an indirect form of discrimination, I believe. It's brought the Mexican American community [together and made it] a lot stronger. [It has] made me more motivated to try to succeed [in my education] and help the community.

Regardless of how students stood on issues related to affirmative action and immigrant rights, the perception of such initiatives as being unfair and unjust clearly sensitized individuals to the political process and how political legislation can influence their life chances (or those of their ethnic group) as persons living in an ethnically/racially stratified society. These findings are in line with earlier research that suggests that ethnic political consciousness can be triggered by the perception of an illegitimate ethnic status hierarchy and persons questioning the political process that maintains or threatens the status quo (Hurtado & Gurin, 1995).

Political consciousness and ethnic awareness paved the way for expression of collective activism in some college students, which was associated with greater ethnic pride and esteem (Kuo & Roysircar-Sodowsky, 1999).

Proposition 187 has awakened the giant, and the giant meaning the Latino community, which I am a part of. I am also [talking about] affirmative action, which is in the process right now. This has motivated me to become active in what I can, which is to be involved in *Ferias de la Cuidad Unida* [Festivals of the United City], which helps [Latino/a] residents in the process of becoming citizens. (Latina/o)

Likewise, an Asian American woman discussed her personal involvement in activism on campus and within her ethnic community related to immigration rights. She discussed how, through her involvement in the PEACE (Filipinos Educational and Cultural Experiences) Club, she helped to start an Asian class on campus (CU) and had participated in many activities to support the rights of Filipinos.

> I got involved [in] the rallies that Filipinos held. I was a part of it. It was in Los Angeles, and they were trying to shut down immigration [for Filipinos to enter the United States]. Some of us from the Filipino Club went and rallied. We went and held signs.

Furthermore, a Latino/a student reflected on the political activism she saw on campus: "Latinos here at RU are more aggressive in fighting for their rights, more so than what I have seen of Latinos at home." Likewise, another Latino student observed, "In the last four years that I've been here, our numbers have been increasing, so, I mean, we're more visible." He added, "Many of the dominant Latino organizations are more visible, more vocal . . . it's made the university pay more attention to us." Still another Latino student commented on his political experience on campus, "When I was at [another university] everybody was more isolated, but here there is more identification, a lot of pride, a lot of us working together." Arguably, political activism and ethnic consciousness were powerful ways students could affirm their ethnic identities and a proactive means of responding to past and present discrimination. For many of these students, awareness of the sociohistorical and political factors that contribute to ethnic inequalities in American society influenced how they experienced their ethnic identity.

Students also discussed how interactions with diverse others encouraged them to turn outward and consider the social and political circumstances of other ethnicities. It is interesting to note that, when asked if they would be willing to work to advance the political, economic, and social rights of other ethnic groups, 56% of Whites, 68% of Asians, 72% of Latinos/as, and 78% of African Americans said they would.[4] Some of these students reflected on the importance of affiliating with other ethnic groups and forming coalitions to engage in political-social activism. As one African American student stated, "Proposition 187 is wrong and I would stand up with them [Mexican

---

4. Because this was a general question posed to participants, it was difficult to ascertain whether their response was influenced by the university experience. However, because this question related directly to having political ethnic consciousness, we believe that the findings were relevant.

Americans]. Everybody needs health care, you know. Regardless of what your nationality is, if you're sick you need help. I would stand up and fight with them."

Likewise, a White student spoke of his activism for the Latino/a community: "I've have done some paintings and literature promoting for the Hispanic culture for some friends of mine" because it was for a "good cause." Similarly a young White woman reflected on this issue and said, "I would be particularly interested in working with Native Americans because I feel personal reverence [for] and connection to their culture. I studied it a bit, [I have] done some work, you know, understanding it." Still another student commented: "I would be willing to work to assist the Latino/a community in pursuit of better immigration rights . . . What I'm reacting to is a need to redefine our border, communities, and lines. So it just so happens that the Latino community is in a position to make some of that happen."

The following statements further illustrate students' politicized view of ethnic identity that encompassed a sense of political awareness of and activism targeting the circumstances other ethnicities faced. However, these students' stories also reflect a sense of kinship with other ethnic minority groups because of shared experiences of oppression and discrimination. "I perceive myself as a person of color, and I think all people of color have a great deal in common [in regard to dealing with discrimination], and we should seek out and stress the commonalities between us" (African American). This politicized sense of kinship with ethnic others was voiced most frequently by African Americans (43%), followed by Latinos/as (31%) and Asians (17%).

> I came here and started learning about politics from friends and became interested in going to [political] rallies. . . . I have been involved in a lot of their [Latino/a] political things. I feel we [Latinos/as and Asians] share a common history in America. When Asians came over, they came over to work on the railroad. I mean, I've studied a lot of their political history and things like that. We share pretty much a common background. Historically, Asians came over here as workers, not to get educated. That was the same reason why Latinos/as came over here. They both got discriminated against. (Asian American)

> My interactions with Latinos/as are pretty good actually. I have some Latina friends and Latino friends. I almost feel there's almost kind of a bond with them, too. Actually with Prop. 187 just happening, and the stuff they are doing with affirmative action, you have to stick together because the

minority people in this world are going to get more screwed up than they have been in the past if they don't. (African American)

I feel like especially Hispanics and Blacks really need to get together because we are facing the same problems. Welfare reform will affect both. Teen pregnancy affects both of our cultures. We have a lot of the same background. There are a lot of Black Hispanics. There is a lot of Black blood in the Hispanic lineage. Some of the Hispanics don't want to admit it or don't know or they haven't learned. But our blood is pretty much mixed, or there's a lot of mixing going on between Blacks and Hispanics. So I think we need to stop letting people divide us and come together, and if we come together, we can really do a lot. We can advance ourselves politically, socially, financially. (African American)

Reflected in many of these students' commentaries is how a strong ethnic identity was related to having positive attitudes toward ethnic-others. These positive out-group attitudes stemmed, in part, from students' growing awareness of social injustices based on ethnic stratification (Phinney & Devich-Navarro, 1997), which contributed to their political consciousness and led them to work not only for the rights of their own ethnic group but for other ethnicities as well. This finding is consistent with those reported earlier in reference to multiple perspective taking and is consistent with the findings of Gurin and colleagues (2002). Many students expressed a broader sense of civic mindedness and political awareness, which was associated with a sense of empathy and concern for social issues and problems other ethnicities faced and with a willingness to engage in democratic social change (Hurtado, 2002). Arguably, the development of such skills not only benefits students' cognitive and personal development but is necessary for effective participation in an ethnically diverse society. As Hurtado (2001) notes, "students who have the ability to develop a societal perspective, exhibit empathy, and acquire a capacity to evaluate alternative perspectives on complex social problems are better prepared to take on social roles as decision makers and negotiators of different perspectives" (p. 197).

Ethnic Organizations and Ethnic Studies Courses Help Students Learn More About Their Own and Others' Ethnicity

This theme focuses specifically on the impact of formal structures of institutions such as student ethnic organizations and course curriculum on students' ethnic identity. This is important for two reasons: (1) Student organizations are a formal structure within the university that are sanctioned by and funded by the university, and (2) they serve as a visible, publicized space for students to come together regardless of their residential status or primary friendship circles. The positive influences of formal structures of the university context—student organizations and course curricula—on students' ethnic identity and personal development was a theme students of color voiced somewhat more frequently (African Americans, 35%; Latinos/as, 38%; and Asians 39%) than did White (18%) students. Hence, it appears that these structural characteristics of the university were more salient and positive forces for the development and growth of students of color as *ethnic* individuals.

Student ethnic organizations and activities often served as vehicles by which individuals came to understand and explore their ethnic identity, cultural values, and traditions. One student reported that the activities organized by the Black Student Association at RU (such as bringing Jesse Jackson to campus) enabled her to show pride in her ethnic group, which sustained her commitment to the group (African American). Likewise, an Asian student commented, "I think that there is a defined group of Filipinos. Having an organization [on campus] makes me proud that we have that." Likewise, the following students reflected on how campus-organized events and student ethnic organizations influenced their growth as ethnic individuals and their integration into a campus community:

> I am in a Latina sorority. It's like another family. I've gotten to know these people, and it's just that I spend so much time with them that I can't help feeling comfortable [on campus]. The majority of the people in my group are either in the [Latina] sorority or in the [Latino] fraternity. . . . I consider them more family than some of the family that I do have. (Latina/a)

> I see a lot of support for Mexican people here at this school. This other day, this man was passing out fliers for this convention about Aztec language, and I thought that was so neat because my grandmother speaks [the language] . . . and my dad understands, but my dad doesn't speak it. And I thought that was so neat. (Latino/a)

> For *Cinco de Mayo*, they had *mariachis*, and I love that. That's something I totally enjoyed and I thought it was wonderful. And the dancers, I like

watching that a lot. There were a lot of people out there, and I like the fact we were all there. (Latino/a)

I am in a dance group. I dance Mexican traditional dance, called *Ballet Foklorico*. So that's a big part of my life here at RU. It's a campus group. So I'm doing that [to express my ethnicity]. (Latina/a)

These students illustrate that ethnic-based, campus-sponsored events and ethnic organizations validated students' ethnic identities within the university setting and gave them an important space for learning and expressing ethnic pride. Other students said that, once they began an exploration process, they sought out student organizations to continue that process in deeper ways. The following students shared this perspective:

This campus is very positive with MEChA (*Movimiento Estudiantil Chicano de Aztlán*) and Casa (community service organization). They have a lot of participation and they want to include you and they want you to know, to realize where you come from. To be proud, you know. It's been really good. (Latino/a)

Some of my friends, we've all pursued some kind of club or organization. They've gone to their [groups], like the Korean Student Association, Chicano, or Latino ones, Indian. When they all did that, it supported me. Like, "Oh, I can do this." This is because I didn't feel like they thought that I was abandoning them. In that way, we all kind of mutually supported each other, and we can all come together still. Because of my friends [I have been able to get more involved in my culture]. (Asian American)

Campus student organizations not only had an impact on the "target" students (those of the same group), but they also served a function similar to that of diverse ethnic peers. Students who attended the activities of other student organizations learned more about other ethnic groups and cultures. Students also discussed the influence student organizations of other ethnic groups had on their own ethnic identity development, indicating that cross-group contact was meaningful. One Mexican American student reflected on how, through her involvement with the multicultural center on campus, she had gained greater awareness and information about other ethnic groups and how the center had been instrumental in uniting students regardless of ethnicity. She said that through her experiences with the multicultural center she learned, "We don't have to segregate. We can have [diverse ethnic] friends, whoever they are." Another student discussed how he viewed the campus as very culturally diverse and how he appreciated being able to participate in different clubs:

> I really like it, because it's not like too many Mexicans or too many Whites or too many Blacks. Overall there is a balance. I don't think it's difficult at all to interact with people of other races. There's the ASIA (Associated Student Incorporated Association), there's the BSA (Black Student Association), and the NHBA (National Hispanic Business Association). There's MEChA. There's a lot of ways for people to interact. (Latino/a)

Much as with coethnic peers, diverse peers who actively explored their ethnicity were role models and mirrors for students to whom they could compare themselves.

> My interactions with Latinos are pretty good. I'm in a couple of groups on campus, African American groups, and we interact with the Latino groups on campus. It works out really good, because it's almost like we have a common goal to uplift each other's races. I feel they get just as much hostility as African Americans do. (African American)

Enrollment and active engagement in formalized curricula had a similar effect on students' ethnic identity, as did campus ethnic organizations. A strong sense of ethnic identity and exploration of ethnicity and culture was reported by students who took ethnic studies and language courses. Being able to speak their native languages and learn about their history, origins, and roots made students feel proud and enabled them to identify strongly with their ethnicity.

> I can't speak Korean very well, so right now I'm realizing that when I was younger I should have taken more Korean school. So I volunteered to take Korean classes to find out more about my history, into more East Asian culture. You know, find out more about the history. (Asian American)

> I didn't used to say I was Mexican American, I was just American. When I got here, it changed a lot. I became more familiar with my identity. I'm taking Chicano Studies courses and I became more in tune with my identity. It means a lot to me now, my family means a lot to me. They are always telling us, you know, about our culture and stuff, and that is starting

to be significant in my life. I want to pass that on to my kids. Since taking those courses, being Chicano is more significant to me. (Latino/a)

I took the history of India fall quarter. It was an amazing class. I learned so much. Then I took the art history of India. Art and history are very interwoven in India. Art tells you a lot about the culture and explains things I never understood before . . . that definitely had a strong influence on me. It made me very proud of my culture instead of being embarrassed of it. (Asian American)

We were the first civilization. Everybody basically had to learn from us. You're not taught that in school until you're in college. Then you hear some stuff. . . . Learning that African Americans were the first civilization makes me feel proud. They try to say we're savages and all that, but we're the first ones to start a civilization. We brought civilization to the Europeans and to Europe, basically. (African American)

Before I started taking Black history classes and learning about my true heritage, I was not very proud of being African American. But now that I've read a lot of history and do all this studying, I'm very proud to be African. . . . As I learned more about being Black and [about] Black history, I really changed. It's really made me proud of being who I am. There's a lot of pride in me. That we Black people have accomplished a lot, we've overcome a lot. I do have a definite self-identity. (African American)

Students in this study demonstrated the snowball effect that taking classes in a formal setting can have on their ethnic identity. Not only does taking classes and learning about one's culture strengthen self-esteem from a psychological point of view, but it also reinforces students' identity, pride in their culture, and sense of belonging. For some, it made them cognizant of the adverse effects that deculturation, which stemmed from years of exposure to inaccurate knowledge about their group, has had on their identities. One Latino student spoke directly to this issue:

By reading books, like Chicano authors or Mexican American authors, they seem to write about your [personal] experience. I think now, by reading these books, you face these problems. Before you're in college, you really didn't deal with the effects of assimilation and discrimination. (Latino/a)

Similarly, one African American student stated: "I used to kind of believe Whites were superior to Blacks as far as education goes. . . . I used to feel inferior, put it that way. Not anymore, not since I've been in college." Likewise, reflected by the following student, is an astute understanding of how a lack of ethnic studies courses in high school affected several aspects of her life.

> I was never taught true history. All I was ever taught was that Black people were brought over here as slaves, and it was a good thing that happened, too, because we weren't very civilized. Once I came to college, I became interested in African American history and African history. It really changed me. It changed everything about my life because then I was proud of my identity. I'm proud to be Black, proud to be African. I didn't realize the transformation at first, but as I look back and saw how my thinking started to change as soon as I started taking African American history classes . . . I probably would have done better in school, maybe I would have had a 4.0 and gotten a scholarship to a better school or a different school. (African American)

Similarly, another African American student discussed her evolution into greater ethnic awareness through reading books and scholarly work: "I think reading books about my ethnic identity has helped me. . . . I learned that we as African Americans are in such a position that we should grab all positive influences and move forward as a group." She also reflected on how reading and writing literature about African Americans contributed to her ethnic identity:

> I think that reading and writing of literature about African American[s] has helped me to learn more about my people and helped me understand my identity better. I have fully embraced all of the positive things and reevaluated who I am in my own terms. I have stopped attempting to define myself by the terms that the mainstream society puts out because, when I was doing that, I could never perceive myself in a positive way. Once I was able to do that, I began to have positive feelings about myself. (African American)

The experiences of these students emphasize the empowering nature ethnic studies courses can have on ethnic identity development. These courses validated students' cultures by supplying content needed to gain a full sense of history and by asserting the importance of that knowledge by making it a formal part of the curriculum.

The positive influences derived from participating in university-sponsored, ethnic-based curricula were also voiced by White students (18%). Although White students did not talk about these courses in reference to their own ethnic identity development, they did acknowledge how they benefited, and grew as individuals, and achieved greater multicultural and ethnic awareness.

> I think that White people should educate themselves more about what it's like to be Black in the United States. . . . Just like taking the Development of the Black Child classes. I think we have to do that. I think that definitely helps you understand what it is like to be Black. It has helped me a lot to understand another culture's point of view. I think that everybody needs to do that. Other cultures are forced to understand how to get along in mainstream; White America and White people are never forced to do that.

> I remember [taking a] literature class last year [with diverse ethnic peers]. It was Black literature, and I remember hearing all of these different ethnicities. That opened and left different feelings for me, like their ethnic backgrounds and how they are different but how you can still relate [to them]. So I think just, like, being in class and hearing the different [ethnic] voices [affected how I feel about myself]. I value the fact that I am open to others, and that makes me feel better about myself. I can accept a lot of different people. I guess understanding what different [ethnic] people go through, that changed me. I can see their different struggles. It is not just about me but what other people have gone through. Ever since I took that course, I am interested in different ethnic authors. Like reading their work.[5]

Taken together, these findings highlight the positive psychological correlates and emotional gains that come from active engagement in campus ethnic organizations and through formal education about one's ethnicity. Particularly in the case of ethnic minority students, self-esteem and pride in one's ethnic group increased when students were allowed and encouraged to explore and strengthen their ethnicity in a college environment that supported and embraced diversity. This finding is corroborated by the survey

---

5. This student spoke of a literature course taken her senior year in high school that influenced her later choice of reading material in college. We include it to illustrate the positive influence of a diversity curriculum on students' development and growth related to the educational context.

data, which indicated that a strong ethnic identity (private acceptance, membership esteem, and a well-integrated ethnic identity) was positively associated with healthy self-esteem in students. Likewise, those students who had a strong membership ethnic identity also reported experiencing a high level of college self-efficacy in being able to navigate the social and academic spheres of a university setting. These findings certainly speak in favor of formalized university initiatives that support a climate of diversity through clubs, ethnic organizations, and departments of ethnic and cultural studies. However, as a caveat to the positive correlates of institutionalized multiculturalism discussed here, we note that, in the case of some students, especially White students, multicultural curricula and campus racial discourse (i.e., sponsored by ethnic clubs and organizations) were quite difficult to negotiate at times.

Negative Effects of a Multicultural Context

Students also commented less positively about campus diversity, which sometimes affected their experiences of ethnicity on campus negatively. As illustrated in Table 7.1, themes 7 through 10 analyze the negative aspects of greater ethnic diversity on a university campus, which can create the perception of an unfriendly and/or chilly campus climate. For some students, campus diversity engendered (1) feelings of discomfort and unease in regard to their ethnicity; (2) perceived discrimination against their ethnic group; (3) a learning environment where racial/interethnic tension was real and palpable; and (4) more visible ethnic segregation. Hence, in this section we examine the negative ramifications associated with campus diversity for students' development and interethnic campus dynamics.

Diversity Engenders Feelings of Ethnic Inadequacy and Discomfort

One of the most salient negative aspects of campus diversity was that such environments triggered a sense of ethnic inadequacy and ethnic discomfort in students. Feelings of unease and discomfort with the experience of one's ethnicity on campus was a theme voiced most frequently by White students (57%), followed by Latino/a (31%), Asian (22%), and African American (4%) students.

In the case of White students, encountering a diverse campus environment was disconcerting at times and made many feel a sense of ethnic discomfort with and disconnect from the university. Although White students were represented in comparable numbers as were other ethnic groups at both institutions, taken together, students of color were clearly in the numerical majority. Because of the demography of the two campuses studied, for some White students, a "minority status" was one of the most salient aspects of their experience of being White on campus. A young woman discussed how she did not feel positive about being "White" and expressed this sentiment: "I feel I stick out on this campus." Similarly, other students said: "It's kind of like being a minority . . . you kind of spot the White people here [and there]." "I have only been here a semester, and I definitely see that White people are in the minority." "I don't think statistically it's true, but I do feel like a minority because I see a lot of different groups around. A lot of Hispanics, Asians, and African Americans, and I don't necessarily see a lot of Caucasians tying together." Other related observations by White students included what they felt was a lack of opportunity "to express your ethnic identity" on campus.

> I am not sure really [about being] White on this campus. There are so many functions, like Black History Month, the *Cinco de Mayo* celebration, and there's not really a White celebration. In one of my classes I was required to see [a Black speaker], which was very interesting, but I don't really see anything on this campus for my culture . . . I kind of feel left out.

Students also noted that feeling like a minority in various campus situations gave them a sense of ethnic discomfort, especially when they interacted with diverse ethnic peers. "Sometimes I feel uncomfortable in lab if they [Asian peers] start talking to each other in another language because it makes me go like, 'What are they talking about? Me? Are they making fun of me?'"

> You definitely feel like you're in the minority. It definitely makes you feel different, and I think that we should feel that way. But I also feel like, let's say in the [Black studies class], you are trying to learn something new while everybody else is trying to validate what they already know. I also don't want to open my mouth because I don't want to have fifty Black people looking at me, like, "Are you crazy?" It does make you feel a little ill at ease.

> I have never been around so many different races, especially African Americans, until I got to this school. I don't know how to act. I don't know how

to talk. I don't want to say anything wrong. That's the big thing is, I'm very much interested in learning about African American culture and so I'm afraid I'm going to say something to offend them. Like a perfect example is if you say, somebody did something, people just say, "Oh, this girl did this or this boy did this," but often, if it's a Black person I'll say, "Oh, this Black guy did this." And then I'll think, is that wrong? Is that being racist? I mean, why didn't I just say the person. Things like that. Just because you say the person, should you assume that they're White, or should you identify them? So I get real nervous because I don't want to offend them. (Black peers)

It is clear that the structural diversity of the college context made White students more conscious of their ethnicity. In the case of the students above, this consciousness was associated with mixed feelings about their campus experience. Students perceived that their ethnicity, personal needs, values and interests as White individuals were not being addressed adequately or simply were ignored by the university. Furthermore, these students felt out of synch with their ethnic peers and with the campus culture, which made them feel like outsiders and made it difficult for them to negotiate being White in a diverse context. Unfortunately, the views of these White students mirror those of ethnic minorities attending predominantly White universities, which potentially place them at risk for psychological distress (Wright & Littleford, 2002); poor adjustment to college (Solberg, O'Brien, Kennel, & Davis, 1993); and academic failure (Olenchak & Hebert, 2002). It is important to point out, however, that although some White students did say that campus diversity made them feel like a "minority" and/or engendered a sense of ethnic discomfort, there were also those who said that, in time, they were able to move beyond this perception, had adjusted well, and appreciated being in a diverse university environment.

At first it was really weird. I was just like, "I'm a minority," because of the diversity. Because I went to a university back East, too, that was just all White. I didn't know with the diversity how I would be accepted as a White. Because when I first came onto campus, it's like everybody was Black or everybody was Asian. You know, that is what you see at first glance because I'm White. [What made me feel more at ease?] Just going to classes and having a Black person come sit next to you and talk to you. They don't see any differences in me and I don't in them. (White American)

Another response by White students to a diverse context was to experience a sense of cultural vacuum when they compared themselves to their multiethnic peers. This perspective was offered by the following students.

> Like, there was this *Cinco de Mayo* week, and that was kind of interesting to be a part of that and watch from a distance. They [Latinos/as] have such a strong tie. . . . It still makes me long for a strong tie with my ethnic group and my culture. . . . We don't have the same culture ties as Hispanics and African Americans and Asians do.

> What interests me is that people who are tied to their [ethnic] background, they have such a sense of history about themselves and I'm just sort of here. I think [having those ties] is a good thing. They are aware of where they come from.

> [I feel inadequate] when I have to come up with something about my culture. Like, last night in class I was in, I was supposed to write down a name of a food that was from my culture that I would bring to a party. I couldn't think of anything except Portuguese sausage and only because it had the name Portuguese in it. I don't think it's [even Portuguese]. It's just the name. If someone asked me to name Japanese stuff, I could name hundreds of stuff, and that's kind of embarrassing. It's like you know so much more about other cultures but nothing about your own.

This finding is consistent with having a weak or diffused ethnic identity, which is common in a cultureless or normalized identity in the case of Whites. As noted in chapter 6, the cost of having a normalized identity for Whites is the loss of a cultural/ethnic identity, which some students saw as an inherent source of strength in their ethnic minority peers.

Unlike their White peers, "minority status" was not a dominant theme related to the experiences of ethnic inadequacy on a college campus of students of color; however, a few students did note it. The following individuals spoke pointedly about experiencing *minority status stress* that affected their college experience (Saldaña, 1995) and, more specifically, interactions with White peers:

> I guess I feel more comfortable with other minorities on campus. I feel that we share some type of discrimination, and I can't say I share that with Anglos. They just lead a different lifestyle than me. A lot of them are well

off, and I can't really fit in that way. A lot of times I feel that they're a lot smarter than me. Maybe it's because they went to better high schools and private schools [and I didn't]. So that kind of makes me feel uncomfortable. I just think they're so different than me, the way they grew up, their value system. (Latino/a)

There is a difference that I can't [cross]. I feel that I couldn't really share my true feelings with them [White peers] about what I have shared with you to the extent that I feel that I bought into White values and, to some extent, because of the past, at times I feel that being Black, I'm less than them. Okay, I can't tell them that. (African American)

These students' sense of ethnic insecurity stems from living in a racially stratified society where they have been accorded and have experienced a lower status than the White majority. Hence, when engaging in social comparisons with White peers, these students voiced an insecure and/or negative ethnic identity related to having a "minority status" (Phinney, 1990). This finding is consistent with studies of ethnic minority students who attend predominantly White colleges (Saldaña, 1995; Wright & Littleford, 2002).

Most commonly, however, minority students' feelings of ethnic discomfort and unease stemmed from the realization that they knew little about their culture and who they were as ethnic individuals. Students who came from predominantly White communities voiced their concern with not being "ethnic enough" and expressed a desire to experience their ethnicity more fully.

What affects me as to whether I'm Korean enough is the language. We have these college group meetings, and they are run in Korean. So I get the gist of it, but I really don't understand the specifics, so I'm always whispering trying to get a translation. The language is the key thing that makes me feel like I'm not as Korean as I should be. (Asian American)

My sister went to UCD four years before me, and she joined an Asian sorority, and I remember watching her go through all that and she was so proud of being Asian. I loved seeing that in her because in high school she was very superficial and, you know, when she got into college and she was really proud about being Asian and I thought that was very cool. She had all these new Asian friends that she never had in high school, but for me, I tend to be friends with Caucasians, you know. I just feel guilty that I am not part of an Asian community as much as I could be. Here [at RU], I feel like I'm in between. I feel like an Asian token. When I see an Asian group, I think how it might feel to be part of an Asian group because to me it seems like it's two different cultures. I'm like [the] opposite [of] my sister. I don't think I feel as Asian as she did in college. I still have Asian friends, but I don't exclusively hang out with them and do cultural things that have to do with my ethnicity. (Asian American)

Hence, a common thread in the commentaries of minority students who came from predominantly White communities was a sense of having lost a part of their native cultural heritage. Attending a university that was structurally diverse and encountering peers with strong ethnic identities made them realize how little ethnicity had shaped who they had become as young adults, which engendered in them feelings of ethnic inadequacy. This finding reveals how the meaning and importance of ethnic identity shifts for students when they transition from high school to college and the difficulties they face in defining themselves ethnically in a diverse context (Saylor & Aries, 1999).

Accordingly, minority students also voiced feelings of guilt and ethnic discomfort if they felt they had failed to meet coethnics' expectations regarding their involvement in campus organizations and their level of commitment to the ethnic group.

When I came here, it was different because there are so many Asians everywhere and I was like, "Oh, my God," I am not the only one. I kind of went through a guilty stage because my friends were still Caucasians and I joined the sorority and it wasn't an Asian sorority. And I started to feel guilty. Like, I don't know. I would feel guilty, like, if I was wearing my letter for my sorority. Asians would look at me like [and think], "What kind of an Asian are you?" You know? (Asian American)

Furthermore, among Americanized ethnic minorities, interactions with coethnics who had strong politicized and/or cultural identities were difficult to negotiate at times and created feelings of ethnic inadequacy and insecurity.

I don't speak Spanish very well. I get uncomfortable [when] I stumble over the grammar. I feel like they (coethnics) are judging me or something. They probably think I'm a lousy excuse for a Mexican or something. Also, just on this campus, those groups (MEChA) seem to be kind of radical and I'm not into the whole "Go People" or something. (Mexican American)

It really [made me] sad, because when I came here I joined an Asian sorority and I was constantly around all these Asian people. It really hurt me because they were, "Have you met Susan? She acts so White." They would say, "I can't believe she joined an Asian sorority." . . . It's true. I'm really whitewashed. I'll joke about it, but it hurts when it's someone that is supposedly your own race . . . saying that about you. You know? That hurts a lot. Like, I'm trying you know. I joined an Asian sorority because I wanted to become more culturally aware, and it's like I realized I didn't like them. They were too hard core. They were racist in their own way. They would be like Asian power. (Asian American)

When using the [label] Latina in describing myself, I do it with a grain of salt. If I call myself that, and they (coethnics) know that I don't speak Spanish and I don't do that, they look at me [differently]. They won't say I'm not Latin American, but they'll look at me differently. I can feel it [in the] classroom. It's in the attitude. When they find out I don't do these things, [they think] she['s] on the outside. It's more, like, she is against us. (Latino/a)

To some extent these students' feelings of ethnic insecurity stemmed from a certain level of rejection by coethnics. Students illustrate that, in some cases, members of ethnic minority groups were critical of Americanized coethnics (i.e., perhaps perceiving them as sellouts).

In a similar vein, two Latinas also reflected on their struggle to define themselves on a college campus and the conflict they experienced when they failed to meet coethnics' expectations of them. These women discussed how the ethnic label they embraced as Latinas contradicted the identity of the peer group. One mentioned how her friends from MEChA wanted her to change her ethnic identification from Mexican to Chicana. "I've had friends who are in MEChA here on campus . . . [who tell me that Chicanos] have done so much [for our people] and I agree with that. That is true. But that doesn't mean that I have to change from being Mexican to [being] a Chicana." Another Latina woman also shared this perspective and discussed how she felt coethnic peers expected her to be more like them.

I think I should associate with everybody, not just be, you know, not just exclude myself from [Whites] because they're of a different race. 'Cause I notice that most of the Mexican girls here, the majority, hang around with Mexican girls. And I'm not like that. So they kind of don't like that with me . . . and I didn't like the term Chicano, because I always heard it's derogatory, so I didn't like the term myself. . . . So I raised my hand and said, "Well, you know what, I like being called Mexican American," and that was our discussion. . . . A lot of people really harped on me because I said that. (Latina–Mexican American)

Heard in these women's experiences is the importance of ethnic labels for individuals and their links to specific meanings and political viewpoints, which can create conflict among coethnics regarding the appropriate ethnic label for the group. The problem for these two women was that they defined their ethnicity primarily in terms of a cultural identification (i.e., Mexican or Mexican American), while their coethnics embraced a politically oriented identification (i.e., Chicano/a), which these women felt uncomfortable assuming. Finally, one student spoke candidly about the frustration she experienced when coethnics and diverse peers questioned her choice of major and her loyalty and commitment to her ethnic group:

I wanted to study Russian. That's when I had these Latin American people, even my friends, these people who I have no qualms with, but even these people who were supposed to be accepting of me were like, "Why are you going to do that?" So many people were telling me that there are enough Europeans who study European things; you need to study your own culture. It really made me angry. It was another expectation that was put on me. Even my friend, he is Black and he's studying a lot of African American stuff, told me, "You need to study Latin America." I've never gotten more frustrated. I mean, I started crying and spiritually I spent a lot of time praying. I told my friend about it and she said, "You're praying about your major?" And I, like, said, "You don't understand. I'm trying to choose a major here and I want to choose something I want to do. But I also don't want it where every time I mention it people ridicule me." It's not just the ridicule but [that it's seen] as a [negative] personal reflection. (Latino/a)

Taken together, the findings in this section point to the conflictive and problematic nature of ethnic identity development for young people within a context where race and ethnicity are salient. Regardless of ethnic background, it's clear that such environments can make students feel uneasy and uncomfortable as they struggle to define themselves as ethnic persons within a culturally and racially diverse learning community.

Perceptions of Discrimination Affect Ethnic Identity

The perception of race-based discrimination on campus was another theme to emerge from students' commentaries. Although students belonging to the four ethnic groups voiced this theme, the perception of discrimination was more evident in White students (43%) than it was in ethnic minorities (African American, 26%; Latinos/as, 31%; and Asians, 22%). A common theme in White students' narratives was the perception that racial double standards existed on campus that favored ethnic minorities (Gallagher, 1995). The following White students highlight the nature of their perception of reverse discrimination. One student said there was discrimination on campus because minorities "get better treatment" in terms of the programs (i.e. tutoring) available to them: "I would get rid of every special group or ethnic advantage there is, first of all." Likewise, other students stated: "You are treated as a minority. You get prejudice, like, with respect to graduation and graduate school." "I think that there is reverse racism going on now, and I think more people need to speak out about it." "The jobs that I see on this campus, the classes, a lot [of] classes seemed to be geared towards African Americans. That kind of bothers me." "Sometimes I feel discriminated [against] for stuff I didn't do, and I don't think it's good because it makes me bitter, like in applying for school. Right now, I'm thinking of that and I think we're all the same qualified, so why does it even have to be an issue?" Other students discussed reverse discrimination as well:

> We are pretty much prejudiced against. I mean as far as all that stuff that is associated with being a minority, we are prejudiced against. I don't mean as far as numbers go, I think. But, for instance, I notice it more as a Greek fraternity, which is sort of White, whatever. And I think, like, affirmative action applies to almost everybody except Whites, and it's fine to be in a Korean association, Vietnamese association, but not a Greek 'cause that is a White association. And that is racist.

> My first semester at RU I wasn't accepted. I was accepted [for] winter quarter. I had good grades, whatever. I had good enough grades to get in, but I just didn't get in the first quarter; they sent me to winter quarter. And I

believe that if I was Black or African American or Latino, I would've have gotten in.

An Asian American student from the research university, where Asians are not considered to be underrepresented, voiced similar sentiments:

> I feel discriminated [against] with school. You know, because getting accepted and stuff has to do with nationality. For example, like my brother, like he's a 4.2 and he got thirteen-something on his SAT and he didn't make it into Berkeley because of the fact that he was Korean. So you feel really discriminated [against] for that because you work so hard in school to get the grades. You can't go where you want because of race. (Asian American)

Another Asian American student at CU reflected on this issue and spoke of racial double standards related to the educational system:

> I just feel that being an Asian minority is limiting. Like, you know. If you're supposedly going to UR, there's a lot of Asians there, or like at UCI. You might have a better GPA than another person of a different ethnic group that you hardly see at that school, [but] they'll get in before you because of their ethnic background and race. I thought that was pretty unfair. Well, I can see that colleges are concerned with trying to get more diverse groups of people on the college campuses, but, you know, it's still unfair to the ones that are trying to get in and can't get in because of race. [There is discrimination in the application process] in getting into the schools.

These comments demonstrated how ethnic and racial diversification have increased competition for educational resources on campus (clubs, admission to graduate programs, campus jobs, and access to certain student services). These findings correlate with predictions made by race-relations theorists (Blalock, 1967; Wellman, 1977) who proposed that, as student enrollments diversify, minority-majority conflicts and tensions are likely to heighten. Likewise, other researchers have also noted (Hurtado, 1992; Reid & Radhakrishnan, 2003) that the larger the relative size of the minority group, the more likely it is that there will be minority/majority conflict and philosophical clashes regarding multiculturalism as well as policies and practices that promote racial diversification. When students believed that particular groups had special privileges or received special attention, the potential for ethnic tension and social distance intensified. This type of negative psychological campus climate undermines the potential benefits of an ethnically diverse learning community. Hence, institutions must set the tone for a more congenial and positive campus climate by committing to student aid initiatives and student development programs and services that preserve an environment of support for all individuals, regardless of race (Hurtado, 1992).

Another theme among White students had to do with their perception that they felt negatively stereotyped by peers because of past-present, minority-majority, interethnic relations. A White student said she felt that ethnic minorities assumed that all "Whites are prejudiced" and in being White, she was put in that category. Two other students offered a similar perspective:

> It's politically incorrect to be White. . . . There's a lot of stigma attached to being White . . . it's something like an oppressor type. . . . It makes me wonder, every time I meet someone new, do they think I am that way?

> There are so many [negative] stereotypes [about Whites] that I don't think people recognize it. "White people are racist," "White people are prejudiced," and I think that it is almost getting embarrassing to be White.

It is clear that these students felt stigmatized by the perception of them as "Oppressor[s]" of minorities, which hindered at times their experiences of ethnicity on campus. For some, this resulted in ambivalence and conflict about the meaning and expression of their ethnicity, which hampered their interactions with diverse peers.

The nature of perceived discrimination that ethnic minority students reported ironically mirrored, in many ways, the feelings of White students. For instance, one Latina said she felt that her ethnic group was discriminated against on campus as a minority group because its members didn't stand out as much as other ethnic groups' did: "I don't know. You see, like, other ethnic groups [on campus], they have their clubs or groups. You hear more of them than you do of Mexican groups. I think they [Mexicans] are still shoved away in a corner." She went on to say, "I rarely see them [coethnics], like, in my classes everybody is blonde. I hardly ever come across them." While attending RU this Latina student became more aware of the stigma associated with her ethnic background and was unable to find positive feedback for her ethnic identity. Likewise, the following Latina thought it was somewhat discriminatory that Latinas did not have their own sorority on campus:

> I noticed that and it made me aware, like wow, there's not a Mexican sorority. Yet there is an Asian sorority, a Black sorority, and White sororities. Everyone can participate, but, you know, what about the Mexicans, you know. We really don't have a group, a sorority, so I thought that was odd.

Still another Latina student said she felt that her ethnic group was discriminated against on campus because of political initiatives that hindered her group's ability to pursue a college education:

> Affirmative action and Proposition 187 makes you really focus on where you came from; it makes you more aware of how politics run. It's almost as though they're putting us at the bottom. I was upset because a lot of students were being told that they were going be denied the education. A good friend of mine, when she first came to this university, she was granted three thousand dollars in grant money to come through financial aid. She's an immigrant [and] she is very bright. She deserved every bit of that. She works very hard. A couple of weeks after the semester began, she received a letter stating that she was going to have to pay all that money back.

Accordingly, ethnic minority students also felt limited by others' negative perception of their ethnic group. Heard in the comments of ethnic minority students was a sense of frustration with being stereotyped negatively and how this perception restricted their experiences on campus and their interactions with diverse peers. The following statements illustrate this point:

> I wonder if they are thinking. Oh, she's just another Asian girl and she's just in her Asian world and stuff like that. Or, she is just competitive, and she just wants to study all the time, and she doesn't have a life. You know? She can't talk to me socially or anything like that. Or maybe she is just a normal person. She is just like me.

> I feel like if you're African American and male, that you are put in a category. Well, he's an athlete. You know. If you see an African American on

campus, then you know he is an athlete. He didn't get in here just as a student. A lot of other students stereotype African Americans like that. For the most part, it's sad, but it's true. But, you know, there are some cases that it is not true. I just think it is unfair to be stereotyped like that. (African American)

The bottom line is that they (White peers) do not perceive me as being on their level. They perceive me as being less intelligent because I am African American. I am not saying that this is true of everyone. I know that it's not true of everyone, but I think there are still far too many that think along those lines and they communicate that. Maybe not directly but indirectly. Yes, I feel that has been communicated to me many times. (African American)

Sometimes I just feel stigmatized because of the tutoring courses. So many other ethnicities feel that if you use a tutoring course, you do not have the ability. I had the course and I have a good SAT score and I have good GPA. . . . I feel sad, that the system, how you're labeled, like here at RU, you know. If you're Mexican American, it's like [ethnic-other peers think], "Oh, you got in because of affirmative action," not knowing that I did pretty good [in high school]. (Latino/a)

I wouldn't say discrimination, but there is a difference in the way people treat each other. If they (diverse ethnic peers) see I'm Latina, sometimes they don't expect much, they don't have high expectations of you. So it's really important to me to make myself look good and represent Latinos/as [well].

These students' apprehension at being stereotyped negatively by peers stemmed from what they perceived as views of their in-group as somewhat inferior to other ethnicities on campus—that is, subordinate in terms of interpersonal social skills, academic and intellectual potential, and/or sociopolitical status within the campus and larger society. As in the case of White students, stereotyping produced feelings of unease and discomfort among minority students when they interacted with diverse peers.

Taken together, it is clear that all students, regardless of ethnicity, can and do experience discrimination. Although some students were clearly more adept at deflecting the negative effects of perceived discrimination and moving past it, it left others with a negative view of their college experience and what it meant to be a member of their ethnic group on campus. Experiences of discrimination on campus can be serious barriers to students' sense of belonging and inclusion that can compromise their academic success and adjustment to college (Cabrera et al., 1999; Smedley, Myers, & Harrell, 1993).

Campus Diversity Makes Interethnic Tensions More Palpable

Although diverse university settings offer unique and multiple opportunities for extended interethnic contact among various groups of students, they also have become the focus of interethnic conflict and tension. Universities are certainly not immune to the racial politics that affect the larger society, and their political discourse is often heavy influenced by such forces. As noted by Mack and colleagues (1997), "colleges and universities often reflect the unease and hostility that have been growing in American society" (p. 256). Indeed, the perception of interethnic and campus racial tension was discussed by students belonging to three of the ethnic groups (African Americans, 23%; Latinos/as, 23%; and Asians, 13%), but more so by White students (43%). The perception of racial and interethnic tensions resulted in a chilly and/or hostile campus climate for some. Echoed in the following students' comments are the realities of ethnic tension experienced at both university campuses:

> Caucasians move back a little to let you (African Americans) through. They do this to prevent any type of conflict between African Americans and Caucasians. I can understand because I've seen a lot in my life. Maybe a Mexican girl bumping into a Black girl, by accident, and she just turns around and blows her head off, you know, verbally. So I guess I can understand that they just want to avoid a conflict. But I am not that kind of person. I mean, if I accidentally bump into someone, I am not going to act rude and obnoxious. I am just going to say, "Excuse me." But they (Whites) act as though, gosh, you know, they (Blacks) might try and beat me up or something. (African American)

> There is a lot of activism on campus but I try to avoid it. I have been approached by people who say, "Your people did this to my people," you know. I'm thinking my people didn't come here until 1930. We didn't do anything to your people. In that respect, you get prejudice coming from that direction. (White American)

Other students also commented on the nature of campus interethnic dynamics:

> They suck! The Latino people are having hunger strikes in the quad to get their way. . . . Everybody is just so angry. There is too much anger going on campus. It could all be avoided if everybody just simply realized that this is a university, a place of learning, not a place of social upheaval. (White American)

It is evident that an ethnically/racially threatening campus climate played a role in how these students experienced their ethnicity and how they reacted to prejudice and racial/ethnic bias. Unfortunately, the lack of positive interethnic contact experienced by some of these students does nothing to change their negative ethnic attitudes (Wright & Littleford, 2002). For some of these students, the perception of interethnic tension on campus contributed to an atmosphere of social distance with multiethnic peers where potential conflicts were avoided by adopting a protective and guarded stance. As one White student noted, "before I came to RU I had friends from all races . . . but having been to RU, I've become a bit racist because everybody emphasizes the differences so much that I would say [that now] I tend to choose friends from my own ethnic group." Because of the discomfort and tension this student experienced on campus, she was reluctant to interact with peers outside her own ethnic group.

A few students also pointed out the interethnic discomfort and unease engendered by race-based, multicultural discourse and curricula.

> Well, I'm taking U.S. history, and all I hear about is the typical slave history and how the White race is responsible for a lot of oppression. And I know that there's a lot of damage, but after a while . . . I hate feeling that there is animosity just because of color. If someone has animosity towards me, I would like to know what it is, how I can fix it, and how we can get past it. So, sometimes I feel it's just because I'm White—they're thinking that, as a whole, White people really hurt them, and they are putting me in that category without even knowing me. (White American)

> My friend took a Latin American course, and I thought that was so cool that they were willing to take that step. But they made her feel totally ostracized. They (Latin Americans) and African Americans get upset because we're uneducated and don't try to do something, but when you do, they don't welcome you at all. I mean as a group. I've met a lot of individuals

who complain about it all the time. It's wrong. People come to the Latin stuff and I totally support them. Individuals will be totally supportive of people trying to experience another culture. But as a group they're like, "Who are you? You're not Latin. You don't know what you're talking about." We [are] trying to figure out where you're coming from, but you don't welcome us sometimes. (Asian American)

One class particularly that I'm in now, there is more of the radical [type of student] and it's not the majority of the class by any means. But there is still that younger mentality that, well, I'm Black and you suppressed me and I'm not going to let you do that anymore . . . an I am better than you attitude. (White American)

Clearly, classroom discussions regarding race-related issues can spark inter-ethnic tensions and feelings of racial anxiety. While the ultimate goal of diversifying university campuses is important for achieving social justice and democracy in a pluralistic society, these findings demonstrate that the road to achieving this objective can be rocky. As noted by Hurtado and colleagues (Hurtado, Engberg, Ponjuan, & Landreman, 2002), because controversial issues related to ethnicity and race inevitably arise when taking multicultural courses, much greater consideration must be given to intergroup relations and helping students learn how to negotiate and transcend social differences and cope with uncertainty. It is interesting to note, however, that although many White students in particular felt uncomfortable when ethnicity and race issues arose, some still voiced a willingness and a desire to "fix or make right" existing social differences so that ethnic groups could "get past that and move forward" in a pluralistic society. This suggests that, despite the unease that surfaced among the various ethnic groups on campus, the opportunity to talk with diverse peers did make students aware of the importance of making democratic changes that favor greater ethnic equality. Through civic education, university officials can facilitate this process more proactively by encouraging students to engage in formal and intellectually rational deliberation and analysis of these issues.

Taken together, the findings in regard to interethnic tension on campus are of concern given the results of a recent longitudinal study of college friendships. The study found that students who reported greater out-group biases and interethnic anxiety at the end of the first year of college were less likely to develop cross-ethnic friendships in subsequent years (Levin, Van

Laar, Sidanius, & Levin, 2003). Furthermore, earlier research of multiethnic campuses indicates that students who perceive the campus climate to be racially threatening are more likely to experience alienation from and lack of attachment to the institution (Cabrera & Nora, 1994; James, 1998). This has been found to have an adverse impact on persistence rates in both White and ethnic minority students (Cabrera et al., 1999; Hurtado et al., 1999).

Campus Diversity Can Contribute to Interethnic Segregation

Students belonging to all four ethnic groups studied (percentages ranged from 17% to 32%) talked about interethnic segregation on the university campus: "I see people cluster in their little ethnic groups, and these groups exclude other people and they don't get the chance to really explore the campus" (African American). "It seems a bit segregated, but it's by choice. You don't see, like, three Whites and two Asians and a Black all standing in a group chatting very often" (White American). "The way it is for me is that the [ethnic] groups are very separate . . . I don't find them mixing at all. So, I mean . . . socially it is not a diverse school, through my experience of it" (African American). "On campus I see Hispanics kicking back with Hispanics and Blacks hanging out in their own places, and Whites spread out. I just see everybody having their own spot [separate space on campus]" (Latino/a). "I walk down the [center of campus and it's] like the real world. Everyone is out for their own race, 'in higher learning.' Mexico is over there, and Asia over there, and Africa over there. And it's so sad" (Asian American). These comments are in line with Buttny's (1999) findings concerning the construction of ethnic/racial boundaries among students, which have contributed to the emergence of a "new segregation"—a climate of racial and ethnic separateness—on university campuses. Although many students recognized that ethnic segregation on campus interfered with the various groups' ability to associate, White students' interpretation of campus segregation was somewhat more negative and threatening than it was for ethnic minority students. Three White students offered these perspectives:

> There's a lot more groups. It's more around you on campus. When I walk around on campus, I always see groups of certain Asian Americans, African Americans, Latinos, and even Armenians. At RU, I pretty much see it wherever I walk. The groups tend to separate themselves. It's not that I

don't believe that it shows ethnic pride, but I don't believe it does anything positive for the whole picture. (White American)

I think I would like to see more mixes because, personally, I would like to see less racial tension. I think that if there were more interaction among members of different ethnic groups then that would heal the racial tension. Not that I don't agree with Hispanic groups or Black groups. There were two Black fraternities out in the campus today. If only there were more groups that were not solely Black or solely Hispanic or solely Asian, which I think there are groups of each. I've never heard of a solely Caucasian group, and anyone who tries to have a solely Caucasian group is looked at as being really bad. You can't have White pride, but you can have a Black pride group. I don't think there should be any pride group. There's enough ties with a person's culture in the home normally, an education of that culture. I think that more people of different ethnic groups could easily become friends or become tied with groups. (White American)

The [younger African American students] kind of segregate themselves and separate, and they're causing it [segregation] all over again as far as I'm concerned. They (African Americans) tried so hard to become one nation with everybody and it was starting to work. It never got fully there. Racism never ended, but now it's like, well, I'm Black and I'm proud. Well, that's wonderful. I'm White and I'm proud, but you don't go segregating yourselves. You need to be proud and still love other people and not separate yourselves That's what a lot of them are doing, and that's what I see on this campus and it just makes me fume because, be Black, be proud, but be American and work with the people who are out there. Don't shut yourselves out, because you're pissing us off. We're really trying hard. I'm trying hard and then all I see is the ones who just don't want to have anything to do with White people and it's like, "What are you doing?" (White American)

Conversely, we also heard how the following two ethnic minority students offer a less negative interpretation of ethnic segregation:

Having a Filipino group [on campus] has really helped me to develop socially on campus. But I see how the different groups on campus exclude from one another. I walk into the cafeteria, and the Filipinos are here, African Americans over here, and Americans over there. And it's like, God, you know. But as far as the Filipinos go, they are very close and that's good, just as long as they don't, like, put everyone else aside. (Asian American)

I am happy to be here. I am glad there are a lot of Koreans on this campus and you feel a link to them. But there's a negative aspect because, if you're with Koreans too much, then you tend to exclude other nationalities and you are not interacting with them. I hope to do that, but it's kind of hard because you tend to just hang out with Koreans. (Asian American)

What some students saw as ethnic and/or racial segregation others were more inclined to view as a mode of obtaining support within the larger institution (Hurtado, 1992). This certainly creates a quandary for university officials: ethnic segregation can promote a climate of "ethnic separateness," which can interfere with promoting meaningful and positive interethnic contact on campus; conversely, segregating students by ethnicity can be construed as a means of affirming one's ethnic identity within a context where race is salient while, at the same time, providing vital social support. As Saylor and Aries (1999) note, many students of color actively seek new means of supporting their ethnic identities when transitioning to the university by joining ethnic clubs and organizations. This facilitates their adjustment to college by allowing them to become involved in the larger campus community. Hence, the challenge is to create a more hospitable campus climate for all students, one that promotes group pride across ethnic groups and embraces a superordinate identity that unites all students regardless of ethnic, racial, or cultural background (Baron & Byrne, 2003).

Summary and Conclusions

Taken together, the findings reported in this chapter illustrate how students' ethnic identity changed while in college because of the university context. Students challenged, confirmed, or reconfigured their ethnic identities as a result of having experienced a diverse campus environment. Notwithstanding the negative aspects of diversity identified in this chapter, the findings of the survey and qualitative data highlight the largely beneficial effects that ethnically diverse learning communities can have on students' personal, social, intellectual, and academic development. For many students, experiencing an ethnically and culturally diverse campus community gave them a positive and enriched sense of ethnic identity and personal self-esteem that supported their adjustment to college. Indeed, the survey findings positively linked students' ethnic identity to having positive self-esteem and healthy academic and social adjustment to the university. These results are consistent with those found by other researchers (Astin, 1993; Chang, 2001; Hurtado, 2001) who report that active engagement in "multiculturalism" (i.e., ethnic courses, cross-ethnic socialization, ethnic clubs, and organizations) is associated with positive academic and social self-concepts in college students.

It is noteworthy that campus diversity engendered a sense of ethnic belonging and inclusion in a large number of students. Especially in this case, campus diversity facilitated the integration and adjustment of ethnic minority students, in particular, into a community of learning. Contact with coethnics gave students a sense of ethnic pride and belonging within the university (Murguia et al., 1991) and was instrumental in their explorations into ethnicity and greater cultural awareness. In the case of students who had not considered the meaning of their ethnicity deeply before college, coethnics as well as diverse peers often served as teachers and role models in this process. In addition, the opportunity to experience an ethnically diverse learning community was a key factor contributing to the development of multicultural competence in students. Experiences with campus diversity were associated with a number of positive interpersonal changes in students, such as a greater level of comfort with and confidence in being able to engage in positive interethnic relations with ethnic-others, as well as to establish meaningful relationships with peers from different ethnicities. In terms of acculturative experiences, students spoke of the multiple influences that various cultural groups had on their personal identities and what they gained from these encounters. Analysis of the survey data substantiates this argument. Regardless of ethnic background, as a group, White, African American, Asian, and Latino/a students did not differ in terms of their social, academic, and overall adjustment to college.

Formal structures of the institutions, such as student organizations and course curriculum, played an important role in student ethnic identity development. Students noted how learning about one's culture in a formal college setting through ethnic-based curricula helped solidify for them the importance of their ethnic identity. Hence, it was through learning that pride in ethnic and cultural heritage increased, as did students' self-esteem. Likewise, involvement in campus organizations not only provided places of support for students to integrate into the campus community, but they also often helped contextualize the political nature of ethnicity for students and challenged them to become more committed to the political aspects of their ethnic group membership through engaging in political activism. Similarly, participation in events organized by other ethnic groups gave students important opportunities to explore other cultures, learn about the sociopolitical issues affecting other ethnicities, and engage in meaningful cross-ethnic interactions.

It is not surprising that the experience of studying and living on an ethnically diverse campus community resulted in changes in students' views about race and ethnicity. Consistent with earlier research (Astin, 1993; Chang, 2001; Gurin et al., 2002), many students said that attending a multicultural campus had made them more open to diversity and its challenges and allowed them to achieve a greater understanding and knowledge of ethnic-others. Students spoke of how campus diversity had encouraged a worldview of interethnic connectedness with diverse peers and a sense of inclusion that went beyond one's immediate group. Likewise, an ethnically diverse learning community prompted a greater commitment by students to social justice and race issues and a willingness to embrace more civic and democratic values (Hurtado, 2001). This form of multicultural perspective taking was voiced by students belonging to all four ethnic groups, as was the desire to be an advocate for the rights of ethnic-others. These findings highlight how university campuses with a significant number of ethnic minorities can have important positive influences on students' development, primarily in "liberalizing political views" and promoting greater ethnic understanding (Hurtado, 2001).

Conversely, the unfortunate side of campus diversity is that such learning communities can also make ethnic tensions more visible, foster feelings of ethnic inadequacy, and create a climate of competition for educational resources and the perception of ethnic separateness. These negative aspects of campus diversity were voiced by students belonging to the four ethnic groups at both RU and CU, but more so by White students and RU students. It is clear that this type of perceived interethnic campus dynamic can undermine the positive benefits of experiencing an ethnically diverse learning community. Although some students were more adept at deflecting the negative aspects associated with negotiating an ethnically diverse learning environment, for others, the perception of an ethnically adversarial and/or chilly campus climate negatively colored their experiences of ethnicity on campus.

Campus diversity was associated with qualitatively different manifestations of ethnic insecurities among the various groups studied. Students of color were more likely to have experienced *minority status stress* and to have felt insecure about how they should express their ethnicity on campus and what role it should play in their lives. Some voiced feelings of guilt about not being "ethnic" enough and frustration when they believed they had failed to meet coethnics' expectations of them. On the other hand, White students' experiences of ethnic inadequacy stemmed primarily from the sense that they were a "minority" on campus and that a diverse context resulted in a cultural vacuum for them. Many White students voiced frustration that the university did not give them the same opportunities afforded to minorities to develop and celebrate their ethnic identity, and that campus diversity made them feel like outsiders. Likewise, more White students reported experiences of discrimination and racial anxiety related to campus multicultural racial discourse (i.e., course requirements and interethnic campus racial politics). The perception of reverse discrimination (i.e., exclusion from certain programs or opportunities on the basis of ethnicity) and experiences of interethnic conflict on campus were also more commonly heard from White students. It should be noted that these findings are consistent with previous survey studies of multiethnic campuses, which indicate that White students' perceptions of racial tension on campus (Hurtado, 1992) and sense of ethnic victimization (Rothman, Lipset, & Nevitte, 2003; Sidanius, Van Laar, Levin, & Sinclair, 2004) were related to higher ethnic minority enrollment. White students in this study scored lower on all ethnic identity measures than did their ethnic minority peers, which may reflect the contextual difficulties they experienced as university students. As noted by other researchers, the perception of a negative campus climate can interfere with students' cognitive and affective development and contribute to a sense of isolation from faculty, peers, and campus organizations (Hurtado, 1992, 1994; Cabrera & Nora, 1994; Smedley et al., 1993). In spite of this, the negative correlates of campus diversity observed for some White students must be tempered by the fact that, for many such individuals, a diverse learning community proved to be meaningful to their developing multicultural interpersonal competence (71%) and relevant to their evolution into greater cultural/ethnic awareness (32%). More specifically, not reflected in the survey findings is that many White students discussed how a diverse learning community had enriched their understanding of ethnic-others and their sensitivity to ethnic issues, and that being in a diverse setting and interactions with diverse peers had prompted them to consider their own ethnicity. This is arguably a crucial step in the process of developing a positive ethnic identity and White ethnic consciousness (Hardiman, 2001). Indeed, many White students (56%) voiced a political interethnic consciousness by expressing a willingness to be advocates for the rights of other ethnic groups.

To conclude, the findings reported in this chapter highlight the unique and shared experiences of students who attend ethnically diverse university campuses as well as the different obstacles they face because of their ethnic background. As Reid and Radhakrishnan (2003) note, "different individuals can—and do—experience the same school in dramatically different ways" (p. 264). Evident from the findings is that the diversification of universities in and of itself will not be a panacea for substantially improved ethnic relations on college campuses; however, it does lay the critical and necessary foundation for bridging cultural differences and offering students an enriched community of learning (Hurtado et al., 1998). Hence, the reality of interethnic tension and discrimination on college campuses must not become the primary factor that prevents students from connecting with the university and experiencing the personal and social advantages that multiculturalism can offer. Many university officials share the goal of creating campus environments and communities of learning that promote students' ability to participate effectively in an increasingly ethnically and racially diverse society (Chang, 1999). Consequently, the onus now falls on institutional leaders to strengthen the psychological climate of their campuses, so that *all* students can capitalize on the benefits of a diverse community of learning and its positive associations with developing healthy ethnic identities in young people, along with the skills, values, and dispositions that are necessary to engage successfully in a pluralistic society (Hurtado et al., 1998).

THE ETHNIC EXPERIENCE
OF COLLEGE

I didn't have a lot of close friends who were Black, and so I didn't have a very strong ethnic identity at all. I don't think I had any ethnic identity at that time. It wasn't until I got into situations as a young adult entering college when I realized for a lot of non-Black people the bottom line was that I would always be Black, regardless of "You're my best friend" or "You're my girlfriend." When it comes right down to it, I always felt like it was going to be Black and White issues that are divided. I think when I became older, because of these experiences when I was younger, I began to seek out my cultural identity. [I felt that to] really know, I should get information to try and make myself positive about who I was. [Reading books] helped me better understand my identity, and I have fully embraced all of the positive things and reevaluated who I am on my own terms and not attempted to define myself by the terms that the mainstream society puts out. [Now I feel] stronger and I feel beautiful for the first time, inside and out . . . nothing will stop me from achieving my goals.

In this study of more than 100 students from two different universities in Southern California, it was apparent that ethnicity played a key role in how students experienced college. As students considered how ethnicity fit into their overall identity, we found that it was either emerging for the first time or was a reexamination of an ethnicity the student had explored earlier. This was enabled by the university context, new to all students, but also by the typical developmental forces in late adolescence and young adulthood where students strive toward a coherent and cohesive identity. In this process students negotiated influences from parents and families, interactions with coethnic and diverse peers, and external societal forces that made ethnicity and race salient. Students chose to take courses and participate in student organizations that formalized exploration and provided learning opportunities that strengthened cognitive, affective, and interpersonal skills and development. The survey data used in the study demonstrated the link between ethnic identity and college self-efficacy—academic and social self-efficacy—in students; that is, strong or well-developed ethnic identities facilitated students' ability to manage various elements of the college environment effectively. A part of ethnic identity, public acceptance of one's ethnic group, emerged as a factor that contributed to students' confidence in handling academic challenges. When considered with the interview data, we also saw that this public acceptance was related to positive perceptions of the campus environment and a healthy exploration of ethnicity, personal growth, and development.

It is important to consider the findings from this study in their context. Southern California has significant populations of all ethnic groups participating in this study. A steady flow of immigrants and residential segregation has allowed ethnic groups to maintain a sense of coherence that is often lost as these groups move into mainstream culture in other parts of the country. Students in the study had a broad range of experiences with diversity before their college experience. Some grew up in neighborhoods that were composed primarily of members of their ethnic group, or perhaps neighborhoods dominated by two ethnic groups. They often attended high schools that were relatively less homogenous, but where college-bound students were more likely to be segregated into predominantly White college-prep classes. Media and cultural activities in Southern California reflect this diversity, where ethnic groups are able to consume news, entertainment, and religious institutions that are specific to their own groups, thereby reinforcing their ethnicity. Thus, students from Southern California were not encountering diversity for the first time when they entered the college environment, nor were they necessarily considering their ethnicity for the first time. For students who did not grow up in the region, the diverse college environment did provide unique challenges and opportunities to reflect on their own ethnicity and their ability to interact with members of other ethnicities.

In this chapter is our final analysis of the ethnic experiences of diverse students. We begin by discussing the contributors to ethnic identity development for different groups of students and the meaning that being Asian, or

African American, or Latino/a, or White had for these separate groups of young adults. We also reflect on the unique lessons learned from students about the complexities of ethnic identity development and the implications of our findings for research and theory. Students' experiences of ethnicity within a diverse college environment and the barriers to contact that prevent formation of positive interethnic relationships are discussed as well. Students offered strategies for improving interethnic contact that they have used or they believed would facilitate positive interethnic dynamics. We conclude by providing recommendations for institutions for sustaining individuals' ethnic identity and promoting a holistic and successful multicultural campus culture.

Contributors to Ethnic Identity

Chapters 3–6 provide in-depth accounts of unique factors that contributed to ethnic identity for each of the ethnic groups studied. Although we had expected overlapping patterns in ethnic identity progression, we found that the various ethnic groups followed distinct pathways that reflected the different sociohistorical and psychological experiences of those groups in the United States. The distinct contributors for each group are summarized in Table 8.1.

Asian American Identity

Asian American students in the study came from specific ethnic backgrounds that were more important to their ethnicity than was the pan-ethnic term typically used to identify students and the group. All students were clear in their preference for their specific ethnic group label and were adept at discerning differences among Asian ethnic groups. More so than in any other ethnic group of students—for instance, Latinos/as—Asian students were specific in discussing the differences that exist across Asian subethnicities in language and racial history, which at times created divisions and ethnic distance among the various Asian subgroups. This was to be expected, as Asian Americans were the most diverse of the ethnic groups in the study.

Asian students expressed their ethnicity through language, food, customs, religion, and family structure. Students also demonstrated the impact of generational status on ethnicity. When students were closer to their families' immigration or actually part of the immigrating family group, their ethnicity was stronger because of their language fluency, their ability to traverse

TABLE 8.1
Contributors to Ethnic Identity

Asian American	African American	Latino/a	White
The Impact of the Family System on Ethnic Identity	Forming Racial and Ethnic Identities	Ethnic Labels & Issues of Ethnic Self-Designation	Who Am I? Labels Used to Define a White Ethnic/Racial Identity
Cultural Attributes Contributing to Ethnicity	Expressions of Ethnicity	Expressions of Ethnicity	The Meaning of a White Identity
Transforming Culture: Becoming American	The Complex Relationship Between Racism & Oppression	Family as a Collectivistic Entity	Implicit Expressions of a White Identity
	Optimistic Prospects for the Future	Ethnic Identity Processes	White Identity in an Intergroup Context
		Emerging Political Consciousness & Awareness	
		Acculturation: Becoming Americanized	

both the culture of origin and American culture, and their connection with family members who continue to live abroad. Family played a critical role in both the transfer and maintenance of ethnicity and the way in which students experienced college and young adulthood. Nearly all students, regardless of ethnic background, thought that enmeshed family structures were unique to their ethnic group. They felt that tight family systems caused students to remain closer to their families; the students continued to live with family in and after college and allowed family norms and expectations to determine life decisions (e.g., choice of partner) and planned lifestyles. They saw these actions as characteristic of their culture and identified the obedience implied in such decisions as another cultural characteristic. In fact, many felt their respect for their families and the obedience shown them distinguished them from their "American" peers. There was the strong perception that strong family endorsement of education was another characteristic of Asian families. Students felt incredible support and high familial expectations for their educational success. They also felt a sense of obligation as many family members had made sacrifices for these students to attend college.

Students were also very aware of the acculturation process they were undergoing as they grew up in the United States. Some looked forward to taking on "American" characteristics, especially the changes in gender roles, the family system, and adherence to strict parenting and discipline. They were also aware that language, a primary external marker of a strong ethnic identity, was being lost as they participated more fully in American culture. Peers sustained and supported ethnicity by modeling involvement in ethnic student organizations or ethnic studies classes and providing avenues for speaking native languages and engaging in other cultural activities. They also served an evaluative role in which students felt that their peers judged them negatively for "acting White." Despite what many students reported to be a positive acculturation process, nearly all took great pride in their ethnic group. This pride came from their knowledge of historic pasts, but also from current challenges as immigrants in a new society. This level of pride, associated with support of ethnicity in the universities and communities, seemed to allow students to look forward to an acculturation process that included the best of two cultures. They felt that, although their language might subside, their ethnicity would remain strong and they would make an effort to pass along that pride and ethnicity to the next generation.

African American Identity

The vast majority of African American students spoke of a Black identity with a sense of pride in the group. This was true even among those who at times were critical of the behavior of the group. The experience of overcoming the struggles of the past and present helped African American students to develop pride in the accomplishments of the group and to set goals for themselves individually and for the group as a whole. A Black identity was linked to a politicized, racialized identification for students, and many talked about their personal immersion experiences and the importance of taking an active leadership role to change the status of the ethnic group. They also experienced ethnic practices and expressions as contributors to their positive feelings about being African American. Students spoke of their connection to family and the strength they derived from faith and religion as vital supports for achieving their goals.

The consistency of African American students' carefully constructing identities that were strong and filled with pride, and their ability to identify specific efforts and experiences that brought them to this point, was a prominent theme among these students. More than the other groups in the study, they were able to connect the anti-Black attitudes or tendencies toward self-hatred (both characteristic of Cross's Preencounter stage) and the discoveries and realizations they made during their immersion experiences, which ultimately led to the development of ethnic pride (Cross, 1991). The discoveries related to relearning history and uncovering the sociopolitical forces in this country that have limited opportunities more covertly for African Americans were direct catalysts for the achievement of healthier and stronger ethnic identities.

Students spoke of a collective group identity as a special type of kinship that united all Black people because of their shared history of oppression and racism. Students reflected on the importance of strengthening this collective identity through educating more people about true African American history and the limiting sociopolitical forces that have affected, and continue to affect, the group. Shared experiences of miseducation and struggles that included slavery have prompted African Americans to reconstruct a culture while confronting contemporary racism and discrimination. Students felt empowered when they realized that, as a group, they have accomplished a great deal despite great odds. The ongoing development of a culture that includes reconstruction of African identities, the unique expression of religion and spirituality, the role of extended and inclusive families, and the formation of a unique dialect, demonstrates that African American ethnicity and culture retain a fluid characteristic where its members feel they make significant contributions to development of the culture. When individuals believe they can make such contributions, they are much more likely to see that their own individual actions and achievements affect the destiny of the ethnic group as a whole. These students definitely saw themselves as capable and active participants in achieving that destiny.

Latino/a Identity

Latino/a participants in the study were primarily Mexican in origin and were very close to the immigrant experience, with a vast majority being either immigrants themselves or children of immigrants. Additionally, most were the first in their families to attend college. Latino/a college students constructed ethnic/racial and cultural identities that were the result of intersecting developmental processes and sociohistorical and political forces. To illustrate, ethnic self-designations tended to be flexible and contingent on the social context, with specific ethnic labels chosen to confer an explicit cultural, ancestral, or political connotation (e.g., Mexicano/a, Mexican American, or Chicano/a). The process of naming the ethnic group was not always easy, and some students struggled with finding the "right" ethnic self-designation, especially when others questioned the legitimacy of an assumed ethnic identification (i.e., the phenomenon of in-between spaces). Furthermore, encounters of mistaken identity (e.g., other identified as White) forced some students to have to "claim" a Latino/a ethnic identification.

Ethnic expressions of a Latino/a identity were associated with ethnic pride and strength among college students. Although students spoke of engaging in many ethnic practices, language, family, and religion emerged as central and overarching themes in defining a Latino/a cultural identity. There were resources in the communities, in families, and on campus that promoted maintaining ethnic practices and expressions, and students in this group took great pride in being both bilingual and bicultural, which they viewed as one of the inherent strengths of their ethnic group. Some who had lost the Spanish language expressed embarrassment and shame (e.g., "I'm a lousy excuse for a Mexican") and spoke of reclaiming that element of their cultural identity through formal study.

Family as a collectivistic entity was a defining and fundamental aspect of students' ethnic self-concept. The *familial* self-concept was articulated in students' reflections of their values regarding *respeto* for and within the family, *personalismo*, and deference to authority, especially parents and elders— values that were reinforced through religious beliefs about morality and proper behavior and the importance of not shaming one's family, community, or ethnic group. In the case of young Latinas, their more liberal gender roles regarding education, social behavior, dating, and enacting certain life plans often clashed with the more traditional expectations of their parents' native culture, so they experienced tremendous pressures to conform to those traditions. Nonetheless many saw themselves as different from their mothers, and through higher education they were redefining the roles they would assume in the future as Latina professionals, wives, and mothers. The importance of education was at the heart of the immigrant experience and of the sacrifices family had made to ensure the success of the younger generation. Students felt strongly supported by their families to pursue a higher education. Many who were first-generation college students felt a great sense of responsibility to guide their younger siblings through the educational process, which ultimately would ensure the success of the family in the United States.

Students articulated how their ethnic identity changed over the years and what things either challenged or supported that identity. They spoke of elements in the college environment—the presence of coethnics and participation in ethnic courses and organizations—that helped them strengthen their ethnic identity and learn about their group. Likewise, students experienced challenges from society (i.e., racism and negative images of the group) and within the university context that tested their ethnic identity and presented challenges to achieving a positive ethnic self-concept. Ultimately, Latino/a students associated a strong ethnic identity with having a sense of confidence that enabled them to tackle life's challenges and struggles. Many Latino/a students also spoke of developing greater political consciousness and awareness that was collectivistic in nature. As such, an emerging and developing political consciousness prompted students to see their actions and future plans as important to improving the status and power of the ethnic group. Education was seen as a primary vehicle for achieving this aim. Finally, experience with acculturation strongly shaped and transformed students' ethnic identity and views about how they would enact their futures. Latino/a students spoke of becoming Americanized and forging a new hybrid culture they found to be personally and collectively beneficial, one that did not entail sacrificing valued and treasured elements of their Latino/a culture and heritage.

White Identity

Our analysis of White identity revealed the struggles and conflicts students faced when framing Whiteness in terms of its cultural or ethnic meaning versus Whiteness as a racial identification in relations to other groups of color. In describing their ethnic backgrounds, these students referred to an elusive identification based on European ancestry or simply labeled themselves White or Caucasian. However, there were many who in the end embraced an "American" or "White American" identity as an ethnic or racial identification and articulated White to be what Devos and Banaji (2005) term a cultural default for an American. Students made explicit references to American political ideological beliefs related to freedom, justice, and equality and embraced values consistent with having an independent and autonomous self-concept associated with individualistic cultures.

Students constructed Whiteness as a cultureless identity, which meant that they were nonethnic. As such, they embraced a racially or ethnically *neutral* identity and defined themselves simply as persons, individuals, *human beings.* "Minorities" were seen to have ethnicity and culture but Whites were not, and in this sense, Whiteness signified a social location in relation to groups with ethnicity. Related to a cultureless identity were ideological views regarding how Whites, as the dominant group, should relate to ethnic minority groups in an ethical, moral, and unprejudiced way that defined for students what it was to be a good, nonracist White person. Furthermore, students also conceptualized Whiteness as "normal," "ordinary," and "invisible" and hence an identity with little psychological significance in living one's daily life. Linked to a normalized and cultureless identity, Whiteness was described as an intangible, an elusive social identity where specific cultural expressions and practices were difficult to identify and articulate. Still, more than half of the students were able to identify at least one practice they tied to their culture and ethnicity as White ethnic persons. However, this seemed to be expressed more as an ethnic identity of leisure, one reserved for holidays and/or special occasions, and not one that was directly "linked or obligated" to specific cultural "communities organized around ethnicity" (Gallagher, 2003, p. 145). Some students viewed having a cultureless identity to be more favorable in that to be "too ethnic" could interfere with one's ability to be rational and unprejudiced. This is consistent with color-blind ideologies that stress that race and ethnicity should be deemphasized in favor of pan-human characteristics as well as the notion that ethnic identity should not be "too excessive" but more of "a private affair" (Gallagher, 2003, p. 145). However, in the case of other students, a normalized and cultureless identity left them with a sense of cultural vacuum and longing for what they perceived to be the strength of ethnic minority groups.

Conversely, when a White identity was framed within an interracial context, students no longer articulated Whiteness as being invisible but discussed it as a psychologically salient racial marker and a meaningful aspect of their social identity. Within the context of multicultural discourse and racial politics that occur inside and outside the university, race mattered for White students, and personal meanings attributed to Whiteness became more problematic, conflictive, and defensive. As a racialized identification, students spoke of Whiteness as a privileged status and the conflicts and dissonance shaped an identity that linked to racial oppression. The acknowledgment of White privilege engendered negative affective reactions (i.e., White guilt) in many that were associated with a loss of group esteem. Personally relevant encounters of White discrimination (especially toward ethnic minority friends) were critical consciousness-raising experiences for students, making it impossible to deny the existence of White racism. We observed among some of these students an attempt to reconstruct and reinvent Whiteness as a positive, nonracist identity based on their own personal reeducation. However, there was a tendency among some students to dismiss White racism naïvely or selectively and trivialize racial and ethnic disparities in American society as a thing of the past. Most pointed was the construction of Whiteness as a victimized identity. Here students defined Whiteness to be an identity of nonuniform privilege, where one is also the victim of race-based discrimination, current forms of multicultural and academic discourse, and campus racial politics. The reinvention of Whiteness as a victimized identity was made possible by espousing color-blind ideologies coupled with students' belief in an egalitarian and merit-based society where minorities are now granted the same opportunities as are Whites.

It is clear that negotiating the cultural/ethnic meanings of Whiteness and its racialized connotations within a context of racial and ethnic diversity was more problematic and challenging for White students. In this regard White students lagged behind their ethnic minority peers in ethnic and racial identity development. The various meanings students attributed to Whiteness pointed to an identity that is in a state of transition and dissonance, one that was contextually and sociohistorically based and often expressed in contradictory ways.

Intergroup Impressions

The above synopsis points to the distinctive elements that contribute to ethnic identity development in various ethnic groups of students. Although students clearly varied in how visible and significant their ethnicity was to them personally, the vast majority of them were able to articulate cultural expressions they attributed to being Asian, Latino/a, African American, or White. Even among White students, we note that Whiteness was not altogether invisible or cultureless, thus expressions of ethnicity were common among all groups. The development and expression of ethnic pride was a central theme in the articulation of ethnic identity among Asian Americans, African Americans, and Latinos/as, which was a result of their families' and groups' overcoming barriers in society. Such constructions of pride and ethnicity were heard less frequently from White students, who stated this indirectly in terms of being a proud American. Also observed was that acculturation forces and family systems were significant to the formation of ethnic identity among Asian and Latino/a students, which affected their values related to familial expectations, gender roles, and life decisions. It is important to highlight, however, that family was central to the values of students belonging to the four ethnic groups studied, but its influence was expressed differently across ethnicities. An American identity and its associated correlates were an important identification for White students and were central to the ethnic evolution for other groups as well. Asians seemed to grapple the most with becoming more or less American, but Latinos/as also experienced this in terms of their awareness that living in America was transforming their cultural expressions, and by African Americans in that some expressly resisted taking on mainstream practices and values.

It was not surprising that the importance of education proved significant across ethnic groups but was intertwined most closely with Asian students' definition of their ethnic self. While White students discussed education in terms of personal fulfillment and individual upward mobility, both Latinos/as and African Americans perceived education as a vehicle for collective change for the betterment of their ethnic community, and Asians viewed it as a source of pride among one's family members. We note that African Americans and Latinos/as explained educational racial disparities differently. African Americans understood institutional racism as a cause for their group's educational underachievement—an analysis that mirrors Ogbu's (1987a) theory of involuntary, caste-like minorities in American society. Latinos/as on the other hand, located that deficiency in their families—"they don't have an education"—not within the educational system and/or within institutions; hence they felt responsible for guiding younger members through the educational pipeline. Finally, African American, Latino/a, and

White students spoke pointedly about societal forces related to oppression and discrimination, external powers that were critical to shaping students' construction of themselves as ethnic and racial persons. In particular, Black-White interracial tensions and conflicts emerged as defining themes in the racial identity development of both African American and White students. Taken together, the findings summarized here underscore how generic models of racial and ethnic identity development may prove to be inadequate in capturing the distinctive pathways and formative life experiences that influence ethnicity identity development of various groups of young people.

Lessons From College Students About Ethnic Identity Development: Implications for Theory

When looking across the ethnic experiences of the four groups as they encountered educational systems, family, society and the universities, we found five dimensions that were characteristic of ethnic identity development processes for college students. Our intent here is not to explain an entire ethnic identity progression but to add to the current state of knowledge and to well-established theories. Identifying these dimensions adds greater depth to our understanding of the complexity of ethnic identity development that current theories fail to describe clearly and/or demarcate within their conceptual frameworks. The five dimensions include:

- Loss and Reclamation of Ethnic Identity
- Peer Influences on the Development of Ethnic Identity
- Intersections of Ethnic and Young Adult Developmental Processes
- Influences of Sociohistorical Forces on Ethnic Identity
- Distinctions Among Racial, Cultural, and Ethnic Identity

The influence of these five psychosocial and historical dimensions became salient under specific contexts and at different times. They emerged as relevant to the manner in which ethnic identity evolved for young persons and the distinct *pathways* that individuals within and across ethnic groups choose to pursue in their development as ethnic and racial individuals. Syed, Azmitia, and Phinney (2007) have begun to speculate that, indeed, we should consider within-group differences as divergent pathways toward ethnic identity. The five dimensions discussed in this section represent how ethnic identity changed and took on different meanings for students as a result of intersecting conventional developmental factors, new experiences, and new social contexts as well as sociohistorical forces that brought their social identity as ethnic beings into the foreground.

Loss and Reclamation of Ethnic Identity

A consistent finding across participants was the experience of losing one's ethnic identity in response to experiences in high school, living in monoethnic communities, and the consistency of familial strategies to maintain cultural practices and knowledge. A common denominator for many students in the study was participation in college preparatory courses during high school that were predominantly White. Because adolescence marks a time when young people greatly desire to fit in with the peer group and not stand out, Asian American, African American, and Latino/a students tended to adapt to the high school experience by assimilating with their White peers. The strong push to assimilate influenced in some students their choice of friendship groups, social activities, and adopting an "American" standard for attractiveness. In addition, the strong desire to blend in with the dominant peer group that was largely White caused some students to minimize the expression and importance of cultural practices. Structural and contextual features of the high schools attended (i.e., being in college preparatory courses), combined with developmental pressures to fit into a White peer group, resulted in a decrease in ethnic identity for such students during high school.

Conversely, other students had somewhat opposite experiences, in that they lived in communities and attended high schools that were composed primarily of members of their own ethnic group. In this environment the cultural practices and expressions of the ethnic group would be "normal," thus indiscernible in how students would be perceived to be unique in more multicultural environments. In essence, just as White students in the study experienced White culture as largely invisible as a distinct culture, to some extent so did students from other ethnic groups who lived in monoethnic communities and who attended relatively segregated high schools. This resulted in an unexamined ethnic identity based on the meanings that family and community ascribed to that identity, essentially resulting in a foreclosed identity, as described by Phinney (1995; Phinney, Jacoby, & Silva, 2007).

Many families encouraged specific activities to teach and maintain cultural knowledge and awareness. These may have included family involvement in ethnic-specific religious communities and activities, ethnic and language schools, use of the native language in the home, and reinforcement of reading history and literature related to the ethnic group. While all of these established a strong foundation for the development of healthy cultural and ethnic identities, familial participation in these cultural activities and traditions tended to diminish in frequency as children aged. Although some persons, families, and communities were able to maintain these practices, some students experienced a sense of cultural loss that came about through coming into contact with new educational institutions and American youth culture, all of which coincided with developmental phases related to adolescence. Students were at a developmental point when their focus was turned outward as they constructed identities where peers, rather than families and parents, were the primary referent group. In attempting to become adept at dealing with external agents (such as educational institutions, other-ethnic friends), they disengaged from those practices and value systems that sustained cultural and ethnic identity up to that point. Since college admission depends on success in high school, socialization into this important societal institution carries much higher stakes for students. This entire process led to a loss of cultural and ethnic identity that students came to acknowledge once they entered the college environment.

The college years represented a reawakening of the importance of one's ethnic identity and a desire to strengthen and explore a dimension of the cultural self that had been lost during high school. Students questioned the meaning of their ethnicity, which led them to an active search for knowledge and understanding through peer influences, engagement in ethnic clubs and organizations, voluntary and required matriculation in ethnic studies courses, and political and civic engagement. In this regard, the college experience was unique for these students because it gave them multiple opportunities for ethnic rediscovery through various structural features of the institution—that is, a diverse student body, multiple ethnic clubs and organizations, and ethnic studies programs. Because universities have structural features that intersect with the developmental push to consider identity in a sociohistorical context (Chickering & Reisser, 1993), or more directly consider ethnic identity (Phinney, 2006), this makes for an especially dynamic time for students. Although students in this study did not usually seek out activities with the specific intent to strengthen ethnic identity, this happened. They declared that the development of their ethnic identity resulted in outcomes such as increased self-esteem and self-confidence, goal commitment, civic mindedness, and academic success.

Matriculation in ethnic studies courses was an important vehicle by which students explored their ethnic identity. Such courses were instrumental in helping students to recognize internalized racism and to acknowledge the cost of assimilation. Students were challenged to reexamine their views on race and ethnicity by having access to accurate knowledge of group history. Furthermore, through such courses, students attained the tools to evaluate critically the systems that maintain racial stratification in American society. Students spoke of K–12 educational disadvantages that were linked to discriminatory practices as well as the limited opportunities some ethnic groups experience in political arenas. More important, taking courses in a formalized setting and learning about one's ethnicity and culture further reinforced ethnic pride and self-esteem.

Likewise, the influence of coethnics was of key importance to all students' ethnic identity, but especially for Latinos/as and Asian Americans. Peers served as role models and vehicles of support in the process of ethnic identity exploration. Because of the significance of cultural scripts (behavioral expectations) related to *personalismo* (being open to influence from authority figures and role models) and interdependence, we believe that Latinos/as and Asian Americans were more likely to address the peer influence in their narratives (Marin & Marin, 1991). We also saw the effect of peers in general in the role student organizations played in students' ethnic identity. When students saw their peers participating in ethnic student organizations, they were encouraged to do the same. The extensive network of student organizations on these campuses, especially at RU, enabled students to participate in highly specific groups that matched multiple social identities (e.g. Korean Christian Student Association); levels of acculturation (e.g. the Chinese student association for native speakers); and social goals (e.g. ethnic fraternities and sororities).

White students awakened to a racial and cultureless identity prompted by social comparison processes and a context that emphasized and made salient ethnicity and race. We note that in the case of White students, this awakening was much more conflictive and entailed negotiating internal issues—experiencing a cultural vacuum as well as a desire to know more about one's ethnicity. This was coupled with external factors, such as being in an environment where ethnicity was emphasized, yet students felt they were not allowed to ask questions or explore this identity freely as their ethnic peers could do. The campus environment provided no tools for them to explore Whiteness, or rather, no tools that these students reported to be useful. Where their ethnic-other peers saw their student organizations as tools and places to develop ethnicity, White students did not even see predominantly White student organizations as "theirs," nor did they see these as vehicles where Whiteness could be acknowledged or celebrated. This resulted in a feeling of a cultureless identity, where they were spectators and not participants in the ethnic identity process that seemed so visible and important to their ethnic-other peers. Associated with this dynamic was the racial identity process White students were undergoing, which required them to consider such issues as White privilege, racism, coping with "White guilt," and feelings of victimization. They expressed a sincere desire to become a "good White person" free of prejudice and a transcendence of race that was positive and allowed them to encounter individuals and the campus environment free of the "baggage" that has accompanied the legacy of racism and oppression in our society.

Peer Influences on the Development of Ethnic Identity

In addition to the modes in which peers interacted with the college environment discussed above, peers also functioned as instruments of ethnic identity development in three important ways. First, the peer group gave students a location for peer-to-peer learning about culture and ethnicity. Second, peers provided a safe haven from a sometimes turbulent campus environment and from society in general. Finally, peers also served as evaluators of individual merit to "enter" the ethnic group.

The multiple influences of the college peer group on students' growth and development cannot be understated. In many ways it was exposure to coethnics and diverse ethnic peers that gave students the impetus to begin their ethnic identity search. Because most students came from highly segregated high schools, encountering a learning environment comprised of multiethnic peers encouraged them to consider their own ethnicity in ways that were linked more deeply to their sense of self than they had been in the past. Likewise, peers—ethnic others as well as coethnics—with strong identities played a pivotal role in this process because they served as role models for explorations of ethnic identity. A strong presence of coethnics often strengthened ethnic identity in students because those who were actively exploring their ethnicity encouraged others to do the same. Peers modeled cultural activities (speaking the native language, participating in ethnic student organizations, and cultural traditions) and exposed avenues for engagement in community activism that benefited ethnic groups. Hence, the presence of coethnic peers facilitated students' examination of ethnicity and affirmed their ethnic identity within the university. This same dynamic played out with ethnic-other peers. Consequently, we see how peer groups comprised of coethnic and diverse-ethnic peers challenged students to evaluate their identities as ethnic persons, make decisions about the role ethnicity would play in their lives, and decide how they would express that identity. Peer-to-peer learning in this regard was clear.

The ability of an ethnic group to achieve a critical mass on campus provided a *safe haven* for students in a number of ways. Such a critical mass of coethnics allowed students to feel a sense of belonging. Many students spoke of how comforting it was to see others like them in the college environment. This comfort was as simple as just seeing others on campus and as substantial as providing opportunities to develop significant relationships with coethnic peers. For example, several students were able to live with roommates from their own ethnic group, which allowed them to speak their native language daily; engage in social activities specific to their group; and participate in more commonplace ethnic expressions, such as preference for food, music, and media. Student organizations served a similar function as same-ethnic living arrangements, but they were formal structures in the university in which students could participate regardless of their residential status or location. For many students ethnic student organizations were places where they could integrate socially that provided the protective subsystem necessary for persistence in the larger community; the importance of this is described by Tinto (1993).

However, these student organizations and their members often also played an *evaluative role* in the developing ethnic identities of students who came in contact with them. The evaluative role coethnic peers played tended to result in one of two outcomes. When students were made to feel naïve and uninformed about their ethnicity and race, they were compelled to seek out and learn more about their ethnic group and related interracial dynamics. In this way they recognized how ethnicity had been lost to them or how they had been previously misinformed. Peer evaluations also played a more judgmental function in students' sense of belonging to their ethnic group. For instance, if students were unable to speak their native language, peers may have judged them to be not "ethnic enough." Students in the study seemed to be highly self-conscious when they felt coethnic peers were evaluating the ethnic identity of others. The microscopic evaluation students experienced produced a sense of shame and guilt from not having placed more importance on language and culture. In essence, the coethnic evaluators served as gatekeepers for membership in the ethnic group. The strong feelings of isolation and rejection were dramatic for some students. This was even more critical for students who reported that the only discrimination they experienced on campus was from their own ethnic group. This dynamic of negative peer evaluation also occurred in the classroom and other campus support units where student communities exist.

Recent survey studies conducted by Hurtado and colleagues (Saenz, Ngai, & Hurtado, 2006; Hurtado, 2007) has given much attention to the positive effects of cross-ethnic peer socialization on student development, primarily in terms of multicultural competence. However, much less attention has been paid to how these relationships are often the primary impetus for young adults' evolution and transformation of ethnic identity where such interactions prompt students to question, challenge, and transfigure their self-concepts as racial and ethnic persons. Hurtado and Guavain (2007) argue that "it is important to address the benefits that students can accrue from same-race peer environments, including social integration and comfort in addition to learning and democratic skills" (p. 188). By using a multi-method approach, this investigation addresses this gap in the literature by delineating more clearly the role that same-race peers, as well as diverse ethnic peers, have on the evolution of ethnic identity for students during the college years.

Intersections of Ethnic and Young Adult Developmental Processes

Another component of the ethnic identity process is how this process intersected with other developmental issues in becoming a young adult. We note the complexity of ethnic identity development for these students in terms of the ongoing influences of acculturative forces—negotiating between competing belief structures related to home and the institutional culture—and other specific adult developmental processes associated with career choice, partnering, and future parenting. Student narratives spoke to the multifaceted ways in which ethnicity and culture interacted in meaningful and transformative ways with important adult developmental tasks and decisions related to autonomy, gender, integrity, and generativity (Erikson, 1968).

Accordingly, in the case of Latino/a and Asian American students, becoming an adult meant moving away from family and acquiring new values and beliefs that emphasized autonomy and independence while at the same time grappling with the importance of retaining valued elements of their native culture such as familialism and collectivism. Some worried that, in this process of acquiring new belief systems, they would turn against their native culture and lose an inherent and critical aspect of their cultural self. Furthermore, becoming young adults signified for these students moving away from an interdependent family unit, which forced them to negotiate the acculturative dynamics of becoming more independent while at the same responding to the familial cultural expectations related to gender roles and family loyalty. Like college students who experienced conflicts between retaining and rejecting parental influences, many others also thought that some of the new belief systems they were acquiring were desirable. For example, most Asian American women and Latinas looked forward to leaving behind male-dominated family systems and embracing more equitable male and female relationships.

Compared to African American and White students, Latino/a and Asian American students experienced more minority status stress in mediating between the university culture and the home culture. Important cultural discontinuities existed between the home culture and the institutional culture for these students (Bernal, Saenz, & Knight, 1995). Although Chickering and Reisser (1993) described the development of interdependence as a desired outcome of developing autonomy, higher education emphasizes the importance of making individual decisions and being independent. In this area we note the push-pull for Asian American and Latino/a students regarding parental control. Students were transitioning to college and entering a society where they were seen and treated as adults, yet family was still intervening in what are perceived to be adult decisions. There was also pressure for students to remain close to home. So, regardless of the ethnic diversity of the campuses attended, the institutional cultures adhered strongly to American values, norms, and behavioral expectations where the developmental agenda is to reproduce "American" values of what it means to be a young adult. These institutional norms at times clashed with the collectivistic, interdependent, and hierarchical family orientations of the Latino/a and Asian American home culture.

Ethnic identity intersected with career development issues and decisions as well. The development of ethnic political consciousness pushed students into considering new career options by changing their value systems in ways that resulted in more collectivist and generative values. Their attempts to achieve a sense of congruence between personal values and the values of their possible careers were paramount in how they were considering their futures. They became concerned with how they would implement their new value system in their work life but, more important, in their life purpose. They envisioned themselves as leaders who could, through their individual actions, "bring up" their ethnic group, by improving its opportunities and status in U.S. society.

In the case of Latinas and Asian American women, gender role expectations at times conflicted with their role as students and how they envisioned their futures. Gender roles prescribe protecting the girls within Latino/a and Asian cultures and keeping them subservient within the family. This clashed with their role as college students and expectations of them to be assertive, competitive, and self-reliant in the university context. These women spoke of giving up the opportunity to study at more prestigious universities because their families expected them to remain close to home. Some were unable to participate fully in the college experience because of cultural scripts that expected women to live at home until marriage. Latinas, in particular, constructed career plans where they were purposely deviating from the life experiences of their mothers, who were likely to have less education and to be subservient in the family home. They saw themselves completing their college educations, having successful careers, and then beginning their families.

An important developmental task of the college years is forming integrity (Chickering & Reisser, 1993) and making commitments about values that will guide the adult years (Perry, 1970). We observed how students' values were changing when they considered their career options or life purposes, and, in terms of acculturative dynamics, we witnessed how students were reconstructing their cultural values. Developing an independent, examined set of values is considered a normal process of young adult development, but for African Americans, Latinos/as, and Asian Americans, this process also required reexamining their groups' cultural values and deciding which to keep, resulting in acculturation outcomes. More specifically, students spoke purposefully of which ethnic cultural values they intended to maintain or modify and which to reject and, in addition, which mainstream values they intended to incorporate into their ethnic identity. For example, Latina women spoke of the importance of marrying in white, a symbol of purity exclusive to women, but also of liberalized gender role expectations in regard to family structure, particularly for the traditional roles of mothers and wives.

Asian American students experienced career decision making and familial expectations in conflictive ways. Cultural values of familial obligation, deference to elders, and the importance of bringing honor to the family called for career choices that were highly valued for prestige and income-earning potential. When students' choices veered from these career options, they felt they had, indeed, brought shame to the family and left parental expectations unfulfilled.

Plans for partnering and parenting also reflected a developmental task of the college years, and for identity development in general, which is also associated with Erikson's (1968) stages of intimacy and generativity. For students in the study, their experiences with their own ethnic identity development prompted them to consider such things as their choice of life partner and how they would raise their children. It was important for some students to maintain cultural and ethnic identity through dating and, perhaps, ultimately marrying same-ethnic partners. Particularly in the case of Asian Americans, some made this decision because of family pressure to partner within their own ethnic group, virtually making it taboo to date outside one's ethnic group. When students forecast what their own families would be like, it was important for many to raise children with strong cultural and ethnic identities who would carry on traditions and values. There were other manifestations of ethnic identity when students saw themselves as parents. Although students seemed to value some elements of parental control and sought to reproduce those in their own families, they rejected the use of physical punishment and other forms of control that might limit opportunities for their children.

Influences of Sociohistorical Forces on Ethnic Identity

Sociohistorical forces continued to make salient ethnic and racial issues for all students in ways that raised their political consciousness. Although the literature assumes the importance of social, historical, and political factors—

that are inferred from responses to a few items on ethnic or racial identity measures—as pivotal to ethnic identity development, in this study we see students actually making the connection between these forces and group pride, strength, and individual motivation. Students' ability to make meaning of sociohistorical factors in different ways yielded a shift in perspective that allowed them to convert negative experiences into motivational forces that resulted in pride, a healthy self-concept, and, ultimately, a drive to succeed. For example, when students understand how the educational system has served them badly, and when they can connect their own experiences to an overlying system of oppression, the resultant change of consciousness transforms how they view themselves and their group. Much like Freire's concept of *conscientizacao* (1993), where critical reflection on social forces transforms the oppressed, the cognitive shift students made through their own critical reflection caused them to consider themselves and the experiences of their groups in a different light. This diverges from more traditional views of the encounter and immersion processes that Cross and others (Cross, 1991; Helms & Cook, 1999) describe where, through a largely emotive experience (hurt, anger, shame), students are propelled to immerse themselves experientially in their cultures. This immersion, which is behavioral but also highly emotional (militant, joyful, and defiant of mainstream society), eases as the individual progresses toward integration. In contrast, we found the conversion experience to be much more of a cognitive task.

Latino/a students found that sociohistorical and ongoing political forces linked to immigration promoted pride in their group's resilience and its ability to persevere despite adversity. They also developed political consciousness around immigration policies and affirmative action. For African Americans, the legacy of slavery and overcoming daily struggles with racism were salient themes in the development of Black pride. In addition, the continued salience of race and ethnicity was reinforced through parental socialization that was intended to prepare young African Americans to cope in a racist society. Political consciousness was developed primarily in two ways for African Americans—through readings promoted by their parents and through the negative portrayal of African Americans in the media—something that was noted by a number of students in the sample, African American or not. In the case of Asian American students, the continual arrival of immigrants and the presence of ethnic enclaves kept ethnicity salient and reinforced cultural expressions. They developed their political consciousness in response to feelings of reverse discrimination regarding affirmative action (Asian Americans are not a protected class under many affirmative action policies) and in response to the political situations in their home countries (such as Vietnam, Cambodia, the Philippines, etc.). White students discussed how sociohistorical forces continue to have a negative impact on interracial relations between their group and other ethnic groups in society. Issues related to affirmative action also resulted in feelings of victimization and perceptions of unfair and unjust treatment. We note that the challenge and eventual demise of affirmative action in California catalyzed the development of political consciousness—albeit in different ways—for each ethnic group.

A vast number of students spoke to relevant past and present sociohistorical forces that continue to affect ethnic/racial groups in American society, including Whites. When students talked about disadvantages other ethnic or racial groups face, most addressed the existence of racial oppression and racism and the difficulty of overcoming and negotiating negative racial stereotypes. Students from all ethnic groups discussed experiences of stereotype threat. We were surprised that ethnic minority students mentioned how they felt that Whites today also face this issue in that many are stereotyped unfairly as being racist. They also spoke of the contradictory advantages that had been afforded to them, and not to their White peers, in the form of educational scholarships and access to special academic programs because of their minority status. Some students were matter-of-fact in this regard and recognized these as vehicles for leveling ethnic disparities in American society. Others were conflictive and empathized with their White peers, who they perceived were being excluded from important opportunities.

Distinctions Among Racial, Ethnic, and Cultural Identity

One of the persistent problems in the literature on racial, cultural, and ethnic identity is the relative ease of using these terms synonymously, which confuses all but the most theoretically astute. In this study, the experiences of students as they navigated complex environments where ethnicity, race, and culture were prominent at different times, and where difficulty in one area challenged students in others, made distinctions among the three processes clearer.

Racial identity primarily reflected how students made meaning of what it meant to be a member of their ethnic group in a society where discrimination and prejudice are based on phenotype and ethnic group membership.

Students shared their experiences with discrimination, stereotyping, racism, and the process of social stratification, which landed their ethnic groups in unwelcome places. For some, the university was a site of refuge from experiences with these and, for others, the university was a place where they suffered discrimination and prejudice from members of their own groups. All students came to understand themselves as racial beings. This was most profound for White students, who spoke of reverse discrimination through observing the college admissions process or support services on campus. However, many White students also reported that, for the first time, they were coming to know themselves as racially privileged in our society. This conflict, at times feeling victim, at times feeling privileged, was a significant area of dissonance for students. Although students, especially African Americans and Whites, recollected a naïve position regarding racial identity as children and resisted the notion of identity based on phenotype, they could not deny that racial identity was flushed out through their encounters with racially based discrimination, prejudice, and privilege.

Students demonstrated *cultural identity* through their participation in cultural activities, the expression of culturally related values, and a desire to maintain or reclaim cultural elements they risked losing. In general, students from the four ethnic groups were able to speak of values, practices, language, religion, arts, history, politics, music, etc., related to their cultures. Many of these artifacts can be judged against somewhat objective criteria, given that many of the cultures are relatively intact—meaning that we can examine countries of origin and their cultural practices or refer to ethnic studies literature for accounts of practices of the ethnic groups in the United States. Therefore, we can make claims about whether students possess a symbolic cultural identity, one about which they may not have accurate knowledge of cultural practices or their meanings, but one where those practices have significance to individuals' sense of being a part of that culture. Students who were raised in families that supported a cultural identity realized they had experienced a loss of cultural knowledge or language over the years and sought to become involved in activities that retaught or strengthened cultural attributes that had waned. Students who felt they were raised with little cultural knowledge had a desire to learn more, to become proficient in the native language, to learn the literature or history of their groups, etc. In general, students hoped to build their sense of culture and then transfer that pride and knowledge to future generations.

The results of the study confirmed the *ethnic identity* description of Jean Phinney (1995), that is, students reported different levels of *belonging* to their ethnic group and feelings of *affirmation* by that group. They spoke of *ethnic pride*. They *self-identified* in different ways as members of their ethnic group, which signified individual constructions of ethnicity. For example, Latino/a students spoke of the meaning chosen labels had for how they defined and expressed their identity—a Chicano/a ethnic identity was different from a Latino/a identity, and a Dominican identity differed even more. Students also evaluated the strength of their ethnic identity and judged the ethnic identity of their peers by the degree to which they and others were *involved in practices* associated with their ethnicity. Taking these together resulted in an overall sense of ethnic identity that also mirrors Phinney's concepts of ethnic identity *exploration, achievement,* and *resolution.* The primary difference between ethnic identity and cultural and racial identity is that ethnic identity was *constructed by students.* Students determined the meaning, significance, or salience of ethnic identity that prompted them to claim—or not claim—ethnicity as an important social identity. As this was constructed by students, many times as a result of their experiences with racial identity and cultural identity, students saw their group membership along a positive-to-negative continuum. Their level of commitment to the group also intersected with their political consciousness that developed (or not) during the racial identity process. Ethnic identity was *student-defined,* making it more of a subjective phenomenon.

Each of these distinct processes developed in the context of different forces. Racial identity did not necessarily happen within the family, but had more to do with social forces. Those forces were global in nature, such as political propositions, educational policies, or the effects of societal institutions, or were more personal in nature, such as experiences of microaggressions (ongoing, subtle, and seemingly innocuous acts of discrimination). Cultural identity occurred as a result of socialization by the family or cultural institutions. For example, the family distributed cultural identity by maintaining language or other practices, visiting the home country, instilling culturally related values, etc. In addition, cultural institutions, such as churches, Japanese schools, or the Polish Boy Scouts, distributed and maintained cultural identity. Students were introduced to these primarily by their families, but some maintained their membership and activity without family influence. Ethnic identity was developed and preserved through family, peer, and community socialization, along with intentional activity and goal setting by the individual students. Their own motivation to develop and maintain ethnic identity was spurred by encountering family members, coethnic and ethnic-other peers, and opportunities in the university and community.

The five dimensions outlined in this section emerged as common psychosocial and historical forces that influenced the ethnic identity development of young adults. These overarching dimensions that defined ethnic identity for young adults in a diverse context are illustrated in Table 8.2. Also highlighted are the unique contributors to ethnicity groups experienced that resulted in unique pathways that drive this ethnic identity process. Hence, our findings add to the body of literature by explicating more clearly the distinct *pathways* that students took toward achieving ethnic identity. These pathways were subsumed formerly within the identification of five overarching theoretical dimensions that defined identity development across different ethnic groups—theoretical dimensions that have been overly simplified or not clearly demarcated in current conceptualizations of ethnicity. For example, the literature is rife with references to the importance of family in the development of ethnicity, but here we explained how family systems enact varied influences on ethnicity when we highlighted the desire for change in gender roles within families and how students constructed this desire as a move away from ethnicity, but we also credited family as a place where ethnicity is encouraged and sustained. As Syed and colleagues (2007) argued recently, future ethnic identity studies must use qualitative methods to elucidate the various ethnic identity *pathways* people undertake and the multiple challenges and mechanisms of support that are relevant for this development—"family, peers, school, community" and ethnic sociohistory—as a "window into the actual processes of ethnic identity development" across ethnicities and within specific ethnic groups (p. 175). In this study, through qualitative interview data, we were able to see the impact of all of these factors on students and their construction of ethnicity.

Lessons From College Students About the Ethnic Experience Within a Diverse College Environment

The results of this investigation described how students' ethnic identity changed while in college in reaction to the various elements of the university

TABLE 8.2

Key Dimensions That Interfaced With Ethnic Identity Development Across Ethnic Groups

	Loss and Reclamation of Ethnic Identity	*Peer Influences on the Development of Ethnic Identity*	*Intersections of Ethnic & Young Adult Developmental Processes*	*Influences of Sociohistorical Forces on Ethnic Identity*	*Distinctions Among Racial, Cultural, & Ethnic Identity*
Asian American	Cultural Attributes Contributing to Ethnicity	Cultural Attributes Contributing to Ethnicity Transforming Culture: Becoming American	The Impact of the Family System on Ethnic Identity	Cultural Attributes Contributing to Ethnicity	Cultural Attributes Contributing to Ethnicity
African American	Expressions of Ethnicity	Presence of Coethnics Engenders Feelings of Inclusion on Campus	Optimistic Prospects for the Future	The Complex Relationship Between Racism & Oppression Optimistic Prospects for the Future	Forming Racial & Ethnic Identities Expressions of Ethnicity The Complex Relationship Between Racism & Oppression Optimistic Prospects for the Future

TABLE 8.2 (Continued)

	Loss and Reclamation of Ethnic Identity	*Peer Influences on the Development of Ethnic Identity*	*Intersections of Ethnic & Young Adult Developmental Processes*	*Influences of Sociohistorical Forces on Ethnic Identity*	*Distinctions Among Racial, Cultural, & Ethnic Identity*
Latino/a	Ethnic Identity Process	Ethnic Identity Process Acculturation	Familialism		Expressions of Ethnicity Familialism Intersections with Societal Forces
White	The Meaning of a White Identity	The Meaning of a White Identity White Identity in an Intergroup Context	Implicit Expressions of a White Identity	White Identity in an Intergroup Context	Who Am I? Labels Used to Define a White Ethnic/Racial Identity Implicit Expressions of a White Identity White Identity in an Intergroup Context

context. Students challenged, confirmed, or reconfigured their ethnic identities as a result of having experienced a diverse campus environment. In chapter 7 we discussed the largely beneficial correlates of campus diversity for students' personal, social, and intellectual growth as well as the less positive aspects of negotiating such campus environments. Although for some students, experiences with campus diversity were either predominantly positive or negative, others spoke of mixed encounters with diversity that pointed to the complex dynamics associated with living and studying in an ethnically diverse context. Also noted were that different students do, indeed, experience the same college environment in dramatically different ways. We summarize below the positive and negative features associated with ethnically/racially diverse university campuses and their influence on student development.

As noted in the previous section, most significant for students was that attending an ethnically diverse campus community engendered a sense of belonging and inclusion within the institution that was associated with a more positive and enriched sense of ethnic identity and adjustment to college. This was especially true in the case of ethnic-minority students. Equally important, however, was that an ethnically diverse learning community emerged as a critical factor for the development of multicultural competence in students. A vast number of students across the four ethnic groups spoke of the importance of diversity for their multicultural cognitive, social, and personal development. Students voiced greater confidence when interacting with diverse peers as a result of attending diverse campuses and in being able to establish meaningful cross-ethnic relationships. Accordingly, campus diversity was associated with philosophical changes in students' views about ethnicity and issues regarding social justice and equality, which related to greater cognitive flexibility on their part and the ability to consider multiple perspectives. Students reflected on how attending a multiethnic campus had made them more open to diversity and its challenges, which promoted a greater understanding and knowledge of ethnic-others that left them with a greater sense of intercultural sensitivity and multicultural self-efficacy.

These findings were supported by formal structures of the institution such as student organizations and course curricula, which played an important role in ethnic identity development and provided spaces for increasing multicultural competence in students. Likewise, campus diversity made salient for students explorations into ethnicity and encouraged greater ethnic awareness and political consciousness. In some, ethnic political consciousness was related to activism. Most interesting is that a large number of students across the four ethnic groups expressed a willingness to advocate for the rights of ethnic-others. This spoke to a greater sense of civic-mindedness and positive political dispositions in these students. Related to a politicized view of ethnicity, students of color describe having a sense of kinship with other ethnic minorities because of shared experiences with discrimination and oppression. These findings highlight how university campuses with a significant number of ethnic minorities can have important positive influences on students' development, primarily in liberalizing political views and promoting greater ethnic understanding and positive interethnic attitudes. In all, these findings point up the development of more mature, healthier, and more secure ethnic identities for these individuals. These findings are consistent with recent findings reported by Phinney and colleagues (2007) that linked a secure ethnic identity to "positive interethnic attitudes and mature intercultural thinking" in young persons (p. 478).

Students also spoke of the challenges and conflicts they encountered when attending diverse university campuses. The unfortunate side of campus diversity is that such learning communities can also foster feelings of ethnic discomfort in persons (i.e., in the case of White students feeling "like a minority," and for students of color not being "ethnic enough"); be associated with discrimination by out-group and in-group members; make racial tensions and ethnic segregation more visible and palpable; and promote a climate of competition for educational resources that is related to a sense of ethnic victimization in students. These themes were, indeed, voiced by students belonging to the four ethnicities studied at both institutions, but more so by White students. It is not surprising that, in these situations, the perception of a "hostile" campus climate negatively affected students' college adjustment and how they experienced their ethnicity on campus. Although some students were more adept than others at deflecting the negative aspects associated with negotiating multicultural racial discourse on campus, it was clear that this type of perceived interethnic campus dynamic can seriously undermine the positive benefits of experiencing an ethnically diverse learning community.

In addition to talking about their campus experiences with ethnicity, students were asked to reflect on the barriers to interethnic contact that kept them from forming a close connection with diverse people. Integrated into this section are students' personal observations of the most significant barriers to developing close interethnic relationships. Most pointed were students' narratives of the continued legacy of interracial tension as a serious obstacle to establishing meaningful ties with ethnic others. As one White student noted, "There are like vibes there, a lot of generalization. Like, there is still a lot of anger there [and] racial conflict that makes it not possible for there to be acceptance." Likewise, an African American student reflected: "In some sense I always feel a racial strain with most other groups from their standpoint, but not individually, but as a group. It seems like there is so much tension." Related to students' discussion of racial tensions was a sense that there were "invisible barriers" that inhibited groups from connecting. One African American offered,

> As far as me being able to establish a bond, I might be able to establish a bond with an individual. But for some reason, I always feel like there's this thin line that one cannot cross among ethnic or racial groups. But, yes, I feel a bond [with an individual].

Students highlighted the difficulty of negotiating the continuum from the intrapersonal to the intergroup in race/ethnic relations and forming bridges that break down implicit and explicit barriers to a positive sense of interethnic connectedness. The cultural differences between ethnic groups accentuated ethnic and social distance among groups and made it difficult to establish a connection with diverse others.

> It's just difficult to relate. I guess there's so much we don't know about each other. It's kind of a task to have to go through all of that, and that's the barrier. Things are different that make up another culture in other groups. Just dealing in completely different situations, you'll have a different ideology and different understanding of life.

Despite the diversity of the two campuses studied, some students reflected on a lack of opportunities for meaningful interethnic contact that went beyond superficial interactions:

> I don't know many [diverse others]. There are many [diverse ethnic peers] in this school, but I don't have the opportunity of knowing them [personally]. I don't just go up to them and say, "Hi, what's your name?" Because they might say, who is this crazy guy? What does he want?

In sum, students' perceptions underscore an important point regarding interethnic contact in diverse contexts. The diversification of universities, in and of itself, is not a panacea for substantially improved interethnic relations, nor will it guarantee meaningful and substantive interethnic contact among students. However, with the evidence provided in this investigation, we argue that such university environments do provide the necessary and critical foundation for bridging cultural differences between ethnic groups and for cultivating other important learning. Given the positive psychological correlates of campus diversity for students outlined here, educators and university administrators must make the most of these benefits and work to dismantle perceived ethnic divides and "invisible racial barriers" that prevent diverse persons from connecting. We recognize that students will vary in their propensity to interact with diverse peers and in the extent to which they will take advantage of diversity-related opportunities. Consequently, the impetus falls to universities to work concertedly to create a wide range and multiple opportunities for positive and substantive interethnic contact within their campuses that would appeal to different types of students.

Institutional Support for Students' Individual Ethnic Identity Development and Multicultural Competence

Ethnic and cultural diversity on university campuses allows students to "retain their personal identities, have a sense of belonging, take pride in their own heritage, and foster an appreciation of diversity among the entire college community" (Lee & Janda, 2006, p. 28). The diversity of the university has the potential to uphold a society where all people are regarded and respected equally and encourages a commitment to preserving their human dignity. Many argue that the importance of espousing such multicultural ideologies is central to the mission of present-day universities, which are responsible for preparing students for life in a pluralistic and increasingly changing society (Hurtado, 2007). Consistent with a recent study by Phinney, Jacoby, and Silva (2007), the findings of our investigation support the premise that "learning about one's ethnicity and making a commitment" to one's ethnic group "is part of a broader [developmental] process of gaining understanding of ethnic diversity [that] allows people to be more open and accepting of people from other ethnic groups" (p. 489). In the remaining sections of this chapter, we make a number of recommendations for promoting the development of multicultural campuses that not only support students' individual ethnic identity development but also work to defuse prejudice and interracial tensions and conflicts. We note that some of these recommendations are supported by observations made by students themselves as strategies for improved interethnic dynamics and multicultural environments.

Diversifying the Student Population

The most significant structural feature of the two institutions studied is that they both had truly ethnically and racially diverse student bodies. As such, they both provided multiple opportunities for students to reawaken, explore, and commit to their ethnic identity. As noted earlier in this chapter, the critical influence of coethnics and diverse peers on students' development and success across multiple levels must be underscored. It is through exposure to a diverse "college peer group" that ethnic identity flourished and students were afforded the needed space "to gain experience, experiment and learn to negotiate differences in background and perspectives that are an inevitable part of contemporary society" (Hurtado, 1999, p. 26). Therefore, it is vitally important that universities continue to make concerted efforts through proactive institutional policies to diversify their student bodies across a broad spectrum of ethnicities and provide subcultures to retain and enable the academic and social success of these students.

The admissions and outreach offices at most colleges and universities are already adept at coordinating recruitment events such as college fairs or open house days on campus for prospective students. Those campuses serious about diversifying student populations need to look critically at the areas and regions that yield most of their students. If these are predominantly White high schools and communities, then admissions and outreach should build or strengthen partnerships with high schools that service diverse communities. Building relationships with high school college counselors, hosting recruitment events on campus, and offering workshops to assist students and their families to complete federal financial aid forms are all ways that admissions and outreach can work from within the university to enlarge recruitment pools. Universities must consider as well partnering with middle schools to assist in the formation of college aspirations of those students. In middle schools, admissions and outreach can conduct workshops where students are introduced to the idea of going to college and informing them of course and grade requirements for college admissions in their states. While campus visits are critical to the recruitment of high school students, they can be especially critical to the future recruitment of middle school students and the development of their college aspirations.

Most admissions and outreach operations spend the bulk of their time and money on recruiting students into the applicant pool. The presence of low-income or first-generation college students in the applicant pool is, indeed, an accomplishment, but what should be important to the institution is that those students actually matriculate. This is also significant because it optimizes students' college-going opportunities. In our experience, students who may have been admitted initially to the top university system in the state chose to begin their college careers at community colleges because they did not think their families could afford to pay the more expensive university tuition. Therefore, yield activities sponsored by admissions and outreach are just as valuable in efforts to diversify student populations.

Yield activities may consist of campus visit days, especially those that include overnight stays in campus housing where admitted students are paired with current students and that include a host of workshops informing them of campus resources, including financial support programs. Workshops also might include such topics as ethnic identity; lesbian, gay, bisexual, trans-gender (LGBT) issues; art and culture; and graduate school opportunities. When on-campus visits can be coordinated with annual programs offered by these ethnic student organizations, efforts in yielding students of color have the greatest chance of success. Involving ethnic student organizations is often key to telling admitted students about on-campus support communities. Regional events are also effective for introducing admitted students to other students, faculty, and staff. One private university's admissions personnel hold meetings for parents in the homes of other parents whose children currently attend the university. This demonstrates to parents that the university is a safe place to send their children (Mina, Cabrales, & Juarez, 2004). Providing literature written in the ethnic languages of the institution's service area is also important to involve and educate non-English-speaking parents to the college-going and decision-making process. Even simple efforts such as having admissions counselors make phone calls to admitted students are often helpful to students in making and solidifying their decisions. All of these efforts are attainable, even in states where anti–affirmative action legislation may prevent institutions from spending public monies to recruit specific ethnic groups.

Student retention plays an instrumental role in diversifying colleges and universities. Conventional concepts of retention have focused on the students' ability to integrate into the academic and social spheres of the institution (Tinto, 1993) or to become involved in the life of the university both psychologically and through time spent in activity associated with college (Astin, 1993). These continue to be important to college student success, but when considering retention of students of color and low-income or first-generation college students, *how* these forces have some bearing on students is paramount. For example, academic integration is often compromised by academic policies on remediation at the college level. Students who come to college lacking preparation in basic skills (which accounts for an increasing number of students) may need to take as many as six courses before reaching college-level math or English courses. Not only does this devastate the academic self-esteem of students, it also causes them to fall behind quickly in credits for graduation and may even jeopardize their ability to remain at the university if they do not complete their courses within a specific period. Academic integration into majors or other courses that may be closer to the students' actual intellectual or career interest may also be delayed because remedial courses must be taken during the first year.

Academic integration is also threatened by poor performance in courses, because, for many students, retention relies on maintaining good academic progress. Early-alert programs that signal when a student is at risk for academic probation or disqualification bring academic advisors and faculty into the rescue effort to help ensure that students get the support services they need. Goal clarity and commitment also play an important role in retention. Too often we assume that career development activities should be reserved for upper-division students, and we restrict career development in the early years to choice of major. For first-generation students, especially those whose parents are immigrants, a college education is not only an intellectual pursuit, it is also the gateway to a profession and a well-paying, respectable job. Bridge or early outreach programs help to acclimate students to campus sooner. Programs such as the ethnic-based academic support services (e.g., RISE-SCORE, Minority Access to Research Careers, McNair Scholars) that are designed to prepare underrepresented groups for advanced studies in the biological and social sciences use multiple interventions to assist students in developing their academic and professional skills and offering financial support to students in the form of stipends. Therefore, for these students, early career development activities can assist them in selecting appropriate majors and may strengthen their commitment to their education as a means to obtaining their goals.

Social integration is also a challenge for students who find themselves outside the critical mass at their institutions. Increasing students' involvement on campus is often difficult when they are required to work to help pay for college and living expenses. Helping students to work on campus strengthens their connection and commitment to campus. Making sure that students are aware of all available financial aid makes them less reliant on excessive amounts of paid work. It is also important to realize that there is a great deal of resistance to assuming student loans among many low-income, first-generation students, so student services personnel need to be more diligent in making students aware of scholarships and other incentive programs to ease their financial burden. Financial aid counselors and other student affairs personnel need to help students discover the opportunity costs of excessive work compared to assuming student loans. Students often forgo time needed in college to fully integrate socially and academically, which puts their persistence at risk and leaves them without important qualifications for the job market by working up to 40 hours a week because they are loan-averse. Helping them understand how loans they take out in college can actually give them the time to participate in important academic (independent study), career (internships), or social (clubs and organizations) activities is a needed component in student success programs.

Student Activities and Ethnic Student Organizations

Equally important was that both universities had institutional structures in place—departments of ethnic studies, required multicultural course curricula, and ethnic clubs and organizations—that solidified and validated for students the importance of their ethnic identities. These institutional features often served as vehicles for expressing ethnicity, which reawakened and strengthened students' cultural and racial identities. Furthermore, such institutional entities provided places of support for students and multiple avenues for integrating into the campus community. These venues also allowed for the development of subsystems, crucial for students who may not see themselves as central to the university culture. Ethnic studies courses and ethnic student organizations are also places where students can find community that helps them feel as if they matter to the university. The university has such structures in place for this, which is key to Schlossberg's concept of marginality and mattering (1989). When students feel they matter to the university, they are more likely to succeed. Therefore, it is vital to allocate sufficient university resources to ensure the sustenance and vitality of diversity-related institutional structures and that these venues remain prominent features of the university landscape as evidence of the institution's commitment to multiculturalism and pluralism.

It is important to recognize that many of the institutional features that sustained students' ethnic identity were created by the students themselves. For instance, ethnic clubs and organizations such as Latino/a Business Association, the Korean Student Association, and ethnic fraternities and sororities were founded on the initiative of students. Because of the positive psychological benefits of these institutional features as mechanisms of valuing and vehicles for retention, similar to Rendón's (1994) validation theory, we recommend that universities play a more active role in supporting students' attempts to start specific ethnic clubs and/or organizations. More specifically, at institutions where such student ethnic organizations are limited in scope or are not thriving, university officials must become more proactive in promoting these student organizations to become established features of the institution and viable entities for student engagement. To illustrate, although pan-ethnic Asian organizations exist at both universities studied, RU was unique in that it provided students with multiple options for participation in ethnically based organizations. Various ethnic subgroups of Asian clubs and organizations were present at RU (i.e., the Korean Student Association, the Japanese Student Organization) that allowed students to integrate more meaningfully into the larger campus community by affording them defined locations of support and involvement.

Equally important to a multicultural campus is having mechanisms in place to reduce ethnic separateness and social distance between the various ethnic clubs and structural features of the institution. Other scholars (Sidanius, Van Laar, Levin, & Sinclair, 2004) have argued that creating ethnic clubs and organizations does indeed strengthen ethnic identity in persons, but they also accentuate ethnic divisions and out-group biases in students. While some studies suggest that student engagement in ethnic clubs and organizations was associated with greater cross-cultural activities (Hurtado, Milem,

Clayton-Pederson, & Allen, 1999), others have argued that these institutional structures contribute to a climate of ethnic segregation. Hence, student activities personnel and staff members must make concerted efforts to promote a sense of common student identity among the various ethnic organizations and clubs. Frequent and sustained interactions between members of various ethnic organizations requiring interdependent and collaborative efforts to achieve a superordinate goal would expand students' sense of social inclusiveness in the university. Such desegregation methods have been found to increase positive out-group attitudes and reduce intergroup conflict and tension (Baron & Byrne, 2003). In fact, recent research suggests that just witnessing coethnics interacting and befriending diverse others is enough to lessen racial biases and negative out-group attitudes in persons (Baron, Byrne, & Branscombe, 2006).

Therefore, "student affairs administrators need to find ways to assess the relevance of their student activity programming and its effectiveness in promoting multicultural learning" (Cheng & Zhao, 2006, p. 30) that prepares students for life in a "multicentric democracy" (Thompson, Engberg, & Hurtado, 2006, p. 450). Students recognized the benefits of forming cross-ethnic coalitions and friendships through greater interdependence among the various ethnic clubs and organizations:

> Some of the girls in my sorority were invited to go to one of the Black Student Union meetings . . . because we like to do a cultural thing every month. We were trying to decide when we could go to one of their meetings as a group, just so we could see what they're about, see what their meetings are about. And it's an easy way for different cultures and ethnicities to learn about each other.

> I was involved in many campus organizations, and one of the things that we've always wanted to do was get involved with other organizations to interact [with them]. There is a large Filipino organization here on campus that you know [is] social. We could establish friendships and get to know each other.

Models already exist in some colleges and universities that provide locations for formalized interethnic contact between groups. Cultural diversity or multiethnic centers offer opportunities for multiple student organizations to come together to support the work of their own organization, and to partner and coprogram with other student organizations. The model of the Panhellenic or interfraternity councils that bring together leaders from all Greek organizations can also be used with ethnic student organizations. Likewise, the Stanford University student program—Leading through Education, Activism and Diversity (LEAD)—brings together four ethnic-based campus organizations in a joint leadership development program for students to form cross-ethnic coalitions. In other words, university leaders must have in place "umbrella programs" affirming institutional norms that promote "cross-racial cooperation and learning" among the various student ethnic/racial organizations through "interorganizational involvement" as a formalized feature of the institution (Milem, Chang, & Antonio, 2005, p. 29).

Another important initiative for promoting effective multicultural campuses is to educate students purposefully from an experiential perspective on the dynamics of prejudice. This can be achieved through student participation in ethnic/race awareness workshops and campus dialogue programs to increase communication and reduce interethnic anxiety (Milem et al., 2005). Participation in such activities should not be left up to students but should be made an inherent component of the university experience and a part of students' civic development (Lee & Janda, 2006). Implementing interethnic group dialogue programs must be a visible component of a university's intellectual offerings, where students are granted academic credit for engaging in these activities and/or integrated into existing course requirements. Finally, in the case of students who may resist participating in such extracurricular activities, universities must design diverse programs that would also appeal to different types of individuals (Cheng & Zhao, 2006). Students articulated the importance of providing such designated spaces for persons to learn ways to fight their own prejudicial attitudes and acquire the tools they need for reducing racial anxiety. A Latina explained:

> If I developed good relationships with [African Americans], with at least somebody that I could say, "Why do I have to feel this way?" and then I'd have to hear a response. I feel that they feel that I discriminate against them. I don't know why. Like when guys try to talk to me or try to get my number or something like that, I tell them, "You know, I have a boyfriend." They say I do that because they are Black. I get scared, I don't want to do that [to them] because I would not want them to do that to me. [I'm scared] because it might be partially true, and I don't want them to feel that way. I want to feel comfortable with them.

The highly successful intergroup dialogue projects at the University of Michigan and the University of Massachusetts provide models for other institutions that are committed to improving the ethnic/racial climate of their campuses to emulate. Likewise, other innovative and empirically based dialogue/discussion university programs include the Intergroup Relations Center at Arizona State University and the Conflict Mediation Program at the University of California at Los Angeles (for short descriptions of each, see Hurtado et al., 1999).

Ethnic Studies Courses and Pedagogy

Enrollment in ethnic courses proved to be critical to students' ethnic identity development. Students spoke of the transformative effects of multicultural course curricula on their ethnic identities and personal growth. Such courses challenged students to alter their views of the racial and ethnic self and supported their journey to achieve a strong, positive, and healthy ethnic/racial identity. Taking classes in a formal setting and learning about one's culture and history strengthened self-esteem from a psychological standpoint and reinforced students' identity, pride in ethnicity, and sense of belonging. Most interesting, these transformations in ethnic identity proved important to students' academic self-efficacy and retention within the university. Based on these findings, we recommend that when encountering students who are struggling academically, university advisors direct them to take ethnic study courses as a medium for retention by sustaining these students' interest in college and promoting their academic success. In sum, the empowering nature of ethnic studies courses for student development cannot be underestimated because they validate students' culture by supplying the needed content and asserting the importance of that knowledge by making it a formal part of the curriculum. These courses also help students to deconstruct the societal forces that have limited the progress of their ethnic groups. Again, this speaks to the importance of creating systems of valuing and mattering within the institution as vehicles for retention and healthy student development.

Because ethnic studies classes proved to be so important for students in the study, and many expressed a need for opportunities to improve their ability to interact with other groups, it is clear that promoting a successful multicultural campus must include requiring students to engage in multicultural education (Lee & Janda, 2006). We note that both institutions studied did require students to enroll in multicultural courses. However, Lee and Janda (2006) have noted that some universities still offer multicultural courses as electives rather than making them required coursework for graduation and/or professional certification. These scholars argue for extending multicultural course requirements beyond the student level to include "staff, professors, and even administrators," who also should be mandated to enroll in multicultural training, and that such training must be offered "in all undergraduate, graduate, and specialization programs" (p. 30). Because of the strong evidence presented in this investigation regarding the benefits of multicultural education, we support such initiatives as key to a university's commitment to multiculturalism and to a campus culture that endorses pluralism. We note that students themselves acknowledged the importance of diversity-related course curricula as vehicles for increasing their intercultural awareness and interethnic understanding.

> I really don't know about [African American] background. In Mexican families, family is really important. Well, how is it in Black culture? Is it really important, or is it just kind of there? The same thing with Asians; what are their beliefs and traditions?

Despite the positive benefits of multicultural and ethnic courses for students, it is also important to discuss the difficulties this type of curriculum can present for students. Particularly in the case of White students, it was clear that ethnic studies and cultural pluralism courses were difficult to negotiate at times. Although some students recognized the importance of such curricula, others dreaded these courses and saw them as opportunities for the institution to engage in White-bashing. With regard to the pedagogy of teaching ethnic and multicultural curricula, individual faculty members must acknowledge that the course content may be difficult for White students to process, so they should provide nonthreatening opportunities for White students to deal with race-related information and issues of White privilege and racism. In other words, White students must be given the opportunity to discuss how they feel about the content presented. This can be done through written assignments, ethnically homogeneous group discussions, and guided mixed-group deliberations. It is important for White students to move from feeling solely like spectators when taking such courses to being active participants in the learning process. In doing so, such courses could better serve as channels for empowering all students, including Whites, to recognize racism and work to dismantle it. As noted earlier, only a few White students denied that racism existed, and many acknowledged the benefits received from being White, yet they felt powerless in terms of what form of activism they can engage in to dismantle racism.

Another strategy to consider when working with students who may not see the benefits of engaging in multicultural education, or who see themselves as being cultureless, is to implement activities recommended by Ortiz and Rhoads's Five-Step Multicultural Education Model (2000). In this model, activities help to direct students in developing an understanding of culture through exploring other cultures, which ultimately assists them in identifying the cultural aspects of their own background and identity. The assumption is that, once all see themselves as cultural beings, acceptance of and participation in multicultural activities is welcomed. Their model is designed specifically to promote the deconstruction of Whiteness by bringing White students into the discourse in ways that respect, not shame them, and that help them to decipher the complexities of culture, racism, and privilege in our society. Likewise, Jackson and colleagues' (Jackson, Warren, Pitts, & Wilson, 2007) recent paper on this topic states the significance of incorporating into multicultural education historical and contemporary White political activists who can serve as role models for White students, thereby facilitating their acquisition of a positive antiracist White identity.

It has been argued that a potential danger of multicultural curricula is that they can contribute to ethnic isolation among different groups of students because race-based teaching approaches reinforce racial distinctions to the exclusion of other important reciprocal interests and commonalities (Henry, 2005). Accordingly, Henry (2005) has argued that multicultural pedagogy should do more than simply provide the "educational space wherein individual students' identities are fostered" but it must also "create opportunities for students to see their interdependencies and witness how such connections emphasize the moral nature of the classroom environment" as a symbol of a society's commitment to pluralism and overarching humanistic goals (p. 1074). This perspective is reinforced by students themselves, who recognize this limitation of multicultural courses. An African American male observed:

> I have a multicultural pluralism class, and I know where he [professor] is coming from, and I really appreciate the approach, but he's basically teaching me Black history and talking about the Black movement. When you

go to the Hispanic teachers, they're talking about Hispanic culture. If you go to the Asian [teachers], they're talking about Asian culture. But the reality is that this world keeps on turning and these [ethnic] divisions are driving us farther and farther apart and at some point you have to start thinking about what is good for us collectively, as a group of people. Not as a group of Asians, Africans, Eurasians, but as a group of people. No [ethnic] borders. I am interested in anything where the focus is on multiethnic pluralism.

Just as campuses do not become multicultural simply by diversifying their student populations, ethnic studies courses and requirements do not diversify the curriculum merely by being present in the class schedule. Attention needs to be paid to the content of ethnic studies courses. If the course is intended to be a survey of ethnic groups in the United States, then time should be allocated for a thorough treatment of each. If the course focuses on a particular ethnic group, care must be taken to make sure that students outside that group are welcomed and included in the class. Foremost, in all ethnic studies classes, faculty members must be ready to deliver high-quality content and must be highly skilled at mediating difficult discussions and helping students to develop effective intergroup communication skills.

Multiculturalism Across the Curriculum

The college classroom affords students critical opportunities for diversity engagement (Thompson et al., 2006). Consequently, we underscore the importance of increasing the depth and substance of students' exposure to multiculturalism across the curriculum and to pedagogical approaches (i.e., cooperative and participatory learning techniques) that provide frequent opportunities for students to interact with diverse peers on an equal-status basis and in meaningful ways (Cohen, 1994). These in-class interactions must be substantive in quality and number and be reinforced through extracurricular multicultural activities. In terms of classroom teaching, studies have shown that students exposed to these types of participatory learning groups report: (1) more cross-ethnic friendships outside the classroom; (2) enhanced critical thinking/problem-solving skills and academic achievement; (3) improved interpersonal and leadership skills; and (4) fewer prejudices and greater tolerance for diverse perspectives and acceptance of ethnic-others (Cohen, 1994; Hurtado, 2001; Slavin, 1995). Students in this study voiced the importance of having these types of opportunities to interact and socialize with diverse peers for decreasing their sense of interethnic discomfort and feelings of ethnic distance from diverse others. A Latina said, "I just think that [Anglos] are so different than me in the way they grew up, the things they have, [and] their value system. If I were to share more things with them, find more things in common, then I would feel a lot more comfortable." Likewise, students who said they knew quite a bit about a particular culture felt that what they lacked was not more cultural knowledge but opportunities to develop friendships. The increased use of participatory group-learning techniques in the classroom, reinforced with multicultural curriculum, can serve this critical function for students and contribute to sustaining an overall positive campus climate.

Students also reflected that they felt personally attacked at times during multicultural and racial dialogue in classroom discussions. As faculty, we recognize the difficulty of mediating such discussions and the discomfort and tension that such discourse can engender. Hence, as educators we have a responsibility not only to teach content, but to ensure civil conversation among students during class discussions. Faculty development programs need to play a more active role in providing faculty who teach such content with pedagogical and instructional tools that facilitate controversial discussions of race more effectively so that the well-being of all students is respected. For instance, the Center for Research on Learning and Teaching at Michigan State University provides many useful resources for faculty who teach controversial topics on how to create and facilitate an inclusive college classroom (see http://www.crlt.umich.edu). However, it is also important to recognize that some unease on the part of students (and faculty) should be seen as a necessary and vital part of the learning process as students grapple with difficult questions about race and their personal growth and development. Furthermore, structured and mediated racial discourse in the context of academic courses should be viewed as important opportunities to teach students vital interpersonal communication skills for negotiating intergroup conflicts and managing ambiguity and complex issues effectively.

In sum, the empirical evidence demonstrates that incorporating diversity into the curriculum through content and structured interactions helps students learn to "negotiate and communicate across differences while overcoming the inherent challenges of working with diverse others" (Nelson, Engberg, & Hurtado, 2005, p. 449). Hence, it is important that universities as centers of higher learning take advantage of the benefits to be gained from multicultural education by reinforcing them with the classroom structures, content, and pedagogical tools most likely to meet the ideological objectives of such curricula. In the case of some universities, this may entail a significant transformation of curriculum and general studies models to include diversity as a core dimension of students' educational experience.

Faculty and Staff Development

We have stressed the importance of faculty and staff development for enacting diversity-related initiatives within an institution. Hence, greater resources must be allocated to institutional offices specializing in faculty development and training. Significantly more instructors must be trained in the use of participatory and experiential learning techniques that support the learning objectives of multiculturalism, and such pedagogy should not be left primarily to ethnic minority faculty and women (Hurtado, 2001). As Nelson and colleagues note, "It is likely that many instructors will need assistance in making these changes, especially in preparing to facilitate the dialogues that transpire within an increasingly diverse campus community" (2005, p. 471). The learning outcomes for faculty and staff development are many. Faculty and staff need training in the pedagogical skills to facilitate discussions of difference, race, and ethnicity, and they need to know more about students on their campuses, especially students from all ethnic groups. For instance, do the experiences of students on their campus mirror or contrast with the students' experiences outlined in this book? Faculty and staff also need to know the histories of ethnic groups in this country, whether or not they are teaching ethnic studies classes. Knowledge of their own groups' history and political circumstances was critical in the ability of students in this study to view themselves and their ethnic groups positively. These lessons should not be confined to the classroom. With staff development activities, this content can be spread through the cocurriculum.

These faculty and staff development programs can take a variety of forms. At Rowan University, interdisciplinary teams of faculty participated in an intensive, five-day workshop exploring identity, citizenship, and diverse democracy, and then designed and cotaught first-year seminar courses with a focus on interdisciplinary diversity (Lindman & Tahamont, 2006). Kent State University is planning a center for diversity studies to train faculty, staff, and students in diversity and cross-cultural pedagogy, in addition to organizing a support system for faculty members who teach diversity courses (*Kent State University Strategic Diversity Plan*, 2006). While these initiatives directly address courses emphasizing diversity, other faculty and staff development initiatives can focus on skill development in active learning pedagogies. These strategies give students an opportunity to interact purposefully with peers they may not encounter in their extracurricular lives and may give students who do not participate in diversity-oriented activities or courses opportunities to interact with peers from different ethnic groups.

Likewise, faculty and staff who are active in facilitating these racial dialogues and workshops on campus must be rewarded. Grant programs can encourage individual faculty to diversify their course content or to create new courses to enhance cross-cultural dialogue and multicultural education. Grant programs can also promote team teaching and collaborative development of new diversity-oriented courses (Lindman & Tahamont, 2006). Grants awarded to departments can facilitate training an entire department in active learning pedagogies, intergroup dialogue, and diversifying course content. Milem and colleagues (2005) found that

> successful programs tend to offer faculty course reductions and/or summer salary incentives for the development, implementation and assessment of new pedagogies. To institutionalize these pedagogies, tenure and promotion guidelines that reflect the institution's commitment to engaging in diversity also need to be implemented. (p. 25)

Sustaining Ethnic Identity While Promoting a Holistic Campus Climate

E pluribus unum becomes a challenge not only for a nation, but for a campus as well. College campuses that strive to create an inclusive climate that welcomes, nurtures, and promotes the holistic development of all students must simultaneously develop the talents and goals of individuals while creating a unique institutional culture that represents its members—from many, a campus becomes one. As we noted previously, there is no shortage of critics who caution against the development of group identities because they threaten the development of a common identity. How do we encourage the development of ethnic identity without threatening the development of a strong institutional identity? How do we transform institutional sagas from legacies that reflect homogeneity to ones that honor the individual and subgroups while still preserving and perhaps improving the whole? We have no doubt that the answers to these questions are many and controversial, but they are at the heart of what it means to have a multicultural or pluralistic campus.

Through this multisite investigation, we have illustrated how diverse university contexts provide a rich and fertile environment for fostering student development across a range of important civic, interpersonal, affective, and cognitive skills. The findings underscore the importance for university leaders to construct supportive, "diversity friendly" institutions that offer multiple "opportunities to bring together students from different backgrounds" (Cheng & Zhao, 2006, p. 31). The times could not be more suitable for educational leaders to capitalize on the human benefits to be gained from diversity and to strengthen the psychological climate of their campuses by respecting the separate identities of groups and yet still promote an integrative and holistic campus culture.

It is interesting to note that students from all four ethnic groups spoke of the college environment as a unique place where discrimination and prejudice was less likely to occur. Many stated specifically that the university was a safe haven where diverse people could come together as students with similar goals, ambitions, and aspirations without fear of rejection or discrimination. Students were explicit in noting that this was not necessarily the case outside the boundaries of a liberal academic setting, where they encountered discrimination by other racial/ethnic groups as well as racial discomfort and unease. For instance, some Latino/a and African American students talked about the racial tensions they have experienced outside the university when they come into contact with other racial communities or ethnic circles (i.e., ethnic-specific nightclubs and homogeneous ethnic communities). A number of students stated that it was within the context of the university where interactions with other ethnicities were encouraged and acceptance was more possible. For instance, a Korean American student spoke of the hostility he had felt toward the African American community because of the Los Angeles riots. He added that he had been able to work through these hostilities while in college by interacting with Black peers who then became his friends. Hence, these universities enabled unique opportunities for diverse individuals to come together and engage in a type of exchange that we seldom see outside the college experience. The findings emphasize the importance of campus climate for promoting a sense of belonging and inclusion among diverse groups of students that goes beyond one's ethnic group and fosters interracial understanding. These exchanges occurred on multiple levels. Students found a sense of connection with diverse others on the basis of their student identity and their mutual quest to achieve a higher education. Therefore, such interactions occurred at the intrapersonal level where ethnicity was not the focal point for students coming together. Students also connected with diverse others at the intergroup level by transcending their own ethnic/racial identities, empathizing with the plight of other ethnicities, and expressing a willingness to act on their behalf to end injustice. Taken together, the work presented here illustrates the relevance of multiethnic interactions that span the intrapersonal-to-intergroup continuum for giving students the necessary tools "to navigate a multicentric democracy—a democracy that recognizes both the connectivity and distinctness inherent in a community predicated on multiple and simultaneous forms of identity, power and privilege" (Nelson et al., 2005, p. 450).

In line with the vision presented by Nelson and colleagues, we argue here that promoting a common identity model among students can serve as a vehicle for integrating all students, regardless of race, through development of a campus culture and institutional saga that are sustained over time. In his classic work on institutional saga, Burton Clark (1972) highlights how five campuses developed unique and long-lasting sagas that came to define those institutions. The benefit of an institutional saga is that the narrative, the ethos, is ingrained so heavily in the institutions' history, traditions, criteria for member selection, reward systems, etc., that new members of the institution are socialized into the saga with relatively little overt effort. The values and practices of the saga are taught to new members through their interactions with virtually every agent of the institution. For an institution whose saga reflects inclusion and pluralism, norms would be in place that guide the behavior, attitudes, and values of faculty, staff, and students. What does this kind of organizational saga look like? The students in this study told us it's one where they felt accepted by their other-ethnic and coethnic peers, regardless of how they chose to define their ethnicity. They expected that there would be opportunities to explore different aspects of their ethnicity, such as learning or relearning languages, learning about their groups' history or politics, learning and practicing cultural traditions, etc. They wanted places where they felt safe from the discriminatory and prejudicial experiences they experienced in the "outside" world. They expected to find classrooms where inquisitiveness and ignorance can be displayed without ridicule. They wanted opportunities to learn from diverse persons and establish meaningful and lasting cross-ethnic friendships. An institution where this kind of saga is present can rely on its members, culture, and structures to sustain these values and transfer them to new members.

The difficulty comes in how to lay the foundation for developing a pluralist institutional saga. Again, we can take cues from Clark's (1972) work. In his study of the five institutions, he states that sagas were created when a new, influential leader took the helm. New presidential leadership is an opportunity for pluralism to take shape. Another opportunity is in a time of crisis. The process of recovery provides a time for reflection, redefinition of institutional values, and redirection of focus. The founding of an institution is an obvious opportunity to invest heavily in such a saga through selecting an institution's first leaders, first faculty, first students, physical plant, organizational structure, etc. While these opportunities are infrequent, we can translate this lesson to developing new curricular and cocurricular programs or revising long-standing programs requiring a systemic change at all levels of the institution.

It would be naïve to present the notion that changing campus cultures, improving campus climate, or creating vibrant, pluralistic institutional sagas can be accomplished through the typical conventions of university process and governance. Predominantly White institutions, even if they are no longer predominantly White, have leaders, structures, policies, faculty, programs, and physical plants that assume they are predominantly White. The dominant culture at all but the most specialized institutions of higher education (historically Black colleges and universities [HBCUs], tribal colleges, colleges for the deaf or blind, women's colleges) is predominantly White. The U.S. Department of Education's Title V Hispanic-Serving Institution grant program assists colleges and universities that have recently achieved Hispanic-Serving Institution status to develop their institutional capacity to serve Latino/a students. With these grants, campuses find that changing their structures, the disposition of their predominantly White faculty and administrative staff, and the perspective of student services to serve Latino/a students better is a long, difficult process because these measures involve a fundamental change in campus culture. Indeed, as Ortiz outlines in her writing on *The Collegiate Ideal* (1999), when there is a strong campus culture based on the stereotype of the *collegiate* ideal—a notion of what college should be (residential, prestigious, youthful, school spirit abounds, etc.)—many facets of the institution support that ideal. Students, activities, services, faculty, administrators, and alumni all work to perpetuate that culture, making transformation difficult.

It can be argued that the creation of an institutional saga that embraces diversity will necessitate the appointment of an office of the provost on diversity and academic initiatives (Lee & Janda, 2006) that coordinates with all units within an institution. Not all universities have such offices in place or accord them the importance needed to sustain a positive multicultural campus. Institutions are advised to hire nationally recognized experts on diversity to serve as their chief officer and/or consultant. Among its objectives, the Office of Diversity and Academic Initiatives should be charged with the task of "identifying racial problems" unique to its institution and "propos[ing] policies and strategies to improve" campus climate as well as the "academic and employment opportunities for under-represented populations" (Lee & Janda, 2006, p. 30). Working in conjunction with all agents of the institution, this office would be responsible for articulating a comprehensive set of diversity goals and objectives specific to its institution, setting realistic benchmarks, and performing regular progress evaluations. As Lee and Janda (2006) note, institutions "need to conduct ongoing, systematic evaluations each year on multicultural curriculum, training, environment, special events and programs, and the level of diversity commitment in order to promote more idealistic diversity in both academic courses and non-academic events" (p. 29). It is vital that universities and colleges define concrete and achievable goals to enhance the substance and magnitude of their diversity initiatives. Equally important is that institutions set the tone for a less ethnically adversarial campus climate by committing to student aid initiatives and student development and services that preserve an environment of support for all individuals, regardless of ethnic background (Hurtado, 1992). As noted earlier, we found in this study that ethnic divisions among groups were accentuated when students saw that some ethnicities benefited from educational resources and opportunities that were not available to all groups. This will require a university-wide effort with various student-related offices working in unison.

For present-day universities, diversity is certainly a work in progress demanding continued development and assessment where all agents within the institution—university leaders and administrators, admissions and financial aid officers, student affairs personnel, faculty, and students—play a vital role in influencing the institution's success. It is important to recognize that, although hiring a chief diversity officer within or establishing an office of diversity is a critical first step, it does not mean that an institution's work is done. Universities committed to diversity must develop a top-down strategic plan that articulates the interconnections among the various institutional entities and their supporting agents for creating and sustaining a successful and effective learning community for all students and an institutional saga that embraces diversity at its core (Hurtado et al., 1999).

The Association of American Colleges and Universities (AAC&U) has articulated several promising diversity models for institutions to emulate. The AAC&U provides a wealth of resources and publications for university officials, administrators, faculty, and staff committed to transforming or expanding diversity within their institutions (see www.aacu.diversity.web .org/diversity). For instance, in a seminal report, entitled *Diversity Blueprint: A Planning Manual for Colleges and Universities* (1998), the AAC&U stipulated five planning principles for institutions undergoing diversity reform—accountability, inclusiveness, evaluation, shared responsibility, and institutionalization—that help put into place the organizational/structural features as well as the behavioral and psychological dimensions necessary to create a positive diverse campus climate. To ensure that diversity becomes and remains a central priority of an institution's mission, these planning principles are put into practice through the implementation of specific programs and priority actions. The AAC&U affirms that an institution's planning priority actions should include, but not be limited to, the following: (1) effective and committed leadership that imparts a clear vision, mission, and cultural legacy that encourages a systemic change at all levels of the institution endorsing diversity as a core value; (2) recruitment and retention of ethnically and racially diverse administrators, staff personnel, and faculty at all levels within the institution and of student groups that have been excluded previously; (3) curricular and cocurricular transformation through revised general education models and courses as well as interdisciplinary and disciplinary specific diversity programs; (4) campus partnerships and connections with diverse communities in the larger society; and (5) institutionalized diversity support programs for faculty, staff, and students to improve campus climate and student learning and skill development in issues of conflict and community. For a description of other similar models for creating and sustaining institutional diversity, we refer the reader to a number of other empirically informed reports provided by the AAC&U: *Enacting Diverse Learning Environments: Improving the Climate for Racial/Ethnic Diversity in Higher Education* (Hurtado et al., 1999); *Toward a Model of Inclusive Excellence and Change in Postsecondary Institutions* (Williams, Berger, & McClendon, 2005); *Making Diversity Work on Campus: A Research-Based Perspective* (Milem et al., 2005); *The Campus Diversity Initiative: Current Status, Anticipating the Future* (Smith, 2004); and, finally, *Greater Expectations: A New Vision for Learning as a Nation Goes to College* (AAC&U, 2002).

The AAC&U (1995) has stipulated that one of the primary objectives of higher education for today's students is that they "learn, in every part of their educational experience, to live creatively with the multiplicity, ambiguity, and irreducible differences that are the defining conditions of the contemporary world" (p. xxii). As such, it is clear that institutions must continue to be deliberate agents of socialization and commit to student- and diversity-related initiatives specifically aimed at reducing biases, promoting ethnic understanding, and fostering an institutional saga of common identity that all students can meaningfully embrace (Hurtado, 2001). If creating institutional sagas that endorse and affirm core values of diversity produce "citizens and leaders who are more engaged in social action" and better prepared to participate effectively in a highly complex and increasingly changing global world, "then higher education will be fulfilling its role in society as instigators of progress" and change (Nelson et al., 2005, p. 471).

The Future of the Ethnic Experience in College

By all accounts, the future of the ethnic experience in college will only become more complex. The diversification of American higher education provides challenges in providing a place where students can develop and express their ethnic identity and thus reap the positive outcomes the students in this study experienced. A number of forces have been put in place since the time of this study that already threaten and prevent pluralist institutional sagas from taking shape by placing constraints on universities' ability to change the ethnic and racial composition of their campuses. The most obvious is the erosion of affirmative action policies across the country. For instance, the passage in 1996 of Proposition 209 [in California, which] banned the use of race as a criterion for admission to the state's public university, led to a drop in the entry rate of Hispanic [and African American] students at both [the] University of California [UC] and California State University [CSU] system. (Erisman & Looney, 2007, p. 34)

Only 16% of native and foreign-born Latino/a students who graduated from California high schools met the criteria for *eligibility* in the California State system, and less than 7% did so for the University of California system. The intent of the CSU system is to admit the state's top 33% of graduating students, and the UC system admits the top 13%. The shortage of Latinos/as in these top groups further illustrates the scope that race/ethnicity plays in access to higher education, especially for persons from low-income groups and who are graduates of low-performing high schools—namely, immigrants and persons of color (Erisman & Looney, 2007). At one of the campuses where this study was conducted, the population of African American students has slipped from 6% at the time of the study to less than 3% of the total undergraduate population, making this group highly underrepresented. This means that positive effects of having a significant number of coethnics on campus becomes difficult to achieve. Underrepresentation of African Americans also makes difficult the interethnic dialogue that is so important for ultimately solving many of the inequities that face our society.

Despite local, state and federal government efforts, we are no closer to meeting our goals concerning equity in accessing quality education in K–12. No Child Left Behind legislation has not resulted in better education for the nation's most needy students (Darling-Hammond, 2007). Even the American Civil Liberties Union's victory (*Williams v. The State of California*, 2004) in California, where public schools are now mandated to provide resources for schools in low socioeconomic areas equal to those in their higher socioeconomic counterparts, has not changed the ability of such students to receive adequate education. How might this affect the future of the ethnic experience in college? Many urban, four-year institutions are growing impatient with the increasing number of students who need to be remediated in math and English to make progress toward their degrees. Some have taken measures to shift the responsibility for remediation to the community colleges, thus mandating that students begin their college careers outside the university. While community colleges are places where students have been able to achieve their dreams of obtaining a higher education, it is well known that students have a far better chance of graduating if they begin their college careers at four-year institutions (Erisman & Looney, 2007). With more low-income students (who are likely to be newly immigrated persons, Latino/as, or African Americans) needing remediation (Alliance for Excellent Education, 2006; Erisman & Looney, 2007), and four-year universities less likely to offer them this opportunity in the future, their numbers on those campuses will decline. As noted by Williams and colleagues:

> Systematic educational and societal inequities leave many low income, first generation students, and students of color underrepresented to attend and succeed in postsecondary education, an "achievement gap" that remains in place at both the secondary and postsecondary levels. Compounding academic challenges is the rising cost associated with postsecondary education that often makes [the] baccalaureate degree unfeasible for students historically underrepresented in higher education. (2005, p. 7)

To illustrate, according to the *Chronicle of Higher Education* ("The States," 2007), tuition rates were set to climb by 7% at the University of California campuses and by 10% at the California State University campuses. This increase in tuition fees is likely to have a negative effect on college enrollments, especially immigrants, Latinos/as, African Americans, and nontraditional students.

Many believe that the high number of immigrants from California, Texas, Florida, and New York will slowly cast their populations across the country as immigrant groups move to other sections of the country where greater economic opportunities are possible. This has historical precedence, as similar movements were seen in the late 19th and early 20th centuries as immigrant groups entering the East and West Coasts began to move inward. Many small Midwestern and Southern towns are already experiencing large influxes of Latinos/as, and ethnic enclaves of newly immigrated Asian American groups can be found in cities around the country. States such as Georgia and North Carolina have already experienced a more than 200% increase in their immigrant populations (Migration Policy Institute, 2003). Ultimately, one hopes, these migrations will result in more of these students on predominantly White campuses in those states. As Williams and colleagues (2005) argue, projected increases in immigration rates from Asian, Latin American, and Caribbean countries will provide colleges and universities with "unprecedented opportunities to diversify their student populations and draw on this diversity as a vehicle for learning for all students" (Williams et al., 2005, p. 5). Ideally, ongoing debates regarding educational reform, affirmative action, and immigration policies will not deter the diversification of these institutions.

In a similar vein, the immigration policy debate, especially as it relates to the Mexican/U.S. border, could also have an impact on the future ethnic experience of college. According to an Institute for Higher Education Policy report (Erisman & Looney, 2007), "immigrants make up 12% of the undergraduate population—a percentage comparable to students with disabilities, Hispanic students and Black students" (p. 5). Of those who are immigrants, 30% of the student population is Latino/a (most of whom are of Mexican heritage), a proportion that dramatically underrepresents their numbers at the national level. Actions restricting immigration, not only from Mexico, but from other countries as well, threatens the likelihood that those individuals will find their way to a college campus. Unlike previous federal legislation that served to broaden access to higher education through enhancing access for women and minorities, proposed legislation to limit immigration brings with it the likelihood that colleges and universities will actually become less diverse. In fact, federal legislation has already made it more difficult for undocumented immigrants to participate in higher education by denying them access to in-state tuition unless that benefit is afforded to *all* U.S. citizens. While many states have designed policies that do allow undocumented immigrants access to in-state tuition, only a few also provide access to state-sponsored financial aid, presenting a significant burden for such individuals by essentially barring their access to higher education.

In this study, only three students noted that they had mixed-race heritage, but during the interview, they self-identified as monoracial. We know that this is not representative of the growing number of mixed-race students on college campuses (Renn, 2004; Smith, Moreno, Clayton-Pederson, Parker, & Teraguchi, 2005). Renn and Lunceford (2004) argue that we, in fact, underestimate the number of mixed-race individuals in the United States because of the manner in which the U.S. Census Bureau collects data on race and ethnicity. The proportion of students at American universities classified as unknown—many who are *assumed* to be of mixed-race heritage—has increased dramatically, from 3.2% in 1991 to 5.9% in 2001, underscoring the complex ways in which the U.S. student population is diversifying and the importance of attending to this growing segment of "unknown" students (Smith et al., 2005). There is currently little uniformity across universities in regard to handling student data when race/ethnicity is left blank or when students mark "other" or more than one ethnic/racial classification. In a recent study of three universities in California, Smith and colleagues (2005) evaluated a method for determining "the racial/ethnic backgrounds of [unknown] students by comparing existing enrollment data to a second, independent data set" that included a Multiracial Classification System— *MRCS* (Smith et al., 2005, p. 5). They reported that the ethnic and racial makeup of institutions was distorted when a large segment of the student body was classified as unknown, and found that a significant proportion of students classified as "unknown" under the standard IPEDS format (Department of Education's *Integrated Post-secondary Education Data System*) were White or of mixed-race heritage. They advocate changes at the institutional and national level where the IPEDS is amended to include multiracial classifications, as was done in the 2000 census, and that the MRCS be used when reporting national educational student outcomes. With the call for greater institutional accountability for student educational and learning outcomes, it is vital for institutions to have accurate and precise numbers of the ethnic/racial composition of their student body. Hence, the numbers matter with regard to educational policies and institutional reform (Renn & Lunceford, 2004). Therefore, identifying specifically who comprises the "unknown" student group is part of the larger effort to assess whether institutions are, indeed, achieving student diversity and ensuring that positive academic outcomes are met across various racial/ethnic groups that represent our nation's student body. Most significant, these numbers come to bear and are of consequence for an institution's "mission, planning, curriculum and pedagogy, program and services, hiring and resource allocation toward all students' high achievement" (Smith et al., 2005, p. 3).

Mixed-race students will also present challenges to our current understanding of ethnic identity development as most models assume a monoracial identification. As students experience more freedom to construct their ethnic identity to include multiple associations and the flexibility to express ethnicity differently in various contexts, ethnic identity, as we theoretically know it, will change. Renn's (2003, 2004) study of mixed-race college students reported that students identified multiracially, used more than one monoracial category, identified situationally, selected one monoracial category, or opted out of racial categorization. Complicating this theoretical finding is that most students assumed three or more of these classifications during their time in college. As the college students of the future arrive on campus, who arguably will be increasingly multiracial, our understanding of ethnicity and its impact on the development of students will require revision, and our programs and practices will need to adapt nimbly to this significant change.

In conclusion, what a privilege it is to have insight into these students' experiences as they traversed the often messy domain of ethnic identity and ethnic or racial dynamics on their campuses. African Americans converted negative experiences into sources of strength, pride, and internal motivation for pursuing college and for enacting future change for the betterment of the group. Latinos/as spoke of education as a vehicle for enhancing the status of the group and of becoming role models and leaders for siblings and future generations. Asian Americans genuinely looked forward to a future that retained their ethnicity and identification with a specific ethnic group while also assuming the best of American culture. Although Whites spoke of their struggles to be part of a diverse learning community, they also reflected on their transformation into greater multicultural competence. Students from all four ethnic groups learned something valuable by being a part of an environment where ethnicity could be challenged, explored, and strengthened. In this area of their lives, these students changed in positive ways, which is one of higher education's ultimate goals.

OVERVIEW OF STUDY DESIGN AND METHODOLOGY

Study Sites

Comprehensive University (CU), one of the 25 campuses of the California State University system, is located in the greater Los Angeles area. It sits in the center of a major technological, industrial, and transportation complex in the middle of a highly diverse area. At the time of the study (1995–1999), the university catalogue described the college as "in a population that is international and multiethnic, [and] cultural pluralism is a major characteristic of the university" (Institutional Catalogue, 1994). Although the campus was built on a large, old Spanish California rancho, it feels small, with the academic and administrative buildings clustered together in grassy areas surrounded by eucalyptus trees.

CU is fully accredited by a number of agencies and, at the time of the study, offered 37 undergraduate majors. There were nearly 7,000 undergraduate students and nearly 3,000 graduate students. Of the undergraduates, 16% were transfers, primarily from community colleges, and 38% were part-time students. Entrance to CU was described as "moderately difficult," in that it accepted 60% of its applicants. In addition, 75% of its first-year students were in the top half of their high school class and had scored more than 900 on the SAT (Peterson's Guide, Inc., 1992). The average age of undergraduate was 29. Because of the high number of part-time students, it is not surprising that only one-third of first-year students graduate within six years (Straughn & Lovejoy-Straughn, 1998). The proportion of part-time students is also a good indication that the university is primarily a commuter campus. Only 6% of the students lived on-campus.

The ethnic composition of the student population at CU reflects the diversity of the area surrounding the campus (see Table A.1). There is truly no majority group on campus, and, unlike Research University, Asian Americans are not a numerically dominant part of the student population. Only 11% of students were Asian Americans, and many of those are Pacific Islanders or Southeast Asian, not Chinese or Japanese. Thirty percent of the

TABLE A.1
Ethnic Composition of Study Sites

	Research Institution	
Ethnic Group	*CU*	*RU*
African Americans	30%	6%
Asian	11%	35%
Latinos/as	26%	16%
Whites	32%	37%
Other	1%	6%

Note: CU = Comprehensive University; RU = Research University.

students were African American, Whites comprised 32% of the student population, and Latinos/as made up 26% of the student body.

Research University (RU), part of the University of California System, has grown to be one of the top research universities in the country. The campus houses a large medical complex, majestic old buildings, and quad areas. On a fall afternoon, the marching band practices in the background, reminding students of the "big-time" athletics that characterize this institution. RU is located in Southern California.

Of the 23,600 undergraduate students attending the campus at the time of the study, over half were in the top 10% of their high school class. Entrance to RU is described as "very difficult" (Peterson's Guides Inc., 1992). Students can choose from 109 majors, and 60% of students continue on to graduate or professional schools. Seventy percent of RU's first-year students finish their bachelor's degree in five years. While RU also draws nearly all its students from California, almost a quarter of them live on-campus, indicating that RU is much less of a commuter campus than is CU (Straughn & Lovejoy-Straughn, 1998).

The ethnic composition of RU's student population is similar to other elite universities in California in that it has a large Asian American population. At the time of the study, Whites and Asian Americans were the clear majority at RU, with Whites comprising 37% and Asian Americans accounting for 35% of the student population. Latinos/as made up only 16% of the student population, but still approached their proportion at CU. The starkest contrast between the two schools, in addition to the difference in the Asian American population, is the fact that African Americans only account for 6% of RU students. It is a traditional student body, with most under-graduate students ages 18 to 24 years and attending school full time.

Study Participants

A total of 120 students were recruited for the study. The survey sample (*N* = 120) was comprised of 36 Whites (30%), 34 Latinos/as (28%), 24 African Americans (20%), and 26 Asians (22%). Table A.1 presents the ethnic break-down for the student sample for each institution attended. The qualitative interview sample consisted of 103 students of the 120 who completed the sur-vey questionnaire. Because of technical difficulties—that is, poor sound qual-ity in recording and/or damaged audiotapes—we were unable to transcribe all 120 interviews. Hence, the final 103 coded interviews included 30 Whites (29%), 26 Latinos/as (25%), 24 African Americans (23%), and 23 Asians (23%). Fifty-nine percent of the overall student sample came from CU, and the remaining 41% from RU. Sixty-four percent of the participants were female, and 36% were male. The majority of students were single (86.7%), in their late teens to early 20s (88.2%), enrolled in college full time (94%), and work-ing full time and/or part time (76%). Twenty-one percent of students reported being first generation in the United States; 28%, second generation; and 51% reported that their families had been in this country for three or more genera-tions. Sixty-seven percent of the participants were native English speakers, and 79% were born in the United States Table A.2 presents a detailed overview of the study participants' demographic characteristics, and Table A.3 illustrates the preferred ethnic labels these students ascribed to themselves.

A Multimethod Research Design

We used a multimethod approach to address the varied influences of ethni-cally diverse university and neighborhood communities on students' ethnic identity and personal development. The qualitative interview data provided insight into students' ethnic identity in terms of specific university contexts and how interactions with coethnic and multiethnic persons before and dur-ing college are important to this development. Furthermore, the collection of survey data allowed us to examine the extent to which participants constructed their ethnic identity with respect to established overarching components of ethnicity and how these components are related to students' personal self-esteem and adjustment to college. A description of interview protocol and survey measures follows.

TABLE A.2
Sample Demographic Profile

Demographic Variables	Percent of Students
Class Standing	
Freshman	25.7
Sophomore	12.4
Junior	28.3
Senior	31.0
Graduate	2.7
Work Status	
Full-time	40.7
Part-time	35.6
Not working	23.7
Living Arrangement	
Family	41.5
Apartment	39.0
Dormitory	23.7
Generational Status in United States	
First	21.2
Second	28.0
Third	12.7
Fourth	8.5
Fifth	29.7
English Native Language	
Yes	67.2
No	32.8
Born in United States	
Yes	79.0
No	21.0
Father's Level of Education	
Elementary school	12.6
Some high school	8.4
High school	11.8
Trade school	10.9
Some college	27.7
Some graduate school	02.5
Graduate/professional	26.1

TABLE A.2 (Continued)

Demographic Variables	Percent of Students
Mother's Level of Education	
Elementary school	15.0
Some high school	05.8
High school	19.2
Trade school	09.2
Some college	26.7
Some graduate school	10.0
Graduate/professional	14.2
Family Class Standing	
Working class	24.6
Lower middle class	13.6
Middle class	33.1
Middle upper class	22.9
Upper class	4.2

Semistructured Interview Protocol

We used semistructured interviews to provide a holistic picture of the meaning of ethnic identity for students attending multiethnic universities. The interview protocol included questions in four areas: Ethnic self-identification; feelings about one's own ethnic group or ethnic group self-esteem; impact of intergroup contact on ethnic identification and ethnic group self-esteem; and transformation of one's ethnic identity as a result of multicultural experiences. Some questions were used as probes to allow students to elaborate on or explain their answer to the question asked. The probes follow each lead question below.

I. Ethnic Identification

The following questions represented measures of ethnic identification:

1. Tell me about your ethnic background. What does your ethnic identity mean to you?
   a. How do you feel about being a member of your ethnic group?
   b. How would you be different if you were a member of another ethnic group?
2. Are there any cultural practices or behaviors that you engage in on a regular basis that allow you to express your ethnic identity?

TABLE A.3
Preferred Ethnic Labels Selected by White, African American, Latino/a, and Asian Students

Ethnic Groups	Percent of Students
Whites	
American	13.9
Caucasian	13.9
White	38.9
Australian	02.8
German	08.3
Irish	05.6
Italian	08.3
Jewish	02.8
Polish	02.8
Latinos/as	
Mexican American	21.2
Mexican	45.5
Mexicano/a	03.0
Chicano/a	06.1
Ecuadorian	03.0
Puerto Rican	09.1
Hispanic	03.0
Latino/a	03.0
Spanish	03.0
African Americans	
African American	66.7
Black	29.2
Ethiopian	04.2
Asians	
Chinese	12.0
Cambodian	16.0
Filipino	16.0
Japanese American	08.0
Japanese	12.0
Javanese	04.0
Korean	16.0

3. What is important to you in living your life?
   a. How are these values expressed in your life?
   b. Where did they come from? Did they come from any specific sources?
   c. Would you say these values are generally shared by others of your ethnic background? How do you know that?
4. Are there any advantages or disadvantages to being a member of your ethnic group?
5. Have there been any social, political, or historical forces which have impacted you as a member of your ethnic group?
   a. How has this affected the way you feel about yourself as a member of your group?
6. Are there any ethnic groups, including your own, that you are willing to work with to advance their political and/or economic rights? Why? Why not?
7. We have talked a lot about ethnicity and what it means to you in different contexts, so to wrap up the interview I'd like you to summarize the importance of ethnic identity in the development of your personality or identity.

The first two questions are fairly obvious; they measure a person's ethnic identity. In question one participants indicate their ethnic identity in terms of a label and then elaborate on its importance. Question two determined whether the participant's ethnic identity is practiced or simply *symbolic*, meaning that ethnicity is an identifier that has few behavioral aspects or consequences.

Question three attempted to determine whether participants perceived their most relevant values to be related to their ethnic identity and/or ethnic group. Responses to this question also shed light on the assumption that certain values are related to particular ethnic groups (e.g., Latinos/as and the importance of family).

Question five allowed for the possibility that a person's ethnic identity might not be influenced necessarily by family or community experiences, but that other forces may have been the catalysts for identity formation. This was especially relevant with a college sample, since many students took ethnic studies and history courses in which they learned about such forces.

Question six in this section helped to assess the connection between ethnic identification and political action. This relationship is also a part of the ethnic identity theories discussed in chapter 2, and it is sometimes assumed that one is not a "true ethnic" unless he or she is willing to enact a political agenda. The summary question (7) was used to see whether the participants altered or added to their original conceptions of their own ethnic identities based on the questions asked before. The self-reflection and analysis required to answer the preceding battery of questions may have triggered additional thoughts on their ethnic identity.

II. Ethnic Group Self-Esteem

This series of questions sought to explore the impact of other ethnic groups on one's own sense of ethnic group self-esteem. They helped answer questions such as: does affiliation with members of other ethnic groups lessen the amount of attachment to one's own group, or what interactions or settings contribute to developing relationships with members of other ethnic groups?

1. Have you ever experienced a strong affiliation or bond with a person or people from ethnic groups other than your own?
   a. When have you experienced this? What led to this relationship?
   b. What was unique about those situations or experiences that led you to bond with this person or ethnic group?
   c. Has this affiliation or bond affected the way you feel about yourself? Your ethnic group? Other ethnic groups?
   d. If no, what do you think has prevented you from having strong affiliations with people who are members of other ethnic groups?
2. Do you feel that hanging out with, talking to, or becoming close to people from different ethnic backgrounds affected or changed you as a person?
   a. Have you adopted values and beliefs of other ethnic groups?
   b. Have you adopted behaviors or cultural practices of other ethnic groups?
   c. Have the ties to your own culture changed as a result of these interactions?
3. Are there positive or negative aspects of being a member of your ethnic group?
   a. Are there positive or negative aspects of being a member of the other ethnic groups?

Questions under 1 and 2 measured the impact of significant relationships with members of other ethnic groups on their ethnic group self-esteem. Together, these questions explored the potential positive influences of relationships and contacts with members of other groups on the development of their own ethnic identity. They also sought to explore whether affiliation with members of other groups lessens one's own ethnic identification (Atkinson, Morten, & Sue, 1993; Cross, 1971).

III. Intergroup Contact

These questions addressed the effects of intergroup contact on ethnic identity development. Students were asked to confirm or challenge the assumption of the existence of negative feelings and experiences with other ethnic groups that have been considered to be necessary in ethnic identity development (Atkinson et al., 1993; Cross, 1971).

1. What would you say are the two or three ethnic groups that you have the most contact with besides your own?
   a. How would you characterize your interactions with these groups?
   b. In general, how do you feel? Do you feel at ease? Do you feel accepted? Does that change in different settings?
   c. Do you communicate well with members of these groups?
   d. When you are interacting with members of that group, what do you think they are thinking/feeling about you?
   e. Do you feel differently when you are interacting with people you know very well versus people you are only acquainted with?
2. Why do you think you **don't** interact more frequently with _____? (Insert any of the following groups they did not mention: Asian Americans, African Americans, Anglos, Latinos/as.)
   a. Would you like to improve the way you interact with any of the groups we mentioned? **If yes,** how might this happen? **If no,** why not?
   b. What do you think would help you to feel more at ease?
3. What is it like to be a member of your ethnic group on campus?

These questions also provided insights about the state of multicultural activity and understanding among college students today. They were especially critical in answering the second set of research questions, which examined how one's ethnic identity influences interactions with members of other ethnic groups.

Survey Instrument—Ethnic Identity and College Adjustment Survey

The *Ethnic Identity Survey* was designed to assess the relationship between ethnic identity processes and students' psychosocial adjustment to college in terms of self-efficacy, social integration, and self-esteem. What follows is a description of the measures included in the survey.

Ethnic Identity

Luhtanen and Crocker's (1992) Collective Self-Esteem Scale (total scale alpha = .78) was used as a multidimensional measure of ethnic identity. The scale taps into components of ethnic identity, such as private acceptance, perceived public acceptance, overall membership esteem, and the importance of ethnicity to personal identity. Each subscale is comprised of four items answered on a 7-point rating scale, ranging from "Strongly disagree" to "Strongly agree." Specifically:

1. *Private acceptance* (alpha = .73) measures the degree to which ethnic identity is accepted by the person him- or herself. Items include "I often regret that I belong to the ethnic group I do" and "I feel good about the ethnic group I belong to."
2. *Public acceptance* (alpha = .65) taps into one's beliefs of how others perceive and judge his or her ethnic group. Sample items are "Overall, my ethnic group is considered good by others" and "In general, others respect the ethnic group I belong to."
3. *Personal identity* (alpha = .70) evaluates the importance of ethnic identity to a person's self-concept. Items include "Overall, my ethnic group has very little to do with how I feel about myself" and "In general, belonging to my ethnic group is an important part of my self-image."
4. *Membership identity* (alpha = .74) items measure how good or worthy a person feels as member of his or her ethnic group. For instance, "I feel I don't have much to offer the ethnic group I belong to" and "I am a cooperative participant of the ethnic group I belong to."

College Adjustment

The Solberg, O'Brien, Kennel, and Davis (1993) College Self-Efficacy questionnaire was used to measure students' adjustment to college. The questionnaire (overall alpha = .93) is a 20-item scale that measures students' perceived ability to handle the demands of college life. Items are answered on a 7-point rating scale, ranging from "Not at all confident" to "Very confident." The scale taps into 3 areas:

1. *Social self-efficacy* (alpha = .83) measures students' level of confidence in interacting with peers and professors. Sample questions include "Make new friends in college," "Talk to your professor," and "Ask a teacher a question outside of class."
2. *Course self-efficacy* (alpha = .86) taps into students' level of confidence in handling coursework and related academic requirements. Sample items are "Take good class notes," "Research a term paper," and "Understand your textbook."
3. *Roommate self-efficacy* (alpha = .84) measures students' level of confidence in negotiating living arrangements with roommate(s). Items include "Get along with your roommate(s)" and "Divide chores."

Self-Esteem

The Rosenberg's Self-Esteem Scale (alpha = .89), a 7-item instrument that provides a global measure of one's self-worth, was used as an overall indicator of students' individual self-esteem. Sample items include "I feel that I am a person of worth, at least on an equal basis with others," "I feel that I have a number of good qualities," and "I feel that I do not have much to be proud of." This scale was answered on a 7-point rating scale, ranging from "Strongly disagree" to "Strongly agree."

Ethnic Makeup of Neighborhood and High School

Two questions were used as indicators of students' level of interethnic contact prior to attending college. Students were asked to report on the ethnic makeup of the neighborhood in which they grew up and that of the high school they attended. This was measured in terms of the percentage of African Americans, Asian Americans, Latinos/as, and Whites who resided in their home neighborhood and had attended the student's high school.

Training of Interviewers

Before data collection, all interviewers participated in 4–6 hours of training in how to conduct individual interviews. Since many of the research assistants were involved in developing the interview protocol, they had a good understanding of the theoretical underpinnings of the questions and an idea of what would constitute a complete answer to each question in the protocol. We also felt that having student peers as part of the team would enhance the genuineness of responses on the assumption that students are more truthful with each other and better able to understand each other's experiences. Fourteen individuals (8 women and 6 men) representing the 4 ethnic groups studied served as interviewers; this group included the 2 authors and 6 graduate and 6 senior undergraduate research assistants.

Data Collection Procedures

Participants were recruited from undergraduate psychology courses at both university institutions and received class credit for their participation. Students were treated in accordance with ethical guidelines stipulated by the respective institutional review boards and assured that their taped commentaries and survey responses would remain completely anonymous and confidential. Participants were informed that the purpose of the study was to gain more insight into the factors that influence ethnic identity development by hearing directly from students of varied backgrounds and experiences. Authenticity in dialogue was facilitated by matching participants to an interviewer of the same gender and ethnic and/or socioracial background (Dunbar, Rodriguez, & Parker, 2002). This was done to encourage rapport and openness, especially when interviewees were asked about perceptions of and experiences with members of other ethnic groups. Interviews took approximately 45–90 minutes; they were taped and later transcribed. The interviews were conducted in private offices by one member of the research team. Upon completing the interviews, the students then answered the survey measures so they would not be "primed" for the interview by the questions and emphases of the paper-pencil measures.

Data Analysis

Qualitative Analysis

We used the constant comparative method to identify major themes and commonalities in the data (Lincoln & Guba, 1985). This analytical method involves comparing narrative data from different individuals to identify themes among each participant's data. Repeated comparison leads to revision of themes and collapsing of themes. Based on this initial process of the primary researchers' reading and rereading verbatim transcripts, a coding thesaurus was created that identified 19 general themes as being relevant to students' experiences of ethnicity; see Table A.4.

As researchers in the field, we are immersed in the ethnic identity literature and cognizant that knowledge of existing paradigms could have colored our interpretation of the data in developing the coding thesaurus. Hence, it was important to have outside persons code the data as well to verify the reliability and validity of the Ethnic Identity Coding Thesaurus. Two research assistants, who were not part of the original research team or who had expertise in the study of ethnic identity, assisted with this verification phase of the qualitative analyses. These coders not only brought an outsider's perspective to the project, but, as university students, they also endowed the study with a unique insight regarding the meaning of participants' narratives that the two primary investigators might have overlooked. We used the method of inter-rater agreement to confirm the reliability and validity of the Ethnic Identity Coding Thesaurus. The two graduate research assistants were instructed to use the 19 themes outlined in the thesaurus to code a subset of the interviews. This resulted in a 69% agreement in the coding of the data. These two graduate students then coded the remaining interviews.

TABLE A.4
Ethnic Identity Coding Thesaurus

1. Expression of Ethnicity	11. Incorporation of Other Cultures
2. Thoughts and Feelings About Ethnicity	12. Perception of Other Groups
3. Ethnic Heritage	13. Barriers to Intergroup Contact
4. Family Issues	14. Impact of Historic, Political, Social Events
5. Values	15. Willingness to Take Action
6. Sources of Values	16. Phenotypic Issues
7. Religion	17. Ways to Improve Intergroup Contact
8. Perception of Interpersonal Relationships	18. Influences of the College Environment
9. Context of Interpersonal Interactions	19. Current Issues
10. Acculturation	

Use of this peer debriefing method supported the reliability and validity of the thesaurus as a coding device.

Student narratives were then compiled to represent the 19 themes and were put into separate binders by ethnic group. In writing the chapters, we used this data management technique to first outline the chapters, and then we reread the original transcripts and searched for additional data themes that may have been missed in the original coding process. This resulted in a further refinement of the general themes into specific subthemes, categories that ensured that the data presented in the book reflected the focus and purpose of each chapter and the experiences of specific ethnicities. Taken as a whole, we believe this process allowed us to analyze the data in a manner that represents the peer debriefing method described by Lincoln and Guba (1985) and the internal auditing process discussed by Fassinger (2005). The use of matched ethnicity interviewers, multiple coders, and computation of thesaurus inter-rater reliability, and the internal auditing method used at various phases of the content analysis, all represent rigorous triangulation of qualitative data, as recommended by Lincoln and Guba (1985).

Quantitative Analyses of Ethnic Identity Survey

We used the Statistical Package for the Social Sciences (SPSS) to analyze the survey data. A series of correlational analyses were performed among the measures of ethnic identity, college self-efficacy, and self-esteem. These correlational analyses were intended to highlight the multidimensional facet of ethnic identity and how its components may relate differently to various aspects of psychological functioning in students. Likewise, we conducted a number of one-way analyses of variances on the ethnic identity measures, the college self-efficacy measures, and self-esteem by ethnic background of students. The purpose of these analyses was to identify group differences on these measures based on the ethnic background of students. Finally, we computed cross-tabs frequencies on ethnic composition of neighborhood and high school attended by ethnic background of students to determine the levels of interethnic contact students had before college. The results of these analyses are discussed in chapter 1.

REFERENCES

Alba, R. (1990). *Ethnic identity: The transformation of White America.* New Haven, CT: Yale University Press.

Alliance for Excellent Education. (2006). *Adolescent literacy.* Retrieved from http://www.all4ed.org/files/archive/publications/ReadingNext/AdolescentLiteracyFact Sheet.pdf

Allen, W. (1992). The color of success: African-American college student outcomes at predominantly White and historically Black public colleges and universities. *Harvard Educational Review, 62,* 26–44.

Alvarez, A. N., & Helms, J. (2001). Racial identity and reflected appraisals as influences on Asian Americans' racial adjustment. *Cultural Diversity and Ethnic Minority Psychology, 7,* 217–231.

Ancis, J. R., Sedlacek, W. E., & Mohr, J. J. (2000). Student perceptions of campus cultural climate and race. *Journal of Counseling and Development, 78,* 180–185.

Araujo, B. Y., & Borrell, L. N. (2006). Understanding the link between discrimination, mental health outcomes and life chances among Latinos. *Hispanic Journal of Behavioral Sciences, 28,* 245–266.

Arce, C. H., Murguia, E., & Frisbie, W. P. (1987). Phenotype and life chances among Chicanos. *Hispanic Journal of Behavioral Sciences, 9,* 19–32.

Ardilla, A. (2005). Spanglish: An Anglicized Spanish dialect. *Hispanic Journal of Behavioral Sciences, 27,* 60–81.

Arminio, J. (2001). Exploring the nature of race-related guilt. *Journal of Multicultural Counseling and Development, 29,* 239–252.

Association of American Colleges and Universities (AAC&U). (1995). *American pluralism and the college curriculum: Higher education in a diverse democracy.* Washington, DC: Author.

Association of American Colleges and Universities (AAC&U). (1998). *Diversity blueprint: A planning manual for colleges and universities.* Washington, DC: Author

Association of American Colleges and Universities (AAC&U). (2002). *Greater expectations: A new vision for learning as a nation goes to college.* Washington, DC: Author.

Astin, A. W. (1993). *What matters in college? Four critical years revisited.* San Francisco: Jossey-Bass.

Atkinson, D. R., Morten, G., & Sue, D. W. (1993). *Counseling American minorities: A cross cultural perspective* (4th ed.). Madison, WI: Brown & Benchmark.

Baker, P. B. (2005). The impact of cultural biases on African American students' education: A review of the literature regarding race based schooling. *Education and Urban Society, 37,* 243–256.

Baron, R. A., & Byrne, D. (2003). *Social psychology* (10th ed.). Boston: Allyn & Bacon.

Baron, R. A., Byrne, D., & Branscombe, N. R. (2006). *Social psychology* (11th ed.). Boston: Allyn & Bacon.

Bernal, M., & Martinelli, P. (Eds.). (1993). *Mexican American identity.* Encino, CA: Floricanto Press.

Bernal, M. E., Saenz, D. S., & Knight, G. P. (1995). Ethnic identity and adaptation of Mexican American youth in school settings. In A. Padilla (Ed.), *Hispanic psychology: Critical issues in theory and research* (pp. 71–88). San Francisco: Sage.

Berry, J. (1990). Psychology of acculturation. In J. Berman (Ed.), *Nebraska Symposium on Motivation: Vol. 37. Cross-cultural perspectives* (pp. 201–234). Lincoln: University of Nebraska Press.

Berry, J. (1993). Ethnic identity in plural societies. In M. Bernal & G. Knight (Eds.), *Ethnic identity: Formation and transmission among Hispanics and other minorities* (pp. 272–296). Albany: State University of New York Press.

Blalock, J. M. (1967). *Toward a theory of minority-group relations.* New York: Wiley.

Boyd-Franklin, N. (2003). *Black families in therapy: An African-American experience* (2nd ed.). New York: Guilford.

Brown, L. M., & Johnson, S. D. (1999). Ethnic consciousness and its relationship to conservatism and blame among African Americans. *Journal of Applied Psychology, 29,* 2465–2480.

Bryant, A., Jr., & Baker, S. B. (2003). The feasibility of constructing profiles of Native Americans from the People of Color Racial Identity Attitude Scale: A brief report. *Measurement and Evaluation in Counseling and Development, 36,* 2–8.

Buriel, R. (1987). Ethnic labeling and identity among Mexican Americans. In J. Phinney & M. Rotheram (Eds.), *Children's ethnic socialization: Pluralism and development* (pp. 134–152). Newbury Park, CA: Sage.

Buriel, R., & De Ment, T. (1997). Immigration and sociocultural change in Mexican, Chinese and Vietnamese American families. In A. Booth & A. Crouter (Eds.), *Immigration and the family: Research and policy on U.S. immigrants* (pp. 165–200). Hillsdale, NJ: Erlbaum.

Buttny, R. (1999). Discursive constructions of racial boundaries and self-segregation on campus. *Journal of Language and Social Psychology, 18,* 247–269.

Cabrera, A. F., & Nora, A. (1994). College students' perceptions of prejudice and discrimination and their feelings of alienation: A construct validation approach. *Review of Education, Pedagogy, and Cultural Studies, 16,* 387–409.

Cabrera, A. F., Nora, A., Terenzini, P. T., Pascarella, E., & Hagedorn, L. S. (1999). Campus racial climate and the adjustment of students to college: A comparison between White students and African-American students. *The Journal of Higher Education, 70,* 134–160.

Cardona, J. R. P., Busby, D. M., & Wampler, R. S. (2004). No soy de aqui ni soy de alla: Transgenerational cultural identity formation. *Journal of Hispanic Higher Education, 3,* 322–337.

Carter, R. (1990). Racial identity attitudes and psychological functioning. *Journal of Multicultural Counseling and Development, 19,* 105–114.

Carter, R. T., Helms, J. E., & Juby, H. L. (2004). The relationship between racism and racial identity for White Americans: A profile analysis. *Journal of Multicultural Counseling and Development, 32,* 2–17.

Casas, J. M., & Pytluk, S. D. (1995). Hispanic identity development: Implications for research and practice. In J. G. Ponterroto, J. M. Casas, J. M. Suzuki, & C. M. Alexander (Eds.), *Handbook of multicultural counseling* (pp. 155–180). Thousand Oaks, CA: Sage.

Chan, S., & Wang, L. C. (1991). Racism and the model minority: Asian-Americans in higher education. In P. G. Altbach & K. Lomotey (Eds.), *The racial crisis in higher education* (pp. 43–68). Albany: State University of New York Press.

Chang, M. J. (1999). Does racial diversity matter? The educational impact of a racially diverse undergraduate population. *Journal of College Student Development, 40,* 377–395.

Chang, M. J. (2001). Is it more than about getting along? The broader educational relevance of reducing students' racial biases. *Journal of College Student Development, 42,* 93–103.

Charles, C. Z. (2000). Residential segregation in Los Angeles. In B. Lawrence (Ed.), *Prismatic metropolis: Inequality in Los Angeles.* New York: Russell Sage Foundation.

Chen, G. A., LePhuoc, P., Guzmán, M. R., Rude, S. S., & Dodd, B. D. (2006). Exploring Asian American racial identity. *Cultural Diversity and Ethnic Minority Psychology, 12,* 461–476.

Cheng, D. X., & Zhao, C.-M. (2006). Cultivating multicultural competence through active participation: Extracurricular activities and multicultural learning. *NASPA Journal, 43*(4), 13–38.

Cheryan, S., & Monin, B. (2005). "Where are you *really* from?" Asian Americans and identity denial. *Journal of Personality and Social Psychology, 89,* 717–730.

Chickering, A. W. (1969). *Education and identity.* San Francisco: Jossey-Bass.

Chickering, A. W., & Reisser, L. (1993). *Education and identity* (2nd ed.). San Francisco: Jossey-Bass.

Clark, B. R. (1972). The organizational saga in higher education. *Administrative Science Quarterly, 17,* 178–194.

Codina, G. E., & Montalvo, E. F. (1994). Chicano phenotype and depression. *Hispanic Journal of Behavioral Science, 16,* 296–306.

Cohen, E. (1994). *Designing groupwork: Strategies for heterogeneous classrooms* (2nd ed.). New York: Teachers College Press.

Cohen, G. L., & Garcia, J. (2005). "I am us": Negative stereotypes as collective threats. *Journal of Personality and Social Psychology, 89,* 566–582.

Comas-Diaz, L. (2001). Hispanics, Latinos, or Americanos: The evolution of identity. *Cultural Diversity and Ethnic Minority Psychology, 7,* 115–120.

Crocker, J. (1999). Social stigma and self-esteem: Situational construction of self-worth. *Journal of Experimental Social Psychology, 35,* 89–107.

Crocker, J., Luhtanen, R., Blain, B., & Broadnax, S. (1994). Collective self-esteem and psychological well-being among White, Black, and Asian college students. *Personality and Social Psychology Bulletin, 20,* 503–513.

Crocker, J., & Major, B. (1989). Social stigma and self-esteem: The self-protective properties of stigma. *Psychological Review, 96,* 608–630.

Cross, W. E., Jr. (1971). The Negro-Black conversion experience: Toward a psychology of Black liberation. *Black World, 20,* 13–27.

Cross, W. E., Jr. (1991). *Shades of Black: Diversity in African-American identity.* Philadelphia: Temple University Press.

Cross, W. E., Jr., & Fhagen-Smith, P. (1996). Nigrescence and ego identity development: Accounting for differential Black identity patterns. In P. B. Pedersen, J. G. Draguns, W. J. Lonner, & J. E. Trinble (Eds.), *Counseling across cultures* (4th ed., pp. 108–123). Thousand Oaks, CA: Sage.

Cross, W. E., Jr., & Fhagen-Smith, P. (2001). Patterns of African American identity development: A life-span perspective. In C. L. Wijeyesinghe & J. B. Bailey (Eds.), *New perspectives on racial identity development: A theoretical and practical anthology* (pp. 242–270). New York: New York University Press.

Cross, W. E., Jr., & Strauss, L. (1998). The everyday functions of African American identity. In J. K. Swim & C. Strangor (Eds.), *Prejudice: The target's perspective* (pp. 267–279). San Diego, CA: Academic Press.

D'Andrea, M., & Daniels, J. (2001). Expanding your thinking about White racism: Facing the challenge of multicultural counseling in the 21st century. In J. G. Ponterotto, J. M. Casas, L. A. Suzuki, & C. M. Alexander (Eds.), *Handbook of multicultural counseling* (2nd ed., pp. 289–310). Thousand Oaks, CA: Sage."

Darling-Hammond, L. (2007, May 21). Evaluating "No Child Left Behind." *The Nation.* Retrieved December 13, 2007, from http://www.thenation.com/doc/20070521/darling-hammond

Devos, T., & Banaji, M. (2005). American = Whites? *Journal of Personality and Social Psychology, 88,* 447–466.

Dolbly, N. (2000). The shifting ground of race: The role of taste in youth's production of identities. *Race, Ethnicity and Education, 3,* 7–23.

DuBois, W. E. B. (1990). *The souls of Black folk.* New York: Vintage Books/The Library of America.

Dunbar, C., Rodriguez, D., & Parker, L. (2002). Race, subjectivity, and the interview process. In J. F. Gubrium & J. A. Holstein (Eds.), *Handbook of interview research: Context and method* (pp. 279–298). Thousand Oaks, CA: Sage.

Durrett, M. E., O'Bryan, S., & Pennebaker, J. W. (1975). Child rearing reports of White, Black and Mexican American families. *Developmental Psychology, 11,* 871.

Eichstedt, J. L. (2001). Problematic White identities and a search for social justice. *Sociological Forum, 16,* 445–470.

Elhoweris, H., Mutua, K., Alsheikh, N., & Holloway, P. (2005). Effect of children's ethnicity on teachers' referral and recommendation decisions in gifted and talented programs. *Remedial and Special Education, 26,* 25–31.

Ellis, P. (2004). White identity development at a two-year institution. *Community College Journal of Research and Practice, 28,* 745–761.

Elshoff, J. D., & Snow, R. E. (1971). *Pygmalion reconsidered.* Worthington, OH: Charles A. Jones.

Erikson, E. (1968). *Identity: Youth and crisis.* New York: Norton.

Erisman, W., & Looney, S. (2007). *Opening the door to the American dream: Increasing higher education access and success for immigrants.* Washington, DC: Institute for Higher Educational Policy.

Falicov, C. J. (1998). *Latino families in therapy: A guide to multicultural practice.* New York: Guilford.

Fassinger, R. E. (2005). Paradigms, praxis, problems, and promise: Grounded theory in counseling psychology research. *Journal of Counseling Psychology, 52*, 156–166.

Felix-Ortiz, M. (1994). A multidimensional measure of cultural identity for Latino and Latina adolescents. *Hispanic Journal of Behavioral Sciences, 16*, 99–116.

Ferdman, M., & Gallegos, P. I. (2001). Racial identity development and Latinos in the United States. In C. L. Wijeyesinghe & J. B. Bailey (Eds.), *New perspectives on racial identity development: A theoretical and practical anthology* (pp. 32–66). New York: New York University Press.

Fleming, J. (1984). *Blacks in college.* San Francisco: Jossey-Bass.

Frankenberg, R. (1993). *The social construction of whiteness: White women, race matters.* Minneapolis: University of Minnesota Press.

Freeman, K. (1997). Increasing African Americans' participation in higher education: African American high-school students' perspectives. *Journal of Higher Education, 68*, 523–550.

Freire, P. (1970, 1993, 1999). *Pedagogy of the oppressed.* New York: Continuum.

French, S. E., Seidman, E., Allen, L., & Aber, L. J. (2000). Racial/ethnic identity: Consequence with the social context and the transition to high school. *Journal of Adolescent Research, 15*, 587–602.

Gallagher, C. (1995). White reconstruction in the university. *Socialist Review, 24*, 165–187.

Gallagher, C. A. (2003). Playing the White ethnic card: Using ethnic identity to deny contemporary racism. In A. W. Doane & E. Bonilla-Silva (Eds.), *White out: The continuing significance of racism* (pp. 145–148). New York: Routledge.

Gandara, P. (1995). *Over the ivy wall. The educational mobility of low-income Chicanos.* Albany: State University of New York Press.

Garcia, J. (1982). Ethnicity and Chicanos: Measurement of ethnic identification, identity, and consciousness. *Hispanic Journal of Behavioral Sciences, 4*, 295–314.

Giles, H., Bourhis, R., & Taylor, D. (1977). Towards a theory of language in ethnic group relations. In H. Giles (Ed.), *Language, ethnicity, and intergroup relations.* London, UK: Academic Press.

Giroux, H. A. (1997). Rewriting the discourse of racial identity: Toward a pedagogy and politics of whiteness. *Harvard Educational Review, 67*, 285–320.

Goldberg, D. T. (1993). *Racist cultures: Philosophy and the politics of meaning.* Cambridge, UK: Blackwell.

Gomez, G. (2001). The continual significance of skin color: An exploratory study of Latinos. *Hispanic Journal of Behavioral Sciences, 22*, 94–104.

Gurin, P., Dey, E. L., Hurtado, S., & Gurin, G. (2002). Diversity in higher education: Theory and impact on educational outcomes. *Harvard Educational Review, 72*, 330–336.

Gurin, P., Hurtado, A., & Peng, T. (1994). Group contacts and ethnicity in the social identities of Mexicano and Chicanos. *Personality and Social Psychology Bulletin, 20*, 521–532.

Halgunseth, L. C., Ispa, J. M., & Rudy, D. (2006). Parental control in Latino families: An integrated review of the literature. *Child Development, 77*, 1282–1297.

Hall, R. E. (1994). The bleaching syndrome: Implications of light skin for Hispanic American assimilation. *Hispanic Journal of Behavioral Sciences, 16*, 307–314.

Hardiman, R. (2001). Reflections on White identity development theory. In C. L. Wijeyesinghe & J. B. Bailey (Eds.), *New perspectives on racial identity development: A theoretical and practical anthology* (pp. 108–128). New York: New York University Press.

Haritatos, J., & Benet-Martinez, V. (2002). Bicultural identities: The interface of cultural, personality, and socio-cognitive processes. *Journal of Research in Personality, 36*, 598–606.

Harrison, A. O., Wilson, M. N., Pine, C. J., Chan, S. Q., & Buriel, R. (1990). Family ecologies of ethnic minority children. *Child Development, 61*, 347–362.

Helms, J. E. (1990). *Black and White racial identity: Theory, research and practice.* Westport, CT: Greenwood Press.

Helms, J. E. (1995). An update of Helms' White and people of color racial identity modes. In J. G. Ponterotto, J. M. Casas, L. A. Suzuki, & C. M. Alexander (Eds.), *Handbook of multicultural counseling* (pp. 181–199). Thousand Oaks, CA: Sage.

Helms, J. E., & Cook, D. A. (1999). *Using race and culture in counseling and psychotherapy: Theory and process.* Needham Heights, MA: Allyn & Bacon.

Helms, J. E., & Talleyrand, R. M. (1997). Race is not ethnicity. *American Psychologist, 52*, 1246–1247.

Henderson, E. A. (1996). Black nationalism and rap music. *Journal of Black Studies, 26*, 308–339.

Henry, S. E. (2005). A different approach to teaching multiculturalism: Pragmatism as a pedagogy and problem solving tool. *Teachers College Record, 107*, 1060–1078.

Hughes, J. N., Gleason, K. A., & Zhang, D. (2005). Relationship influences on teachers' perceptions of academic competence in academically at-risk minority and majority first grade students. *Journal of School Psychology, 43*, 303–320.

Hurtado, A., & Gurin, P. (1995). Ethnic identity and bilingual attitudes. In A. Padilla (Ed.), *Hispanic psychology: Critical issues in theory and research* (pp. 89–106). Thousand Oaks, CA: Sage.

Hurtado, A., Gurin, P., & Peng, T. (1994). Social identities: A framework for studying the adaptations of immigrants and ethnics: The adaptations of Mexicans in the United States. *Social Problems, 41*, 129–151.

Hurtado, S. (1992). The campus racial climate: Contexts of conflict. *Journal of Higher Education, 63*, 539–569.

Hurtado, S. (1994). The institutional climate for talented Latino students. *Research in Higher Education, 35*, 21–41.

Hurtado, S. (1999). Reaffirming educators' judgment: Educational values. *Liberal Education*, 24–31.

Hurtado, S. (2001). Linking diversity and educational purposes: How the diversity of the faculty and student body impacts the classroom environment and student development. In G. Orfield (Ed.), *Diversity challenged: Legal crisis and new evidence*, 187–203. Cambridge, MA: Harvard Publishing Group.

Hurtado, S. (2002). Are we achieving the promise of diversity? *Liberal Education*, *88*(2), 12–13.

Hurtado, S. (2007). Linking diversity with the educational and civic missions of higher education. *Review of Higher Education*, *30*, 185–196.

Hurtado, S., & Carter, D. F. (1997). Effects of college transition and perceptions of the campus racial climate on Latino college students' sense of belonging. *Sociology of Education*, *70*, 324–345.

Hurtado, S., Engberg, M. E., Ponjuan, L., & Landreman, L. (2002). Students' pre-college preparation for participation in a diverse democracy. *Research in Higher Education*, *43*, 163–168.

Hurtado, S., Milem, J. F., Clayton-Pedersen, A. R., & Allen, W. R. (1998). Enhancing campus climates for racial/ethnic diversity: Educational policy and practice. *Review of Higher Education*, *21*(3), 279–302.

Hurtado, S., Milem, J., Clayton-Pedersen, A., & Allen, W. (1999). *Enacting diverse learning environments: Improving the climate for racial/ethnic diversity in higher education*. (ASHE-ERIC Higher Education Report, Vol. 26, No. 8). Washington, DC: The George Washington University, Graduate School of Education and Human Development.

Hurtado-Ortiz, M. T., & Guavain, M. (2007). Postsecondary education among Mexican American youth: Contributions of parents, siblings, acculturation, and generational status. *Hispanic Journal of Behavioral Sciences*, *29*, 181–191.

Ingram, D. (2005). Toward a cleaner White(ness): New racial identities. *Philosophical Forum*, *36*, 243–277.

Inman, A. G. (2006). South Asian women: Identities and conflicts. *Cultural Diversity and Ethnic Minority Psychology*, *12*, 306–319.

Jackson, C. L., & Neville, H. A. (1998). Influences of racial identity attitudes on African American college students' vocational identity and hope. *Journal of Vocational Behavior*, *53*, 97–113.

Jackson, R. L., Warren, J. R., Pitts, M. J., & Wilson, K. B. (2007). "It is not my responsibility to teach culture!": White graduate teaching assistants negotiating identity and pedagogy. In L. M. Cooks & J. S. Simpson (Eds.), *Whiteness, pedagogy, performance: Dis/placing race* (pp. 67–86). Lanham, MD: Lexington Books.

James, R. (1998). The perceived effects of social alienation of Black college students enrolled at a Caucasian southern university. *College Student Journal*, *32*, 228–239.

Juang, L. P., Nguyen, H. H., & Yunghui, L. (2006). The ethnic identity, other-group attitudes, and psychosocial functioning of Asian American emerging adults from two contexts. *Journal of Adolescent Research*, *21*, 542–568.

Jussim, L., & Harber, K. D. (2005). Teacher expectations and self-fulfilling prophecies: Knowns and unknowns, resolved and unresolved controversies. *Personality and Social Psychology Review*, *9*, 131–155.

Kawaguchi, S. (2003). Ethnic identity development and collegiate experience of Asian Pacific American students: Implications for practice. *NASPA Journal, 40*(3), 13–29.

Keefe, S. E. (1992). Ethnic identity: The domain of perceptions of and attachment to ethnic groups and cultures. *Human Organizations, 51,* 35–43.

Keefe, S. E., & Padilla, A. M. (1987). *Chicano ethnicity.* Albuquerque: University of New Mexico Press.

Kent State University. (2006). *Kent State University strategic diversity plan.* Retrieved December 10, 2007, from http://www.kent.edu/Administration/President/strate gicinitiatives/StrategicPlan/

Kim, J. (1981). *Process of Asian American identity development: A study of Japanese American women's perceptions of their struggle to achieve positive identities as Americans of Asian ancestry.* Unpublished doctoral dissertation, School of Education, University of Massachusetts, Amherst.

Kim, J. (2001). Asian American identity development theory. In C. L. Wijeyesinghe & B. W. Jackson III (Eds.), *New perspectives on racial identity development: A theoretical and practical anthology* (pp. 67–90). New York: New York University Press.

Kim-Ju, G. M., & Liem, R. (2003). Ethnic self-awareness as a function of ethnic group status, group composition and ethnic identity orientation. *Cultural Diversity and Ethnic Minority Psychology, 9*(3), 289–302.

Kincheloe, J. L. (1999). The struggle to define and reinvent Whiteness: A pedagogical analysis. *College Literature, 26,* 163–196.

Kincheloe, J. L., & Steinberg, R. S. (1998). Addressing the crisis of Whiteness. In J. S. Kincheloe, S. R. Steinberg, H. M. Rodriguez, & R. E. Chenault (Eds.), *White reign: Deploying Whiteness in America.* New York: St. Martin's Press.

Knight, G., Bernal, M., Cota, M., Garza, C., & Ocampo, K. (1993). Family socialization and Mexican identity and behavior. In M. Bernal & G. Knight (Eds.), *Ethnic identity: Formation and transmission among Hispanics and other minorities* (pp. 105–130). Albany: State University of New York Press.

Knowles, E. D., & Peng, K. (2005). White selves: Conceptualizing and measuring a dominant-group identity. *Journal of Personality and Social Psychology, 89,* 223–241.

Kohatsu, E. L. (1992). *The effects of racial identity and acculturation on anxiety, assertiveness, and ascribed identity among Asian American college students.* Unpublished doctoral dissertation, University of Maryland, College Park.

Kuh, G. D. (1996). The other curriculum: Out of class experiences associated with student learning and personal development. *Journal of Higher Education, 66,* 123–155.

Kuo, P. Y., & Roysircar-Sodowsky, G. (1999). Political ethnic identity versus cultural ethnic identity: An understanding of research on Asian Americans. In D. S. Sandhu (Ed.), *Asian and Pacific Islander Americans: Issues and concerns for counseling and psychotherapy* (pp. 71–90). New York: Nova Sciences.

LaFrambroise, T., Coleman, H. L. K., & Gerton, J. (1995). Psychological impact of biculturalism: Evidence and theory. *Psychological Bulletin, 114,* 395–412.

Lee, G., & Janda, L. (2006). Successful multicultural campus: Free from prejudice toward minority professors. *Multicultural Education, 14*(1), 27–30.

Lee, L. C., & Zane, N. W. S. (Eds.). (1998). *Handbook of Asian American psychology*. Thousand Oaks, CA: Sage.

Lee, R. M., Falbo, T., Doh, H. S., & Park, S. Y. (2001). The Korean diasporic experience: Measuring ethnic identity in the United States and China. *Cultural Diversity and Ethnic Minority Psychology, 7*, 207–216.

Lee, S. J. (2006). Additional complexities: Social class, ethnicity, generation, and gender in Asian American student experiences. *Race, Ethnicity and Education, 9*, 17–28.

Lemon , R. L., & Waehler, C. A. (1996). A test of stability and construct validity of the Black Racial Identity Attitude Scale, Form B (RIAS-B) and the White Racial Identity Attitude Scale (WRIAS). *Measurement and Evaluation in Counseling and Development, 29*(2), 77–85.

Levin, S., Van Laar, C., Sidanius, J., & Levin, S. (2003). The effects of ingroup and outgroup friendship on ethnic attitudes in college: A longitudinal study. *Group Processes & Intergroup Relations, 6*(1), 76–92.

Lieber, E., Chin, D., Nihira, K., & Mink, I. T. (2001). Holding on and letting go: Identity and acculturation among Chinese immigrants. *Cultural Diversity and Ethnic Minority Psychology, 7*, 247–261.

Lincoln, Y. S., & Guba, E. G. (1985). *Naturalistic inquiry*. Beverly Hills, CA: Sage.

Lindman, J. M., & Tahamont, M. (2006). Transforming selves, transforming courses: Faculty and staff development and the construction of interdisciplinary diversity courses. *Innovative Higher Education, 30*, 289–303.

Luhtanen, R., & Crocker, J. (1992). A collective self-esteem scale: Self-evaluation of one's social identity. *Personality and Social Psychology Bulletin, 18*, 302–318.

Mack, D. E., Tucker, T. W., Archuleta, R., DeGroot, G., Hernandez, A. A., & Oh Cha, S. (1997). Inter-ethnic relations on campus: Can't we all get along? *Journal of Multicultural Counseling and Development, 25*, 256–268.

Mahalik, J. R., Pierre, M. R., & Wan, S. S. C. (2006). Examining racial identity and masculinity as correlates of self-esteem and psychological distress in Black men. *Journal of Multicultural Counseling and Development, 34*, 94–104.

Marcia, J. (1980). Identity in adolescence. In J. Adleson (Ed.), *Handbook of adolescent psychology* (pp. 159–187). New York: John Wiley.

Marin, G., & Marin, B. V. (1991). *Research with Hispanic populations*. Newbury Park, CA: Sage Publications.

Martin, J. K., & Hall, G. C. N. (1992). Thinking Black, thinking internal, thinking feminist. *Journal of Counseling Psychology, 39*, 509–514.

Martinez, T. A. (1997). Popular culture as oppositional culture: Rap as resistance. *Sociological Perspectives, 40*, 265–286.

McDermott, M., & Samson, F. L. (2005). White racial and ethnic identity in the United States. *Annual Review of Sociology, 31*, 245–261.

Migration Policy Institute. (2003). *Data sources on the foreign born and international migration at the U.S. Census Bureau*. Washington, DC: Author.

Milem, J., Chang, M., & Antonio, A. (2005) *Making diversity work on campus: A research-based perspective*. Washington, DC: Association of American Colleges and Universities.

Mina, L., Cabrales, J. A., & Juarez, C. M. (2004). Support programs that work. In A. M. Ortiz (Ed.), *New directions for student services: Addressing the unique needs of Latino American students* (pp. 79–88). San Francisco: Jossey-Bass.

Miville, M. L., Constantine, M. G., Baysden, M. F., & So-Lloyd, G. (2005). Chameleon changes: An exploration of racial identity themes of multiracial people. *Journal of Counseling Psychology*, *52*, 507–516.

Miville, M. L., Koonce, D., Darlington, P., & Whitlock, B. (2000). Exploring the relationships between racial/cultural identity and ego identity among African Americans and Mexican Americans. *Journal of Multicultural Counseling and Development*, *28*, 208–235.

Mobasher, M. (2006). Cultural trauma and ethnic identity formation among Iranian immigrants in the United States. *American Behavioral Scientist, 50*(1), 100–117.

Morales, A., & Hanson, W. E. (2005). Language brokering: An integrative review of the literature. *Hispanic Journal of Behavioral Sciences*, *27*, 471–503.

Murguia, E., Padilla, R. V., & Pavel, M. (1991). Ethnicity and the concept of social integration in Tinto's model of institutional departure. *Journal of College Student Development*, *32*, 433–439.

Negy, C., Shreve, T. L., Jensen, B. J., & Uddin, N. (2003). Ethnic identity, self-esteem, and ethnocentrism: A study of social identity versus multicultural theory of development. *Cultural Diversity and Ethnic Minority Psychology*, *9*, 333–344.

Nelson, T. L., Engberg, M. E., & Hurtado, S. (2005). Modeling accentuation effects: Enrolling in a diversity course and the importance of social action engagement. *Journal of Higher Education*, *76*, 448–476.

Neville, H. A., Heppner, P. P., & Wang, L. (1997). Relations among racial identity attitudes, perceived stressors, and coping styles in African American college students. *Journal of Counseling and Development*, *75*, 303–311.

Nghe, L. T., & Mahalik, J. R. (2001). Examining racial identity statuses as predictors of psychological defenses in African American college students. *Journal of Counseling Psychology*, *48*, 10–16.

Nghe, L. T., Mahalik, J. R., & Lowe, S. M. (2003). Influences on Vietnamese men: Examining the traditional gender roles, the refugee experience, acculturation, and racism in the United States. *Journal of Multicultural Counseling and Development*, *31*, 245–261.

Niemann, F. Y. (2001). Stereotype about Chicanas and Chicanos: Implications for counseling. *Hispanic Journal of Behavioral Sciences*, *29*, 55–91.

Ogbu, J. U. (1987a). Variability in minority school performance: A problem in search of an explanation. *Anthropology and Education Quarterly*, *18*, 312–334.

Ogbu, J. U. (1987b). Variability in minority responses to schooling: Nonimmigrant vs. immigrants. In J. P. Vincent (Ed.), *Advances in family interventions, assessment, and theory* (Vol. 1, pp. 128–176). Greenwich, CT: JAI.

Okagaki, L., & Frensch, P. (1998). Parenting and children's school achievement: A multiethnic perspective. *American Educational Research Journal, 35,* 123–144.

Okech, A. P., & Harrington, R. (2002). The relationship among Black consciousness, self-esteem, and academic self-efficacy in African American men. *Journal of Psychology, 136,* 214–224.

Olenchak, R., & Hebert, T. (2002). Endangered academic talent: Lessons learned from gifted first generation college males. *Journal of College Student Development, 43,* 195–212.

Olsen, L. (1997). *Crossing the schoolhouse border: Immigrant students and the California public schools.* San Francisco: California Tomorrow.

Ontai-Grzebik, L. L., & Raffaelli, M. (2004). Individual and social influences on ethnic identity among Latino young adults. *Journal of Adolescent Research, 19,* 559–575.

Ortiz, A. M. (1999). The student affairs establishment and the institutionalization of the collegiate ideal. In J. D. Toma & A. J. Kezar (Eds.), *New directions for higher education: Reconceptualizing the collegiate ideal* (pp. 47–58). San Francisco: Jossey-Bass.

Ortiz, A. M., & Rhoads, R. A. (2000). Deconstructing Whiteness as a part of a multicultural educational framework: From theory to practice. *Journal of College Student Development, 41*(1), 81–93.

Padilla, A. (2006). Bicultural social development. *Hispanic Journal of Behavioral Sciences, 28,* 467–497.

Parham, T. A. (1989). Cycles of psychological Nigrescence. *The Counseling Psychologist, 17,* 187–226.

Parham, T. A., & Helms, J. E. (1985a). Attitudes of racial identity and self-esteem in Black students: An exploratory investigation. *Journal of College Student Personnel, 26,* 143–147.

Parham, T. A., & Helms, J. E. (1985b). The relationship of racial identity attitudes of self-actualization and affective states of Black students. *Journal of Counseling Psychology, 32,* 431–440.

Pascarella, E. T., & Terenzini, P. T. (1991, 2005). *How college affects students: A third decade of research.* San Francisco: Jossey-Bass.

Perry, P. (2001). White means never having to say you're ethnic: White youth and the construction of "cultureless" identities. *Journal of Contemporary Ethnography, 30,* 56–91.

Perry. W. G., Jr. (1968, 1970). *Forms of intellectual and ethical development in the college years: A scheme.* New York: Holt, Rinehart, & Winston.

Peterson's (1992). *Peterson's complete guide to colleges.* Lawrenceville, NJ: Peterson's.

Phelps, R. E., Taylor, J. D., & Gerard, P. A. (2001). Cultural mistrust, ethnic identity, racial identity, and self-esteem among ethnically diverse Black students. *Journal of Counseling and Development, 29,* 209–216.

Phinney, J. (1989). Stages of ethnic identity development in minority group adolescents. *Journal of Early Adolescence, 9,* 34–49.

Phinney, J. (1990). Ethnic identity in adolescents and adults, review of research. *Psychological Bulletin, 108,* 499–514.

Phinney, J. (1992). The Multigroup Ethnic Identity Measure: A new scale for use with adolescents and young adults from diverse groups. *Journal of Adolescent Research, 7,* 156–176.

Phinney, J. (1993). A three-stage model of ethnic identity development in adolescence. In M. Bernal & G. Knight (Eds.), *Ethnic identity: Formation and transmission among Hispanics and other minorities* (pp. 61–80). Albany: State University of New York Press.

Phinney, J. (1995). Ethnic identity and self-esteem: A review and integration. In A. Padilla (Ed.), *Hispanic psychology: Critical issues in theory and research* (pp. 57–70). Thousand Oaks, CA: Sage.

Phinney, J. (1996). When we talk about American ethnic groups what do we mean? *American Psychologist, 51,* 918–927.

Phinney, J. (2000a). Identity formation across cultures: The interaction of personal, societal, and historical change. *Human Development, 43,* 27–31.

Phinney, J. (2000b). Racial and ethnic identity: Ethnic identity. In A. Kadin (Ed.), *Encyclopedia of psychology* (pp. 254–259). Washington, DC: American Psychological Association.

Phinney, J. S. (2005). Ethnic identity in late modern times: A response to Rattansi and Phoenix. *Identity, 5*(2), 187–194.

Phinney, J. (2006). Ethnic identity exploration in emerging adulthood. In J. Arnett & J. L. Tanner (Eds.), *Coming of age in the 21st century: The lives and context of emerging adults* (pp. 117–134). Washington, DC: American Psychological Association.

Phinney, J., & Alipuria, L. (1990). Ethnic identity in college students from four ethnic groups. *Journal of Adolescence, 13,* 171–184.

Phinney, J., Cantu, C. L., & Kurtz, D. (1997). Ethnic and American identity as predictors of self-esteem among African American, Latino, and White adolescents. *Journal of Youth and Adolescence, 26,* 165–185.

Phinney, J., & Chavira, V. (1992). Ethnic identity and self-esteem: An exploratory longitudinal study. *Journal of Adolescence, 15,* 271–281.

Phinney, J., & Chavira, V. (1995). Parental ethnic socialization and adolescent outcomes in ethnic minority families. *Journal of Research on Adolescence, 5,* 31–53.

Phinney, J., & Devich-Navarro, M. (1997). Variations in bicultural identification among African American and Mexican American adolescents. *Journal of Research on Adolescence, 7,* 3–32.

Phinney, J., Ferguson, D. L., & Tate, J. D. (1997). Intergroup attitudes among ethnic minority adolescents: A causal model. *Child Development, 68,* 955–969.

Phinney, J., Jacoby, B., & Silva, C. (2007). Positive intergroup attitudes: The role of ethnicity. *International Journal of Behavioral Development, 31,* 478–490.

Phinney, J., & Kohatsu, E. L. (1997). Ethnic and racial identity development and mental health. In J. Schulenberg, J. L. Maggs, & K. Hurrelmann (Eds.), *Health risks and developmental transitions during adolescence* (pp. 420–443). Cambridge, UK: Cambridge University Press.

Phinney, J., Madden, T., & Santos, L. J. (1996). Psychological variables as predictors of perceived ethnic discrimination among minority and immigrant adolescents. *Journal of Applied Psychology, 28,* 937–953.

Phoenix, A. (1997). "I'm White! So what?" The construction of whiteness for young Londoners. In M. Fine, C. P. Linda, L. W. Powell, & L. M. Wong (Eds.), *Off White: Readings on race and power in society* (pp. 187–197). New York: Routledge.

Pizarro, M., & Vera, E. M. (2001). Chicana/o ethnic identity research: Lessons for researchers and counselors. *Counseling Psychologist, 29*, 91–118.

Ponterotto, J. G., Casas, J. M., Suzuki, L. A., & Alexander, C. M. (Eds.). (1995). *Handbook of multicultural counseling.* Thousand Oaks, CA: Sage.

Pope-Davis, D. B., & Ottavi, T. M. (1994). The relationship between racism and racial identity among White Americans: A replication and extension. *Journal of Counseling and Development, 72*, 293–297.

Portes, A., & Bach, R. L. (1985). *Latin journey: Cuban and Mexican immigrants in the United States.* Berkeley: University of California Press.

Portes, A., & Rumbaut, R. G. (1996). *Immigrant America: A portrait.* Berkeley: University of California Press.

Portes, A., & Stepick, A. (1993). *City on the edge: The transformation of Miami.* Berkeley: University of California Press.

Pryor, J. H., Hurtado, S., Saenz, V. B., Santos, J. L., & Korn, W. S. (2007). *The American freshman: Forty year trends.* Los Angeles, CA: Higher Education Research Institute, UCLA.

Ramirez, M., III, & Castaneda, A. (1974). *Cultural democracy, biocognitive development and education.* New York: Academic Press.

Reid, L., & Radhakrishnan, P. (2003). Race matters: The relationship between race and general campus climate. *Cultural Diversity and Ethnic Minority Psychology, 9*, 263–275.

Rendón, L. I. (1994). Validating culturally diverse students: Toward a new model of learning and student development. *Innovative Higher Education, 19*, 33–51.

Renn, K. A. (2003). Understanding the identities of mixed-race college students through a developmental ecology lens. *Journal of College Student Development, 44*(3), 383–403.

Renn, K. A. (2004). *Mixed race students in college: The ecology of race, identity, and community on campus.* Albany: State University of New York Press.

Renn, K. A., & Lunceford, C. L. (2004). Because the numbers matter: Transforming postsecondary education data on student race and ethnicity to meet the challenge of a changing nation. *Educational Policy, 18*, 752–783.

Rhoads, R. A. (1998). *Freedom's web: Student activism in an age of cultural diversity.* Baltimore, MD: Johns Hopkins University Press.

Richardson, T. Q., & Silvestri, T. J. (1999). White identity formation: A developmental process. In R. Hernandez-Sheets & E. R. Hollins (Eds.), *Racial and ethnic identity in school practices* (pp. 46–69). Mahwah, NJ: Lawrence Erlbaum.

Roberts, R. E., Phinney, J. S., Masse, L. C., Chen, Y. R., Roberts, C. R., & Romero, A. (1999). The structure of ethnic identity of young adolescents from diverse ethnocultural groups. *Journal of Early Adolescence, 19*(3), 301–322.

Robinson, L. C. (2000). Interpersonal relationship quality in young adulthood: A gender analysis. *Journal of Adolescence, 35*, 775–784.

Romero, A. J., & Roberts, R. E. (1998). Perception of discrimination and ethnocultural variables in a diverse group of adolescents. *Journal of Adolescence, 21,* 641–656.

Rosenberg, M. (1979). *Conceiving the self.* New York: Basic Books.

Rosenthal, D. A., & Feldman, S. (1990). The acculturation of Chinese immigrants: Perceived effects on family functioning of length of residence in two cultural contexts. *Journal of Genetic Psychology, 151,* 495–514.

Rosenthal, R., & Jacobson, L. (1968). *Pygmalion in the classroom: Teacher expectations and student intellectual development.* New York: Holt.

Rothman, S., Lipset, S. M, & Nevitte, N. (2003). Does enrollment diversity improve education? *International Journal of Public Opinion Research, 15,* 8–26.

Rowe, W., Behrens, W. J. T., & Leach, M. M. (1995). Racial/ethnic identity and racial consciousness: Looking back and looking forward. In J. G. Ponterotto, J. M. Casas, L. A. Suzuki, & C. M. Alexander (Eds.), *Handbook of multicultural counseling* (pp. 218–236). Thousand Oaks, CA: Sage.

Rowe, W., Bennett, S. K., & Atkinson, D. R. (1994). White racial identity models: A critique and alternative proposal. *Counseling Psychologist, 22,* 129–146.

Rumbaut, R. (1995). The crucible within: Ethnic identity, self-esteem, and segmented assimilation among children of immigrants. *International Migration Review, 28,* 748–794.

Russell, K., Wilson, M., & Hall, R. (1992). *The color complex: The politics of skin color among African Americans.* New York: Harcourt Brace Jovanovich.

Ryan, R. M., & Deci, E. L. (2003). On assimilating identities to the self: A self-determination theory perspective on internalization and integrity within cultures. In L. R. Leary & J. P. Tangney (Eds.), *Handbook of self and identity* (pp. 253–272). New York: Guilford.

Saenz, V. B., Ngai, H. N., & Hurtado, S. (2006). Factors influencing positive interactions across race for African American, Asian American, Latino, and White college students. *Research in Higher Education, 48,* 1–38.

Saldaña, D. H. (1995). Minority status stress. In A. Padilla (Ed.), *Hispanic psychology: Critical issues in theory and research* (pp. 43–56). Thousand Oaks, CA: Sage.

Sanchez, D., & Carter, R. T. (2005). Exploring the relationship between racial identity and religious orientation among African American college students. *Journal of College Student Development, 46,* 280–295.

Sanchez, Y. M. (1997). Families of Mexican origins. In M. K. DeGenova (Ed.), *Families in cultural context: Strengths and challenges in diversity* (pp. 61–80). Mountain View, CA: Mayfield.

Santiago-Rivera, A. L., Arredondo, P., & Gallardo-Cooper, M. (2002). *Counseling Latinos and la familia: A practical guide.* Thousand Oaks, CA: Sage.

Santos, S. J., Ortiz, A. M., Morales, A., & Rosales, M. (2007). The relationship between campus diversity, students' ethnic identity and college adjustment: A qualitative study. *Cultural Diversity and Ethnic Minority Psychology, 13,* 104–114.

Sax, L. J., Astin, W. A., Korn, W. S., & Gilmartin, S. K. (1999). *The American college teacher: National norms for the 1998–99 HERI Faculty Survey.* Los Angeles, CA: Higher Education Research Institute, UCLA.

Saylor, E. S., & Aries, E. (1999). Ethnic identity and change in social context. *Journal of Social Psychology, 139*, 549–566.

Schlossberg, N. K. (1989). Marginality and mattering: Key issues in building community. In D. C. Roberts (Ed.), *Designing campus activities to foster a sense of community* (New Directions for Student Services, No. 48, pp. 5–15). San Francisco: Jossey-Bass.

Schooler, D., Ward, L. M., Merriwether, A., & Caruthers, A. (2004). Who's that girl: Television's role in the body image development of young White and Black women. *Psychology of Women Quarterly, 28*, 38–47.

Sellers, R. M., Rowley, S. A., Chavous, T. M., Shelton, J. N., & Smith, M. A. (1997). Multidimensional inventory of Black identity: A preliminary investigation. *Journal of Personality and Social Psychology, 74*, 715–724.

Sidanius, J., Van Laar, C., Levin, S., & Sinclair, S. (2004). Ethnic enclaves and the dynamic of social identity on the college campus: The good, the bad and the ugly. *Journal of Personality and Social Psychology, 87*, 96–110.

Silvestri, T. J., & Richardson, T. Q. (2001). White racial identity statuses and neo personality constructs: An exploratory analysis. *Journal of Counseling and Development, 79*, 68–76.

Sinclair, S., Hardin, C. D., & Lowery, B. S. (2006). Self-stereotyping in the context of multiple social identities. *Journal of Personality and Social Psychology, 90*, 529–542.

Slavin, R. (1995). Cooperative learning groups and intergroup relations. In J. A. Banks & C. A. McGee Banks (Eds.), *Handbook of research on multicultural education* (pp. 682–634). New York: Macmillan.

Smedley, B. D., Myers, H. F., & Harrell, S. P. (1993). Minority-status stresses and the college adjustment of ethnic minority freshmen. *Journal of Higher Education, 643*, 434–452.

Smith, C. E., & Hopkins, R. (2004). Mitigating the impact of stereotypes on academic performance: The effects of cultural identity and attributions for success among African American college students. *Western Journal of Black Studies, 28*, 312–321.

Smith, D. G. (2004) *The campus diversity initiative: Current status, anticipating the future.* A James Irvine Foundation Report. San Francisco: James Irvine Foundation.

Smith, D. G., Moreno, J., Clayton-Pedersen, A. R., Parker, S., & Hiroyuki Teraguchi, D. (2005). *"Unknown" students on college campuses: An exploratory analysis.* A James Irvine Foundation Report. San Francisco: James Irvine Foundation.

Sodowsky, G. R., Kwan, K. L., & Pannu, R. (1995). Ethnic identity of Asians in the United States. In J. G. Ponterotto, J. M. Casas, L. A. Suzuki, & C. M. Alexander (Eds.), *Handbook of multicultural counseling* (pp. 123–154). Thousand Oaks, CA: Sage.

Solberg, S. V., O'Brien, K., Kennel, R., & Davis, B. (1993). Self-efficacy and Hispanic college students: Validation of the college self-efficacy instrument. *Hispanic Journal of Behavioral Sciences, 15*, 80–95.

Spanierman, L. B., & Heppner, M. J. (2004). Psychosocial Costs of Racism to Whites scale (PCRW): Construction and initial validation. *Journal of Counseling Psychology, 51,* 249–262.

Straughn, C. T., & Lovejoy-Straughn, B. (1998). *Lovejoy's College Guide.* New York: Arco.

Steele, C. (1997). A threat in the air: How stereotypes shape intellectual identity and performance. *American Psychologist, 52,* 613–629.

Stonequist, E. V. (1937). *The marginal man: A study in personality and culture conflict.* New York: Scribner's.

Sue, D., Mak, W., & Sue, D. W. (1998). Ethnic identity. In L. C. Lee & N. W. S. Zane (Eds.), *Handbook of Asian American psychology* (pp. 289–323). Thousand Oaks, CA: Sage.

Suinn, R., Ahuna, C., & Hknoo, G. (1992). The Suinn-Lew Asian self-identity acculturation scale: Concurrent and factorial validation. *Educational and Psychological Measurement, 52,* 1041–1046.

Sullivan, R. E. (2003). Rap and race: It's got a nice beat, but what about the message? *Journal of Black Studies, 33,* 605–622.

Suyemoto, K. L. (2004). Racial/ethnic identities and related attributed experiences of multiracial Japanese European Americans. *Journal of Multicultural Counseling and Development, 32,* 206–221.

Swim, J. K., & Miller, D. L. (1999). White guilt: Its antecedents and consequences for attitudes toward affirmative action. *Personality and Social Psychology Bulletin, 25,* 500–514.

Syed, M., Azmitia, M., & Phinney, J. (2007). Stability and change in ethnic identity among Latino emerging adults in two contexts. *Identity: An International Journal of Theory and Research, 7,* 155–178.

Tafoya, S. M. (2004/2005). Shades of belonging: Latinos and racial identity. *Harvard Journal of Hispanic Policy, 17,* 58–78.

Tajfel, H. (Ed.). (1978). *Differentiation between social groups: Studies in the social psychology of intergroup relations.* London: Academic Press.

Tajfel, H. (1981). *Human groups and social categories.* Cambridge, UK: Cambridge University Press.

Tajfel, H., & Turner, J. C. (1986). The social identity theory of intergroup behavior. In S. Worchel & W. G. Austin (Eds.), *Psychology of intergroup relations* (pp. 7–24). Chicago: Nelson-Hall.

The states. (2007, August). *The Chronicle of Higher Education, Almanac Issue 2007–08, 9*(1), 38–95.

Thompson, C. E., & Carter, R. T. (1997). An overview and elaboration of Helms' racial identity development theory. In C. E. Thompson & R. T. Carter (Eds.), *Racial identity theory* (pp. 15–32). Mahwah, NJ: Lawrence Erlbaum.

Thompson, F., Engberg, M. E., & Hurtado, S. (2006). Modeling accentuation effects: Enrolling in a diversity course and the importance of social action engagement. *Journal of Higher Education, 76,* 448–476.

Tinto, V. (1993). *Leaving college: Rethinking the causes and cures of student retention* (1st ed.). Chicago: University of Chicago Press.

Tokar, D. M., & Swanson, J. L. (1991). An investigation of the validity of Helms' (1984) model of White racial identity. *Journal of Counseling Psychology, 38,* 296–301.

Tracey, T. J., & Sedlacek, W. E. (1987). The relationship between noncognitive variables to academic success. A longitudinal comparison by race. *Journal of College Student Personnel, 26,* 177–184.

Tsai, J., Mortensen, H., & Wong, Y. (2002). What does "being American" mean? A comparison of Asian American and European American young adults. *Cultural Diversity and Ethnic Minority Psychology, 8,* 257–273.

Tsai, J., Ying, Y. W., & Lee, P. A. (2001). Cultural predictors of self-esteem: A study of Chinese American female and male young adults. *Cultural Diversity and Ethnic Minority Psychology, 7,* 284–297.

Uba, L. (1994). *Asian Americans: Personality patterns, identity and mental health.* New York: Guilford.

U.S. Census Bureau. (2000). *Profile of general demographic characteristics, 2000.* Retrieved May 1, 2005, from http://censtats.census.gov

Vera, H., & De Los Santos, E. (2005). Chicana identity construction: Pushing the boundaries. *Journal of Hispanic Higher Education, 4,* 102–113.

Walker, T. (2001). Arizona State University Intergroup Relations Center founding proposal. Retrieved from http://www.usu.edu/provost/intergroup/geninfo/pro posal.htm

Walsh, J. J., & McGrath, F. P. (2000). Identity, coping style, and health behaviour among first generation Irish immigrants in England. *Psychology and Health, 15,* 467–482.

Warren, J., & Hytten, K. (2004). The faces of Whiteness: Pitfalls and the critical democrat. *Communication Education, 53,* 321–339.

Water, M. (1990). *Ethnic options: Choosing identities in America.* Berkeley: University of California Press.

Weis, L., Proweller, A., & Centrie, C. (1997). Re-examining "A moment in history": Loss of privilege inside White working-class masculinity in the 1990s. In M. Fine, L. Weis, & M. L. Wong (Eds.), *Off White: Race, power and society.* New York: Routledge.

Wellman, D. T. (1977). *Portraits of White racism.* New York: Cambridge University Press.

Williams, D. A., Berger, J. B., & McClendon, S. A. (2005). *Toward a model of inclusive excellence and change in postsecondary institutions.* Washington, DC: Association of American Colleges and Universities.

Wilson, J. W., & Constantine, M. G. (1999). Racial identity attitudes, self-concept, and perceived family cohesion in Black college students. *Journal of Black Studies, 29,* 354–366.

Wolsko, C., Park, B., Judd, C. M., & Wittenbrink, B. (2000). Framing interethnic ideologies: Effects of multiculturalism and color-blind perspectives on judgments of groups and individuals. *Journal of Personality and Social Psychology, 78,* 635–654.

Wong, C., & Cho, G. E. (2005). Two-headed coins or Kandinsky's: White racial identification. *Political Psychology, 26,* 699–720.

Wright, M. O., & Littleford, L. N. (2002). Experiences and beliefs as predictors of ethnic identity and intergroup relations. *Journal of Multicultural Counseling and Development, 30,* 1–20.

Yeh, C., & Huang, K. (1996). The collectivistic nature of ethnic identity development among Asian-American college students. *Adolescence, 31,* 645–655.

Yeh, C. J., Carter, R. T., & Pieterse, A. L. (2004). Cultural values and racial identity attitudes among Asian American students: An exploratory investigation. *Counseling and Values, 48,* 82–95.

Yeh, T. L. (1997). *Asian American racial and ethnic identity: Theoretical and empirical distinctions.* Unpublished master's thesis, University of Maryland, College Park.

Yi, K., & Shorter-Gooden, K. (1999). Ethnic identity formation: From stage theory to a constructivist narrative model. *Psychotherapy, 36,* 16–26.

Yip, T. (2005). Sources of situational variation in ethnic identity and psychological well-being: A Palm Pilot study of Chinese American students. *Personality and Social Psychology Bulletin, 31,* 1603–1616.

Yip, T., & Fuligni, A. J. (2002). Daily variation in ethnic identity, ethnic behaviors, and psychological well-being among American adolescents of Chinese descent. *Child Development, 73,* 1557–1572.

Yuh, J. (2005). Ego identity and its relation to self-esteem and ego identity among college students in a multiethnic region. *Journal of Applied Social Psychology, 35,* 1111–1131.

INDEX

AAC&U. *See* American Association of Colleges and Universities
acculturation
    Asian Americans and, 85–95
    definition of, 33
    Latinos/as and, 151, 185–191
    models of, 32–36, 35*f*
    university context and, 257–265
active reintegration, 48
activism, university context and, 274–275
adolescence
    developmental processes in, ethnic identity development and, 324–327
    identity in, 6–10
affirmative action
    erosion of, 358–359
    Latinos/as and, 182–183
    university context and, 273–274
    White Americans and, 238–239
African American(s), 98–129
    demographics of, 4
    identity development theory on, 42–47, 51–53
African American identity
    contributors to, 310*t*, 311–312
    functions of, 101
    pathways to development of, 333*t*
American Association of Colleges and Universities (AAC&U), 357–358
American Civil Liberties Union, 359
American identity, White Americans and, 199–200
Asian American(s), 62–97
    demographics of, 4
    identity development theory on, 45–46, 53–55
    participants in study, demographics of, 63
    term, 62
Asian American identity
    contributors to, 309–311, 310*t*
    pathways to development of, 333*t*
assimilation, 33–34, 35*f*
    See also acculturation
attitudes
    in ethnic identity, 22, 24
    White, types of, 57–58
autonomy, 49–50

biculturalism, 35–36, 35*f*
    Latinos/as and, 141–142, 190–191
    bilingualism, Latinos/as and, 141–142
    Black. *See* African American(s)
    Black Student Association, 5, 278

bonding, 101
boundary crossing, ethnic, Asian Americans and, 93–95
bridging, 101
buffering, 101
busing, 11–12

California, demographics of, 4, 308
campus climate
    definition of, 249
    and ethnic identity, 249–251
    factors affecting, 250
    holistic, sustaining ethnic identity in, 352–363
code switching, 101, 142
coethnics
    Asian Americans and, 80–85
    and college experience, 321
    critical mass of, 323
    and ethnic discomfort, 290
    and examination of ethnic identity, 265–270
    and feelings of inclusion, 253–257
    Latinos/as and, 132–133
    White Americans and, 221
cognitive effects, university context and, 257–265
collectivism
    African Americans and, 125–127
    Asian Americans and, 68
    Latinos/as and, 146–164, 179–180, 183
college
    ethnic experience of, 307–363
    and ethnic identity development, in Latinos/as, 165–170
    future of ethnic experience in, 358–363
    ideal of, 355–356
    See also university context
college adjustment
    diversity and, 248–306
    survey instrument on, 375
college students, identity and, 6–10
color-blind perspective, 59, 202, 231–232, 241, 315–316
confidence, growth in, Latinos/as and, 174–175
conflictive interracial relations
    awareness programs on, 345–346
    university context and, 293–294, 297–300
    White Americans and, 232–237
conformity status, 43
connection
    African Americans and, 125–128
    Asian Americans and, 80–83

397

Also available from Stylus

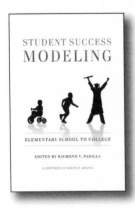

Student Success Modeling
Elementary School to College
Edited by Raymond V. Padilla
Foreword by Sarita E. Brown

"What I find of greatest value about this book is the introduction of a model of student success that is sensitive to contextual circumstances and focuses on student agency to overcome barriers to their success. As Ray Padilla alludes, there are hundreds of correlational studies on pre-college characteristics as determinants of student success but we know very little about what goes on inside institutions that is enabling or disabling of students who lack the normative profile of the successful college student. Padilla's model provides a critical perspective on student success: He takes it for granted that institutions are filled with visible and invisible obstacles that stand in the way of historically marginalized student populations. Accordingly, rather than asking the typical question: What student characteristics predict college success? he instead asks: What expertise do marginalized students possess that enables them to overcome institutional barriers to success?"—*Estela Mara Bensimon, Professor of Higher Education in the division of Educational Policy and Administration, and Director of the Center for Urban Education, University of Southern California*

Sentipensante (Sensing/Thinking) Pedagogy
Educating for Wholeness, Social Justice and Liberation
Laura I. Rendón
Foreword by Mark Nepo

"Teaching the whole student begins in clarity of language, but to even glimpse the possibility of stepping beyond knowledge (facts, figures, theories) toward the cultivation of wisdom, it must honor means of communicating that lie beyond language and do so with the same commitment to clarity— that is to say, honesty—that Nida's essay calls for. Rendón's pedagogical model takes a courageous step in that direction."—*James Rhem, Executive Editor, The National Teaching and Learning Forum*

"What would happen if educators eschewed the silent agreements that govern institutions and established a new set of working assumptions that honor the fullness of humanity? In this visionary study, Laura Rendón lays the groundwork for a pedagogy that bridges the gap between mind and heart to lead students and educators toward a new conception of teaching and learning. Grounding her work in interviews of scholars who are already transforming the educational landscape, Rendón invites the reader to join a burgeoning movement toward more inclusive classrooms that honor each learner's identity and support education for social justice. Her book is vital reading for anyone seeking to create more inclusive institutions for students and teachers alike."—*Diversity & Democracy (AAC&U)*

22883 Quicksilver Drive
Sterling, VA 20166-2102

Subscribe to our e-mail alerts: www.Styluspub.com